# THE SOUTHWEST

*Books by David Lavender*

Winner Take All: The TransCanada Canoe Trail

California: A Bicentennial History

Nothing Seemed Impossible: William Ralston and Early San Francisco

David Lavender's Colorado

California, Land of New Beginnings

The Rockies

The American Heritage History of the Great West

Climax at Buena Vista: American Campaigns in Northeastern Mexico
   1846–47

The Fist in the Wilderness

Red Mountain

Westward Vision: The Story of the Oregon Trail

Story of the Cyprus Mines Corporation

Bent's Fort

Land of Giants

Trail to Santa Fe

The Big Divide

Golden Trek

Andy Claybourne

Mike Maroney, Raider

Trouble at Tamarack

One Man's West

# THE
# SOUTHWEST

*David Lavender*

*A Regions of America Book*

**HARPER & ROW, PUBLISHERS**

NEW YORK

| | | |
|---|---|---|
| Cambridge | | London |
| Hagerstown |  | Mexico City |
| Philadelphia | | São Paulo |
| San Francisco | *1817* | Sydney |

FIRST EDITION

*Designer: C. Linda Dingler*

Library of Congress Cataloging in Publication Data

Lavender, David Sievert, 1910–
The Southwest.

(A Regions of America book)

1. Southwest, New—History. I. Title.

F799.L38    979    78-69622
ISBN 0-06-012519-5

80 81 82 83 10 9 8 7 6 5 4 3 2 1

To MILDRED
For sharing and sustaining

# CONTENTS

MAPS

## SOUTHWEST INVOCATION

*Oh, our mother, the earth; oh, our father, the sky,*
*Your children are we, and with tired backs*
*We bring you the gifts that you love.*
*Then weave for us a garment of brightness;*
*May the warp be of the white light of the morning,*
*May the weft be of the red light of evening,*
*May the fringes be the falling rain,*
*May the border be the standing rainbow.*
*Thus weave for us a garment of brightness*
*That we may walk fittingly where the birds sing,*
*That we may walk fittingly where the grass is green,*
*Oh, our mother the earth; oh, our father the sky.*

—Tewa Indian chant as recorded
at the Museum of New Mexico,
Palace of the Governors, Santa Fe

THE SOUTHWEST

# An Introduction:

## THE PEOPLE, THE LAND, THE BLAZING SKY

*Southwest Pepper Pot*

One of history's most gripping and at the same time most dimly understood adventure stories deals with the peopling of the Americas by immigrants from Asia, their adaptation to the new land, and their ultimate defeat by latecomers from Europe. Physically the American Southwest occupies only a small part of the stage on which the drama took place. It is a significant part, however, because the region's semiarid climate, which delays decomposition, has made it a rich source of aboriginal records. In addition, it is here that troops from the United States and Mexico at last combined to bring about the final defeat of the long-resistant native peoples. Defeat—but not destruction. The point needs emphasis. The Indians of the Southwest are still a force to be reckoned with.

*Item.* More Indians live in the Southwest than in any other section of the United States, and since 1948 they have been allowed to vote. (Elsewhere in the United States Indian voting dates from 1924.) As a result, local politicians pay at least some attention to this new body of constituents.

*Item.* Indian reservations occupy 26 percent of the land area of Arizona, plus another 9 percent in New Mexico. Valuable natural resources have been discovered on some of the reservations, and tourists attracted by the Indians' handsome crafts and colorful ceremonies add appreciably to the economic well-being of both states. Local chambers of commerce seldom forget either point.

*Item.* Since 1946, the United States has allowed all tribes that wish to do so to sue the government over violations of treaties dealing with the original taking of their lands. Many of the southwestern tribes have won substantial compensation. Taught by those cases how to utilize the law for remedying early wrongs, Indian lawyers are now asserting tribal rights to water whose potential value is, at current writing, incalculable. Whatever the figure, it has set a lot of Anglo heads to aching.

*Item.* Although internal difficulties have at times disrupted inexperienced tribal governments (fostered since the 1930s by the United States), Indian leaders in general have not been made complacent by their successes. They know that tribal unemployment rates far exceed the national average, that much housing is substandard, that health and educational programs fall far short of meeting what whites would consider minimal requirements. In conjunction with federal agencies designed to combat such inequities for all underprivileged Americans, the tribal governments are trying to attack the problems. As we shall see later on, some of their programs are highly imaginative and solidly rooted in Indian, not Anglo, ways of looking at things. For that reason they may succeed where earlier Anglo programs, most of which aimed at the assimilation of the Indians into the mainstream of American culture, did not. Even so the specter of white advisers telling Indians what Indians are supposed to be like continues to hang over reservation affairs.

Meanwhile the Indians quietly maintain their own values. Each year traditional ceremonies lure back to the homeland, for recharging as it were, hundreds of off-reservation Indians who have learned in the cities to wear American clothes, repair American cars, dance to American rock bands, drink American beer—but not how to be Americans, which most of them don't want, anyway. Or, as an acquaintance said to me at the supermarket in Window Rock, headquarters of the Navajo tribe, as we watched a mother in a traditional velveteen blouse and voluminous calico skirt put a box of Pampers into her shopping cart, "It doesn't matter where the shit lands. That baby will grow up Navajo."

Even more numerous than the Indians and boasting the region's next longest span of history are the Southwest's Spanish-speaking people. Their first colonists settled beside the Rio Grande in northern New Mexico in 1598, nine years before the Virginia Company moved into Jamestown. Although immigration to New Mexico was snail-slow for the next two and a half centuries, natural increase was brisker. By 1850, two years after the war between the United States and Mexico, some 60,000 Hispanic peoples lived in the newly conquered region, enough to qualify New Mexico for statehood. They were too exotic a people for American tastes, however, and sixty-two more years passed, enlivened by unneighborly infighting between New Mexico and Arizona, before either territory was allowed by Congress to declare itself a sovereign member of the union.

Meanwhile immigration from south of the border was quickening. During the early part of the twentieth century, revolutions swept Mexico, triggering fear and paralyzing many industries. Either as fugitives from persecution or in search of jobs, thousands of dark-skinned people crossed the international border to work in American mines, on farms, railroads, and urban construction projects. During World War II and its cold-war aftermath, when American demands for workers soared, the northward movement was stimulated still more by the "temporary" importation of *braceros* to labor in the vast fields of American agribusiness. Similarly, "green-card" permits allowed unnaturalized Mexicans to hold low-paid positions in garment factories, food processing plants, hotel kitchens, and the like.

And still the pressures mount. Although the Mexican government has for some time been pushing industrialization, the country's factories cannot yet provide enough jobs to care for the maturing young people of a nation beset by one of the world's highest rates of population growth. The desperate surplus, hundreds of thousands strong, pile up against the porous border in the fond belief that somewhere beyond, in the rich Estados Unidos, where so many of their countrymen already live, there must be a place for them. Each year the lawful quota of immigrants allowed to migrate permanently across the border is completely filled. How many more cross without visas is unknown, but during the past three decades the number of "wetback" (illegal) entries must have soared far into the millions.

The grievous situation has created in the United States a new body of citizens and would-be citizens unlike any other in this country. Irishmen in Boston, Italians in Chicago, Japanese rice farmers in the Sacramento Delta—all are conscious of their origins and often celebrate them with native food and rituals. But they are also conscious of the ocean that separates them from their sources, and this separation has done much to quicken their adoption of American customs. By contrast, Mexican immigrants are not cut away from their homeland. Whether they travel legally or illegally, they can and do return easily for visits that reinforce their native ways. Their *colonias* and *barrios* within the United States are constantly replenished by streams of relatives and friends to whom the aura of the home village clings undiminished. They are truly foreign, unassimilated, often unwanted; yet the borderlands where most of them pause for at least a time before moving on to Los Angeles, Denver, Chicago, or wherever—these broad lands were once their people's possession. They do not forget. And all the while new collision courses are developing between them and American labor unions, agricultural groups, uneasy politicians, and even naturalized Mexicans fearful of wetback competition.

As early as the opening decades of the twentieth century, the old-line Spanish-speaking people of the Southwest had sensed the scorn with which the new arrivals were being greeted by many Americans. Accordingly, they sought to keep the taint away by referring to themselves, in their contacts with Anglos, as Spanish-Americans. Concurrently, newcomers who achieved United States citizenship sought comparable protective coloration by calling themselves, in conversation with Anglos, Mexican-Americans. The rest, of course, were plain Mexicans. Yet *all* were Mexicans, proud of the uniqueness of their culture.

How could they indicate this pride without giving up their parallel satisfaction in the American citizenship they had acquired or hoped to acquire? Many of the younger ones, fired by the widespread militancy of the 1960s and early 1970s, took to calling themselves Chicanos, published their own newspapers, and at the very time they were most stridently demanding their rights as Americans flaunted their Indian heritage by means of banners bearing fiery representations of the Aztec eagle. Others, repelled by the militancy, yet attracted by the dream of a culturally united minority north of the border, have tried to find solidarity in what they call La Raza Unida, a union of all Spanish-speaking people within the United States, no matter what their origins.

Faced with such a salad bowl, one becomes arbitrary about descriptive terms. This account will follow several illustrious predecessors in using "Hispano," normally a word with a very broad reach, to single out those Spanish-speaking people of European descent whose forebears lived in the Southwest before the American acquisition. Those outside that circle will be referred to as Mexicans, Mexican Americans, or Chicanos, as circumstances warrant. The hope is to keep careless stereotypes from robbing subgroups of their backgrounds and aspirations.

But that is not the end of the trouble, for the term "American" contains its built-in ambiguities, too, especially in the Southwest. For one thing, the Mexicans and Indians who share the country with us scoff at our pretensions of being the only "Americans" inhabiting the continent. They prefer to call us Norteamericanos or Anglo-Americans, or plain Anglos, or *gringo,* from *griego,* literally Greek, but now a derogatory term for any oddball foreigner—like Polack, say, or greaser.

And what of our own subcultures? Tucson's annual folk festival—in large part the creation of Big Jim Griffith, six and a half feet tall, bearded like a pard, in his spare hours a professor of anthropology at the University of Arizona and the rest of the time an entertainer and singer of folk ballads (that festival, molded, too, by Big Jim's vibrant wife Loma)—draws not just the Yaquis, Pápagos, Apaches, Navajos, and the mercurial Sonorans from south of the border that you would expect, but also Yugoslavs, actual Greeks, Scots, Scandinavians, Austrians, Asiatics, and whatnot. Yet despite this breadth of field, the festival has no slots for two bodies of migrants that southwestern Anglos, Mexicans, and Indians all recognize as being distinctive—Texans, who after the Civil War swept with their cattle and virulent anti-Mexican prejudices throughout every grazing section in the area; and the persistent Mormons, who, beginning in the late 1870s, marched south out of Utah to found tight little communities along the upper drainage of the Salt and Little Colorado Rivers in Arizona. And so again this account will follow local custom by referring to English-speaking residents of the Southwest as Anglos, yet qualifying the term when advisable by those quasi-ethnic definitions "Texan" and "Mormon"—plus, in more recent connections, "Californian."

## Separations

In case the distinctions listed above seem like ethnic hair-splitting, consider the Rimrock Project, one of the notable anthropological studies of our era. In 1940, several outstanding scholars under Clyde Kluckhohn of Harvard University invaded a small area near the New Mexico–Arizona border and sought to learn whether five different groups that had been living there side by side for many decades really did march to different drums. The people studied were two Indian "communities" (Zuñi and Navajo), two Anglo (Texan and Mormon), and one Hispanic. The papers that resulted, published finally in 1966 as *People of the Rimrock*, not only set scientifically viable standards for isolating and defining basic cultural values but also confirmed what the people involved sensed well enough without study: In spite of small surface borrowings, each *was* different, here in what is supposed to be the most homogenizing nation on earth. Such are the things that give the pepper pot its flavor.

Cherished feelings of separateness have endured in the Southwest for several reasons. One is the widespread differences in language, dialects included—a Texas drawl in the heart of Arizona, for instance. Another bulwark against sameness comes from each ethnic group's sharp image of itself; the Mormons, to use their own words, are "a peculiar people." Related to such group images is shared historical experience—and that brings back another Window Rock memory.

Several score Navajos, both men and women, angry at a decision of the tribal council, were marching in protest along a street leading to the council's handsome headquarters building, its rugged hexagonal shape and massive beams artfully designed to capture a sense of modernity while retaining the architectural elements of a traditional hogan. Among the demonstrators was a beautiful young woman. She was tall and slim. Her jet black hair dropped down her back to her waist. Her white skirt almost touched the ground but was of Anglo rather than Navajo cut. She wore modishly large, round sunglasses tinted blue. But no one would mistake her for an Anglo. The placard she carried above her head declared in strong letters:

WE WALK FOR
THE LONG WALKERS

That memory! In 1864 troops of the United States Army, seeking to end Navajo marauding, had forced 8,491 men, women, and children on a long walk almost across New Mexico to an early-day concentration camp beside the Pecos River. After four miserable years, the survivors were given some livestock and allowed to walk home again. Now there are close to 150,000 Navajos, and the walk is more than a century gone, but no child is allowed to forget. It is as if a young American were to hark back, clenched fist raised, to Valley Forge in his insistence on what he believes is just. Such common heritages built granitic convictions of distinctiveness.

Finally there is the land—harsh, demanding, sun-blasted. Repelled by the prospect of hardships in so seemingly barren a country, immigrants did not sweep in great surges into the nation's southwest corner to overwhelm established peoples before they had a chance to adjust. But to understand the full significance of the region's isolation, we need to look more closely at the land itself, experience its sun, sense its vastness.

## Dry Country

Since many geographers insist that most of western America between
the 100th meridian and the Pacific littoral is primarily desert country and
that even the major mountain ranges are mere oases, it is well to start
this section on topography with dryness—with the two huge deserts,
Chihuahuan and Sonoran, that roll northward out of the Mexican states
from which they draw their names. Though relief maps show other
plains and basins known locally as deserts, those two are the granddad-
dies. Along with a pair of dominant mountain clusters, one in north-
central New Mexico and the other drawing a strong diagonal across
Arizona, they set the region's environmental tone. Anything else is an
echo.

In the east the Chihuahuan desert licks up the Rio Grande Valley
almost to Albuquerque. It sprawls in savage rumples across Big Bend
National Park, where the Rio Grande—or as the Mexicans say, El Rio
Bravo del Norte—cuts fantastic chasms through the gaunt Chisos
Mountains. It turns the water of the Pecos River as bitter as greasewood
bark and sweeps on across the whole southwestern protrusion of Texas.

In spite of the rugged Chisos and the soaring prow of the Guadalupe
Mountains in the new (1965) national park of the same name, much of
the Chihuahuan Desert is almost unbearably flat. In the United States
section, this is particularly true of the Deming Plain, which spreads
westward from El Paso for a hundred miles. If you are crossing the plain
on Interstate Highway 10, up north from the border a ways, you will
think nothing changes. But it does. In some places there are broad
communities of runty olive-green creosote bushes, named for the pun-
gent smell the leaves emit when crushed or wet. The pebbly ground
shows clearly between the plants because each one needs a broad root
system for soaking up every drop of moisture that falls, and crowding
would be self-destructive. Such things—the spacing of plants; the stony,
naked ground; the constant reflection of sunlight—give the Chihuahuan
Desert its hard and brittle look.

Along arroyos that flow two or three times a year or on outwash
slopes at the base of mountain canyons, there are no creosote bushes.
Instead there are mesquite trees—short and twisted and thorny, produc-
ers of edible seed pods for cattle and in the old days for hungry humans.
Instead of spreading their roots for water, as creosote bushes do, mesquite trees drive them deep into the earth—as much as seventy-five feet,
it is said. Such tap roots are big and tough. Accordingly, the woodgather-

ers of the borderlands obtain fuel not by chopping down trees but by digging them up.

Here and there other plants appear—blade-leafed yuccas, cacti, agaves, ocotillos, each with its own exotic shape and unfriendly thorns. Now and then a lizard scuttles dryly. There are spine-backed horny toads, rattlesnakes, and occasional lean jack rabbits. Dim on the horizon are barren mountains, as disassociated from each other as creosote bushes. Sometimes their saw-toothed crests appear to wobble in heat waves rising from the sunbaked ground; at other times a haze of dust turns their steep sides to a pale, ethereal blue.

A little short of the New Mexico–Arizona border, the international boundary drops abruptly south for thirty miles before resuming its western course across the shrunken Continental Divide. As elevation increases, short, round-topped juniper trees appear, widely spaced because of the usual competition for water. But at least there is water— small streams that sink into the sand as soon as they near the flatlands. Where they are alive, however, they are bordered by willows and cottonwoods and, higher on the hillsides, by scattered groves of oak trees.

Surprisingly, to outsiders, this is good cattle country, particularly on the Pacific side of the Divide. Though mountain ranges in general remain isolated one from another, some are high enough to draw moisture from the clouds and so cloak themselves in evergreens. Lower down, gramma grass hides the bones of the ground, its tan seed heads shaped, in the fall, like plumes on ancient Greek helmets. Here, too, scattered out on both sides of the international border are some of North America's richest copper deposits.

Many valleys pleat the land. Some lead trickles of water into Mexico, others north toward southern Arizona's great life-giver, the Gila River. As elevations drop, a new desert, the Sonoran, takes over. Much of it seems like the Chihuahuan Desert to the east. The mountains are just as naked, jagged, and tortured by the weather. They are not durable. Exfoliating relentlessly, they are slowly burying themselves in their own detritus. The mouth of each steep canyon exudes a widening fan of decomposing gravel. Adjoining fans merge to create long inclines called *bajadas*, and it is these that give the countryside between the Santa Cruz Valley, where Tucson stands, and the stark Yuma sand dunes its unique quality.

This is the "arboreal" desert, a stunted, twisted forest of eerie growth. Plants that are thin east of the Divide become taller and more convoluted here. On the lower slopes are mesquite thickets and the usual drab creosote bushes, plus green-barked paloverde trees, their branches blazing with golden flowers in the spring. Higher up, whiplike wands of ocotillo reach out as if from a flaring vase toward the hard blue sky, their tips flaunting crimson banners when the rains are right. Century plants, sotol, and yucca, taller than the varieties east of the Divide, are widespread. All three begin as rosettes of needle-pointed blades, but the leaves of the century plant are wide and fleshy while those of the yucca are narrow and flexible. Agitated by the constant wind, the yucca's vibrating green blades flash back the sun until the rosettes look like big balls of shimmering light. After years of slow growth, both the century plants and the yuccas waken abruptly and send up from the hearts of their rosettes tall stalks lined with dazzling flowers. This upsurge is completed within a few weeks and then the plant dies, but the dry stalks form bold patterns against the sky for years to come.

Even more striking are the many varieties of cactus. All are magnificently floral, and two species are additionally notable because of their forms. One is cholla. Its branches grow in segments so loosely jointed that they break off at a touch—and woe to whatever does the touching. Sometimes cholla is called jumping cactus on the basis of an old wives' tale that the detached segments actually leap at their victims. Cholla grows far and wide in the Southwest, but here in the arboreal desert it stands in groves as tall, sometimes, as a man, each plant's many-branched antlers dense with straw-colored needles that gleam like steel in the sunlight. Mingled with these groves are the most famous of all American cacti, the giant candelabra-limbed saguaros, their heavy trunks deeply pleated so that the plant can expand or contract like an accordion while either storing or utilizing water. Although saguaros—some grow forty feet or more tall—have become a popular symbol for the entire Southwest, their range is actually confined to southern Arizona and northern Sonora.

Gradually the mountains that produce the bajadas lose elevation, grow narrower, until they look like the petrified dorsal fins of ancient monsters trapped in bogs of sand. Anyone who wants an awesome glimpse of these wastelands can find it by driving Mexico's Highway 2, which parallels and in places all but touches the international border between Organ Pipe National Monument and the Colorado River.

Before the road was paved, the crossing was called, with justice, El Camino del Diablo ("The Devil's Highway"). Indians pioneered it, Spanish missionaries risked it because it promised a shortcut from Sonora to the west, and during the California gold rush dozens of stampeders, both Americans and Mexicans, died beside it. Along one stretch of almost a hundred miles the only water available lay out of sight in rock *tinajas*, which are great potholes (the literal meaning of *tinaja* is "earthen jar") carved into the bottoms of precipitous gullies by storm waters raging at infrequent intervals down the barren mountainsides.

Although some of the upper tanks may hold as much as ten thousand gallons of water, cooled by the shade of overhanging cliffs and visited by the nimble mountain sheep of the region, the treasure could be made available to saddle horses and other livestock only if travelers scrambled up the dangerous, water-smoothed walls and bailed the liquid from the higher bowls to those lower down. Even that labor did not always suffice. Some stampeders, dragging along under temperatures as high as 120 degrees, found the *tinajas* empty. Others missed them altogether. Later travelers, so it is said, expressed their joy at escaping by arranging in symbolic patterns the bleached bones of those who had perished just short of salvation.

The salvation of water. Dams, canals, and wells along the Colorado and Gila rivers have spotted the northwestern section of the Sonora Desert—it reaches far up the prickly western flanks of Arizona and spills over into the below-sea-level valleys of southeastern California—with emerald quilts worth many thousands of dollars an acre. Fantastic conduits sustain the urban areas of central Arizona and southern California. But as the belated rush to the Sunbelt continues—it didn't really build headway until World War II—the demands on the rivers and on natural underground reservoirs threaten to exceed the supply. When the crisis comes, if it does (we will investigate probabilities later in this account), into what pattern then will the bones of our hopes fall?

## High Country

Two mountain massifs counterbalance the southern deserts. One thrusts south out of Colorado approximately as far as Santa Fe and is divided roughly in half by the sweeping valley of the Rio Grande. The eastern section—which boasts of two peaks, Wheeler and Truchas, that exceed 13,000 feet in elevation—goes by the name Sangre de Cristo. As practically everyone knows, the phrase translates as "Blood of Christ" and derives from the ruddy light that some sunsets spread across the western slopes—a widespread mountain phenomenon that the more matter-of-fact Swiss call, in their country, alpenglow.

The western half of the New Mexico massif is an extension of Colorado's San Juans. In New Mexico the San Juans do not attain the elevation of the Sangre de Cristos, but are made delectable by many fine meadows winding among forests of slim aspens and stately evergreens. Unlike the Sangre de Cristos, the San Juans are riven into northern and southern sections by the highly colored trough of the Chama River, a major tributary of the Rio Grande. The break created by the Chama is pronounced enough so that the mountains south of it have their own name—Jemez, famed for containing one of the world's largest calderas. (A caldera is a collapsed volcano.) Tuff from this long-extinct erupter has been eroded into extraordinary forms by the thin streams that slice through the neighboring plateaus, and geologists say that other beds of ash from the same source were deposited as far away as Kansas. The ancient caldron itself, sixteen miles in diameter, is now ruffled with forests and dotted with peaceful ranches.

The main product of these northern mountains is not volcanic ash —though it is very fertile—or grass or wood, but small rivers. On the east side of the Sangre de Cristos a latticework of creeks gather to form the east-flowing Canadian River, named for a handful of French-Canadian traders who astounded the Spanish in 1739 by penetrating New Mexico from French bases in the Mississippi Valley. A more famous stream, which originates as a crystal dance in a deep V in the southern fringes of the same range, is the Pecos. As it moves south into Texas, its waters turn astringent but still serve to sustain many large cattle ranches and irrigate many thousands of acres.

Two mightier rivers are born in the Colorado section of the San Juan Mountains. The larger, called logically enough the San Juan, barely nicks the extreme northeastern part of New Mexico but contains 70 percent of the surface water available in the state for irrigation and urban use. Inevitably it is destined to play an increasingly important part in the emerging economy of that section of the Southwest, both for Indians and for Anglos.

The other stream is the Rio Grande. After flowing east out of the San Juans into Colorado's wide San Luis Valley, this historic river veers south and enters New Mexico through a profound slit of tan basalt that gradually gives way to narrow riverine plains. The Rio Grande is the only stream to travel entirely across New Mexico.

And that—the Canadian, Pecos, Rio Grande, Chama, and San Juan —is the full list of New Mexico's major perennial rivers (that is, streams that get somewhere before drying up). For the fifth largest state in the union, this is not very much water, especially when one considers that even at flood time none of the rivers will float anything larger than a rubber raft. Nor is Arizona, the sixth largest state, much better off with its engorged Colorado and overappropriated Gila.

Smallness has had one historic advantage in New Mexico, however. The Pueblo Indians first and afterward Hispanic settlers from New Spain could utilize the little streams for irrigation without machinery or big dams. Wherever the foothills opened enough to provide space for a few farms, tiny communities appeared.

For instance, Chimayó, founded about 1700. Once it was a compact town because of fear of Indians. Today it is a "string village," running for three or four miles beside the Santa Cruz River (a small creek actually) that trickles down the pine-clad western slopes of the Sangre de Cristo mountains. The settlement's single continuous street, paved now, is bordered by irrigation ditches cooled by the shade of tall cotton-wood trees. Each little house, bright with hollyhocks, is surrounded by a plot of corn and a few gnarled fruit trees. Sheep bells tinkle; roosters crow; no one hurries. The Spanish you hear has changed very little over the centuries and is sprinkled with archaic Castilian terms.

Here and at nearby Cordova are families of woodcarvers, who have been passing on their craft, father to son, for six generations or more. Here and at Truchas, perched spectacularly on the rim of the mesa above, families of weavers have carried on their trade fully as long; handmade Chimayó textiles are known to collectors throughout the Southwest. (But, according to Harry Cordova, master weaver of Truchas, change may be coming; the vocational courses given at the district high school seem to promise brighter futures to today's young people.)

At the upper end of the town, sheltered beside a small twin-towered adobe chapel that was built in 1815, is a tiny pool whose mud is believed to possess miraculous curative powers. Tewa Indians had been repairing there for a thousand years before the chapel was erected. They and the Hispanos still come, still believing. Plus this: In 1598 New Mexico's pioneering band of colonists ended their months-long journey a dozen miles or so from Chimayó's site. Part of the celebration with which they marked the completion of their trip was the reenactment of a pageant already a century old, Los Moros y los Cristianos, wherein gaily capari-soned warriors on horseback hammered away at each other in a sham battle symbolic of the expulsion of the Moors from Spain. Today in Chimayó a homespun version of that same pageant is presented each August to a crush of local celebrants who have to stand behind a sagging wire fence to watch, for there are no seats beside the field. Though almost surely the free-swinging performance—rearing horses, flowing capes, wooden swords and shields, papier-mâché helmets painted silver

—has not been presented every year since 1598, still Chimayó's Los Moros y los Cristianos has sound claim to being the oldest folk festival in the United States. And its existence is possible because the mountains, the manageable stream, and the narrow strip of irrigable land created an ambience wherein a faith in the rightness of what was being done could endure without competition from other cultures, which would not have understood, would not have wanted to understand, what the bronze-skinned people of Chimayó are reasserting to themselves by means of this ancient rite.

## Flat Country

The central axis of New Mexico has long been mountainous, but in past eons the ranges were loftier and wetter than they are now. Streams laden with silt and gravel roared down the slopes. Those flowing east soon struck flat country. As the water lost speed, the solid materials dropped out, clogged the channels, and forced the river to spread out into multiple new courses. Alluvial fans developed, much like the bajadas described earlier but on a grander scale. Spreading sideways, they merged. Advancing on a broad front, they carried sediment hundreds of miles east, forming from the waste of the mountains the area that we now call the High Plains.

Meanwhile the climate was growing drier. The change was not uniform. More rain fell east of the 100th meridian (the longitudinal line that forms, for part of its course, the eastern boundary of the Texas Panhandle) than falls where the Pecos River now flows. Changes in precipitation created changes in vegetation. More or less at the 100th meridian—the boundaries of climate zones are never precise—tall, rank prairie grasses gave way to short, curling buffalo grass whose myriad roots interlaced to form a highly resistant sod. This expanse of buffalo grass extended west to the present eastern rim of the Pecos Valley. Along the way precipitation averages slowly dwindled, and at the Pecos rim (except that as yet there was no valley), buffalo grass yielded in its turn to bunch grasses of various kinds, spaced out by the competition for water.

Ground covered by buffalo grass was protected from erosion. The rest was not. In the east the High Plains crumbled away, leaving escarpments hundreds of feet high deeply scalloped by cliff-girt canyons (Palo Duro is the most famous) that are still eating their way—inches a century—back into the alluvial earth beneath the sod.

Erosion at the western edge of the High Plains created what is sometimes called the Upland Trough, a broad depression that runs from Wyoming down through New Mexico into southwestern Texas. This trough is not a valley, for its continuity is broken by a series of swells that push east from the mountains far into the High Plains.

One such swell coincides roughly with the eastern section of the Colorado–New Mexico border. (Raton Pass—the famed wagon, railroad, and automobile gateway into the Southwest—is a low point in this rugged barrier.) Small creeks flowing south from the neighborhood of Raton Pass join others draining east out of the Sangre de Cristos. Together they fall into the Upland Trough, form the Canadian River, and strike out as if headed for Mexico. But then, in the vicinity of today's big Conchas Dam, another uplift intervenes and bends the Canadian due east to hew through the High Plains of the Texas Panhandle a flat-bottomed canyon a thousand feet deep.

Where the Upland Trough becomes open again a little north of historic Fort Sumner—scene of the Navajos' incarceration after the Long Walk of the 1860s and of Billy the Kid's nighttime death at Pat Garrett's hands a dozen years later—the Pecos slides in. Enveloped now by the Trough, the river continues south and southeast beside the High Plains to meet the Rio Grande.

And that is what buffalo grass has wrought: an enormous elevated tableland divided invisibly north and south by the Texas–New Mexico border and bounded by the Canadian, the Pecos, and the eastern escarpments in Texas. This unique plateau covers 20,000 square miles (about half the area of Ohio) and would be bigger still if geologists counted in the Edwards Plateau, with which it merges imperceptibly far south in Texas. Although a part of the Southern High Plains, it has been given its own name, Llano Estacado, the Staked Plains. Spanish soldiers probably called it that because its surrounding bluffs looked to them like military barricades built out of long stakes. However, one Anglo tale says that the name came from the habit pioneer homesteaders had of marking their trails with stakes that would guide them home again.

Although the Llano slopes gently toward the southeast, it looks dead flat. One community there has named itself, in resignation, Levelland. Rain falling on those aching, treeless miles of sameness does not run anywhere. It is either evaporated by winds whose average velocity is the highest in the United States—in winter they produce devastating blizzards—or it percolates directly into the ground except where soil compaction prevents. In those areas scores of shallow lakes appear, some a few rods in diameter, some a mile or more. Many are ephemeral but a few last throughout the year. Most are bitter with salts but nevertheless attract during the winter great flocks of one of the West's most appealing birds—long-billed, long-necked, long-winged, long-legged lesser sandhill cranes.

In fairly recent times, deep wells and scientific techniques of dry farming have blanketed the Llano with farms and cattle ranches. In earlier days, however, all people save the Plains Indians had trouble, despite the lakes, in making their way across its dry, featureless miles. The dread Comanches, who followed the teeming buffalo across it, increased the hazards. Thus the Llano Estacado became a barrier, increasing New Mexico's isolation by frustrating attempts to open a trade route from Santa Fe to Spanish San Antonio and on to the sea at New Orleans.

Yet it was not impenetrable, for it lured onto its blank expanses a small, bold class of Pueblo Indians and Hispanic adventurers called Comancheros after their custom of dickering with the dread nomads. At first the trade was limited to trinkets, dried buffalo meat, hides, the crusty bread the Indians loved, and captives taken from other tribes that the New Mexicans could sell at home as slaves. After the Civil War, however, as Texas settlements pressed westward, the Comanches took to running off whole herds of livestock. The Comancheros then became intermediaries in a flow of rustled horses and cattle, stocking many a ranch in New Mexico, and from there moved on to the California and Colorado goldfields. The clandestine business did little to soften the antipathy that has long existed between the peoples of New Mexico and Texas. But, then, to many New Mexicans the Texans also appear as raiders, for they twice tried to extend Lone Star jurisdiction across the Llano Estacado to the Rio Grande before being bought off by the United States Congress in 1850 for $10 million.

Economic penetration has been more successful. During this century so many people have moved from west Texas into the flat, rich oil, cotton, and cattle country of southeastern New Mexico that the area is now known as Little Texas. New Mexico even provides them and their relatives back home with an enticing playground, the Sacramento Mountains, whose main peak, Sierra Blanca, is 12,003 feet in elevation. Well up the Sacramento's eastern slope, at marvelous Ruidoso, sweet-smelling with pines, diligent promoters have built a racetrack that each year offers the world's biggest purse for quarter horses. A social philosopher might grow ruminative about this. The developers of Ruidoso Downs, one of them told me in all seriousness, decided to promote quarter horses because no other race track anywhere offered a world championship for that breed. The venture succeeded so well that the Downs is now conducting world-champion sweepstakes for mules. Mules are indeed worthy, long-suffering, neglected animals. But what one wonders is this: Does the sound of "world champion" so appeal to Texans that they have made a small town in a far-off mountain range a howling financial and social success on no other basis?

## High Country Again

The Sacramento Mountains are the easternmost of the many narrow, parallel, north-south ridges into which the Sangre de Cristo and San Juan Mountains split at approximately the latitude of Santa Fe. To adapt a description originally applied to somewhat similar ranges in Nevada, these uplifts look, on a relief map, like a group of caterpillars humping down toward the international border. Between them lie deep, dry troughs. The more favored of the depressions are grassy enough to support sheep and cattle ranches. Others are bleak with glistening white sand dunes (the world's first atom bomb was test-fired in one of those desolate hollows) or are splotched with scabrous flows of black lava.

Well west of the Rio Grande, the disjointed ridges pull together to form the lower end of the Southwest's second great mountain massif. Its directional cast is unlike that of most other North American chains in that its strike from its starting place in New Mexico is southeast to northwest rather than north-south. Long and rumpled, it has been carved by deep canyons and wide basins into too many sections to bear a single name. Instead it goes by many local designations—the Mogollons (pronounced Muggy-own) in New Mexico, the Whites and Pinaleños in eastern Arizona, followed by the Mogollon Plateau and the spectacular 200-mile Mogollon Rim, until at last it dwindles into wrinkled hills in the vicinity of the Grand Canyon's western extremity. But before the fading takes place, there is a final burst of geologic energy. On the highland's northern side are the loftiest summits in Arizona, the San Francisco Peaks, one of which, Humphrey Peak, reaches an elevation of 12,670 feet. Thanks to this long belt of mountains, Arizona is, visitors are sometimes surprised to learn, an important lumbering state. Boosters claim that it possesses the most ample stand of sunny-barked, long-needled ponderosa pines in the nation.

Be that as it may, the forest-crowned uplift certainly splits Arizona into two radically different sections. South and southwest of it, beyond the profound gorges of the Salt, the Verde, and the Gila rivers are the fringes of the Sonoran Desert, already described. To the north and northwest is the vast, chromatic Colorado Plateau.

By definition a plateau is an elevated plain, and there are indeed monotonous stretches of flat land here. But there are also sudden canyons, valleys bordered by fluted walls of highly colored rock, clusters of bare white-bluish-reddish humps called badlands by realists and the Painted Desert by romanticists, and then, farther north, more weird monoliths, inaccessible buttes, and shaggy, cliff-girt mesas.

The Plateau, which extends into adjacent regions of New Mexico, Colorado, and Utah, slopes inward from its high rims to the canyons of the Colorado River. The transition from one level to the next is often marked by plunging red cliffs. As altitude drops, pines give way to forests of twisted juniper and piñon and then to long reaches of velvety sagebrush. For much of the year it is a cold country, swept by scythelike winds.

Because of its abundance of ancient cliff-dwellings, of Navajo trading posts beside the sometimes desolate roads, and the Hopi villages on and around the jutting fingers of the mesas that wrinkle the heart of their reservation, tour guides like to call this section of the Southwest "Indian Country," just as though Indians live nowhere else. But perhaps the catch phrase is pardonable. For it is a colorful country, physically and metaphorically, and the scene as we will eventually notice, of some remarkable experiments designed to further Indian economic and educational self-sufficiency.

## The Sky Above

"Oh, our mother, the earth; oh, our father, the sky": Such is the opening line of a Pueblo Indian prayer. In another chant the Hopis thank the same duality for color, music, work, and "the understanding of the clouds." For the southwestern Indians know, better than do many whites in the same region, that existence depends on the fragile interplay of the life-giving powers of the land, the air, and the sun.

The uncertain storms come from different sources. The Pacific Ocean sends out winter clouds that provide about half of the precipitation received in the region's northern mountains. The Gulf of Mexico loads the summer's heated air with the restless components of crashing thunderstorms. Late spring and autumn are dry. But there are minor exceptions. The rainy season of the Southern High Plains spreads out from May through October, and southern Arizona is occasionally drenched at any time of year by storms moving unexpectedly northeast from the Gulf of California.

Elevation profoundly affects the amount of moisture that reaches the ground. The deserts near Yuma, Arizona, altitude 100 feet, average between two and three inches a year—and some years receive none. The upper elevations of the Sangre de Cristos may get forty inches. There is a price, however. Mountains tall enough to drain the clouds generally create "rain shadows" that leave valleys and basins on their lee sides panting and desiccated. For instance, the ring of distant mountains around the Colorado Plateau make it the driest part of the Southwest's northern reaches, even though its elevation is high—from 5,000 to 9,000 feet.

Summer thunderstorms are concentrated, erratic, and frequently intense. Because of the regularity with which currents of hot air slide up certain mountainsides, those spots draw the noisiest barrages. Santa Fe is said to attract more wild lightning storms than any region outside the Gulf Coast. And although each area drenched by a summer downpour is small, the weather conditions that produce the precipitation are widespread, so that several storms may be banging away simultaneously. One of the Southwest's magnificent sights is a sky of deep blue pools gleaming among gray-bottomed clouds that seem to rest on solid columns of rain—or, at times, of hail. Then, too, there are "dry" storms —rumbling purple clouds dragging along ragged curtains of rain that blow away without reaching the ground.

The suffering brought on by storms is sometimes extreme. In Santa Fe in the middle 1850s, rows of adobe homes simply dissolved. In 1946 in Carlsbad, southeastern New Mexico, flash floods slapped more than a hundred buildings out of their way in a matter of minutes. The Texas Panhandle is filled with tales about killing winter blizzards.

Individuals sometimes create their own catastrophes. One summer evening in 1878 while rain was sluicing across the Camp Supply region in southeastern Arizona, a young cavalry lieutenant, Austin Heneley, rode his horse into a rapidly rising stream. The animal turned topsyturvy. Seeing the wreck, a fellow lieutenant, John Rucker, raced down past a bend in the stream, spurred in, and reached for Heneley's bobbing body. Rucker's horse was also swept topsy-turvy. Both men were battered to death by water, and after that, Camp Supply was renamed Camp Rucker. The irony is that such floods fade into the sand almost as rapidly as they appear.

Because of a century studded with incidents like that, highway departments have learned to mistrust the ordinary wayfarer's judgment. In southern Arizona especially, warnings are posted where highways dip in and out of normally dry, bridgeless washes: DO NOT ENTER WHEN FLOODED. The grammatical ambiguity amuses English teachers: Who is flooded? But the point should be clear even to jokesters.

At the other end of the weather spectrum are dust storms. Except in the mornings, wind is a constant companion. It piles masses of yellow tumbleweeds against barbed-wire fences. Near human habitations it creates one of the nation's ugliest sights—festoons of tattered newspapers and tissues fluttering from every projection. For an illustration, if you want it, pause at the overlook where eastbound Interstate Highway 10 starts its drop into the Rio Grande Valley near Las Cruces. The distant view of green fields, the small, tree-shaded city, and the leaping backdrop of the Organ Mountains is unforgettable. But to see it you must steel your stomach against the sight of a square mile of nearby bushes writhing with paper tentacles and of ground littered with cans and broken glass.

Although air movement may quicken at any time of year toward gale force, the acceleration is most common during the dry months of spring and during summer droughts when the afternoon clouds release blasts of turbulence but no rain. First come ground streams—ribbons of sand skittering and rustling along the surface. As velocity increases, a yellow haze fills the lower parts of the air. If the rage persists, the dust clouds turn brown and rise as high as 12,000 feet. At such times visitors think they have arrived at the edge of cataclysm, but the occurrences are common enough so that the newspapers scarcely notice. For headlines there have to be near-zero visibility and enough sand seeping through door cracks to spread gritty films across floors, tablecloths, and dishes.

In a land where such winds blow, rainfall figures obviously do not tell much about the amount of available moisture in the earth. The sun, too, is another relentless drying agent. No other section of the United States is so awash with light. Clouds are so rare that 80 percent of the possible sunshine that could reach the earth between dawn and dark falls regularly on southwestern Texas, the southern parts of New Mexico and Arizona, and southeastern California. Furthermore, it is an intense glare, made so by reflection from light-colored soils and pale vegetation.

On the average, Albuquerque experiences only five days each year when the sky is so overcast that no beams slip through. In the winter this means balmy days, cool nights, and opportunity for uninterrupted recreation. Tourists love such weather, and the cities love the tourists. The El Paso newspaper keeps a running sunshine diary on its front page.

The last time I noticed, the record read complacently, "The sun shone today for the 119th consecutive day. The sun failed to shine only two days last year. The sun has failed to shine only 24 of the past 5,521 days." No doubt comparable statistics were in the minds of study-group members from the Société Médicale of Paris, who declared after examining the world's climates during the 1890s that New Mexico's weather possessed "more beneficial characteristics and fewer drawbacks than any other region of the world."

To the drying action of wind and sun must be added transpiration. Transpiration is the process whereby plants draw moisture from the soil, use it, and then pass it on through their pores into the atmosphere. Desert plants have developed many devices to reduce transpiration. Cacti have no leaves; ocotillo and paloverde shed theirs during dry times; some evergreen shrubs either curl up their leaves as temperatures rise or cover them permanently with a waxy exudation that inhibits the passage of water. In very few places do plants stand close together. Even so, a tremendous amount of the erratic precipitation that falls on southwestern soil returns to the air through the land's frugal vegetation.

As a result of these three drying agents—sun, wind, and transpiration—all but the highest mountains suffer from what agronomists call "moisture deficiency." In many places this deficiency exceeds twenty inches. This means that no matter how excellent the soil or how free of frost the nights, unless irrigation water equal in amount to twenty or more inches of rain is spread at appropriate intervals on the fields, crops cannot be grown.

The effect on the patterns of settlement and hence on the characteristics of the people has been profound. Until technology bred environmental arrogance, all races—Indians, Hispanos, Mexicans, Anglos— huddled together in spots where, like the people of Chimayó, they were able, with their limited mechanical resources, to move water out of nearby streams onto tillable fields. Men and women accustomed to laboring this way, using their own hands to bring life to the land, naturally grew to believe that they were better attuned to their needs than outsiders ever could be. Within fairly recent times, however, massive dams, huge canals, and perpetually whirring electric pumps have changed the life-bringing processes without changing attitudes, as a seemingly trivial happening of a few years past painfully demonstrates.

The teller of the tale is Charles Colley, author of a recent biography of one of Arizona's pioneering agricultural experts, Robert H. Forbes. Work in Africa as well as in the Southwest convinced Forbes that as the human race progressed, it had well earned the epithet "desert makers." After retiring from the University of Arizona at the mandatory age of sixty-five he carried this feeling with him into the legislature, where he served for several terms. He did not die until he was a hundred.

As part of his legislative crusade against desert making, Forbes argued ceaselessly for laws to regulate Arizona's rampant exploitation of its finite supplies of underground water. Inevitably he encountered bitter opposition. During the course of one public meeting an irate farmer shouted out that the value of his land depended on the water beneath it and he would be thoroughly damned if he would let his property rights be destroyed by government interference.

Forbes answered patiently that unless pumping were regulated, the property would soon be valueless anyway. The man thereupon stormed, "That's perfectly all right. If I want to destroy my land, I will do it, but I don't want you [meaning the legislature] to do it for me."

The audience erupted into cheers. And the memory of Chimayó, of the Rimrock Project, of the Pampers in the supermarket at Window Rock came back. *That baby will grow up Navajo!* Each southwestern group, its values fortified by shared living in protective pockets of isolation, likes to think the same of its children. But always, one way or another, sooner or later, the pockets have been breached. What then?

That, essentially, is what this book is about—the problems that came during periods of critical change and disillusionment to several stubborn peoples who had been convinced by long habit that their ways were right.

# 1

## BEGINNINGS

*Firstcomers*

Twenty thousand years ago the land's long corrugations of mountain and valley were untouched by man. Animals abounded, for the climate was humid then. Curling streams, sweet-water lakes, and savannas of thick grass supported mammoths, mastodons, elephants, camels, giant ground sloths, and towering early-day bison in numbers almost beyond our conception. Because of such bounties, men eventually did appear from somewhere—not gnarled ancestral prototypes, but true men, erect, intelligent, able to utilize fire and flake pieces of obsidian and flint into deadly cutting edges.

In spite of heated arguments to the contrary, conservative archaeologists are unwilling to date the arrival much before 10,000–12,000 B.C. It was probably a slow penetration by small family bands. By means of primitive warfare the different groups laid claim to exclusive hunting territories through which they wandered as the demands of hunger dictated. Another need, the avoidance of inbreeding, led to fierce raids on neighboring bands for the sake of exogamous mates.

The hunters' lives were short, brutal, and filled with a continuing wonder at and fear of natural phenomena they could neither understand nor control. The fortuitous slaying, generally from an ambush beside a waterhole, of some massive creature brought savage rejoicing to the entire band, accompanied, one imagines, by ululating howls of triumph from the killers. Everyone rushed in. They dulled their first hunger with blood and raw bits of the vitamin-rich internal organs. Sated briefly, they ripped off chunks of meat that they carried to a nearby shallow cave, where they roasted it and at a joyous communal feast gorged themselves close to stupefaction.

If the need for clothing demanded, women armed with stone knives stripped the slain animal's hide from its carcass. With stone scrapers they removed clinging bits of fat and flesh, a process that helped preserve the hide and made it suitable for shaping into garments. At what time the wanderers learned to tan skins by removing the hair and softening the leather with a concoction brewed from the animal's own brain is unknown.

Man's instinctive inventiveness showed itself in the shaping of projectile points. One noteworthy development was the adding of longitudinal grooves to both faces of a spearhead so that blood would flow more freely when the weapon was thrust into its target. Once a satisfactory point had been developed, change came slowly—but it did come. Archaeologists have learned to recognize several types of points and have named them for the sites where each was first discovered—Sandia, Clovis, Folsom. By coincidence all are in New Mexico. It should not be assumed, however, that any given design originated at the site for which it was named, because later discoveries have shown that successful design innovations spread quickly throughout large geographical areas. Some theorists speculate that this uniformity in artifacts means uniformity in race: The Southwest's firstcomers all belonged to the same "tribal" group. Or it may simply mean that useful technological developments are quickly adopted by even antagonistic peoples, as witness, for a single modern example, the transistor radio.

Another archaeological mystery concerns the fate of the early hunters. About 8,000 to 7,000 B.C. the climate turned arid. The luxuriant vegetation that had supported the giant herbivore died out. So, too, did the animals, an extinction hastened by the Paleo-Indians as they desperately hunted down the last herds that were struggling to survive in a dwindling number of favored spots.

Did the predators vanish with their victims? Or did they adapt to environmental change? No one knows. In any event, the Southwest remained populated, either by descendants of the early hunters or by a new influx of people from the outside—or both. Whoever they were, these arid-land dwellers were able to exist on a varied diet—mountain sheep and deer if hunting went well, but mostly seeds, berries, nuts, roots, insects, reptiles, and such small game as rabbits, squirrels, and rodents, which could be killed with a throwing stick or trapped in primitive snares.

Changing from a meat to a partly vegetable diet under the impetus of hunger seems in hindsight an obvious enough step, but before it could be taken considerable ingenuity had to be called into play. Hard seeds cannot be assimilated by the human digestive system unless they are pulverized, in itself a remarkable discovery that came from no one knows where. As pulverizing agents the Indians of the Southwest—and elsewhere—developed grinding stones. The bottom one, which remained stationary, was hollowed out to hold the grain; the other, rounded to fit the hand, was rolled tediously back and forth over the kernels until they were reduced to a powder.

Before the seeds could be ground they had to be gathered. This brought into being beaters, seed trays, baskets transported on one's back by means of a tumpline around the forehead, and woven receptacles for storage. (Pits lined with stones against rodents also served as storehouses.) Another remarkable discovery was the waterproofing of tightly woven baskets with resin or other gums. This made possible the cooking of food in water that was brought to a boil by the addition of fire-heated stones. Once that step had been taken, pulverized grains could be turned into gruel as well as baked into flat cakes.

Because numerous artifacts from this post-big-game hunting period have been unearthed in Cochise County, southeastern Arizona, the culture as it exists in the Southwest has been named Cochise. The term is too limiting, for it implies a restriction of area and a uniformity of peoples that did not exist. The only standardization was in man-made objects, which suggests once more that useful knowledge spreads more rapidly than do feelings of common brotherhood.

At some point, possibly as early as 3,000 B.C. and probably on the broad, grassy highlands where the Continental Divide crosses today's international border, wandering groups of seed-eating Cochise peoples made their initial contacts with native American agriculture, a discovery that had taken place millennia before in central Mexico. Its staples were primitive maize (cobs only two or three inches long have been found in Bat Cave, west-central New Mexico), beans, squash, melons, and, almost as useful, cotton. Another, somewhat later borrowing from the south was pottery.

From these acquisitions a new culture evolved, called Mogollon after the mountains where the first revealing artifacts were found. Like all early changes, this one had been slow. A few families would heap up little mounds of earth, make holes with pointed sticks, drop in kernels, and leave the rest to the weather while they resumed their habitual search for seeds, insects, and small animals. But now there was an anchor. Each fall the wanderers came back to harvest the produce that summer sun and rain had matured. It was the fumbling beginning of what the Spanish later called *rancherias*—villages of scattered huts that were not occupied throughout the year but that had as the basis of their continuity the planted fields around them. Eventually hundreds of *rancherias,* their social and physical organization varying from area to area, were dotted throughout what is now the Mexican Northwest and the American Southwest. A few still remain.

## The Canal Diggers

Gradually, by steps that cannot now be traced, a more sophisticated agriculture developed in the low desert south of Arizona's central axis of mountains. There, in a broad, hot valley, a great gathering of waters occurs. The Gila, Salt, and Verde rivers knife down from the mountains on the east and north, and the San Pedro moves more sluggishly out of the highlands near today's border with Mexico. So much living water in a warm and fertile land drew northward from Mexico a group of prehistoric people known today as Hohokam, a Pima word meaning "all used up" or "vanished."

By the beginning of the Christian era, as Europeans count time, the Hohokam were diverting water from the rivers of the Gila system to spots where its life-giving powers would be productive. The ditches grew until by A.D. 700 some were as much as thirty feet wide at the top, fifteen feet deep, and carried water to fields six to seven miles from their intake points. The labor involved staggers our machinery-oriented imaginations. Without the aid of metal picks or shovels or wheels for moving carts, the Hohokam excavated networks of canals aggregating as much as 150 miles in length. Obviously some kind of power structure was necessary to regulate the work of construction and maintenance and to make sure that farmers on the upper part of the system did not prevent a fair share of water from reaching those lower down. The job was so well done that during the 1860s Anglo pioneers simply repaired and cleaned the old canals and used them to water their own "pioneering" fields. Even today Pima Indians use sections of the old complex for irrigating their crops.

Thanks to that laboriously constructed system, a relatively few Hohokam farmers could feed several times their own number. The energies thus released were devoted to many pursuits. Towns containing a hundred or more houses each grew up. The buildings were simple. First a shallow pit was dug into the earth, the floor hardened, and a dome-shaped roof of posts, brush, and earth erected over it. By A.D. 1000 or so the Hohokam apparently were also heaping up earthen temples shaped like truncated pyramids and were building huge courts with earthen walls wherein a violent game was played with small rubber balls that resemble modern handballs.

Crafts flourished. As the canal network spread, the Hohokam began growing cotton. They mastered intricate styles of weaving. They made buff-colored pottery and small clay figurines that they decorated with a paint of reddish iron oxide. Because they were near the Gulf of California they obtained seashells by trade and fashioned them into ornaments. Their great artistic triumph was learning how to etch designs into the shells with cactus juice, a technique that antedated the discovery of etching in Europe by two or three hundred years.

As so often happens, success proved to be its own undoing. Overuse of irrigation water and lack of drainage in the fields saturated the soil with salts. In search of fresh land, the Hohokam farmers kept moving downstream, a dispersal perhaps hastened by internecine feuds, until diminished returns and diminished hopes finally brought the effort to an anticlimactic end. And incipient urban civilization regressed to a *rancheria* style of living that was followed until modern times by the Hohokams' reputed descendants, the Pimas and Papagos.

## Builders in Stone

Several generations passed before a working knowledge of agriculture spread from the Mogollon and Hohokam people northward into the grudging environment of the Colorado Plateau. The food gatherers there were basketmakers—exceptionally good basketmakers. They had progressed from weaving with coarse materials to using fine vegetable fibers for making soft, seamless bags, dog hair for belts, and human hair for braided rope. During their wanderings they sheltered themselves in the numerous caves that dot the sandstone canyons of the Plateau. The many bands spoke at least four different languages and several dialects of each. Where the different groups came from is another mystery. Some at least seem to have been dissident Kiowas who split away from their main group on the High Plains, roamed westward into the Four Corners area (where New Mexico, Colorado, Utah, and Arizona come together), and there, about A.D. 500 exchanged their nomadic ways for a more sedentary farming existence. The distinctive culture that they and their disparate neighbors developed was so uniform that it resulted (as with

Cochise and Mogollon) in a single term being applied to many people—
Anasazi, a Navajo word meaning "Ancient Ones."

In time the Anasazi moved from their caves to surface sites close
to the Plateau's rare sources of dependable water. There they took to
living in clusters of unimpressive pit houses similar to those used by the
Hohokam.

The largest communities of pit houses took shape on that part of the
Colorado Plateau drained by the San Juan River. North of the San Juan
the favorite streams included the Animas River, McElmo Creek, and,
especially, the deeply canyoned water courses of today's Mesa Verde
National Park. South of the San Juan, other relatively populous settlements grew up beside the trickling Chaco River, a product of the Continental Divide in northwestern New Mexico, and Chinle Wash, which
heads in spectacular Canyon de Chelly, Arizona.

Different kinds of geography in this large block of country called for
different kinds of cultivation. On the high ridges of southwestern
Colorado and on parts of the Hopi tablelands south of Black Mesa,
enough precipitation fell during summers to make "dry" farming possible, especially on alluvial fans where waters draining down mountain
gullies spread out to provide intermittent wetness. Elsewhere controls
were necessary.

The simplest kind was to use small rock walls and earth for creating
planting terraces in normally dry gullies. When rainwater did flow, the
planted terraces were able to sponge up enough moisture to keep the
plants growing. Where perennial streams flowed past bits of arable
ground, gravity irrigation ditches were used. Because creeks and planting patches were small, so, too, were the canals—except in Chaco Canyon. There the Anasazi built irrigation works comparable to the ones
constructed by the Hohokam farther south. In Chaco, too, the Anasazi
farmers learned to build reservoirs, some paved with clay and stone to
reduce seepage.

Although no social organization of any kind linked one community
to another, their technologies developed along similar lines. The people
all learned, very gradually, to replace atlatls (a device for hurling spears)
with more accurate bows and arrows, to make pottery, and to domesti-
cate the wild turkeys that were raiding their crops. Interestingly
enough, the turkeys were kept not for eating (except for some Mesa
Verde people, who apparently enjoyed roast fowl) but for feathers,
which were used for ceremonial decorations and for making fine turkey-
feather robes and blankets.

The Anasazis' crowning achievement was community architecture.

Along toward A.D. 900 a surge of energy swept the Plateau settlements. During the next several generations pit dwellings were abandoned in favor of conjoined masonry apartment houses called pueblos (towns) by the Spanish. Some pueblos apparently grew by simple accretion, cell on cell. Others followed a preconceived plan, their multistoried buildings ranged neatly around one or more central plazas. Most were erected either on mesa tops or in valley bottoms. A few—and these are the ones that most impress modern tourists—were crowded into huge caves in the walls of certain canyons. On encountering one of those cool, silent, cliff-encased ruins, it is impossible not to feel a stab of emotion, for somehow the honey-colored, honeycombed gatherings of stone manage to convey both the poetry of life's timelessness and the mortality of its individual members.

Why were the towns designed as they were? Again no one knows. Cave locations, from which the fields and sources of firewood were hard to reach, suggest considerations of defense. So, too, do the blank walls on the outer sides of the terraced houses built around plazas where the land was flat. Defense against whom? Raiding nomads of whom no record remains? Or from war parties sallying out of one Anasazi pueblo against the inhabitants of another? Or perhaps the residents of the pueblos that were built on flat land simply wanted to be as close as possible to the central plazas, where each village's religious life centered, and therefore they erected their buildings in tiers rather than stringing them out.

Whether the buildings were located in caves or on the top of mesas, their masonry was superb. Structures built in caves often rose from the brink of space for twenty feet or more. Those on flat land were taller and more extensive. Pueblo Bonito in the bottom of Chaco Canyon, designed in the shape of a huge D—its straight wall was 667 feet long, the rounded one more than 800 feet—held 800 rooms arranged in several stories. Nearby Chetro Ketl contained an estimated 60 million stone blocks, along with almost innumerable beams and poles cut with stone axes in the mountains and carried on human backs to the growing village. Captain Perez de Villagra, who traveled through parts of the Southwest with the Oñate expedition in the early 1600s, claims to have seen pueblos seven stories high. The magnitude of such accomplishments can best be appreciated by remembering that apartment houses of equivalent height did not appear in New York City until the advent of structural steel following the Civil War.

Entrance into the lower levels of the terraced dwellings was by means of ladders to the roof and then down through a hole that also served as a flue for the fire beneath. Like the blank rear walls, lack of doorways suggests defense. But it also indicates the hold of tradition on the Anasazi, for their pit houses had also been entered through roof holes. Those ancient dwellings, indeed, became prototypes for the village sanctuaries now known by the Hopi word *kiva.* Large villages contained dozens of small kivas. Sometimes interlocking with each other and with the house walls, they were for clan or family use. Kivas for community use were enormous, up to sixty feet in diameter, their walls gaily painted and their roofs supported by massive pillars.

Kivas were, in the main, subterranean, but they might be partly above ground. As a general thing, they were round, but they might be rectangular or square. Mostly the kiva was the domain of men, but women could enter to bring food, watch ceremonies, or socialize a bit. The early Spanish called the cells *estufas,* hot rooms for sweat baths. The word has often been shrugged aside as a mistake, but archaeologist Edgar L. Hewitt, who spent many years working in Chaco Canyon, thinks the kivas may well have filled that function also.

Whatever their miscellaneous uses, kivas were essentially religious in purpose. Pragmatists may call the small tunnel that extended from under the kiva floor to the surface outside a ventilator shaft, and the slab of stone behind the central fire pit a deflector. But to the Pueblos the shaft provided an approach for the *kachinas,* the spirits of earth and sky, and the deflector was definitely an altar. The kiva also held the sipapu, the symbolic hole that represented the people's place of emergence into the upper world. Finally, the kiva was the storehouse for the sacred paraphernalia of the ceremonial dances.

The dances, which involved the entire populace of a village either as participants or spectators, were held at set times in the plazas. Mostly the rituals were religious. In giving up nomadic habits for the fancied security of agriculture, the Anasazi had locked themselves into an environmental trap. The land and the climate were harsh. Acutely aware of their dependence on the powers of earth and sky, the Ancient Ones sought through a series of elaborate and carefully memorized rituals to propitiate what they could not otherwise control.

Dancing was the principal medium of expression—communal dancing, for in those tightly structured societies there was little room for individual prayer. Indeed, prayer is a poor term for the ceremonies. Their basis was magic—incantations designed to bring about desired happenings. Some of the ritualistic dances were associated with the growth of corn: its planting, its maturing, its harvesting. Others were calculated to force rain from the rare clouds or to keep the sun from going astray at the time of the solstices. If results did not follow, the failure was blamed on some incorrectness in the ceremony.

A further purpose of some of the rituals was the redistribution of wealth. Although the Anasazi, like most Indians, had no concept of the ownership of land in an Anglo sense, families did farm individual plots, and not all reaped equally well. In order that the inequities might be redressed, certain dances were accompanied by a piling up of food items to which the dancers and those in need could help themselves. It was all done in style, and was great fun, too—a thud of drums, the thrum of whirling bull-roarers, the blaze of color from pine boughs and feathers attached to costumes, from ornaments and garish masks.

Theirs was a dynamic civilization. Its architectural influence spread south through central Arizona to the Hohokam and on into northern Mexico, inspiring structures whose remnants are still visible. The bands of the Mogollon Mountains, who may have given the Anasazi their first knowledge of agriculture, received from them in turn new concepts of construction. Beside the Mimbres River in southwestern New Mexico a people now called Mimbreños perfected what some connoisseurs consider to be the handsomest prehistoric pottery in North America.

Such dynamism also fostered embryo commerce and industry. The different groups of Anasazi not only quarried stone, but also mined turquoise for jewelry, obsidian for arrow points, hematite and other colored earths to use in making paint for adorning their bodies, pottery, and ceremonial masks. In New Mexico they harvested salt from deposits left by the evaporation of saline lakes east of the Manzano Mountains, and in central Arizona they used tunnels and at least one shaft for burrowing in quest of the same substance. These products were all used as articles of trade between the various villages. Turquoise was sent deep into Mexico, where the Aztecs revered green objects. In exchange for it, the Anasazi received little tinkling copper bells and live parrots and macaws. Other articles brought in from a considerable distance were coral for beads and seashells.

The principal Anasazi trading center was an astounding complex of towns in Chaco Canyon, northwestern New Mexico. Four main villages occupied the wide, relatively flat canyon bottom. Smaller towns dotted other parts of the depression, between undulating red sandstone cliffs only sixty or so feet tall. Others stood back on the adjoining mesas—a total of forty or so towns housing a combined population of perhaps 8,000. Most of the inhabitants apparently were involved in gathering or making objects of trade or in growing food to support the merchants.

Among the most intriguing of the Chaco remnants are the roads.

The Anasazi had no wheels and hence no carts, yet sophisticated aerial surveys have recently revealed a system of highways, some more than twenty feet wide, radiating from the main center off through an area roughly 200 miles in circumference. Those roads ran straight as arrows; when they turned, they did so at right angles. They surmounted the low cliffs of the region with ramps or steps chiseled into the stone. Some evidence of fill exists in low spots, and it seems that during the height of Chaco's prosperity in the eleventh and twelfth centuries A.D. the highways were kept scrupulously clean of stones and brush. Associated with them, perhaps, were masonry lookout stations. Modern investigators have found that smoke or fire signals emanating from the stations make possible the sending of simple coded messages across miles of desert country in minutes. Often, too, the stations were placed so that persons standing a few yards to one side or another of the direct line of vision could not detect the communications.

The roads linked town to town, and the towns to resource sites—to agricultural fields near water; to pits from which fine clay could be dug for pottery; to the mountains, fifteen or more miles away, where timber grew. The Chaco people used tens of thousands of heavy pine logs in building their multistoried masonry apartment houses. The easiest way for a group of men to transport a log thirty feet long was not to line up single file, but to march abreast, each carrier clutching his part of the log to his chest. So wide, cleared paths made sense for wood carrying. Not all the roads, however, led to the trees, yet they too were carefully engineered and maintained. Why? For ceremonial foot races? (The Navajos raced horses along some of the ancient roads well before whites became cognizant of the lanes.) No one can give an answer—yet.

Another prehistoric pursuit of note was the strip mining of coal from flat seams in Jeddito Basin on the south side of Black Mesa, about 120 miles west and a little north of Chaco Canyon. Using baskets for carrying, the ancestors of today's Hopis removed the overburden and excavated the underlying material for cooking, heating their homes, and firing pottery. (The use of coal for heat was discovered at about the same time in England.) There is evidence that those ancient miners may have also ventured underground. In any event, they extracted from the southern edges of Black Mesa, between A.D. 1000 and A.D. 1500 an amount of coal estimated at well over 100,000 tons. During the past decade, Black Mesa has become the scene of highly controversial Anglo strip-mining activity on a far larger and more destructive scale. But who is to say the Anasazi would not have mined as much a thousand years ago if they could have?

## Regroupings

Astounding vigor—and yet, as seems to happen in all civilizations, the Anasazi culture lost its drive. Fields wore out. The cutting of excessive amounts of timber started erosion cycles that resulted in such deep arroyos that water could no longer be turned easily into irrigation ditches. Possibly a drop in temperature suggested the wisdom of moving to regions that had longer growing seasons. Topping these problems there came, late in the twelfth century, a staggering drought.

The combined blows forced an essentially conservative people to leave their homes in search of new hope. The Four Corners country was abandoned. New groupings took form. In the west there was considerable clustering around the Hopi mesas and at the Zuñi pueblos close to the present Arizona–New Mexico border. A little farther east another community arose on the broad top of the cliff-girt mesa still known as Acoma.

The largest concentrations gathered in the Rio Grande Valley, both beside the main river and along its short tributaries. There the migrants apparently absorbed early farmers of uncertain derivation who until then had been living in simple one-story houses of mud and sticks. Meanwhile other migrating Anasazi continued past the Rio Grande to settle in the Galisteo Basin south of today's Santa Fe, on the relatively moist eastern slopes of the Manzano Mountains, and beside the Pecos River. At each new site they tried, like displaced persons from every other nation, to recreate the civilization they had known earlier, but in none of the new towns did they attain the artistic or architectural excellence of their ancestors.

Spanish estimates indicate that when, about A.D. 1500, stability returned to the area 30,000 or more people were dwelling in 100 pueblos. As before, they spoke several languages, some with bewilderingly similar names—Tiwa, Tewa, Towa, Tano, Piro, Tompiro, and, finally, Keresan. Related groups were not always neighbors. The Tiwa of Taos were separated by many miles from their southern relatives, who chose to come to a halt on both sides of the Rio Grande north of Albuquerque. That branch of the Towas that until the 1830s lived in an extensive complex beside the Pecos River was far removed from related Towas whose communities dotted the western tributaries of the Rio Grande. And so on—a hodgepodge that continues to furrow the brows of archaeologists seeking to untangle the movements of the various groups by means of pottery types, linguistic peculiarities, ceremonial distinctions, and the like. For us the main thing to remember is that the seemingly similar Pueblos are really a salad bowl of unamalgamated peoples, and that even today the residents of neighboring towns frequently cannot understand each other without resorting to either Spanish or English as a common tongue.

At about the time the different Pueblos were coming to new terms with their natural environment, fragmented bands of pure nomads, the Apaches, harried out of the north by stronger tribes, were drifting onto the Southern High Plains of eastern New Mexico and western Texas. Wiry and deep-chested, they moved on foot, of course, but they did use big, wolflike dogs hitched to travois poles for dragging their buffalo-hide tipis and containers of personal possessions from one camp site to the next. Their social organization was extremely loose—twenty or so bands further split into extended family groups with no leaders other than the shamans who directed traditional ceremonies and ambitious young men who now and then put together temporary raiding or hunting parties.

After reaching the Southwest, these many bands began slowly scattering out across even wider reaches of country than the Anasazi-Pueblos had covered during their migrations. To try to be precise about each group would be an exercise in confusion—even if it were possible. Here it is enough to say that the Apache de Navajú (today's Navajo) wandered across the Continental Divide into the San Juan Basin of northwestern New Mexico. The Jicarilla Apache (so named because of their skill in making *jicarillas,* or small baskets) stayed east of the Navajo in the rough country of north-central and northeastern New Mexico. The Mescaleros, who delighted in eating the pit-barbecued hearts of the mescal plant, eventually appropriated as their favorite base the Sacramento Mountains, dominated by Sierra Blanca's hoary head. The Lipans ranged through the rumpled country of southwest Texas and on across the ferocious Big Bend section into Mexico. Still others—Gilas, Chiricahuas, Tontos, and whatnot, now lumped together as Western Apaches— worked their way across New Mexico to find firm lodgment in the shaggy wilds around the upper reaches of the Gila River.

None of them seemed to have caused any particular trouble for the sedentary Pueblos—then. Indeed, all the Apache bands learned some agriculture from their new neighbors and developed a rudimentary kind of *rancheria* culture. On the High Plains, contacts (except possibly with the Piro) extended beyond mere imitation. The Apache there liked Pueblo vegetables and pottery, and the Pueblos liked the dried buffalo meat and buffalo hides that the Apache offered in trade. An easygoing equilibrium, potentially advantageous to both peoples was developing, when, to the total astonishment of both groups, the Spaniards burst onto the scene with guns, horses, greeds, and strange religious assurances. After that, things could never again be the same.

# 2

## DON QUIXOTE'S NEW WORLD COUSINS

### With Wild Surmise

In the spring of 1536 three half-naked Spaniards and the black slave of one of them appeared as if by magic on what was then New Spain's (Mexico's) farthest northwestern frontier. The four had just completed one of the extraordinary odysseys of North American history, and yet the madness of the times was such that the rumors they reported commanded far more attention than did the sober chronicle of their misadventures.

It was a twist that would have absorbed Miguel de Cervantes Saavedra, creator of Don Quixote. For, as Cervantes recognized, the Spanish temperament was given to blurring fact with illusion and then pursuing what resulted with unreckoning persistence. Quixotism: the stuff of comedy. Our smiles are wry, however. For in much of the Southwest it has been, and still is, the stuff of tragic history as well.

Its seeds were sown in the petty kingdoms of the Iberian Peninsula. For nearly 800 years—more than three times as long as the United States has been in existence—those unyielding people battled the invading Moors from North Africa. Whole lifetimes were built around the struggle. Ragged peasants as well as nobles fought ferociously to maintain Christendom against the abominations of Islam, to thrust forward inch by inch the land claimed by the medieval princes to whom they owed allegiance, and, for themselves, to gain recognition and fortune.

Fame came from exhibiting proper mixtures of courage, charisma, craftiness, endurance, and loyalty—at least until treachery became more profitable than loyalty. Prestige arose from owning a bit of ground worked not by one's own hands but by defeated infidels held in *en-*

*comienda,* or trust, an arrangement whereby the *encomendero* protected his charges and trained them in Christian ways in return for the right to exact reasonable amounts of labor and tribute from them. This was pride at its highest. A landowner was a *señor.* If the king smiled, he became a *hidalgo* (literally *hijo + algo,* son of something) and could place the title *Don* in front of his name. Inasmuch as the title was hereditary, pretensions to gentility could continue long after the land itself was lost. By Renaissance times the Spanish Peninsula swarmed with hidalgos who possessed little more than coats of arms and ready swords.

What the centuries of warfare did not instill was a respect for toil, for the careful management of agricultural fields, or the wealth that might have been reaped in the drab commercial ventures that were bringing a new merchant class to the fore elsewhere in Europe. Because of these prejudices, younger sons (landed estates went to the firstborn) had only a few acceptable fields in which they could exercise their talents. Educated as lawyers, they might seek office in the tightly structured bureaucracy that the Spanish monarchs were creating. Educated as clerics, they could enter the increasingly powerful Church or one of its religious orders. Or they might buy army commissions and attach themselves to the banner of some renowned captain.

It so happened that the last Moors were driven from Spain in 1492, the same year that Christopher Columbus opened the gates to the New World. Established families were not particularly impressed by Columbus; they thought their sons should stay in Europe, where Spain was rapidly climbing to the top of the continental power structure. But those on the periphery, those who had not yet attained either status or the raw loot they thought would bring status—they rushed in. There were churchmen dreaming of a wealth of heathen souls to save, and would-be *encomenderos* dreaming of broad plantations tilled by those same heathens. There were office holders, camp followers, sutlers, and just plain pillagers.

All told, their numbers were relatively few, but their accomplishments were not. First came fabulous wealth from sugar fields in the Indies. The natives who worked there died in such numbers from oppression and unfamiliar diseases introduced by the conquerors that replacing them with fresh laborers captured in yet unconquered islands and on the mainland became another source of handsome profit. After that came the wildness for gold, stimulated first by Cortés's looting of the Aztec empire and then Pizarro's brutal subduing of the Incas—a sequence of bulldog battles during which the vastly outnumbered invaders rallied from defeat and, aided by native allies, a few horses, and minimal technological superiority, won victories that even today seem next to unbelievable.

Who were the conquerors? Cortés was the son of an obscure squire who had fallen on bad times. Pizarro's birth was illegitimate, and he is said to have worked for a time as a swineherd. Both came from Spain's poorest province, Estremadura, as did one of Pizarro's principal captains, Hernando de Soto. All three became governors—Cortés of Mexico, Pizarro of Peru, De Soto of Cuba—and all were wealthier than even they could say.

Naturally the adventurers who had come to the New World in quest of just such wonders talked endlessly of the accomplishments—and of the myths that in their exuberance they took to be as real as Tenochtitlán itself. Wide-eyed, they dreamed of El Dorado, the gilded man, whose entire body was dusted with gold at a yearly festival and whose imaginary kingdom has provided a name for counties, towns, cities and metaphors throughout the United States. Of the fantasy (*Las Sergas de Esplandián* by Garcí Ordóñez de Montalvo) that named California: "Know ye that at the right hand of the Indies there is an island named California, very close to the Terrestrial Paradise and inhabited by black women, without a single man among them. [Ah, what a place to overrun!] . . . The island everywhere abounds with gold and precious stones . . ." And the Seven Cities of Antilla, founded by a Christian archbishop and six bishops fleeing with their people from the Moors to a haven provided by Providence in the West—a rich haven, naturally.

Talking so, unattached fortune hunters strolled arrogantly through the streets of the half-rebuilt Tenochtitlán (Mexico City), abused the hospitality of those who took them in, seduced white women, raped the others, and looked for someone to lead them to magnificence. Churchmen complained to the king about them and about the *encomenderos'* treatment of the Indians. King's agents, listening to a thousand rumors about the next coup to be wrought by this riffraff, raised doubts about Cortés's loyalty. He was deposed as governor, and Mexico entered a period of even greater chaos as rival factions struggled to seize the power that had once been his.

The task of cleansing the stables fell on a royal commission headed by the scion of a most illustrious family, Don Antonio de Mendoza. An exemplary bureaucrat, Mendoza was widely admired for his humanistic education, his aplomb, efficiency, affability, and loyalty. To keep him incorruptible, he was given an annual salary that has been estimated as the equivalent in purchasing power of one million of today's dollars. But even Mendoza proved susceptible to that blurring of reality and illusion that was becoming the hallmark of early Mexico.

And so we return to the three whites and the black slave who appeared out of the northern wilds only months after Mendoza assumed his seat of power in Mexico City. For like everyone else in his court the viceroy was fascinated by the story.

Eight years earlier the quartet had been members of a large gold-hunting expedition stranded in Florida. With characteristic tenacity, the conquistadores, many of whom had never before worked with their hands, killed their horses and made boats by stretching the hides over a framework of timber. They melted down spurs, bridles, and other accouterments to obtain necessary metal. They improvised sails and oars and then rowed out past the surf to follow the coastline to Pánuco, Mexico, a new settlement that they supposed was only a few hundred miles away. Near present-day Galveston, Texas, the soggy boats became separated. Some evidently foundered at sea; some wrecked on the shore. Soon only five scattered survivors remained, toiling as slaves of the Indians who captured them. Of the five, one preferred, when an opportunity to escape arose, to stay with his masters rather than face the terrors of the unknown.

After six years of hunger and misery, the other four got together and fled west. Their leading spirit was a nobleman named Alvar Nuñez Cabeza de Vaca, who had left Spain as treasurer of the ill-fated expedition. Somehow the Indians came to believe he possessed miraculous healing powers, and after that the quartet's journey, which lasted two years, was a triumphant procession from one tribe to the next. They encountered and crossed the Rio Grande somewhere in the vicinity of today's El Paso and may have touched on New Mexico and Arizona before bearing south through Sonora and Sinaloa. It was a magnificent epic, but the things they saw—buffalo, many different tribes of Indians, naked mountains, towering cacti—did not interest their listeners nearly as much as things about which they had heard only vague reports. Farther north than they went, it was said, were cities formed of houses containing several stories. The inhabitants wove and wore fine cotton cloth (and no doubt adorned the garments with golden ornaments). They had coral (and it was easy to imagine pearls as well) that came from a sea somewhere to the west. They mined turquoise and emeralds. Five of these emeralds, shaped like arrowheads (probably they were of malachite), had traveled the trade routes to Sonora and there had been given to the travelers by their hosts during that stage of their journey.

These sparse seeds fell on fertile ground. Not long before, the unspeakable Nuño de Gutzmán, pillager, slave hunter, mass murderer, had heard of similar cities from an Indian who claimed to have visited them long before during a trading trip with his father—cities agleam with silver streets and other stock embellishments. Immediately the Don Quixotes of the region had decided that the habitations were the fabled Seven Cities founded by the Christian bishops who had escaped from the Moors, and many had joined Gutzmán as he thrashed through the mountains with his Indian informant, trying fruitlessly to find the wonders. But now here were Europeans, not aborigines, who had been close by and could lead the way!

Mendoza proposed that the quartet do just that—return as scouts to see with their own eyes the things that so far they had only heard about. They refused, and Mendoza had to be content with buying from his owner the slave, Estevánico, or Esteban. He then turned the black over to a remarkable Franciscan friar, Marcos de Niza, who had been in both Guatemala and Peru and knew just how mind-boggling the treasures of the New World could be.

What followed cannot be readily explained. Accompanied by a devoted retinue of Indians, Estevánico strutted off ahead of Fray Marcos but kept himself in good graces by sending back regular reports of the marvels that lay just beyond the next hill. Eventually the black reached multistoried Hawikuh, a Zuñi Indian pueblo in west–central New Mexico. There he somehow offended the inhabitants and was slain. His followers fled pellmell along their back trail until they encountered Marcos at a point near the present boundary between Arizona and Sonora. Ignoring their warnings and proceeding with only two intrepid Indian companions, Marcos pressed ahead, so he reported later, until he could spy on Hawikuh from a nearby hill: A wonder, "larger than the city of Mexico"! After surreptitiously erecting a cross as a sign of Spanish possession, back he scuttled "with much more fear than food."

Few historians believe that Fray Marcos came anywhere near Hawikuh and speculate that he made up the story rather than have a potentially mighty expedition founder simply because a slave had managed to get himself killed. If such were his motives, he succeeded. Mendoza rushed a recommendation to the king that a full-scale *entrada* be authorized.

Many aspirants, Cortés among them, wanted to lead the adventure, even though they would have to pay, as was customary, its full costs and then hope for recompense from whatever they discovered. Mendoza, however, was determined to stay in control—imagine bridling Cortés when the golden gates came into sight!—and therefore suggested that the assignment go to a young favorite who had come to Mexico as a member of his entourage: Francisco Vasquez de Coronado.

## The Conqueror

Coronado was the younger son of a minor nobleman of Burgos. His charismatic talents, brightened by family connections at court, caught Antonio de Mendoza's attention, and at the age of twenty-five he was invited to accompany the viceroy to Mexico. He rose rapidly. He acquired a lucrative estate by marrying the daughter of another Mexico adventurer, Alonso de Estrada, an illegitimate son of King Ferdinand, and shortly thereafter was appointed by Mendoza to the governorship of Nueva Galicia. Its capital, little Culiacán, was a long way from the amenities of Mexico City, but it was a good jumping-off place for anyone who might want to press still farther north.

Plans for the expedition were already well underway when the king's official sanction finally reached Mexico City early in January 1540. By mortgaging his estate, Coronado had raised 50,000 ducats toward defraying the costs. Mendoza had added 60,000 more. How much came from lesser optimists is problematical. One participant who wrote his memoirs many years after the events declared nostalgically that "such a noble body was never assembled in the Indies, nor so many men of quality in so small a body." Other contemporaries paint a different picture. Mexico, said one, was fortunate to be rid of such a crew. Most were unmarried and hence unsettled, bad characters, lazy, without occupation or income. Yet somehow scores of them were able to provide themselves with at least one saddle horse and pack animal each, plus arms and a personal servant or two.

All told, 336 Europeans volunteered. About 275 of them were cavalrymen. Among the footmen were four friars, Marcos at their head. Riding animals—Coronado alone took twenty-three horses—and pack stock numbered roughly 1,100 head. Approximately a thousand Indians were recruited to do camp chores, build trail as necessary, and herd the hundreds of cattle, sheep, and goats that were to provide food along the way. Several Indians took their wives with them, as did three of the Europeans.

Coronado was resplendent in gilded armor and a steel helmet adorned with plumes. Presumably many of the Indians were equipped with the padded cotton body protectors favored by their people in central Mexico. The rest of the army carried a mix of fine Toledo swords, iron-headed lances, bows, and shields of thick leather, but relatively few coats of mail, harquebuses, and wickedly powerful crossbows, for those last-named implements were costly.

The horde spent close to four months straggling through eight hundred miles of mountains, jungle, and flooded streams to the official starting point at Culiacán, located a short distance inland from Mexico's west coast, opposite the lower end of Baja California. Another thousand miles (though of course the Spanish did not use that unit of measurement) stretched ahead to Hawikuh, first of the fabled Seven Cities of Cíbola, as the pueblos were coming to be called.

At Culiacán the first evidence of disregard for reality manifested itself. Melchior Díaz, a hard-twisted officer stationed at the provincial capital, had recently led a small squad of soldiers northward to learn more practical details about the route than Fray Marcos's account had revealed. Along the way he developed doubts about the friar's dependability. Marcos had said that the road lay close enough to the coast so that ships could be used for supplying the land party; Viceroy Mendoza, indeed, was already equipping three small vessels for just that purpose. But by questioning the local Indians closely, Díaz had determined that the coast veered northwest while the trail veered northeast, so that ships and landsmen would be widely separated by the time the latter reached Hawikuh. Marcos had further declared that the trail was smooth and easy. Díaz found it uncommonly difficult. Because of snow in Arizona's central belt of mountains, he had not been able to reach Hawikuh itself, but Indian information implied that neither it nor its neighboring pueblos were nearly as splendid as the friar had said.

Stop everything because of a few discrepancies? Not Coronado—or Mendoza, who was within reach at a place called Compostela and whom Coronado consulted by messenger. Their decision was for the commander to press ahead with a party of eighty superior horsemen, a few well-armed foot soldiers, the four friars, hundreds of Indians, and part of the livestock. The main army was to be held at Culiacán until the evidence became clear-cut. The three supply ships meanwhile groped northward up the Gulf of California as scheduled.

After an arduous march on dwindling rations, the vanguard reached and stormed the defiant pueblo of Hawikuh. After the short, hard fight, during which Coronado was flattened by stones hurled from the rooftops at his plumed helmet, the weary victors examined their prize. Piled-up cells of stone and mud, a barren plaza, skimpy furnishings that would bring scarcely a peso in Mexico City. . . . They poured curses on Marcos.

Grim Coronado, his bruised head still aching, called a meeting of the chief men of the Zuñi pueblos—there were six towns, but Spanish chroni-clers persisted in speaking of seven—and from them sought to learn as much as he could about the surrounding countryside. The Indians, who had no basis for comparison, said the region's cities were big and rich, especially those occupied by the Hopi to the northwest. To top that, a pair of emissaries arrived from a Towa village located beside the Pecos River two hundred miles to the east. The two had heard through the wilderness grapevine of the strangers' arrival and, traveling much of the way at the Pueblo Indians' tireless dogtrot, had hurried west to discover what was going on. From them Coronado learned that the Seven Cities were just a beginning. Pueblos abounded—and surely some were rich.

Spirits soaring, he dispatched one party northwest to gain the submission of the Hopi villages, or, as he understood the name to be, the Kingdom of Tusayan. (Kings, of course, were no part of the social organization of any North American Indian group, but early Europeans insisted on extrapolating their own experiences into New World societies.) Another party continued on past the Hopi pueblos to investigate reports of a great river that flowed west and southwest; just possibly it would furnish means of reaching the supply ships working north along the coast. Simultaneously the visitors from Cicuyé (Pecos) guided a third small party east to look over the cities in that direction.

So far, so good. But Coronado's rekindled optimism could not wait until the reports of his explorers were in. Exuberantly he rushed Melchior Díaz south, along with the discredited Marcos, to start the main army marching north. Díaz was also to found a halfway station along the route that could be used to speed subsequent travelers along their way, for of course there would be many followers. And finally the tough old captain was to find a route to the sea—or at least to the river whose upper reaches were being examined even then—and thus open supply routes to Spain's newest realm.

Díaz did reach the lower Colorado River but missed the supply ships, which by a rash feat of seamanship had ridden a monstrous tidal bore across the mud flats at the delta, from whence long boats had toiled as far upstream, perhaps, as modern Yuma. The captain, Hernando de Alarcón, heard from Indians of other white men a month's journey to the east, but could not recruit companions enough to justify trying to join them. So he had sailed home after leaving messages at the foot of a marked tree that Indians pointed out to Díaz. Meanwhile, the explorers who had been ordered to find the upper part of the river discovered the Grand Canyon. So much for *that* as an easy water route to Cíbola.

Concurrently the explorers working west with the guides from

Pecos—their commander's name was Hernando de Alvarado—reached the Rio Grande at about the site of today's Bernalillo, New Mexico. There they found twelve pueblos surrounded by fields ready for harvesting. The villages looked much like Hawikuh, except that they were built of puddled adobe clay rather than of stone. The name of the cluster, so Alvarado understood, was Tiguex. Today the word is rendered Tiwa.

The inhabitants, who had heard of the battle at Hawikuh, were nervous. Delegations from the different pueblos marched out together, playing flutes and bearing gifts of food, cotton cloth, and dressed animal skins. Let not the pangs of death come here, they were saying. But if they had gold or emeralds, they did not reveal them.

Neither did the other pueblos that Alvarado visited as far north as Braba, later called Taos. Still, it was a pleasant land, its climate milder and its pasturage lusher than at Hawikuh. By letter Alvarado urged Coronado to establish winter quarters near the Tiguex settlements. He then rode off with his men to visit Cicuyé and the buffalo plains beyond.

Agreeing, Coronado marched east through early snowstorms, the army grumbling behind him. Two thousand miles from Mexico City— their route had been roundabout—for this? They'd have been better off going to Peru.

And then, not unexpectedly—for why else were they there?—the thunderclap came. Treasure! At Cicuyé, Alvarado had picked up a captive Plains Indian as a guide for an examination of the plains beyond the Pecos River. Because of the fellow's appearance, the Spaniards called him the Turk and had plied him with their usual questions about the resources of the country. The drift of the interrogation, the tapping of sword hilts, ornaments, and coins with dirt-encrusted fingernails, the repetition of the word *oro* all created their own answers. Why, yes, the Turk said and pointed northeast. Quivira, his home country, had gold— so much that the people used the metal for plates and the king took his siesta under trees whose boughs were hung with twinkling bells of purest gold.

Proof? Certainly. Alvarado's original guides, both of whom were leading figures of Cicuyé, possessed a golden bracelet they had wrenched from him when taking him captive.

Confronted, the pair shook their heads in bewilderment. They had no . . . But the power of wishful thinking being what it is, the Spaniards chose to believe the Turk. They clapped the two men in chains, fought off an attack by their fellow townspeople, and rejoined the army at Tiguex. When spring made travel possible . . . Ay!

At first the timorous people of Tiguex maintained a friendly stance.

But as cold deepened, incidents arose. The residents of an entire pueblo were forced out so that the shivering Spaniards could use the rooms. Requisitions of food and clothing grew exorbitant. There were problems about women. Fighting erupted. As a warning, the outnumbered Spanish seized the most obstreperous of the towns, razed it, and publicly burned thirty of its inhabitants at the stake. Another defiant town was besieged and starved into submission.

As the sun gained strength after the spring equinox, exhilaration filled the Spanish camp. Quivira! In April 1541, almost exactly a year after the departure from Culiacán, the entire force followed the Turk east, bridged the Pecos River, which was roaring with snowmelt, and straggled onto the Llano Estacado. They saw buffalo beyond numbering, encountered a group of nomadic Apaches whom they called Querechos, and, as the featureless miles dropped behind, began to realize that the Turk was showing no great eagerness to reach his homeland.

Grilled at knife point, he promised to do better. But the season was far advanced now, and the pace of the column was snail slow. Coronado ordered the main force to return to Tiguex and stockpile fresh stores of food against whatever developed. Meanwhile he and thirty picked riders, supported by fifty or so Indian footmen, pressed ahead with the Turk to Quivira.

The outcome was one of the most familiar failures in American annals. Seventy-two days out of Tiguex, the expedition reached, in what may have been the central part of present-day Kansas, a few villages of grass huts inhabited by Wichita Indians. Under pressure the Turk admitted that there was no gold. He had lied about it because the people of Cicuyé had promised him rich rewards for luring the Spaniards onto the Llano, where, it was hoped they would perish. Bleakly, Coronado had the prevaricator strangled and returned to Tiguex.

A desolate winter followed, filled with dissension. One day when Coronado was seeking diversion by racing horses with a fellow officer, his saddle girth broke and he was trampled almost to death by his opponent's horse. The fall was symbolic. The beliefs out of which his life had been formed had been shattered, too, by this land over which he was powerless to exert control. During the long march home from Tiguex, he was so ill and depressed that he had to be carried much of the way in a litter.

His companions were equally unsettled. Save for the handful of loyal ones who carried him, they mocked and reviled him and on arriving in Mexico City charged him with criminal mismanagement, gross cruelty to the Indians, and concealing in his own baggage precious materials that had been given him secretly in Quivira. Found guilty, he was fined and deprived of his governorship of Nueva Galicia. Although a review board in Spain reversed the decision, he stayed disconsolate until his death at the age of forty-four. Mendoza on his part lost what he had sunk into the venture—upwards of a year's salary—and was humiliated by the Crown's order that there be no more such nonsense.

## The Colonizer

In 1578–79 England's most famous pirate, Francis Drake, appeared without forewarning in the Pacific, pillaged towns and ships off South and Central America, and then disappeared without a trace. How had he managed?

It seems simple now. He had left the New World by sailing boldly on around the globe to England. But it was a long, hard way. Only Magellan's men had made the trip before; and the Spanish feared that the elusive Drake may have used as a shortcut from Atlantic to Pacific the fabled Strait of Anian that geographers believed lay somewhere north of Mexico. Since England was a mortal enemy, it behooved the dons to find and block the passageway if possible. For that reason dispatches from New Spain's northern frontier began receiving unusually close study.

Dramatic developments were occurring there. In 1546, at Zacatecas on the province's bleak central plateau, four prospectors had made one of the great silver strikes of all time. Instantly northern Mexico was in ferment. Defying hostile Indians and abominable communications, other prospectors pushed doggedly north from Zacatecas, founded the city of Durango, and then continued to the Florida River in what is now the state of Chihuahua. There, in 1567, at a place called Santa Bárbara, another great strike was made, drawing into the area cattle ranchers, farmers, merchants, mechanics, priests, soldiers—everyone needed to support the mines except workers.

Ore was removed by hand labor under dreadful conditions. Most whites refused the toil, and so Indians were pressed into service, first at minimal wages paid in merchandise and then as slaves. (Some blacks were also imported.) The Indians died like flies and had to be constantly replaced. By 1580 raiders were regularly following the Florida River to its confluence with the Conchos, and the Conchos northeast to the Rio Grande, some two hundred miles below El Paso. It was a huge area, and the Spaniards were mounted whereas the Indians were not. Yelling and firing guns—a sound that always stunned Indians hearing it for the first time—they thundered down on the little villages of thatched huts as if hunting rabbits (the simile comes from a viceroy of the times), put the men, women, and children they seized into chains, and herded them south for sale. It was illegal, as a royal cedula of 1573 made sternly clear: No Indian could be enslaved unless he was actually making war on Spanish citizens. But it was not hard to prod potential victims into resistance, and from there on one could bend one's conscience as one wished, as other civilized Europeans were doing during the same period in Africa.

From one of these Indian captives a Franciscan friar in Santa Bárbara, Augustín Rodríguez, heard the same sort of tales that had reached Cabeza de Vaca nearly half a century earlier. In the north were many big cities inhabited by agricultural Indians who made superior pottery and cotton blankets, useful items of trade in the mining camps. Inasmuch as Coronado's expedition had been forgotten on the largely illiterate frontier, Rodríguez supposed he had unearthed new information. His heart leaped. His work among the lowly Concho Indians to whom he had been assigned had proved unrewarding, and the thought of more amenable souls fired his imagination.

He carried his tale to Mexico City and won permission to form a small scouting party to investigate the Indian's report. The group left Santa Bárbara on June 5, 1581, followed the Conchos to the Rio Grande, and turned up that river to Tiguex. From Tiguex they cast east, then west, noticing during the long rides that the inhabited areas of the Pueblo country would appear on a map in the shape of a rough cross. When the military leader of the party said it was time to return to Santa Bárbara, the three friars in the group refused to go, pleading that they must begin their work of conversion and that reinforcements could find them at Paruay, one of the Tiguex towns beside the Rio Grande.

By the time a second party, this one led by a wealthy rancher, Antonio de Espejo, reached the rendezvous in February 1583, the trio were dead, slain by Indians who preferred their own religious customs. Espejo pressed ahead, nevertheless, and far to the west, in the mountains of what is now central Arizona, found indications of silver ore. Eager to come back with royal permission, he invented a term for the entire area—Nueva Mexico—suggestive of another land of fabulous wealth.

Meanwhile the mails had been busy, and before Espejo returned to Santa Bárbara in the fall of 1583, Madrid had learned of the Rio Grande cities and of the thousands of souls ignorant of Christianity. Here was a harvest that could not be neglected—and a self-supporting base from which a search for the Strait of Anian could be launched. Back to the viceroy came orders that he enter into a contract with some substantial citizen who, in return for extensive semifeudal powers, would colonize the new country for Spain. This contract would have to be approved by the king and the Council of the Indies before it became binding, and without a contract no one could legally enter the new province.

The dice were loaded in the Crown's favor. In effect, applicants for the contract bid against each other. Each had to state how many colonists he would provide—and rank and file were hard to find, for Spanish farm workers and craftsmen did not emigrate to the New World in numbers comparable to those that crossed from England during the subsequent century. The successful bidder would also have to arrange for the military support of the colony. He would have to map the nearby shoreline, for it was thought that New Mexico lay near the Pacific, and he would be expected to search for Anian. He would have to assist the friars in their work of conversion, and then fill the rest of his time with the normal chores of administration and justice. Outlines of his views on all this had to accompany his bid.

In return, the successful applicant could search for mines and, after assigning to the Crown its 20 percent cut of any production that resulted, could retain the rest. He would have rights of *encomienda* and *repartimiento*. As suggested earlier, the first allowed him to exact, as a form of taxation, relatively modest amounts of produce from the Indians inhabiting the area allotted him in trust. *Repartimiento* covered rights to conscript, at specified wages, certain amounts of labor from his charges. In a poor land, the emoluments would not amount to much; but New Mexico was not deemed poor.

Outshining these lures was the same fascination that had motivated the first conquistadores—honor. A man would have titles. He could create a court of his own, for he would be allowed to assign *encomienda* rights to his followers and in return demand military service from them. Having attained this prestige, he could then hope to climb to a higher run on the rigid ladder of caste already taking form in New Spain. At its top were the *gachupines*, or *peninsulares*, men born in Spain. Only they could hold the principal offices available in the New World. The *criollos*, those born outside the mother country, were socially inferior, even though the purest Spanish blood flowed in their veins. Still lower were the *castas*, showing the stigma of various mixtures of white, Indian, and Negro blood.

But caste lines that were inflexible in Mexico City were more malleable on the frontier. An exceptional *indio* could become a mounted herdsman, a *vaquero,* rather than a faceless toiler in a field; and a *mestizo* (part *indio,* part white) could acquire a few head of livestock, possibly a small mine. *Criollos* capable of managing extensive properties sometimes achieved greater wealth than most *gachupines* possessed. And if a *criollo* were very rich and very lucky, he might attain one of the prestigious offices—a governorship, say—normally reserved for the arrogant *gachupines.*

Cognizant of these quirks of character, the Crown confidently bet its baubles of honor against the fortunes of ambitious northern *criollos* —and won. In a minor repetition of the rush of the conquistadores to the New World, several aspirants bid for the right to risk everything they had in New Mexico. Fifteen years of frustration then followed. Much of the foot dragging arose from the Crown's sudden determination to build an armada capable of sweeping England's navy from the seas—and then from the panicked adjustment that followed the armada's defeat. Intrigue by the bidders, bureaucratic red tape, and reviews of applications that became necessary when one viceroy succeeded another brought on still more delays.

Hoping to break the logjam, Espejo set out to carry his appeal directly to Madrid but died en route. Another hopeful, Gaspar Castaño de Sosa, brazenly tried to take advantage of technicalities in the colonizing law. Act first, bluff later: With 170 men, women, and children, their equipment carried in a small train of wagons and carts (the first wheels in what became the American Southwest), Castaño blazed a new crossing of the Rio Grande near today's Del Rio, Texas, forged a difficult way up the Pecos River to Cicuyé, and then cut west, back to the Rio Grande. There he was overhauled by troops from Mexico, chained, removed with his people from the province, and exiled to the Philippine Islands. Nor was that the end. In 1593, the year of Castaño's trial, a group of soldiers pursuing renegade Indians found themselves well up the Rio Grande, looked at each other with quick speculation, and decided to keep going. Somewhere on the plains they disappeared like smoke.

Throughout this time, law-abiding suppliants continued their importunities, and late in the 1590s a winner emerged. He was Don Juan de Oñate. His father, Cristóbal de Oñate, had become one of the richest men in Mexico as a result of his participation in the Zacatecas silver discoveries. Young Juan's wife was the daughter of one of Cristóbal's partners in the strike and, on her mother's side, a descendant of both Hernán Cortés and of the Aztec emperor, Moctezuma. Juan himself had been a successful soldier and landowner and had gained control of profitable mines. Nonetheless he was a *criollo* and in his son's veins was that stain of Indian blood, however exalted. And so, after his wife had died, he turned toward the north to fill voids in what other men would have considered a life crowned by fortune.

He was spare, tough, and exacting, and in return for what he was bringing the crown he demanded and received exceptional privileges. He was to be paid 6,000 ducats a year and receive a land grant—he would choose it himself—of thirty square leagues, approximately three quarters of a million acres. He was to have the right to open harbors and bring in two ships a year for handling ore and supplies. Most importantly, to him, he was named civil governor of New Mexico, captain general of the provincial troops, and *adelantado* ("he who goes first"), a designation that lifted him to a plane occupied by the leaders of the New World's other great *entradas*. As presumptive heir to the noble line he expected to found, he took with him to New Mexico his twelve-year-old son. Also in his train were his favorite adult nephews, Juan and Vicente Zaldívar. As hardened physically and morally as their uncle, the pair, in common with the other leading *criollos* and young *gachupines* in the expedition, expected to be named *hidalgos* for their work and be able to pass the title on to their eldest sons—Sancho Panzas, the lot of them, hoping for islands of their own to rule.

The column that started north in January 1598 contained about 400 men, 130 of whom had their families along. Many were Spanish, but of the ordinary soldiers, farmers, and small craftsmen more were *mestizos*. Also included were several civilized Tlascala Indians from central Mexico for doing hard manual work and lulling the suspicions of Indians still unfamiliar with Europeans. The communal herd of livestock—horses, mules, donkeys, cattle, sheep, goats, pigs—numbered about 7,000 head. There were 83 ox-drawn vehicles, many of them carts whose two wooden wheels screeched on axles of pine. Altogether the procession stretched out for about four dusty miles.

To save travel time for the ponderous mass, Oñate avoided the trail down the Conchos River, which all other parties except Castaño's had used, and ordered scouts under Vicente Zaldívar to find a direct way across the Chihuahuan Desert to the Rio Grande. They reached the river a few miles below what is now Ciudad Juárez and turned upstream to a gap that the river had carved between crowding mountains, an opening that in time would become known as El Paso del Norte (the Pass of the North). There, on April 30, 1598, the *adelantado* staged an elaborate ceremony of possession: Spain's land—and his. Then, so that the sight of so large a column would not frighten the Rio Grande Indians into hiding, he went ahead with a small party to receive the submission of the villages.

Sixty miles above the Pass a rim of mountains forced the trail away from the east bank of the river into a desolate valley grisly with blotches of alkali. On this terrible stretch, soon to be called Jornada del Muerto (Journey of the Dead), one of the advance party perished of thirst and others might have experienced a smiliar fate if a little dog belonging to one of the men had not led the riders to springs in a side canyon. It was a marvelous stroke of luck, for now the main column could be warned to enter the Jornada with water enough to last as far as this place of replenishment. Even so the suffering caused by heat, thirst-crazed animals, and carts stalled in the tractionless sand was appalling.

Although the Indians of Tiguex had inflicted trouble on most of the early parties entering the area, they greeted Oñate cordially. At Santo Domingo, seven chiefs who supposedly represented thirty-four pueblos knelt, kissed his hand and that of the friar with him, and swore fealty to king and Church. It is unlikely that the Indians understood the significance of the act, and it is equally questionable, in view of the autonomous nature of the Pueblo villages, that the seven *caciques* (a word for chief that the Spanish had brought from Cuba) represented nearly as many people as Oñate thought. Ignorance was bliss, however. Pleased with what he considered his good beginning, the captain moved on up the Rio Grande to its junction with the Chama. There, after a stay in a pueblo that obliging Indians vacated for the weary families, he founded New Mexico's first short-lived capital, San Gabriel.

A major crisis arose almost at once. Thirty troopers under his nephew Juan de Zaldívar sought to requisition food from the pueblo of Ácoma. (Today Ácoma is called the Sky City in tour brochures because of the way its terraced houses perch on the flat top of a red sandstone butte rising 357 feet from the gray sage of the surrounding valley.) Pretending affability, the Ácomites persuaded all the visitors except for a small horse guard to ascend the narrow crack that formed the principal route up the cliffs to the town. A wild melee followed. During it, Zaldívar and twelve others died. Eight more, fighting desperately, retreated to the edge of the precipice. Three managed to burst down the trail. Five jumped from the rim. One was smashed on the talus below. The others, landing in sand dunes that wind had heaped against the base of the cliffs, lived and were carried to safety by the horse guard.

On January 29, 1599, a punitive expedition of 70 men led by Juan's brother Vicente set forth to humble the town. While the bulk of the force launched a diversionary attack against the main route of ascent, Vicente and eleven others squirmed up another crack on the back side of the butte, and the Indians were then caught between two fires. By the time the madness subsided, between 600 and 800 persons had been slain. Two were Spaniards.

A few of the surviving Indians escaped. The rest—70 or so males and 500 women and children—were taken to the pueblo of Santo Domingo, which had become the missionary headquarters of the region, and were sentenced for the murder of Juan de Zaldívar and his companions. As punishment, 60 young girls were taken to convents in Mexico City, never to see their homeland again. All others were required to give twenty years of service to the Spanish colony. In addition, all males over twenty-five had one foot cut off. Two Hopis who had been visiting Ácoma and who had joined the fighting each had a hand amputated and were sent home to tell their people what happened to those who resisted the invaders.

It was not the end of horror. Two years later, early in 1601, acts of defiance by Indians at Ábo, east of the Rio Grande, led to another punitive campaign by Vicente de Zaldívar. He reported burning three pueblos, killing 900 persons, and seizing 400 prisoners, whom he distributed as slaves among his men. Even granting that the figures were exaggerated and that most of the slaves escaped, the episode suggests what the tension of living in a grudging land 700 miles from help was doing to the colony. The invaders felt cornered by circumstances and showed it in the way they bared their teeth.

At San Gabriel, the settlement near the junction of the rivers, crops were disappointing. Improvidently, the colonists devoured cattle and sheep they should have saved for breeding stock, and then laid heavy requisitions on the neighboring Pueblos, who themselves were short of food. Oñate explored nervously northeast toward Quivira (Kansas), found nothing that seemed of value to him, and was lucky to extricate his men from an attack by the Indians of the plains. Reversing fields, he then made a remarkable march west to the mouth of the Colorado River. Unaware that the salt water into which the stream flowed was fenced away from the Pacific by the 800-mile-long peninsula of Baja California, he returned to San Gabriel boasting that he had discovered a marvelous way station for the rich galleons that were beginning to ply regularly between Acapulco, Mexico, and the Philippine Islands.

High talk, however, was no longer enough. Reality had caught up with Sancho Panza. Even though a rigorous Spanish law declared that once a man had committed himself to an expedition, he was bound to stay with it until formally released, desertions were rife. The fugitives carried bitter accusations with them, including some about Oñate's sexual demands on the colony's married womenfolk and others about his having had two of his critics assassinated. But inasmuch as the tale bearers were deserters, might the accusations be self-serving? Oñate's friends, reinforced by a visit from Vicente de Zaldívar, shielded him, and some reinforcements were even sent north to help. Like the others, however, they fell prey to discontent and soon only forty or so adult Spanish males and their dependents were left in New Mexico.

Aroused finally, the Council of the Indies prepared to abandon the province. At that the Franciscans raised a cry of protest. The friars in New Mexico were at last reaping the rewards of their patience in San Juan, Santo Domingo, Isleta—8,000 converts, it was claimed. Surely this precious salvage was not to be turned back to the forces of darkness. Moreover, some show of occupation was necessary to assert Spanish claim to the land if foreigners did try to move south from Anian.

King Philip II and the Council capitulated. Enough soldiers would stay in the north to protect the missionaries, but not "as an army, nor with the clang of arms," and their captain would function as civil governor as well. The provincial capital was to be moved to a central, militarily strategic site, one where local settlers could be sure of ample grazing for their livestock and where there would be no conflict with Indians over water. The man chosen as governor to oversee the changes was Pedro de Peralta. The town he laid out in 1609–10 was Santa Fe.

Oñate meanwhile had been recalled and in 1608 started south with a few loyal followers. Indians fell on the party as it was crossing the Jornada del Muerto. One Spaniard died. He was Oñate's sole son, twenty-two years old now, whom the father had hoped to make his heir as ruler of Nueva Mexico. They buried him as decently as they could, and, his head bent under the pitiless sun, Oñate rode on to his trial and the stripping away of the honors for which he had given some $4 million in our terms and the ten best years of his maturity.

## The Civilizers

The world was too much with the Franciscan friars of New Mexico during the seventeenth century. Their dubious battle with other claimants competing with them for what the Indians had to offer drained away, during the course of seventy years, the energies of some 250 priests and a disproportionate amount of the Crown's millions of pesos. The result was holocaust.

One way of placing the situation in perspective is to look at the mission system as it evolved in Sonora and Nueva Vizcaya, the latter a long sprawl of desert and mountains that eventually was divided into the modern Mexican states of Durango and Chihuahua. In those areas the proselytizing fathers, both Jesuits and Franciscans, depended for results on suasion rather than on shows of power. In ones and twos, guarded sometimes by a handful of soldiers and assisted by a few Indians who had already been converted, they pushed ahead of the frontier in search of suitable *rancherias* of seminomads. Their initial goal was to turn the loosely structured bands among which they settled into tightly organized communities over which they could exert close supervision.

First they stirred curiosity by passing out gifts and then setting up, in some noticeable spot, a flimsy roof of poles and brush as a shelter for an altar, a crucifix, and perhaps a statue of the Virgin. Robes, stoles, rituals, and chants attracted additional spectators. But the irresistible lure was the friars' promise of help in the unending struggle against hunger: metal hoes, cattle, chickens, and such new crops as wheat, grapevines, and fruit trees. Accustomed already to farming of a sort, the *rancheria* people caught on quickly. It was easy then to organize them into work crews under the leadership of some of their own people and then shift part of the labor away from clearing fields to laying the foundations of a permanent church building. There were schools, too, in basic crafts: blacksmithing, leather working, brick making, carpentry, and the like. The efficiency achieved by even rudimentary organization still left the Indians ample time in which to attend to their own wants.

Indians with an ear for language were taught the catechism and encouraged to help the friars prepare adults for baptism. (If parents consented, small children could be baptized without instruction; this offered a way to reach the mothers and then, more slowly, the standoffish fathers.) All was enlivened by instruction in singing, playing musical instruments, and painting. The interior walls of the churches invited bright colors, and the carving of sacred images challenged woodworkers. Pageants illustrating Biblical stories were common, and the friars, most of whom made a point of learning their charges' tongue, repeatedly explained the meaning of the Ten Commandments and expatiated vividly on Heaven and Hell.

This was not just a religious program. In cedula after cedula, the Crown insisted that the Indians were free men, entitled to full citizenship as soon as they were Hispanicized and Christianized. Their first service was defensive: A mission congregation under the control of an able friar was not likely to attack Spanish ranches, mines, or caravans, and at times could even be called on to help resist the incursion of "unreduced" natives. (Civilizing Indians was called reducing them.) And when citizenship was achieved, the converts, it was hoped, would be able to substitute for Hispanic peasants and artisans who were seldom allowed to leave Spain for the New World because their hands were needed at home.

How long should it take to reorient a people's culture? Utterly convinced of the rightness and therefore the irresistibility of what they were doing, the heads of the main orders—Jesuits, Franciscans, Dominicans, Augustinians—at first theorized that it could be done in ten years. That period completed, the mission community would be secularized. A parish priest would take charge of the church. Tools, land, and livestock would be divided among the Indians, and they would be on their own as newly formed, if second-rate, Spanish citizens.

Experience soon cooled the ardor. Many Indians showed a perverse tendency to cling to their idolatrous beliefs while enjoying, with no sense of incongruity, the showier rituals of Catholicism. Improvident, as most partially educated people are, they were quick to gamble away or sell at a song their shares of the erstwhile mission's property. Worse, with the friars gone, there would be no way to protect them from exploitation by land and mine owners eager to get trained labor at low prices. Finally, the missionaries were as prone as anyone else to hold on to the power bases they had created. As a consequence, secularization came slowly— ten times ten years sometimes—amid acid complaints from frontiersmen about what they called mission monopoly.

Still, in the *rancheria* country, the program did help bring many Indians into the mainstream of New World Spanish culture. In seventeenth-century New Mexico, however, it did not.

Two reasons for the failure stand out. First, a mission church could not easily make itself the organizational hub of a pueblo, for those towns, their social patterns tightly structured, were built solidly around plazas that already provided a focus for every aspect of village life. Physically, the church was all but compelled to play second fiddle as an integrating force. Secondly, civilian economic competitors were on hand to demand their share of Indian labor and tribute. Some were *encomenderos* appointed by Oñate; others were government officials acting on behalf of the Crown—and themselves.

The friars did what they could to break into these tight circles. They made their churches, erected with Indian labor, as tall and massive as possible so that each would command attention even though it was located at the periphery of the pueblo it served. A notable example, still standing, is the Church of San Esteban at Ácoma, the creation of Fray Juan Ramírez, who became the missionary pastor of the cliff-top pueblo in 1629.

By that time, thirty years had passed since the brutal sentences imposed on the villagers by Oñate for the slaying of Juan de Zaldívar and his soldiers. During their servitude, many of the Ácomites may have accepted Christianity; at least they had become familiar with it. Their own sufferings, together with memories of Vicente de Zaldívar's massacre of the Pueblos at Ábo, may have made them wary of what might happen if they resisted the new friar's advances. Legend, however, offers a different explanation for their friendliness. Just as Ramírez was approaching the bottom of the trail leading to the village, so the story goes, a child tumbled from the rim above. Miraculously he caught it, saving it from certain death. Hostility melted, and Fray Juan was allowed to enter the pueblo.

The only spot available for a church was a rough section of the mesa near the edge of a rose-red precipice. Very well, it would do. With amiability and dedication, reinforced by gifts, Ramírez won the trust of the Indians and then their help. First he laid out a vertiginous donkey trail from the valley floor to the mesa top, chipped away enough rock to make it passable, and on the backs of laboring burros brought up load after load of fill material to level the site he had chosen. Next came the bricks. Indians who had learned the craft during their servitude dug up adobe clay, moistened it beside the valley stream—the only water on the mesa came, as it still does, from rain draining into natural rock cisterns —kneaded in straw and dry grass as binding material, placed the mixture in molds, and let the sun bake it hard. Donkeys carried the bricks, too, up the trail, ton after ton. The church's main walls were eight to ten feet thick and thirty-five or more tall. Topping them in front were twin towers that added another twenty-five feet of height and more tons of brick. Beams forty feet long and upward of a foot in diameter supported the roof. Legend declares that relays of Indians brought the huge timbers from the slopes of Mount Taylor, nearly fifty miles to the north, without letting them once touch the ground.

Even today, when a steep black-topped road up the back side of the mesa has reduced the impressiveness of Ácoma's site, the thought of that early cliffside labor, unassisted by anything more mechanical than pulleys, is staggering. And more. For this gaunt, echoing edifice—the hero of Willa Cather's *Death Comes for the Archbishop* understated in describing it as "depressing"—still speaks across the centuries of the chill that seizes the human spirit when a drive to dominate becomes paramount.

Awing the Indians was only part of the Franciscans' sense of mission during those years. They also undertook to champion their charges against the lay officials who, with equal vehemence, claimed priorities of their own.

Land was a perennial bone of contention. The Pueblo Indians had long since occupied the choicest spots amenable to cultivation and irrigation by the means then available. Naturally the invading Spaniards, and especially those who held *encomienda* grants to certain areas, settled as close to those same spots as possible. The missionaries also crowded in. Out on the edges were ordinary settlers trying to get along as best they could.

Encroachments by one group on territory claimed by another led to endless recriminations. Since the friars generally managed to accumulate the largest herds and command the biggest work crews, they bore the brunt of the ill will. Why should a crown-supported order pledged to poverty graze hundreds of cattle and horses while the citizen-soldiers who protected the province found themselves hard put to buy a single mount? The Franciscans retorted that the gains they achieved through superior efficiency were not intended for themselves but for their wards. Could the governors say as much?

The governors could not. Most had taken their jobs in that forsaken part of the world with every intention of making as much profit as possible during their single three-to-five-year terms. They exacted heavier tribute from the Indian towns than the law allowed. They set up sweatshops in the Governor's Palace, a long, low adobe building with a big courtyard behind it that still fronts the north side of the Santa Fe plaza. There captive nomads and Pueblo Indians charged with petty misdemeanors spent every daylight hour weaving textiles that could be sold in the mining communities of Nueva Vizcaya. They sent out other crews to gather piñon nuts, which miners regarded as a delicacy, and salt, which was used in the reduction of ore. Worst of all, they dealt in slaves, attacking Apaches, Navajos, and Utes to obtain that human commodity, reckless of the fierce reprisals brought on by their raids.

The priests fulminated in the pulpits against all this and more; they complained of the personal morals of their opponents and, when tempers grew hot enough, denied sacraments to and excommunicated anyone who dared defy them. The lay officials responded by accusing the friars of physically and sexually brutalizing the Indians under them. They used trumped-up charges to arrest and imprison persons who supported the priests—and sometimes the priests themselves.

One notorious governor, Luís de Rosas (he held office from 1637 through 1641), personally cudgeled and seriously injured two priests who brought him unwelcome news. Later, so it was charged, a different pair of priests were involved in the assassination of one of Rosas' close associates. Eventually Rosas himself was murdered by an "outraged" husband who let his wife be used for setting the stage.

These family quarrels among the Spaniards weakened discipline throughout the pueblos. If New Mexico's civilian population refused to obey the padres, why should the Indians? Rebels at Jémez and Taos killed their priests and destroyed the churches, but were savagely subdued by Spanish soldiers. More dismay came from virulent epidemics of smallpox and measles, and, late in the 1660s, from the onset of a prolonged drought. Hunger also pinched the Apaches, who intensified their raids to such a point that the pueblos bordering the plains east of the Manzano Mountains had to be abandoned. Devastation from all causes was so acute that as the second half of the century began, the ninety or so pueblos that had existed at the time of Oñate's arrival had shrunk by more than half.

Despair gave Indian religious leaders—shamans, or, as the Spaniards called them, "wizards"—an opportunity to regain their former power. Actually, the majority of the Pueblos had never wholly abandoned their religion, but had sought to fuse it with those elements of Catholicism that appealed to them. This suited neither the shamans, whose authority rested on the maintenance of the old rites, nor the friars, who regarded any deviation from their teachings as damnable and dangerous idolatry. As restlessness grew in the pueblos, both groups braced for a showdown.

In 1675 the friars prevailed on a new and unusually cooperative governor to use his troops for extirpating once and for all every form of native worship. The soldiers worked efficiently. In pueblo after pueblo they razed the *estufas* (kivas) that were the center of village ceremonies, destroyed prayer sticks, and burned the elaborate *kachina* masks that were the essence of the ceremonial dances. They also arrested forty-seven known wizards. Three who were regarded as particularly obnoxious were summarily hanged; the rest were flogged and imprisoned.

An extraordinary thing then happened. Seventy Tewa warriors from the north stormed into the Governor's Palace and demanded the release of the prisoners. Otherwise, they threatened, the Tewa pueblos, acting in concert, would either make war on the settlers or would desert en masse to the Apaches. The frightened governor complied, a capitulation not lost on one of the prisoners he released, a shaman named Popé from San Juan Pueblo: If the independent Pueblo villages could be prevailed on to act together, the Spanish yoke might be shattered! For weren't there many more Indians than Spaniards? (Estimates of the number of Pueblos in New Mexico in 1675 vary from 16,000 to 30,000; of Spanish, 2,400, including *castas* of every sort; of Franciscans, 33—exactly half of their authorized total.)

Using restless Taos as his base, Popé plotted slowly and carefully. In the opinion of a modern Franciscan scholar, Fray Angelico Chavez, he was materially aided by a gigantic mulatto with bulging yellow eyes, a by-blow of the Naranjo family, aching for revenge on the Europeans who relegated him to inferiority because of his mixed blood.

Letting himself be glimpsed only occasionally under awesome circumstances, Naranjo pretended to be the personal representative of Pohé-yemo, a sun deity celebrated by all Pueblos regardless of the language and historical differences between them. In this way, working through Popé, Naranjo achieved the unity that the Pueblos needed and, with his knowledge of Spanish customs and psychology, helped plan the details of the insurrection. Promise of help was also obtained from certain Apache bands who hated the Spaniards, wished to resume interrupted trade relations with the outlying pueblos, and so agreed to join the fighting.

Warnings of what portended leaked early in August 1680 to the new governor, Antonio de Otermín. Unable to believe what he heard, he reacted slowly. Not so the Pueblos. Learning that they had been anticipated, they used smoke signals and relays of runners to flash word throughout the area: now!

Close to 400 Spaniards vanished during the first wild sweep against the haciendas (livestock ranches) that were scattered between Taos and Socorro. Most died, but some *castas*, hoping to escape their bonds, may well have joined the Indians. Twenty-one priests were subjected to the grossest of indignities before being murdered. Holy images were desecrated and churches reduced to shambles. While this explosion of hatred was distracting the Indians, fugitives who survived the first onslaught streamed toward two places of possible security—Isleta Pueblo, a little below modern Albuquerque, where a detachment of soldiers was stationed under Lieutenant Governor Alonso García, and Santa Fe. Promptly Indians cut communications between the two spots, so that neither knew whether the other was surviving.

Approximately 1,000 persons, only 100 of them capable of fighting, huddled inside the Governor's Palace at Santa Fe. After the Indians had invested the town, a countercharge resulted in the slaying of an estimated 300 of the attackers and the capture of forty-seven. The captives were immediately and publicly executed. But the rebels succeeded in cutting off water from the Palace, and after a week of suffering and terror Otermín ordered Santa Fe abandoned.

Though no excess baggage could be carried on the flight, the people demanded one object—a crowned wooden statue, not quite three feet tall, of the Virgin Mary, lovingly painted and lavishly gowned, symbol of the one hope that gleamed for them in this darkness of destruction. Normally the figurine stood in the town's parish church, the Parroquia, an adobe building located a short distance from the Palace. Somehow it was retrieved and went with the bedraggled procession of carts, pack mules, saddle animals, and walkers of all ages that on August 21 left the *villa*, as the town was called, and headed south into uncertainty.

Hordes of Indians jeered from the hilltops but made no effort to stop the Spaniards. In time they caught up with the Isleta refugees, who were also fleeing south, accompanied by several hundred Indians from the southern pueblos.

Bickering and complaining, the combined groups moved through the Pass of the North to the Rio Grande's southern bank, where, on the site of modern Juárez, was a mission church surrounded by a straggling town—the original El Paso, which nearly two centuries later shifted to its present location north of the river. Ordered to remain in the vicinity until the reconquest of New Mexico could be undertaken, the dispossessed threw together several communities beside the river and tried to restructure their lives. Twelve grim years passed. Punitive expeditions into New Mexico succeeded in looting and burning a few rebel pueblos but obtained no lodgement. Meanwhile the refugees endured hunger, Apache raids, and an uprising of Manso Indians. Discouragement caused such a melting away that after a decade of delay, scarcely half the original group remained. At that low point, a savior as hungry for fame as Oñate had been a hundred years earlier offered to lead the people home.

He was Don Diego de Vargas, born in Madrid in 1643, scion of an impeccably noble line. He was lean, resilient, and exquisitely elegant, his thin face adorned with hairline mustaches and a narrow goatee. Although he had married into a family as illustrious as his, he was unhappy. At the age of thirty-one he walked out on his wife and sailed to New Spain. Because divorces were impossible in Catholic Spain, the adored woman he found in Mexico City, mother of three of his children, remained unwed. He added grandly to his already immense fortune, and in 1688 offered to return the lost province to Mexico at his own expense.

Endless paper work and difficulty in recruiting troops kept him from launching his invasion until 1692. Not altogether to his surprise, for his sources of intelligence were good, he encountered no active resistance. Popé had turned out to be such an unbearable tyrant that the Pueblo alliance had fallen apart and many of the villages were skirmishing bitterly against each other. Some even welcomed Vargas in the hope of gaining his support in their feuding. He swept through the entire Pueblo country without unsheathing his sword. To prove his peaceful intentions, he went alone and unarmed into several towns, never losing his aplomb even when pugnacious shamans scooped up dirt and threw it into his face. On his return to El Paso four months later, he advised the viceroy that recolonization was now possible.

On October 4, 1693, he started north again with 100 soldiers, 73 families, 18 Franciscans, and a number of Pueblo auxiliaries. A minimum of food, three small cannons, and the carefully crated statue of the Virgin were carried in twenty-one wagons and carts. Bringing up the rear were 4,000 animals—goats, sheep, cattle, mules, and horses.

Unusually cold weather stiffened the resistance that the worried shamans had been stirring up since Vargas's reconnaissance the year before. The Pueblos declined to sell the rations that the Spaniards had counted on and desperately needed. The crisis came to a head outside Santa Fe. Tano Indians from Galisteo Basin had occupied, walled, and partly rebuilt the *villa,* and when Vargas asked them to return to their own pueblo so that his people could have shelter in their former homes, the Tanos refused. For two weeks Vargas dickered. During that time, twenty-two persons, mostly children, perished of cold and hunger in the Spanish camp outside the walls. Outraged finally, Vargas decided to storm the town. While the women uncrated the statue of the Lord's Mother and knelt beside it in the snow, the attack began.

Even though 140 Indians arrived from Pecos to help the Spaniards, two days of ferocious fighting were required to subdue the Tanos—at least the official reports say it was ferocious. One Spaniard was slain, and nine Indians. The real savagery came, or so it seems from today's perspective, afterward. Eighty-one rebels who declined to yield and had to be rooted out of their hiding places were executed. Four hundred others of both sexes who surrendered voluntarily were treated more gently: ten years of servitude to the soldiers and settlers. Another three years passed, marred by murders and ruthless retaliations, before the last of the hostile villages gave in. Except for the Hopis. They never surrendered, and even slaughtered the inhabitants and wrecked the stone houses of one of their own communities, Awatovi, when it seemed on the point of receiving a missionary. The Hopis also gave a haven to Pueblos from the Rio Grande area who preferred to join them rather than live at home under Spanish rule.

Those who did stay won some small gains. *Encomiendas* were abolished; tribute was lightened. Although shamans were sometimes still tried for witchcraft, there were no more mass raids on the kivas, and the missionaries, a less ardent lot than those of the 1600s, either did not notice or pretended not to notice that native religions continued to flourish in secret, their forms brightened, as in the past, with colorful borrowings from Catholic ritual. As the number of Spanish settlers slowly increased, and the number of Pueblo Indians, particularly males, slowly declined, there was some intermarrying. Spanish agricultural practices spread, and numbers of Pueblos were incorporated into the dominant society as workers and part-time soldiers.

The Virgin triumphant: The statuette, renamed La Conquistadora, She Who Conquers, was restored to its place of honor in the Parroquia, where it still stays, though the chapel itself was encased within the Cathedral of St. Francis during that church's construction in the late nineteenth century. In 1712, eight years after Vargas's death, a new governor ordered an annual procession in his honor. Following a solemn High Mass, La Conquistadora was lifted reverently from her niche, placed on a platform, and borne on devout shoulders to the field where the freezing families of De Vargas's soldiers had knelt during the storming of Santa Fe. There she stayed in a crude shelter (later the Rosario Chapel was built for her) during a full novena, after which she was returned. Since then the custom has been neglected at times, but has always sprung alive again. Now, each June, nearly three centuries after its inauguration, you can still watch from sidewalks packed with spectators the procession leave the Parroquia one Sunday and return the next, instead of after nine days as formerly. There are some who will say that in that bejeweled figurine is the core of the Spanish Southwest, its color, devotion, persistence, its clinging to tested faiths.

And during that same June, at spots not far removed from the route of the procession, you can still hear/feel the pulse of Indian drums and chants, and watch the dip and lift of feet and vivid masks as the Pueblos repeat afresh their corn dances. To Don Quixotes from everywhere this has always been a durable and baffling land.

## *The Apostle of Fading Ideals*

During the years that Don Diego de Vargas was planning and carrying out the reconquest of New Mexico, a Jesuit missionary, Eusebio Kino, was advancing that part of the Spanish frontier lying west of the Continental Divide inch by inch out of Sonora into what is now southernmost Arizona. His progress in miles was minimal when compared to the leap the Franciscans had taken out of Nueva Vizcaya into northern New Mexico, and would later take into California. Plans of staggering sweep bubbled from him almost constantly, but few reached fruition. Yet the name Kino, together with that of Junípero Serra, who worked in California two thirds of a century later, is the only one among hundreds of devoted Catholic proselytizers on New Spain's missionary frontier that the average citizen of the Southwest is likely to recognize.

Inevitably the question "why?" arises. What qualities about the man—or perhaps about the Southwest itself—can account for this exaltation? Why, to cite a single instance, did the state of Arizona (a word he probably never heard) honor him as a leading citizen by putting a copper figure of him, its likeness largely imaginary, in the Hall of Statuary under the south rotunda of the national Capitol in Washington, D.C.?

Eusebio Francisco Kino: He wasn't even a Spaniard. Born in northern Italy, he was educated so thoroughly in nearby German universities —his favorite studies were mathematics, astronomy, and map making— that he once remarked he hardly knew whether he was German or Italian. On recovering from what threatened to be a fatal illness, he showed his gratitude to the Lord by entering the Society of Jesus. He dreamed of being sent as a missionary and cartographer to China. Instead he was ordered to help a soldier named Atondo colonize Baja California.

Because Spain had not been in the habit of publishing geographic information, the world's map makers had not learned that Ulloa in 1539 and Alarcón in 1540 had discovered that Baja is a long, narrow peninsula. As for the Spanish, they had forgotten. Cortés's initial concept again held sway: California (there was no distinction then between Upper and Lower California) was the largest island in the world. Thorny, dry, and mysterious, it was inhabited by Indians eking out the most miserable of existences. But they did have souls and there might be pearls in the coastal waters.

Atondo's colonists and the Jesuit missionaries who accompanied them added little to the meager data. Although they spent two years trying to find a habitable location, even crossing to the Pacific side of the "island" during their search, they failed. To Kino's dismay—he wanted to stay with the Indian converts who trusted him and also map hitherto unknown territory—the enterprise was abandoned, and he was ordered to build a mission near the headwaters of the Rio San Miguel in northern Sonora.

The area was strategic. Its heart is a big, rolling, grassy swell of land that gives rise to fingerlings of streams that flow south, west, and north. Their hill-pinched valleys, dotted with occasional broad openings of fertile land, lead through what was then called Pimería Alta, the land of the Upper Pima Indians. The area involved covered about 50,000 square miles, approximately that of England's New York colony, and was inhabited in 1687, the year of Kino's arrival, by an estimated 30,000 naked, seminomadic, unconverted aborigines.

There Kino became one more cog in the carefully organized social machine that had served the Jesuits well during their slow expansion northward. He took Christianized Indians to Rio San Miguel—he named his mission there Nuestra Señora de los Dolores—to do necessary manual work and reassure the natives into whose territory he was intruding. A still more powerful reassurance derived from the sheep, cattle, and horses that the party drove with them, for the Jesuits had long since learned (to borrow a turn of phrase from a modern Jesuit historian, John Francis Bannon) that the way to a heathen's soul was through his stomach: If a missionary expected a band of Indians to settle down to civilized ways, he had to provide a substitute for the wild meat they had once obtained through hunting. Indeed, the guarantee of a stable food supply —the Jesuits also introduced wheat—often led the perpetually undernourished natives to ask missionaries to visit them.

To these lures Kino added the charm of his exuberant personality. He liked Indians. He had scant interest in their religions or customs— after all, he was there to change those things—but he was willing to sit for hours listening to their problems, smiling over their accomplishments, exclaiming over their adventures. He did not stop their dances or rant against the intoxicating liquor they brewed from native plants. In return they grew eager to please and generally followed his advice both about church matters and their dealings with the soldiers and occasional miners who sometimes crowded too close on his heels.

He worked with almost frightening energy. At Dolores he built as his first chapel the usual mud-and-wattle hut, launched farming operations, and then put what labor was available to erecting a more imposing church. (It took six years to complete.) But he was temperamentally incapable of sitting still. As soon as affairs were progressing satisfactorily, he began searching the valleys for other *rancherias* where he could build more missions, even though he knew that the Jesuits were having difficulty recruiting enough priests for their worldwide labors. Ah, but *his* Indians counted; with so great a harvest of souls hanging in the balance, surely he would be sent the manpower he needed. During the next several years he launched eight missions and many *visitas*, which were churches that had no priest but were visited more or less regularly by the missionary in whose district each was located. The three of his establishments most familiar to today's Southwesterners are those located in the Santa Cruz Valley south of Tucson—San Xavier del Bac, Tumacácori, now a national monument, and Guevavi.

Duties poured on him. Indians had to be taught to plow with oxen, harvest wheat with sickles, and thresh the grain by spreading the sheaves inside a corral and hazing horses and mules around on top of the rustling carpet until their churning hooves had freed the kernels. Lean-hipped, heavy-horned, half-wild cattle, which multiplied rapidly in the grassy uplands, had to be rounded up, branded, and, at proper times, butchered, so that the meat could be dried into hard, black, almost indestructible jerky. Horses, too, proliferated lustily, and had to be chased into broad-winged corral traps in order that likely-looking young animals could be lassoed and eventually broken to harness or saddle.

In addition to supervising these activities with the aid of Indian majordomos, Kino and the handful of missionaries who were gradually sent to him had to say mass every day, teach ritual and hymn singing, catechize those seeking baptism, perform marriages and funerals, set up and then oversee a rudimentary governmental organization for the various Indian *rancherias* in their districts, arbitrate quarrels, urge on the lazy, reprimand and sometimes flog sinners, heal physical as well as spiritual hurts, make plans, prepare requisitions, keep accounts, and write endless reports justifying expansions and pleading for the wherewithal to keep on growing.

Living could be difficult. Though winters were mild, spring was parched and windy. Crashing thunderstorms added a steamy humidity to summer's oppressive heat. During the first storms hordes of toads emerged from the earth in which they had buried themselves the previous year. Settlers thought they were spontaneously generated: Semen deposited during earlier seasons was activated by water on warm mud and, presto, the creatures rose into sight as fully formed as Minerva.

Until suitable buildings were erected, the missionary had to live under dirt-and-branch roofs that leaked mud during storms and always harbored hosts of spiders, mice, rats, and evil-smelling *cucarachas,* a kind of winged cockroach. Bats loved to spend their days in the soft gloom of the often doorless, windowless church buildings. Said Ignaz Pfefferkorn, who followed Kino into Pimería Alta by some years, "I sometimes killed two or three hundred with the help of some Indians. Without this unceasing warfare I could not have kept a single altar, image, or decoration clean and unviolated."

In addition, Kino was hard on himself. He mortified his flesh. He wore coarse clothing, added evil-tasting herbs to his ill-cooked food, slept on a sheepskin or sweaty saddle blankets spread on the ground, and sometimes rose in the middle of the night to flagellate himself with whips.

His natural tendency to overreach was triggered in 1691 by the arrival of a superior, Father Juan María de Salvatierra, on a routine tour of inspection. From him Kino learned with a surge of excitement that another missionary *entrada* into Baja California was under consideration. If only the cost and difficulty of feeding the lost souls on that barren land weren't so exorbitant!

Kino's imagination leaped in answer. Soon his missions in Pimería Alta would be producing a surplus of wheat. As for transporting it, he himself would build and launch a schooner from a harbor somewhere nearby.

He really thought he could, even though he knew nothing about shipbuilding and lacked skilled artisans. In 1693 he took a scouting party down the west-flowing Altar River to an Indian *rancheria* called Caborca, shaded by groves of tall cottonwoods. Here was ample lumber for a boat the size he contemplated—33 feet long and 12 wide. Now to find a harbor to which he could carry the prefabricated craft, in sections, on mule back.

On west his party went, into blistered desolation. When hunger and weariness threatened their animals with collapse, he climbed on foot to the summit of a barren hill. Squinting west through the glare, he saw a sheen of water. The ocean! And off beyond the narrow arm, indistinct in the haze, rose the pale blue mountains of California, still unexplored, still unmapped.

When his superiors heard of the chimerical plan, they ordered him to desist. Obediently he returned to the arduous work of proselytizing, but he could not quench the desire to keep on reaching. Whenever he could, and occasionally when he shouldn't have, he left Dolores untended while he explored. Sometimes he traveled with a few Indians, sometimes with a fellow missionary or two, but most often with a squad of soldiers commanded by a man who became a lifelong friend, Juan Mateo Manje, commander of the newly founded presidio (fortress) of Fronteras, northeast of Dolores. Nine times he pushed as far north as the Gila River, reaching it by a variety of routes—along the north-flowing San Pedro and Santa Cruz valleys and even by way of the dread Camino del Diablo, the Devil's Highway, near today's international border.

During the trips he encountered a new group of Indians, the tall, handsome, stark-naked Yumans. As ornaments they valued blue abalone shells, and one man presented Kino with a string of them. The only other abalone shells he had encountered were on the west, the Pacific, side of California, and as he turned the gleaming gift in his hand, a flash of insight struck him. Inasmuch as the Indians had no way of crossing long stretches of open water, the shells must have reached the Yumans by land. California, it followed, was not an island, but a peninsula. The world's maps would have to be redrawn!

To check his theory he made more arduous trips to the Gulf and to the lower Colorado River, whose delta he finally reached. The truth was incontrovertible. Baja California, as it soon became known, was attached to the mainland.

His imagination rioted. The missions that Salvatierra was struggling to start in Baja California could be best supplied not by boat but by mule trains circling the head of the Gulf. And that was only a beginning. If shells could be carried east from the coast, then colonists and merchants could also go west to bays Kino had only read about, bays still uninhabited by Europeans—San Diego and Monterey. Traffic could be developed between the rich mining camps of northern Mexico and top-heavy galleons putting into those bays with exotic wares from the Orient. As settlement spread, the Apaches could be subdued. Communication could be opened with reconquered New Mexico by way of the Colorado River—the realities of the Grand Canyon, like those of the Gulf, had been forgotten—and the stubborn Hopi Indians, who rumor said would accept Jesuits although they refused Franciscans, could be returned to the Catholic fold. Plus untold souls not yet known. Why, a whole new kingdom—Kino had a name for it, the Kingdom of New Navarre—awaited claiming. As its administrative, religious, and military center, he proposed a bustling new *villa*, or city, to be located near the point where the Gila River joins the Colorado.

In proposing all this, he was tilting at what were then impossible windmills—implacable geography, distance, cynicism, lethargy, and an Old World bureaucracy that was struggling by means of endless expensive wars to maintain the fiction that Spain still occupied the top of the

European power structure. Nor was Madrid alone in giving him short shrift. Even in the Mexican Northwest, Kino's enthusiasm drew sneers. He was accused of wanting fame for himself more than enlightenment for the Indians, whom he reportedly baptized in wholesale lots without proper preparation. Moreover, the claims of his missions for grazing and agricultural lands were already closing choice areas to secular settlers and miners. A kingdom? For whom?

If he did not exactly lie about affairs in his district, neither was he wholly candid. He reported only good about the Pimas and Papagos—their gentleness, hospitality, and eagerness for God's word. Later missionaries saw a different aspect. "Cleanliness," wrote Father Phelipe Segesser, "is not found among them." They were covered with lice, which mothers picked out of their children's hair and ate. They drank excessively and spent their nights yowling and dancing, so that the next day all they wanted was to "lounge about unless the father drives them to work like little donkeys." They were polygamous and saw no reason to change: Did not a stallion have more than one mare?

Nor were Kino's descriptions of the land any more realistic. His maps of Pimería Alta labeled as rivers arroyos that were actually dry much of the year. He could speak of riding with other missionaries along the parched Camino Diablo chanting hymns in praise of Our Lady of Loreto while the land about them broke into "pleasantness and beauty of roses and flowers of different colors." Because the episode occurred in March it may have been preceded by light rains that brought on an ephemeral spring flowering, but that explanation was not offered. Rather, readers were left to think that truly fearful trails presented little difficulty.

In spite of these foibles of overoptimism, Anglos have been inclined to take Eusebio Kino on his own terms. He has had a good press from enthralled biographers. Pragmatic Americans appreciate the persistence with which he tested his geographic theories. Like Junípero Serra, he fits well into what has been called the Romance of the Missions: a father touching with kindly palm the bowed head of a kneeling primitive, for he did enjoy Indians, and when clashes threatened, he labored hard to solve them by peaceful rather than military means. But mostly he was the epitome of expansionism, and Anglo-Americans have never known any other approach to the frontier. He glowed with energy, exuded a promoter's confidence that the waiting land could be turned to fruitful uses, and argued (as few Anglos would) that this could be accomplished without annihilating the peoples already there. More than any other popular figure, he represented what seventeenth-century Spain in America was all about.

But he was an anachronism, the Don Quixote of fading ideals. He had outrun his era. He died in 1711, and by then progress northward, except for a final surge in California, had gone as far as Spain could carry it. The next century would be very different, a time when the rim of Christendom was no longer conceived of as a cutting edge but instead as a buffer against shocks from the outside.

# 3

## POROUS FRONTIERS

### Dead Ends

After Diego de Vargas had retaken Santa Fe in 1693 and had soundly thrashed the Pueblos who rose against him three years later, energy on New Spain's northern frontier ran thin. Like the defeated and bewildered Pueblo Indians around them, the colonists who had accompanied De Vargas up the Rio Grande and those who followed him during subsequent years simply dug in and endured.

The most stultifying factor was isolation, town from town in the remote, winding valleys and all of them from the nearest city of consequence, Chihuahua, seven hundred miles to the south. Everywhere there were shortages—of tools, weapons, paper, furniture, cloth. There were no schools. The only doctor was stationed at the Santa Fe presidio to care for the soldiers. Since few could go there to consult him, people had to rely on herbs, *curanderos*—local curers—and superstition.

Local officials were as ignorant as the people. Although the provincial governor, always a high-born outsider with little knowledge of neighborhood affairs, was directed by law to put honorable men who could read and write in charge of New Mexico's eight administrative districts—the administrators were called *alcaldes mayores*—he could seldom find qualified candidates. The job brought no recompense to the holder other than self-esteem and the right to collect small fees for official services, and so, in the words of one contemptuous priest, most *alcaldes mayores* were men who had failed at other work, "paper shufflers and swindlers . . . unfortunates without education or breeding."

The priests? All were missionaries. Except for those stationed in Santa Fe, their headquarters were at one or another of the nineteen pueblos that remained in existence following the conquest. (Coronado had found close to a hundred.) These men of God visited the Hispanic towns in their districts irregularly and caused much grumbling because of the prices they charged for administering the sacraments of baptism, matrimony, and extreme unction.

Most grew old and feeble in office. Vitality degenerated into fussiness. Don't let Indian women go to the fields under pretext of hoeing weeds, Fray Joaquín de Jesús Ruíz of Jémez Pueblo warned a successor in 1776, for what the females really want is to "join the older youths in wanton and wicked dalliance." Don't let the women sit together in church, for they are inveterate gossips, and the church, after all, is "a house of prayer, not of chitchat." And don't let the children who are assembled for religious instruction cover the lower part of their faces with the blankets they wear over their shoulders, "for then they keep eating grains of toasted maize and chewing some nasty stuff they are addicted to."

Nature was fickle and hard. In the mountain valleys of the north, where most of the Hispanos and Pueblos lived, late springs or early frosts could damage the crops. So could bears and crows and gophers. Drought might shrink the streams; flash floods swelled them thunderously. Always there was the dread of raids by the nomadic Indians who ringed the province.

Two outside concerns, their ramifications not always clear to the New Mexicans themselves, kept rumpling this drab local tapestry. One was the Spanish government's dread that imperial rivals—France, England, even Russia—might someday seek to seize the great silver mines of New Mexico, on which Spain's solvency depended. The other was the upheaval in tribal alignments occasioned by migrants from the north—Utes, who sought to drive the Navajos out of northwestern New Mexico, and the voracious Comanches, who did drive the eastern Apaches off the High Plains of New Mexico and western Texas.

During the third quarter of the eighteenth century the two forces entwined, though without the participants willing it so, and Madrid was then forced to reorganize the management of New Spain's northern provinces. In the 113 years that lay between the reconquest of New Mexico and the arrival of Zebulon Pike of the United States in Santa Fe, that shake-up was the one truly significant event that occurred on the frontier. Inevitably it also brought to the fore the only significant frontiersmen that the area saw during the same time span.

## New World Geopolitics

The nature of the forces that brought about the reorganization of the north can be quickly sketched. First, the international rivalries. Almost as soon as France and England had established colonies in North America, Spanish strategists sensed that struggles to control the heartland of the continent were inevitable. Collisions with the English began in the Carolinas and the Florida-Georgia area during the 1670s and 1680s. France intruded in 1682 in the person of Robert Cavelier, Sieur de La Salle, who that year coursed the Mississippi from the Great Lakes area to the Gulf of Mexico. Two years later he established a colony at Matagorda Bay on the Texas coast, no great distance from the mouth of the Rio Grande.

Frantic counterthrusts were ordered. Some historians speculate that Diego de Vargas was commissioned to reoccupy New Mexico not just to save the souls of the Indians but also to erect a barrier in case La Salle tried to ease himself toward Mexico by way of the Rio Grande. Meanwhile Spanish search parties scoured the coast looking for the French colony and at last found to their relief that it had disintegrated and that La Salle had been killed by his own men.

Plans for missionizing Texas as yet another barrier to the French were called off but then reactivated when French settlers occupied the Illinois country and New Orleans. An unnecessary disaster resulted from that expansion. In 1720 a self-satisfied young lieutenant named Pedro de Villasur marched out of Santa Fe with more than a hundred men to investigate reports that Frenchmen had advanced far up the Platte River of Nebraska and were trading guns for fur. Pawnees ambushed him near a stand of "very thick grass higher than the stature of a man" and destroyed almost half his force. As far as is known today, no Frenchmen were anywhere about.

In 1739, Gallic traders, led by the brothers Peter and Paul Mallet, did reach Santa Fe with a few mules loaded with goods. A joyous pealing of bells welcomed them, for the cloth and cutlery they brought were far cheaper than similar articles carried north from Chihuahua with the annual mission supply caravan.

Uneasy about the unprecedented situation, the governor wrote Mexico City for advice and was told crisply that Spanish law forbade trade with foreigners. The Mallets, who by then had sold their stock, were deported. Other traders, hearing of the starved market, soon took to their trail. To escape observation they moved their business to Taos

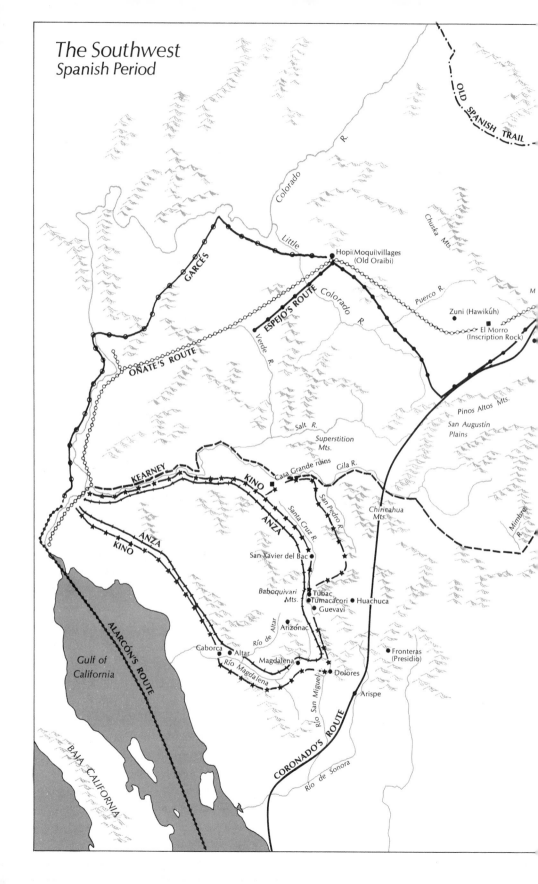

# The Southwest
## Spanish Period

OLD SPANISH TRAIL

Colorado R.

Chuska Mts.

M

GARCES

Little

Colorado R.

Puerco R.

Hopi (Moqui) villages
(Old Oraibi)

ESPEJO'S ROUTE

Zuni (Hawikúh)

El Morro
(Inscription Rock)

ONATE'S ROUTE

Verde R.

Pinos Altos Mts.

San Augustín
Plains

Salt R.

Superstition
Mts.

Casa Grande ruins

Gila R.

KEARNEY

KINO

ANZA

Santa Cruz R.

San Pedro R.

Chiricahua
Mts.

Mimbres
R.

KINO

ANZA

San Xavier del Bac

Baboquivari
Mts.

Tubac
Tumacacori
Guevavi

Huachuca

ALARCÓN'S ROUTE

Gulf of
California

Arizonac

Río de Altar

Caborca
Altar

Magdalena

Río Magdalena

Dolores

Fronteras
(Presidio)

Río San Miguel

Arispe

BAJA CALIFORNIA

CORONADO'S ROUTE

Río de Sonora

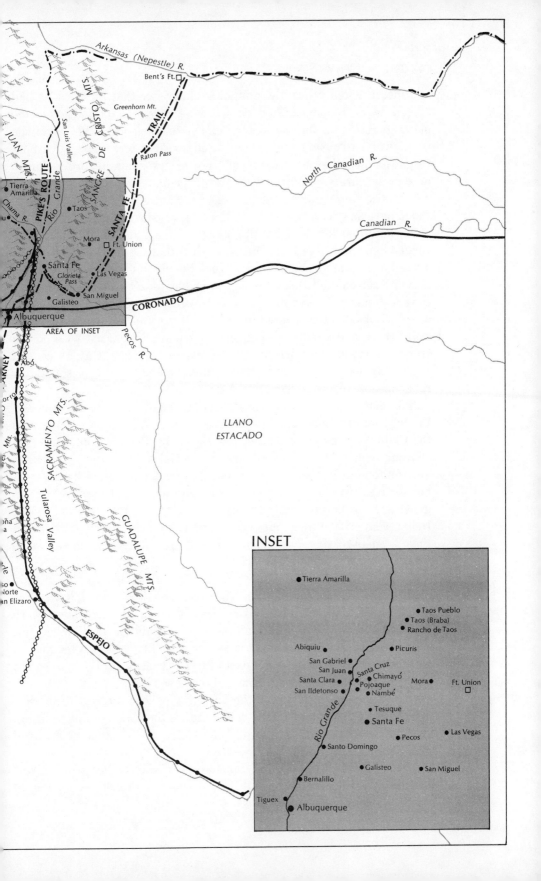

Arkansas (Nepestle) R.

Bent's Ft.

Greenhorn Mt.

San Luis Valley

SANGRE DE CRISTO MTS.

Raton Pass

North Canadian R.

JUAN MTS.

PIKE'S ROUTE

Tierra
Amarilla

Chama R.

Rio Grande

Taos

Mora

Ft. Union

SANTA FE TRAIL

Canadian R.

Santa Fe

Glorieta
Pass

Las Vegas

Galisteo

San Miguel

Albuquerque

CORONADO

AREA OF INSET

Pecos R.

Abó

ARKNEY

orro

LLANO
ESTACADO

SACRAMENTO MTS.

Tularosa Valley

GUADALUPE MTS.

ña

so
Norte
an Elizaro

ESPEJO

INSET

Tierra Amarilla

Taos Pueblo
Taos (Braba)
Rancho de Taos

Abiquiu

Picuris

San Gabriel

San Juan

Santa Cruz

Chimayó

Santa Clara

Pojoaque

Mora

Ft. Union

San Ildetonso

Nambé

Tesuque

Santa Fe

Rio Grande

Pecos

Las Vegas

Santo Domingo

Galisteo

San Miguel

Bernalillo

Tiguex

Albuquerque

and incorporated it into the annual summer fair that for decades had been drawing Hispanos, Pueblos, Utes, Navajos, and the Indians of the plains together under the shelter of a week-long armistice. Soon the event was so rousing an economic and social success that governors forgot its illegality and came north, they said, to maintain order—or, to be more accurate, to skim off whatever profits they could.

The setting was spectacular: the soaring, green-blue backdrop of the Sangre de Cristo Mountains, a dance of crystal streams, a gray sage plain, and then the deep basaltic gorge of the Rio Grande. Trails converged like crooked spokes. During each gathering thousands of horses grazed on a swampy meadow near Taos Pueblo. Its inhabitants, dressed in white cotton, and Hispanos gay in bright serapes, wandered among the encampments with a proprietary air. Utes adorned in necklaces made of grizzly bear claws offered deerskins they could tan better than any other tribe, and hollow-eyed children stolen or purchased with horses from poverty-stricken parents in *rancherias* as far away as central Utah. Navajos brought piñon nuts, blankets, and Spanish prisoners for ransom. Comanches had captive Apaches to sell, plus dried meat, thick buffalo hides, and softer ones that they passed off as white elk skin. The French and growing numbers of traders from Chihuahua—about 1750 the Chihuahuans took over the running of the annual supply caravans —brought in calico, mirrors, vermilion, bridles, metal pots, hatchets, and, quite against the law, guns, powder, lead, and liquor. There were horse races, war dances without war, and exuberant fornications. In general, according to one friar, the New Mexicans got the best of their Indian visitors "because our people ordinarily play infamous tricks on them." Small matter. The Indians evened the balance by robbing some ranch on their way home.

Inevitably the Chihuahua merchants complained to the viceroy about illegal French competition. The viceroy ordered a crackdown. During the early years of the 1750s several astonished Gallic traders were arrested and some were taken all the way to Spain for questioning. But far more instrumental than that in ending the infiltration was the French and Indian War that broke out east of the Mississippi in 1754, spread to Europe two years later, and, renamed the Seven Years' War, lasted until 1763. Naval blockades slowed the flow of supplies into North America, and the French no longer came west because they had nothing to bring. Besides, when Canada was invaded by England, they became involved in the fighting there.

Out of hatred of England, Spain entered the conflict as an ally of France. When it became evident in 1762 that the French were going to be driven from North America, Madrid asked Paris for, and received by secret treaty, the vast expanse of land beyond the Mississippi that Americans would eventually call Louisiana Territory. If California were occupied—and the unexpected appearance of Russian otter hunters on the continent's far northwestern coast made the contingency likely— Spain could then lay claim to the entire western two thirds of what became the United States, from the Mississippi to the Pacific.

Even this mass might not be enough to forestall the victorious British. Peace had scarcely come when Anglo fur traders, most of them natives of the New England colonies, began pushing west through Canada on what might develop into a flanking movement of the upper Mississippi. We smile now, but in those days the vastness of North America was not understood. José de Gálvez himself, the king's personal representative in Mexico City and one of the shrewdest administrators ever to reach New Spain, speculated that the Colorado River might rise in Lake of the Woods, just north of today's Minnesota, and flow to the Gulf of California, a ready-made highway to Sonora and the silver mines. Actually, of course, the Colorado heads a thousand miles southwest of Lake of the Woods on the Pacific side of the Rockies, but where little is known much can be feared. The frontier, it seemed obvious to Spain, needed strengthening against both Russians and British.

It also needed strengthening against the Apaches. Driven off the buffalo plains by the Comanches and desperate for new sources of supply, they were shredding the provinces of Coahuila, Sonora, and, in particular, Nueva Vizcaya almost at will, depopulating ranches and threatening many mines with closure because of the danger they posed to transportation and the movement of labor.

## The Indian Menace

Long before French traders from Quebec and Montreal had appeared in person on the Great Plains of the north, their greed for beaver was upsetting tribal balances of power. Rival groups of Indians fought each other for hunting territories and the right to act as middlemen for the spreading commerce, carrying knives and brass pots far into the West and bringing back pelts to their French suppliers. As one facet of the struggle, Blackfeet and Crow Indians, armed with trade muskets that had reached them along ancient aboriginal trade routes, began pressing on the Shoshoni, who lived along the edges of and within the mountains of Wyoming and Montana.

During this crisis, the southern Shoshoni, the Comanches of historic times, broke away from the northern groups and, band by band, began drifting south. A flight? Not necessarily. They had discovered horses and were as entranced by the possibility of mastering those magic animals as they were frightened by the new weapons in the hands of their enemies.

How the Comanche first acquired and learned to ride the animals is not known. Whatever the process, it was shattering for the Apaches. Once the Comanches had mastered a few horses, they set out with ferocious intensity to get more. Because the Southern High Plains were near the sources of supply and also teemed with buffalo, they swarmed toward and across the Arkansas River. Although they were willing to trade for horses, they preferred stealing them, because slipping into an Apache camp and making off with an enemy warrior's favorite mount was an irrefutable proof of manhood. Or they raided, running off entire herds in one wild dash. If the need arose, they pursued wild horses, roping them sometimes or driving them into hidden corral traps located near water holes. They learned what the Apaches apparently did not; they practiced controlled breeding, gelding some animals but leaving the best as stallions to father better offspring. By such methods a skillful warrior might achieve what, in Comanche eyes, was fantastic wealth—private ownership of as many as 250 animals.

Horses solidified the Comanches' inherent conviction of their own superiority. They were the Nermernuh, True Human Beings, and with this unshakable sense of rightness bolstering them they set out to gain full mastery of the southern plains. They shortened their bows and lances so that the weapons could be used with greater effectiveness when they ran full tilt against either buffalo or human enemies. Unlike the Apaches, they planted no fields that would hold them bound to one place during part of the year.

War parties were capable of striking at targets as far as 800 miles from whatever camp the Indians were occupying at the time. Once a man had covered an important stretch of country he could ever afterward draw a map of his trail on a piece of hide or in the earth with such precision that those who studied the drawing could then follow the route exactly from memory. Harum-scarum young girls and wives, too, often traveled with the men and during battles sniped with bows and arrows from the edges of the melee. Because it was the custom of these mixed parties to start their journeys by moonlight, their potential victims came to dread such evenings and called the moonlit nights of spring, when grass was green and horses were fresh and fat, the time of the Comanche moon.

The outnumbered Apaches, weakened by the attacks of buffalo-hungry tribes living east of them and by Spanish retaliatory strikes from the west, could not withstand the invasion. Some of the northern Apache groups—the Faraones, for example—disappeared entirely. The bloodied Jicarillas of the Arkansas River fled for refuge close to Taos and sent out fruitless appeals for Spanish aid. Rumors reaching Santa Fe in 1725 from still farther east told of other bands, Lipans probably, being crushed by a nine-day battle fought near the Wichita River.

Reeling from the impact, the scattered Apaches holed up in rugged mountain fastnesses they had formerly visited only intermittently during summers for the sake of their fresh water and relatively cool air—the Chisos and Davis Mountains of southwestern Texas and others in Nueva Vizcaya; in the Guadalupes and Sacramentos of south–central New Mexico; and those rugged uplifts farther west where their still unscathed relatives roamed the headwaters of the Gila. Fighting mostly afoot in those tumbled areas, they were able to beat back Comanche incursions, but the only way they could find sufficient food was to wrest what they needed from the Spanish settlements. In Nueva Vizcaya their attacks grew so ravaging that provincial authorities formally declared war on them in 1748.

By contrast, New Mexico benefited from the Apache retreat. At first the newcomers, the Comanches, did not seem formidable. When glory hunters among them tried experimental horse raids in 1716 and again in 1719, Spanish punitive expeditions mauled them severely. Sobered, the chiefs promised to keep the peace, and in the main they did, for tribal energies were taken up with consolidating their gains in Apachería. The Comanches also held French traders at a distance lest they bring guns to the Apaches, and that pleased the authorities in Santa Fe because the interdiction likewise kept Gallic snoopers out of New Mexico—for a time.

As soon as the Apaches had been driven beyond reach of the French, the blockade lost its point and after 1739, as we have seen, traders were able to slip across the plains to Taos. A few years later the Comanches themselves were formally admitted to the annual fair and for a while all seemed well. But a new change came with the outbreak of the Seven Years' War. Deprived of the French goods to which they had grown accustomed and unable because of the competition at Taos to buy as many items as they wanted, the Comanches turned, like the Apaches, to raiding.

Spanish injudiciousness heated the fires. The most notorious instance occurred in 1760 and is described with varying details by church officials who picked up the story during later tours of inspection. Somehow Pueblo Indian auxiliaries fighting with Spanish punitive expeditions laid hold of several Comanche scalps and were allowed to dance over them in front of watching members of the slain men's tribe. The spectators carried reports of the outrage home and a reputed 3,000 warriors (so wrote both Bishop Pedro Tamarón and Fray Atanasio Domínguez) vowed to massacre everyone, Hispanos and Pueblos alike, in the Taos area.

They struck on August 4. Warned of their approach, several families fled for refuge to the fortified hacienda of a leading settler, Don Pedro de Villalpando. He and many of his men were away at the time, and so only seven males—or fourteen (accounts vary)—were available to withstand the assault.

Normally Indians sought to hold down casualties by avoiding frontal attacks. This time, however, Comanche sappers charged under a cover of bowmen to the base of the walls. Whenever a defender leaned over the parapet to shoot down on them, he drew a cloud of arrows. Shielded thus, the Comanches broke through the entry. Several women, Señora Villalpando among them, seized lances and fought beside the men. All who struggled were slain. Afterward, said Fray Atanasio with a shiver, the Comanches, who had suffered heavy casualties themselves, coupled dead male and female Hispano bodies together, burned several nearby farms, and withdrew with sixty-four captives.

A forty-day pursuit by presidial soldiers and militiamen failed to rescue the prisoners. Yet some of them could have been recovered the following year. Several chiefs came to Santa Fe under truce and there offered to negotiate the sale of several captives taken from Taos at unspecified times. Going into a passion over the arrogance, as he deemed it to be, Acting Governor Don Manuel del Portilla y Urrisola had the chiefs killed and then led a surprise attack on the unprepared Comanche camp nearby.

The war of slashing hit-and-run raids did flare then. Outlying haciendas and towns were abandoned, the frontier shrank, Santa Fe filled with refugees. Southward, meanwhile, the Apaches were even more deadly. Between 1748, when the governor of Nueva Vizcaya declared war on them, and 1763, they killed 800 people and destroyed 4 million pesos' worth of farm, ranch, and mission property. They "enter the pueblos" [along the river below El Paso], wrote Fray Atanasio Domínguez in 1775, "steal from them all the horses and mules they find in them, make captives of the little ones who fall into their hands and leave their parents, if not completely dead, without the better half of their lives, which is their children."

Nor were Apaches and Comanches the whole of the story. In 1751 Pimería Alta was shaken by a revolt of Pima and Papago Indians that took a hundred lives. Quick action by presidial troops brought about an appearance of peace, but its shakiness became evident when the Seri Indians who lived along the lower Sonora River went to war against the Spaniards and were joined by resentful bands from farther north—a turbulent situation that the western Apaches were quick to turn to their own advantage.

Clearly defenses had to be strengthened—but not at all costs. Spain's participation in France's war against England had all but bankrupted the empire. The country's distraught ruler, Carlos III, a homely, energetic, mahogany-colored gnome imbued with a reformer's zeal, was determined to restore his country's vitality first by replenishing the national treasury and then by overhauling the entire government structure. These demands would leave little money for the frontier.

How, then, could safety and stability be achieved?

## The Frontiersmen

The first step was the erection, at parsimonious prices, of a line of forts designed to keep the Apaches out of the key ranching and mining areas of Coahuila, Nueva Vizcaya, and Sonora. Locating proper sites in those remote areas turned out to be exhausting. Some of Spain's top military men, engineers, and cartographers spent half a dozen years and rode horseback nearly 20,000 miles preparing a cordon that ended up roughly parallel to and a little south of the present international border. To the architect of the plan, Field Marshal the Marqués de Rubí, this line marked New Spain's real frontier; the provinces to the north—Texas, New Mexico, and, later, California—were expendable. The concept turned out to be remarkably prescient, for those were exactly the areas that fell to the Republic of Texas and then to the Americans in 1836 and 1848.

The next step was the even lengthier one of administrative reform. The full band of northern provinces lying between the Gulf of Mexico and Baja California were split away from the viceregal government in Mexico City and erected into a semiautonomous unity called, by some mysterious twist of Spanish logic, the Provincias Internas—the Internal

Provinces. Administration was placed in the hands of a *comandante-general* who was paid the munificent salary of 20,000 pesos a year (at least $100,000 in terms of today's purchasing power) but ordered to establish his headquarters at the poverty-stricken little mud hamlet of Arizpe, Sonora, because it was deemed to be halfway between San Antonio, Texas, and San Francisco Bay.

Two complications slowed the already snail-like progress. The first was Carlos III's thunderbolt order that every Jesuit in the empire be exiled. This meant the removal, under trying circumstances, of the men in charge of the missions of Sonora and Baja California and their replacement with Franciscans. The second interruption was the almost simultaneous occupation of Alta California as a counter to the British and Russians.

Out of the ruck of people involved in these activities emerged two remarkable frontier figures. One was Juan Bautista de Anza, an army officer. The other was Fray Francisco Garcés, a Franciscan replacement for the banished Jesuit missionary at San Xavier del Bac, a station that Kino had founded a few miles south of the Indian *ranchería* of Chuk Sohn, now Tucson. Two contemporaries could hardly have been more different than Anza and Garcés. It is questionable whether they really liked each other. Yet for part of an eventful decade they were bound together by the sharing of a similar dream.

Anza's grandfather and father, of Basque lineage and inordinately proud of it there in the wilderness, had been army officers in Sonora before him. The father, also named Juan Bautista, yearned for more. Once he had offered to pay out of his own pocket part of the expenses that would be involved in blazing the trail from Sonora to California that Kino had recommended years before. The authorities had been on the point of accepting the proposal when, in April 1739, the captain had blundered into an Apache ambush and had been slain.

At the time, young Juan had been four years old. After being privately tutored by Jesuits, he had enlisted in his father's old post at Fronteras, thirty-five miles south of the present border town of Douglas, Arizona. For two years he served as a common soldier without pay. On July 1, 1755, aged twenty-one, he became a lieutenant. Four and a half years later he gained a captaincy and was put in charge of the presidio of Tubac in the Santa Cruz Valley of what is now southern Arizona. He was married by then and had begun a family. He owned considerable property, much of it inherited from his father, and was snugly ensconced among northern Sonora's elite of army officers, mine owners, ranchers, and churchmen. But though he campaigned endlessly—against rebellious Pápagos to the west, Seris and renegade Pimas to the south, and Apaches to the east—he felt as cramped by the narrow horizons as his father had, and so the elder Anza's dream of California became his dream, too.

Francisco Garcés, four years younger than Anza, was the soldier's opposite—unpolished, undistinguished, and, at the time of their meeting, lacking in frontier experience. A native of mountainous Aragon in northern Spain, Garcés had been a poor student in the local grammar school and later at the Franciscan college of Querétaro, Mexico, where he had been sent after deciding on a missionary career. But humble people liked him, and at Bac, which was within Anza's district, he developed a genius for getting on with Indians. He was of medium height, lean, and dark-eyed, with a sparse black beard showing strongly against his fair skin. On receiving his assignment to Pimería Alta, he had devoured Kino's memoirs as part of his orientation, and now he was on fire to outdo the Jesuit's explorations.

The government's decision to settle Alta California electrified both the priest and the soldier, for the original plan envisioned a march through Sonora to the Gila and down that stream to the Colorado River crossing at the Yuma villages, an operation that would have involved each man. A new uprising by the Seris aborted the idea, however, and the new province was occupied in 1769 by land parties toiling northward along the dreary length of Baja California and by two supply ships bucking adverse winds on their way to San Diego and Monterey bays.

News of the wayfarers' slow progress was flashed across the desert to Tubac by the Indian grapevine. The speed with which the communication came fathered an exciting corollary: The coast could not be as far away as many people supposed. In emulation of his father, Anza wrote hastily to his superiors offering to pay the costs of taking a mule train of provisions overland to Monterey, if permission were given him. His hope was to prove that Alta California could be supplied more easily by land from northern Sonora than by sea from San Blas, far down the Mexican coast. This in turn would provide Sonora ranchers—Anza included—with an outlet for beef and grain. Undoubtedly, too, success in blazing a usable trail to California would result in his being promoted to a higher rank.

Instead the captain was sent south from Tubac to fight the Seris once again.

Garcés meanwhile was consoling himself by following Kino's tracks westward. Often he traveled alone, relying for safety on a rectangular linen banner. On one side of it was painted a picture of the Virgin Mary;

on the other was a gruesome representation of a lost soul writhing in hell. Whenever he neared a *rancheria,* he raised the banner on a standard and let the curious heathens flock around him for an explanation. The device never failed him, he assured Anza, but the captain remained furious. The crazy innocent would get himself killed; there would have to be a punitive expedition and that would bring on still more Indian wars.

Garcés went blithely ahead. During the crushing summer heat of 1771 he managed to cross the Colorado River and reach the sun-blistered trough that would later be called Imperial Valley. There thirst turned him back, but not before he had glimpsed in the mountains to the northwest a pass that he was sure would open a way to the coast.

He told Anza of his discovery. Anza forwarded the information to the new viceroy in Mexico City, Antonio Bucareli, and repeated his arguments about a supply route to California from Sonora. This time he received partial backing. Fray Junípero Serra, head of the California missions, happened to be in Mexico City when Anza arrived and, on being consulted by Bucareli, confirmed that the sea route from San Blas had proved dangerously undependable. A good land route would be a blessing. But Sonora? The friar wanted reinforcements of families for California and the Seris and Apaches of Sonora worried him. He thought that a trail from New Mexico to Monterey might be safer. Surely the Hispanic and Pueblo people of that province could furnish grain and beef as easily as the Sonorans could.

Bucareli replied that he would have both routes tested—the one from Sonora first because Anza and Garcés were ready to go, whereas time would be needed to start things rolling in New Mexico.

Anza's trip was authorized for the winter of 1773–74—thirty-five people altogether, soldiers, friars (one of them Francisco Garcés) and roustabouts. Just before they were scheduled to leave Tubac, Apaches hit the presidio and made off with 130 animals. The loss forced the glum explorers to travel south to Altar for replacements and then, to save time, to follow a route that would never do for the California colonists —the dread Camino Diablo.

At the Yuma crossing, which both Anza and Garcés realized would be a key point on the new trail, they went out of their way to win the friendship of one of the Indians' principal chiefs—big, genial Olleyquotequiebe. The diplomacy paid off. The Yumans helped them transport their baggage across the river, and after a harsh time in the sand dunes bordering Imperial Valley they broke through to Mission San Gabriel, nine miles east of the site of future Los Angeles.

The outcome for Anza was an appointment as lieutenant colonel, with orders to recruit, during the summer of 1775, a mixed group of soldiers, civilians, and their families for founding a new presidio beside San Francisco Bay. Garcés meantime was to do more scouting. After settling a missionary named Tómas Eixarch among the Yuma Indians, he was to participate in the search for a possible trail between New Mexico and Monterey, whose eastern section was being examined that same summer by a young missionary from Zuñi Pueblo, New Mexico. (The missionary's name was Silvestre Velez de Escalante, but Garcés seems not to have known that, though they both were working on the same project.) While Anza went on from the crossing with the California settlers, Garcés was supposed to look over the hoped-for trail's western reaches.

An Apache horse raid marred the start of Anza's trip, too. He went ahead anyway, with 240 poorly mounted people, 165 of them women and children. They marched out of Tubac and headed for the Gila on Monday morning, October 22, 1775. Despite cold weather, sluicing rain, and frequent sickness, Anza got them through to Monterey with the loss of only one woman during childbirth. Both the people and their commander wept when he bade them farewell and started a 2,000-mile horseback ride to Mexico City to report.

He took Olleyquotequiebe with him in order to impress the chief with Spain's might. For both it was a triumphal tour. Anza sat for his portrait, his mustaches curled, his full beard trimmed to a point, and on his head a hat of velvet given dash by an upturned brim and sweeping plume. He introduced the Yuman to society and stood with him as godfather when, rechristened Salvador Palma, the Indian was baptized in the great cathedral beside the Zócolo. As a climax to the heady days, Anza was made a full colonel and appointed governor of New Mexico, which in truth needed a strong hand right then. We will rejoin him there shortly, but now the story belongs to Fray Francisco Garcés and his extraordinary wanderings.

His first goal after separating from Anza at the Yuma villages was to find a way of avoiding that stretch of coastal trail in California that followed the Santa Barbara Channel toward the new mission of San Luis Obispo, gateway to Monterey. The Chumash Indians in the Santa Barbara area (which had not yet been settled by Europeans) were troublesome, and the way itself, pinched tight between mountains and ocean, was difficult. An alternate route might be developed through a certain broad valley, today's San Joaquín, that was said to lie inland from the Coast Ranges. Aided by guides from the Mohave villages 200 miles north of the Yuman towns, Garcés might be able to work out a path across the desert to the San Joaquín, turn north along it to the latitude of San Luis Obispo, and then cut through some handy pass to the mission. Misty though the plan was, he determined to try.

The effort, made during the height of the California rainy season, failed. The streams of the San Joaquín boomed with floods; sheets of water filled the low places. Garcés' Mohave guides balked, and he had no choice but to turn his mule back to their home village a little north of today's Needles.

There, late in the spring of 1776 he found a letter from Anza, brought by Indian courier, that ordered him back to the Yuma crossing. Impossible! Some visiting Walapai Indians who lived to the east had just told him in answer to his questions that, yes, he could reach New Mexico by traveling through their country. And, yes, they would take him that far on their way home. In defiance of both Anza's orders and predictions by his Mohave friends that the Moqui (Hopi) Indians would kill him if he tried to go through their lands, Garcés decided to continue his explorations.

Guides from one village passed him along, still on muleback, to the next, sharing their meager rations without stint. A little beyond a watering place now called Peach Springs (on today's U.S. Highway 66) he veered northeast over mountains covered with piñon pine and across a vast plain sliced by deep canyons. His guides there were Havasupai Indians and they were taking him to their principal village in Havasu Canyon, one of the Grand Canyon's most spectacular tributaries and a stirring trip still.

To get there, he wrote in his journal, "I went along a narrow way . . . some three handbreadths wide with a very high cliff on one side and on the other a hideous abyss. What came next was worse. I had to get down from my mule and the Indians from their horses in order to descend a wooden ladder," while the animals were led down by a much longer route. He stayed in the gorge, hearing the sound of the waterfalls, admiring the irrigated gardens, and asking his endless questions for five days. With a new group of men, women, and children—Yavapais this time—he climbed out of the chasm by a different route. Following trails that Cárdenas might have used in 1540, he reached the South Rim of the Grand Canyon. He named the stupendous gash Puerto de Bucareli for the viceroy—ah, if only Bucareli would help push the Word this far! —and then, swinging southeast, he reached the mesas on which the Hopi villages crouched.

His first stop was Oraibi. Hostile crowds watched from the roofs of the stone houses as he dismounted in the plaza. While one of the Yavapai led his mule to a nearby corral, he tried to lure the Hopis into talk by showing his banner and holding out a handful of sea shells, a treasure that all other Indians he knew coveted. Except for three Indians who turned out to be traders from Zuñi, the villagers stayed aloof.

Evidently the Zuñi trio told him that their young padre—Silvestre Velez de Escalante, but the name still did not percolate through to Garcés—had visited the same village the year before with another party of traders and had encountered the same kind of hostility. Anyway, Garcés promptly wrote "the missionary at Zuñi" a long, incoherent letter about his views and adventures and entrusted it to one of the visitors for delivery. He cooked a meager supper over a fire of corncobs that he gathered from the streets, wrapped himself in a cloak, and passed the night huddled in a corner of the plaza, sniffed at by dogs. The next day he saddled his mule, visited the nearby villages, and met the same cold, silent reception.

Again he passed a waterless night in the Oraibi plaza. At dawn, July 4, 1776, a great throng advanced on him through the streets and across the contiguous housetops, making shrill whistling noises with their flutes and stirring up a clatter by pounding with sticks on wooden bowls. Jumping to his feet in alarm, Garcés held out a Cross "and partly in Yuma, partly in Yavabai [as he spelled it], and partly in Castilian, with the aid of signs," tried to soothe them. To no avail. Threatening gestures ordered him out. One of the Yavapai brought his mule and they rode in dejection off the mesa.

He wanted to continue to Zuñi, but neither he nor his friends had been able to buy supplies in Oraibi, and the Indians insisted that they use the little they had left on their homeward journey. Back to Havasu he went, rested awhile in that delicious red-and-green retreat, then returned through the Mohave and Yuma villages to his station at Bac. By dint of one of the most notable journeys ever taken in America by a single white, he had found a new trail west, but it seemed unlikely that it would ever be commonly used.

The letter he had written in Oraibi reached Escalante in Santa Fe, where the priest had gone to meet his superior, Atanasio Domínguez, to report, among other things, what he had learned concerning routes westward to Monterey. Escalante was pessimistic. The country beyond Zuñi was rough and dry; pasturage for livestock was sparse. Apaches would threaten the road from the south, Navajos from the northeast. The Hopis' cooperation would be essential for success, and they were not likely to extend it—an estimate confirmed by Garcés' letter and by the account of the messenger who brought it. A better solution, Escalante thought, was to work out a trail through the country of the Utes, far north of the Grand Canyon.

Domínguez agreed. Aided by an expert army cartographer, Bernardo de Miera y Pacheco, and guided by prospectors who had already been as far north as western Colorado's Gunnison River, the priests took a small party as far as Utah Lake (just south of Great Salt Lake, which they did not visit), then gave up in the face of coming winter and the grisly deserts to the west. Cutting south to the upper end of the Grand Canyon, they managed to cross a few miles above the point where the Glen Canyon Dam now stands and returned home by way of the Hopi villages. "Those obstinate heathens," Miera y Pacheco fumed in his report. They ought to be cut off from water until they learned the virtues of cooperation. But they weren't, and after almost two centuries of settlement, there was still no way for a white man to get in or out of New Mexico except south through El Paso and Chihuahua.

As for Francisco Garcés, he was transferred from Bac to the two small mongrel settlements, part mission and part town, that were built twelve miles apart among the Yuma Indians to keep the river crossing open. Hostility was growing there, too, partly because the Indians were not receiving the presents they had been promised in return for their cooperation. In July 1781 matters came to a head when a band of California-bound pioneers appeared with a herd of nearly 1,000 horses. The families in the group went ahead to San Gabriel, but the unmarried soldiers and their commander stayed behind to rest animals debilitated by the summer heat. When some of the livestock were let loose in the Indian gardens, the spark flared. Fifty-three men died, Garcés among them, his body pulped by clubs.

After that the only way to reach California by land was through desolate Baja. All in all, it was a strange frontier for a once-mighty empire—a few isolated fingers clutching northward at one of the biggest, richest expanses of raw territory in the world, yet barely able to hang on.

## Seedbed of a New Race

In New Mexico the job of hanging on had fallen to Governor Juan Bautista de Anza. Great things were expected of him. He had dealt with Indians either as a diplomat or fighter most of his life. He was honest and energetic, whereas many of his predecessors in the governor's chair had been indolent bumblers, peculators, petty tyrants, or all three to-gether. More important, he was a frontiersman himself. As such he might understand, as few of the officials before him had, the unique breed of settlers that was taking shape in the cruelly isolated province.

He made his start north from Chihuahua in 1778 after consultation with the new Comandante of the Provincias Internas, Teodoro de Croix, and other frontier strategists. Along with eighteen badly needed friars, he joined the annual northbound supply caravan, which by then was being operated by a brotherhood of Chihuahua merchants. Its progress went like this. After attending the summer bartering fairs at Taos and Abiquiu on the Chama River, buyers repaired with their purchases, including slaves, to a rendezvous south of Albuquerque. Home-based weavers and the little textile factories in Santa Fe sent down mule trains laden with serapes and stockings. (Wagons were no longer used; mules were faster and cheaper.) Ranchers appeared with herds of sheep and, less frequently, cattle.

Often as many as five hundred persons gathered at the rendezvous for the sake of mutual protection on the trail ahead. In addition to merchants, ranchers, and their hired help, there were soldiers, dispatch carriers, friars, and ordinary travelers. Finally there were hangers-on, notably the *trobadores*, who went along to sing for their suppers beside the campfires.

The racial mix was typical of New Mexico as a whole. Among the wayfarers were some whose veins carried pure Spanish blood, though probably not as many of them as the bearers of certain ancient New Mexican names like to claim today. There were occasional pure-blooded Indians from Mexico and Mexican *mestizos*, products of liaisons be-tween the Indian women of New Spain and European immigrants. There were a few blacks and mulattos. Yet another blending came from the union of New Mexicans of all blood lines with female captives seized during retaliatory raids on the outside tribes—Utes, Comanches, Ap-aches, and, most commonly, Navajos.

A distinctive and steadily expanding group were the *genízaros*, Indian children who had been acquired by trade with one of the wild tribes or by raids on their camps. Whatever their origin, the waifs were a common article of commerce, "ransomed" by their purchasers whose justification was that they would give them a Christian upbringing in return for their labor in the kitchens or fields or, in the case of young girls, in the purchaser's bed. Generally, the slaves—for that is what they were really—were freed on reaching adulthood, particularly if they were married by then to one of their own kind or to some humble *mestizo*.

Because *genízaros* had forgotten their own languages and customs and had no families to which to turn, they hung around the settlements, existing as best they could. They were good fighters, having little to lose, so the authorities eventually established some of them in special towns where they could absorb the first shock of raiding Indians. One such *genízaro* settlement was Abiquiu on the Chama. Another was Tomé, south of Albuquerque, where in 1777, the year before Anza's arrival, fifty-one persons had been slain by Comanches—along with another eleven at Albuquerque. They were resilient, though. Historian Fray Angelico Chavez estimates that by the opening of the nineteenth century *genízaros* made up a full third of New Mexico's population.

As Anza would learn, this conglomeration of peoples did not meld completely. Each group maintained inner barriers that others seldom penetrated. Still, there was considerable interchange of customs, skills, beliefs. For most of the settlers of all groups poverty was a common horizon. They became fatalistic, inured to pain and grief, cooperative with neighbors, generous to hungry wayfarers, suspicious of authority. The family unit, which spread out to include cousins and second cousins, godfathers and grandnieces, and the land that they all tilled together— those were the goods of life that held meaning. Until, at the end of their days desire condensed into a single prayer, "God, give me a good death!"

As governor, Anza needed to know something of the legal theories involved in land acquisition. Ultimately, according to Spanish law, title vested in the king. A contrast in the methods by which Americans and Spaniards acquired land will suggest the implications of this. An American citizen, having met the conditions laid down by his elected government, could appropriate varying amounts of the public domain as an inviolable right. A Spanish subject could not. He had to supplicate for the bit of earth he wanted as *merced*—a favor, a gift, a "mercy." Even the Pueblo Indians, who had been living in the area long before the king's assumption, acquired rights to the lands surrounding their towns only as a dispensation of royal mercy. Pueblo grants varied radically in size. The people of Nambé, north of Santa Fe, for instance, were given 13,585 acres, while those of Isleta received 110,080.

In time mercy was shaped by custom into a few set patterns. Hispanic towns, for instance, could be located wherever a provincial governor, acting always under the authorization of his superiors, felt they were needed. Called either *villas* or *pueblos,* according to size (villas were larger), each new town was granted enough land so that every head of a family could have a house lot and a farm plot. Out beyond the farms lay commons on which wood could be cut and livestock grazed.

Santa Fe, established in 1609–10 by Pedro de Peralta, was such a *villa*. Almost a century later Diego de Vargas created a second *villa*, Santa Cruz de la Cañada, twenty-five miles north of Santa Fe, by ordering uncooperative Indians out of two adjacent pueblos and replacing them with Hispanic citizens. In 1706 drums beating in the plazas of settlements throughout the province warned that a circular from the government was about to be read. As bellowed forth by the town crier, the announcement solicited colonists for a new *villa* to be named Alburquerque, after the viceroy in Mexico City. Lured by bonuses of tools and livestock, thirty-five families responded. Those who could write soon dropped the surplus *r* from the *villa's* name. This gave New Mexico a total of four *villas:* Santa Fe, Santa Cruz, Albuquerque, and El Paso, the last of which then stood on the south bank of the Rio Grande, where Ciudad Juárez is now.

Individual grants of land were issued to stock raisers desirous of protecting their grazing lands from encroachment by their neighbors. The tightly grouped buildings of the enterprise, built around a central court and sometimes protected from Indian attack by defensive towers at the corners, were called *haciendas*. Often the owner of a powerful hacienda was, in effect, a feudal lord, holding his *peones* by chains of debt to the soil they husbanded for him like serfs.

Far more common in New Mexico than individual grants were community grants made to a group of people, generally relatives. In the mountainous north, where the bulk of the population lived, the windings of the canyons cut the utilizable land into many isolated pockets. In order that as many farm plots as possible might front on the main irrigation ditch, the holdings were laid out in long, narrow strips. The commons, called the *ejido*, were located out in the hills.

As families grew, the strips were subdivided among the heirs until further slicing became economically self-defeating. At that point a few of the more ambitious members of the community struck out on their own to establish a new settlement, as José de Medina, Manuel de Quintana, Manuel Martín, and Miguel Martín, residents of Chimayó, did in 1743. After finding suitable land, they appealed in headlong Spanish to the governor, who in 1743 was Gaspar Domingo de Mendoza:

That inasmuch as all four of us are burdened with children and wives and without having land in our possession to cultivate for our support, because those which we have are very limited as we have inherited them from our parents and our brothers were so many that we received a piece so small that we can scarcely plant one almud of corn on account of which we have experienced great want and hard work . . . we have decided to register and do register . . . a piece of crown land to which no one has any right. . . . For the love of God grant us the said land, in the name of our majesty, God preserve him.*

Following routines set by law, Mendoza referred the application to the *alcalde mayor* in charge of the pertinent district. The *alcalde* determined that the area was as described and returned the certified appeal to the governor. On deciding that a *merced* was in order, Mendoza directed the *alcalde* to "give them the royal possession that they requested for themselves, their children, and heirs in full right and that in the name of his majesty, God guard him, they may hold, cultivate, and improve it. . . ."

Accompanied by the *alcalde* and their rejoicing families, the grantees then went to the site. There, "shouting aloud the name of the king, they threw rocks, pulled up grass and did the rest within the boundaries they requested," all of which the *alcalde* duly reported "on the present paper since the seal [official] kind is not current in this kingdom"—one more of New Mexico's many shortages.

As soon as the recipients of a community grant were in possession, work began in earnest. First a main ditch, the *acequia madre*, had to be dug—no small matter inasmuch as it might be two or three miles long, from six to twelve feet wide, and three or more feet deep. Everyone pitched in, using metal hoes and wooden shovels. If earth was to be hauled away rather than just thrown over onto the lower side of the canal, it was heaped on a cowhide and skidded off by oxen. Engineering consisted of squinting and arguing. Large trees and boulders caused picturesque but wasteful meanderings, and when the first water was turned through the head gate, it was followed with suspense: Did the canal have proper fall so that the precious liquid would flow gently to the farthest lateral?

For the sake of safety, authorities wanted the community's residence buildings to form a wall around the four sides of an interior square, or plaza, in which livestock could be penned if Indians struck. Indeed, the word *plaza* came to mean fortified town.

Many communities objected to the authorities' instructions. They could not afford to put towns on arable land. Accordingly, a village of the kind the officials wanted would have to be located at a distance from the farms, creating hardship for the women and children, who had to walk out to care for the crops while the men were on militia duty, hunting, or herding livestock. In spite of the law, therefore, the *pobladores* ("townspeople") placed their homes near their fields. Sentries

*From documents translated by Myra Ellen Jenkins, New Mexico State historian, in *Land Title Study*, State Planning Office, Santa Fe, 1971, pp. 219–220.

posted at strategic lookouts were depended on to warn of Indians promptly enough so that workers in the vicinity could flee to a designated refuge. The residents of *villas* could be just as reckless of their own safety and of the law as the *pobladores* were. Anza was regularly exasperated by the refusal of the people of Albuquerque to obey his order that they move from their outlying farms back to the villa's central plaza.

A merchant in Santa Fe or the owner of a prosperous hacienda might duplicate in miniature the ideal shape of a plaza by placing several contiguous rooms around a patio. Such a house looked in on itself; its outer walls were blank and ingress was through heavy double gates large enough to admit the universal two-wheeled carretas.

A poor *poblador,* however, had to make do with a simple cube built of bricks molded from clay dug from the community pit and *vigas* ("roof beams"), which were cut from tall trees in the nearby mountains. The beams spanned the short dimension of the cube and were allowed to protrude a foot or so beyond the walls on either side. On top of the beams was a tight herringbone pattern of sticks that were sometimes peeled and painted in alternating colors, say red and green, and left open to view from below, as were the beams. A mat of brush and twigs was piled on the sticks. Above the mat was a roof of pounded clay surrounded by a low parapet through which protruded wooden *canales* for carrying away storm water. Protruding *canales* and *viga* ends lent aesthetic appeal to the warm, ruddy adobe walls by laying a pattern of strong black shadows across them when the sun was out.

As families grew, additional cubes were added to the original, like a chain of boxcars, until some barrier—a neighbor's garden or an arroyo —prompted a right-angle bend. In a town the string might be fronted by a wooden awning resting on thin wooden pillars. Windows were small and either glazed with thin sheets of translucent mica or barred with sticks. There was no glass in early New Mexico.

Inside, the earthen floors were pounded hard—a mixing in of animal blood increased durability—and covered with locally woven rugs. Except for the rich, who might own a few ornately carved chests and perhaps a glossy table imported from Mexico, wooden furniture was almost nonexistent. Mattresses were placed directly on the floor at night and by day were rolled up against the wall and covered with blankets to serve as seats. (After American trading caravans had appeared, a strip of muslin was often fixed to the lower third of the wall to keep adobe or whitewash from rubbing off on the clothes of those sitting on the mattresses.) Bread was baked outside in beehive ovens. The rest of the cooking was done in an elliptical fireplace set into a corner of the main room on a hearth elevated several inches above the floor. Decorations were limited in the main to gaunt *santos* and *Cristos* carved from soft cottonwood and, in the case of the thorn-crowned, crucified Christ figures, garishly painted with red stripes and dots to represent a gush of blood.

Pleasures were as simple as the homes. A gay fiesta celebrated the birthday of whatever saint the village had chosen as its patron. Horse races were popular, as was a violent game in which each competing rider tried to pull up a rooster that had been buried to the neck in sand. Dances were frequent. Every community had its *trobadores*. Both men and women gambled avidly at cards and smoked cigarettes rolled out of corn husks and a cheap native tobacco. Parents who lived near a mission sometimes hired a priest to tutor their children, but since much of the learning was devoted to religious doctrine and help was needed at home, few young people were sent along that road to literacy. All of which caused Atanasio Domínguez to sniff, during his tour of inspection of New Mexico, "The people of this kingdom are so simple that they do not know the day on which they were born." Yet most of them had mastered an art Domínguez did not know: how to survive with a minimum of conveniences in a formidable land.

New Mexico was so poor that taxes were light. One paid only tithes to the church and irregular *donativos* ("voluntary contributions") levied for a variety of purposes—to send food to a town whose harvest had failed or to support a military campaign either in one's own district or, sometimes, as far away as Europe. In addition, one also had to serve in the provincial militia.

Every adult male—Spanish and Pueblo Indian—was registered on the muster roll of the district in which he lived. During campaigns Hispanic citizens had to supply part of their own rations, necessary horses, and either a gun or bow, arrow, and lance. Pueblo Indians were issued firearms at the beginning of a campaign and afterwards regularly tried to keep them, to the angry frustration of their Spanish officers.

Short campaigns were led by the *alcalde mayor* of the district involved. More ambitious strikes were commanded by the governor, who was also in charge of the presidio at Santa Fe. He brought with him, as the backbone of the combined force, a detachment of regular soldiers dressed for combat in a sleeveless armor called *cuera*. This makeshift uniform reached below a rider's knees, was stitched together from seven plies of bleached, quilted buckskin, and was decorated along seams and pockets with bright red cloth. Each trooper was also burdened with a heavy, smooth-bore musket, a brace of pistols, an iron-bladed lance nine feet long, a sword, a cartridge box, saddlebags filled with provisions, a canteen of water, a cooking pot, heavy boots, and spurs with enormous rowels. Historian Max Moorhead has calculated that the mass of equipment weighed 159 pounds, and so it is understandable why each *soldado de cuera* ("leather-jacketed soldier") needed six horses and a mule to keep him mobile in the field—a troublesome herd of animals attended during the march by some of the Pueblo auxiliaries.

By and large the Pueblo Indians enjoyed the campaigns. They could ride horses and fire guns, privileges that Spain theoretically denied subject Indians. They could share in whatever loot resulted from a victory and often were able to recover livestock and captives that had been stolen from them. And they could count on an ecstatic welcome home if they returned bearing scalps.

On such occasions a triumphant party sent up smoke signals of their approach. In a frenzy of excitement their fellow townspeople bedecked themselves with paint and feathers and rushed out to escort them into the pueblo. The women, wrote Fray Atanasio Domínguez in disgust, would "paw, fondle, flatter, and overwhelm" those who carried the trophies. They would snatch up a scalp and to show their opinion of the enemy would "scornfully touch [it] to their private parts." After giving thanks in the church, a practice that particularly offended the priests, they prepared a feast, sent invitations to nearby pueblos, raised the trophies on a pole, and danced exuberantly around them, giving expression to an ancient joy made more attainable by fighting for the Spanish government rather than against it.

## Peace at Last

Fighting had been the government's main purpose in sending Anza to New Mexico—fighting not just for the sake of the people there but also as part of a broad new plan for containing the Apaches. The line of stationary presidios scattered along the "real" frontier of the north had proved porous. Although patrols regularly scouted the ground between neighboring forts, the Apaches had no difficulty slipping through to continue their raids farther south. Their skills honed sharp by the constant pressures of hunger and danger, they were becoming, despite numerical inferiority, as potent a body of guerrilla warriors as the world has known. Between 1711 and 1776 in Nueva Vizcaya alone small handfuls of them had killed 1,963 people, made off with 68,873 head of assorted livestock, and forced the abandonment of 116 haciendas.

How could they be contained? In search of an answer the new Comandante of the Provincias Internas, Teodoro de Croix, summoned leading frontier citizens and soldiers to meet with him at a series of councils of war during 1777. Anza attended the one at Chihuahua and there received—indeed helped formulate—his instructions.

He was to concentrate first on subduing, by diplomacy if possible but by force if necessary, those bands of Comanches that were harrying New Mexico. (Fellow officers would try to handle the other Comanche bands that were bringing misery to Texas.) As soon as the aggressors saw the light, they would be allowed—for they were inveterate traders —to resume their visits to the Taos fair. Meanwhile they could satisfy their desires for war by joining the Spaniards in campaigns against the Apaches. A similar policy was to be followed with the Navajos.

When Anza reached Santa Fe, he found the north in terror of a new Comanche chief called Cuerno Verde ("Green Horn") because of a green-painted bison horn he wore in his headdress. A Spanish expedition had recently killed his father, and his hatred was implacable. He was, moreover, persuasive and had extended his influence over Comanche bands other than his own, a rare accomplishment among Indians.

Although diplomacy seemed an unlikely approach to such a foe, Anza dutifully tried. He sent Indian emissaries to Cuerno Verde with gifts and proposals that they meet to talk of peace. The chief, whose band ranged the rolling lands where the High Plains butt up against the Rockies south of present-day Pueblo, Colorado, answered with insults. Angrily, Anza turned to force.

Today his strategy seems simple to the point of obviousness: He would carry the battle to the Indians. At the time, however, the approach was innovative. Throughout two centuries of Indian warfare, New Mexico had waged few offensive campaigns. The Santa Fe presidio was chronically short of armament; militiamen resented being called from their tasks at home; and if an offensive thrust across the limitless plains failed to achieve results, how could the local commander justify himself to his superiors? Play safe. Wait for the Indians to strike and then pursue them.

Anza reasoned that Cuerno Verde, accustomed to such tactics, would not expect an unprovoked attack, especially if it were to come from a direction the Spanish had never before used. He planned carefully. After obtaining ample munitions and some fine new carbines from the south, the governor summoned 645 men to a rendezvous in an out-of-the-way spot near Taos. He fortified the pueblo in case it should be attacked while stripped of many of its defenders and then, in August 1779, marched north along the full length of Colorado's San Luis Valley. Most of the way he limited campfires even on cold, rainy evenings and traveled at night to avoid detection.

He reached the plains by a stealthy march over the rough southern shoulder of what was later named Pikes Peak. When he found Cuerno Verde's camp, he surprised it by coming up from behind and shattered it. The chief and many warriors were away, however, raiding Taos. Frustrated by its new defenses, they were returning to their camp when the attackers pounced from ambush and destroyed them. All told, the Spanish force killed the chief, his leading warriors, and nearly a hundred others. When they returned to Taos, they took with them five score pack mules loaded with booty.

Anza could not follow up the victory. Spain joined France in another war against England, a decision that put Madrid on the side of England's rebellious American colonies. For the duration of that conflict, economy was the watchword on the frontier.

Anza settled down to making routine administrative reforms. Because his victory had by no means ended the danger of Indian raids from Utes, Navajos, Apaches, and revengeful Comanches, he forced many of the province's stubborn, scattered towns to pull together around defensive plazas, as they were supposed to. He ordered every citizen to arm himself—with guns if possible but at least with bow and arrows. He refused to let trading parties venture out among the Utes as had been customary, lest they stir up trouble. In order to reduce vagabondage in the province, he issued orders that no one could leave his home town or Indian pueblo without first obtaining a permit, free of charge, from the *alcalde* of his district. He managed to end an incipient Navajo–Gila Apache alliance by promising the Navajos unrestrained access to the trading centers of the Rio Grande if they abandoned their allies. He also enlisted some of them as auxiliaries for future campaigns, promising them booty, payment for each Apache head they cut off and delivered to him, medals and scarlet cloth for brave deeds in battle, and booty for everyone after a successful fight.

As soon as the ending of the American Revolution enabled him to obtain ample munitions again, he formed a crack troop of rough riders and took after the Comanches with a relentlessness they had never before experienced. Bloodied by the attacks and tempted by promises of resumed trade at Taos if they yielded—by then they badly needed that trade—small groups of Comanches began edging into the border towns, grinning and making signs of peace.

Anza refused to treat with fragments. Civilized nations dealt only with whole entities—another nation, as it were—even though the so-called Comanche nation was entirely encased within territory claimed by Spain. Until the Indians themselves selected one individual to represent all groups in the area, the war would continue.

He made the condition stick, although political unity of that sort was foreign to Indian thinking. At a huge conclave beside the Arkansas River, the Comanche bands of the High Plains chose Ecueracape of the Cuchanec group to treat for them. When Ecueracape rode to Santa Fe to deal with Anza, the entire populace rushed out to cheer him through the streets and into the low, porticoed Palace of the Governors. Anza made him a general, heaped gifts on him, and returned with him to Pecos Pueblo, where a solemn assembly of warriors ratified what their delegate had done. The peace thus entered into with the New Mexicans of colonial Spain was never broken in any major way by the participating groups. Not so in Texas and farther south in Mexico, where the Comanches continued for decades to be almost as fearful a bane as the Apaches.

Hoping that his accomplishments would bring him a rewarding appointment, Anza retired from his governorship early in 1788. To his disappointment he was reassigned to Tucson, by then a walled town to which the Tubac presidio had been transferred some years earlier. In December 1788, during a journey to Arizpe to confer with his commander general, he was stricken and died. He was fifty-four years old.

Like the Comanches, the Apaches, too, were being worn down, partly by their Indian enemies and partly by feuds among themselves. Insidious lures, authorized in 1786, played on their weariness. Apache groups that declared for peace were promised plots of land, generally near some presidio, where they could build towns of their own. While they were learning to build houses and cultivate crops, the siren whispers said, they would be fed and provided with basic necessities by the government. They would be given guns for hunting in the hope (this of course was not told them) that they would forget bows and arrows while growing dependent on Spanish gunsmiths to keep their weapons in repair. They would be supplied with liquor, too, both to demoralize them and to make it easy for agents planted among them to learn their plans.

The scheme worked after a fashion. Although many Apaches accepted the handouts only as an expedient and slipped back to their old haunts as soon as they felt safe in doing so, more settled down to the kind of cramped life that would be duplicated many years later on American-style reservations. And so, with many interruptions, two centuries of conflict raveled out into a period of uneasy calm.

The change brought renewed buoyancy to the people of Arizona and New Mexico. Settlers clustered around Tucson and Tubac, growing cattle and vegetables to provide rations both for themselves, the soldiers, and the Indians who were located on a reservation near the Tucson presidio. Generous land grants from the government helped Arizona's livestock industry send down its first roots in the San Pedro, Sonoita, and Santa Cruz valleys. The superb mission church of San Xavier del Bac, often called today The White Dove of the Desert, replaced the adobe buildings Garcés had known. In New Mexico pioneer sheep ranchers pushed into the mountains around Albuquerque. Community settlers in search of less crowded lands probed farther and farther up the Rio Grande and its tributaries. The Pueblo Indians ventured with their flocks across the Sangre de Cristo Mountains onto the eastern slopes that faced the once deadly plains.

Meanwhile Spanish authorities in New Orleans and St. Louis were beginning to take alarm at the thrust of the newly independent Americans westward toward the banks of the Mississippi. One resentful official described the frontiersmen as "determined bandits." Another predicted that if the Americans obtained a foothold on the Missouri River, whose headwaters were deemed to rise near the sources of the Rio Grande, "they will assemble troops of vagabonds [i.e., fur traders] and will unite to go to pillage" the mines of Mexico.

The worry led, among other things, to attempts to open communications between Santa Fe and the settlements farther east—San Antonio in Texas, Natchitoches in Louisiana, and St. Louis near the vital junction of the Missouri and Mississippi rivers. Such roads, it was argued, would not only speed military traffic in the event of war but would also allow merchandise to be imported from Havana, Cuba, to the Mississippi and then transported by mule train to the interior, thus constituting a commercial flank attack that would break the thralldom in which New Mexico was held by the grasping wholesalers of Chihuahua.

The blazing of these trails was assigned to an extraordinary Frenchman, Pierre Vial, known to the Spaniards as Pedro Vial. Apparently Vial had emigrated from France to America in the 1770s. After trading for a time in what is now Kansas and Oklahoma, he fell into the clutches of a band of Comanches who kept him roaming around with them so that he could repair their guns for them. In time he managed to reach San Antonio, and because he knew more about the central plains than any other white man available the government hired him to unravel a series of trails radiating eastward from Santa Fe.

He spent seven years, 1786–1793, at the effort, stumbling at first but in 1788–89 working out with four companions a direct 950-mile route from Santa Fe to Natchitoches and a longer way back through San Antonio to the New Mexican capital. Nothing to it, he reported. "This entire trip is filled with many herds of buffalos, wild cattle, mustangs . . . deers of various kinds, prairie chickens, and other fowls, as well as nuts and wild fruits that are very convenient for travelers." It is a commentary on the limited horizons of the colonists of New Spain's northern frontier that no travelers chose to test the advantages of that delectable route.

Still remaining to explore was the way from Santa Fe to St. Louis. Vial and two companions undertook the arduous trip in 1792. After they had crossed the Arkansas River, Kansa Indians "took possession of our horses and equipment, cutting our clothes with knives, leaving us entirely naked." Except for the intervention of a warrior whom, incredibly enough, Vial had met while trading on the plains many years before, the trio would have been butchered. As it was, they were held captive, stark naked, for six weeks. Then luck smiled again. A French trader happened by, ransomed them, clothed them, and took them in his pirogue to St. Louis.

On his return trip the next summer, Vial wooed the Pawnees toward friendliness with Spain, was nearly slain by mistake when another Pawnee group mistook his party in the darkness for Comanches, and on arriving in Santa Fe told the authorities that if a person's sole aim was to reach Santa Fe from St. Louis, he could do it in twenty-five days.

Again there was no follow-up. But the days when the Spanish frontier could afford inertia were ending. On October 1, 1800, Napoleon, ambitious to restore France's overseas empire, secretly wrested Louisiana Territory back from Spain. To calm the Spanish he promised never to let the huge area fall into the hands of the aggressive Anglo-Americans. Less than three years later he changed his mind and sold the region to the United States for 60 million francs.

New Spain was aghast. If St. Louis was only twenty-five days away, as Vial had reported, how long would it be before godless *contrabandistas* from the United States came tumbling across the new borders into Texas and New Mexico?

# 4

---

# CONQUEST

## *Cat's-paw*

Twenty-seven-year-old Lieutenant Zebulon Montgomery Pike was a natural dupe—earnest, ambitious, dutiful, and naive. As a result, his commanding officer, James Wilkinson, top-ranking general of the United States Army and governor of newly acquired Louisiana Territory, found him a most useful tool.

Wilkinson had joined Aaron Burr in casting covetous eyes on New Spain's northern provinces. The script, it is generally supposed, went like this. War between the United States and Spain seemed imminent during the opening decade of the nineteenth century. If it came, Burr, who was busy raising a private army, would take advantage of the confusion to conquer the lightly defended Spanish possessions bordering on Louisiana Territory and set up an independent empire with himself as its head. Wilkinson was slated to play a principal part in the coup. Presumably Burr did not know that the nimble general was also in the pay of the Spanish government—a triple agent, pretending allegiance simultaneously to the United States, Spain, and Aaron Burr.

One of Wilkinson's responsibilities in the Burr conspiracy was the gathering of data about Spanish defense capabilities on the frontier—primarily in New Mexico since that was the most populous province within Burr's reach.

The mood of the times smoothed the path of the plotting. President Jefferson, eager for information about Louisiana Territory and abetted by Congress, had recently started a major expedition up the Missouri River under command of Meriwether Lewis and William Clark. Other parties were scheduled to explore the Red River on the assumption that when the boundaries of the Purchase were drawn, the stream would mark the dividing line between the United States and New Spain. Madrid, it should be noted, rejected the assumption, arguing that because Napoleon had broken his word about selling Louisiana to the United States, the deal was illegal and title had reverted to the original owners.

To the expeditions that Jefferson and Congress had authorized, Wilkinson added more of his own. In 1805 he sent Zebulon Pike and a handful of men on a difficult winter trip to the sources of the Mississippi, to tell the Indians and British traders in the area that the American government now held sovereignty over the lands to the west of the river. Jefferson had approved of the trip almost automatically after its launching, and Wilkinson supposed, correctly as matters developed, that a similar expedition by the same lieutenant farther south would also escape close scrutiny.

On its face the new project appeared innocuous. Pike was to complete certain errands among the Osage and Pawnee Indians and then continue west toward the headwaters of the Arkansas and Red rivers. He was warned to give no offense to Spain. He thought the trip would be short and did not take along winter uniforms for the men or himself, although the party did not leave St. Louis until July 15, 1806. The oversight would cause great suffering later on.

Just before his departure Wilkinson foisted off on him, as surgeon for the party, an energetic young civilian doctor recently arrived in St. Louis, John H. Robinson. As Pike soon learned, Robinson was also a bill collector—or at least was pretending to be one. In 1804 William Morrison, a merchant of Kaskaskia, Illinois, had staked a French trader, Baptiste Lalande, with $2,000 worth of goods for an experimental trading trip to Santa Fe. Two years had passed with no word from the fellow. Worried, Morrison hired young Robinson to go to Santa Fe, if opportunity allowed, and learn what he could about Lalande's doings.

The doctor could hardly have expected to reach Santa Fe unless the expedition pressed close to the New Mexican capital, which would all but have nullified Pike's written instructions to stay away from Spanish territory. The lieutenant, moreover, must have soon realized that bill collecting was a guise: Robinson intended to spy out New Mexico's defensive capabilities while pretending to be looking for Lalande.

How much Robinson knew of the uses to which Aaron Burr might put his deviously gained information is impossible to ascertain. Years later, when Mexico was revolting against Spain, the doctor fished happily in the troubled waters, and he may have developed his taste for conspiracy on the road to Santa Fe. It is unlikely, however, that Pike was guilty of treason even by association. Straightforward and naive, he would have assumed that the data he helped Robinson gather was for the use of his own country in the event of war with Spain, surely an honorable pursuit for a dedicated soldier.

So off they went, twenty-three men without winter uniforms. The lack still puzzles, for they could have anticipated cold weather even in those southern latitudes. What they could not know was that Spain, in its anxiety and anger over the American advance, was trying to stir up a few blizzards of its own by sending relays of prairie diplomats onto the plains to rouse the Pawnees against all Americans.

The initial thrusts—three of them—were led by that aging trailblazer, Pedro Vial, in association with one José Javert, who passed in New Mexico as a Frenchman but was probably a wandering adventurer from Pennsylvania named Harvey. Their main target was the expedition being led up the Missouri River and on to the Pacific Northwest (where Spain still insisted she had claims) by William Clark and Meriwether Lewis, the latter of whom the Spaniards persistently referred to as Captain Merry. For various reasons all three of the Vial-Javert missions failed, and in the spring of 1806 the anti-American maneuvers were assigned to a professional soldier, Lieutenant Don Facundo Melgares.

A veteran of several skirmishes with the Apaches, Melgares was rich, amiable, competent, and stocky—in time he would grow very fat. Obedient to orders, he rode north from Chihuahua with 100 presidial soldiers. In Santa Fe he added as auxiliaries 500 reluctant Hispanos, *genízaros,* and Pueblo Indians. He requisitioned enough supplies from the New Mexican settlements to last the force six months and gathered together an enormous *caballada* ("horse herd") for carrying men and material—2,075 animals. Folklore insists that every common soldier rode a white horse and every officer a black one, which forms an interesting Spanish variation on the Anglo notion that the leader rides a white horse.

More puzzles now arise. Was the target of this imposing force, by far the largest Spain had ever sent onto the Plains, still Lewis and Clark, as historian Warren Clark has recently argued? Or had attention shifted to Pike, as traditional interpretations would have it?

Pike, who later came to know Melgares well, always believed that he was the Spaniard's quarry and in support of that belief gave a detailed description of the route by which Spanish spies in St. Louis sent word of his intentions through south Texas to Chihuahua. Denigrators of General Wilkinson amend this explanation, charging that the general himself let the Spanish know of Pike's destination. Their argument goes like this: Burr's scheme of an independent empire in the Southwest was collapsing and no reconnoitering of New Mexico was needed. Yet if Wilkinson canceled Pike's expedition, he would have to offer explanations to Washington. To avoid that situation, he let Pike go ahead and then ingratiated himself with his Spanish paymasters by hurrying word of the American "offensive" to Chihuahua, a double-dealing act that put his own men into acute danger.

Impossible, retorts historian Cook. Logistics in backward New Mexico were such that Melgares must have begun putting his grand expedition together even before Wilkinson had ordered Pike to prepare for a trip west. Melgares's target, therefore, could only have been "Captain Merry"—plus, as a side issue, thirty-seven soldiers of another American expedition led by Captain Richard Sparks that was currently toiling up the Red River in two clumsy bateaux.

Except that historians like to be tidy about their facts, there is not much point in debating the matter. What counts is this. Melgares did not need six hundred men to handle Lewis and Clark or Pike or Sparks or all three expeditions put together. The show was designed to impress the Indians. In spite of what any traveling Anglos might try to tell them, the red men were to realize that the King of Spain and not the President of the United States was their Great Father.

Translated, this bluster really meant that only the Indians could now save Spain's overextended frontiers in North America.

In pursuit of this impossible hope Melgares led his unwieldy column across the Llano Estacado and on to the Red River in what became the central part of the border between Oklahoma and Texas. There he learned from red visitors that the Sparks party had already been turned back by Spanish dragoons from the presidio at Nacogdoches, Texas. Relieved of that part of his assignment, the lieutenant swung north to treat with the Pawnees.

Problems with discipline and with his horse herd led him to leave 240 of his men beside the Arkansas River in the southern part of today's Kansas. With the rest he continued north to the vicinity of the Nebraska border. There, beside the Republican River, he found a major Pawnee village—a huge circle of wooden houses sixty feet in diameter and covered with earth, so that each dwelling looked like a small hill.

At that point the Spaniards were within 140 miles of the Missouri, and if they had continued their march they would have reached the river in time to apprehend Lewis and Clark on their homeward journey to St. Louis. Melgares, however, halted. No word of Lewis and Clark's position had reached the Pawnee village. His draftees were mutinous, his horses in bad shape. The Pawnees were suspicious—and winning the Pawnees was, basically, his purpose. So he called the chiefs into a grand council, handed out gifts, and persuaded them to accept Spanish flags. Impressed, the Pawnees agreed to eject any Americans who ventured onto their part of the plains. Melgares then obtained additional horses, picked up his men on the Arkansas, and took the long trail back to Santa Fe, satisfied that he had fulfilled his mission. Actually, as soon became evident, he had simply made things easier for the Americans by leaving what amounted to clear road directions westward.

Pike came across the Spaniards' tracks out on the Kansas plains. Trespassers on American soil! Although it was evident that he was heavily outnumbered—he had sent five men back to Wilkinson with dispatches—he followed the trail to the Pawnee town, arriving there late in September 1806, when there was already a bite in the morning air.

The Indians were truculent. Pike faced them down, saying that if anything happened to him and his friends, "the *great American father*" (as Pike underscored the words in his journal) would send out myriads of young warriors "to gather our bones and revenge our deaths." He maintained this show of confidence until the Indians, who admired courage and in any event saw no gain in risking casualties for the Spaniards' sake, caved in and let the Americans pass.

Up to that point Pike had relied for guidance first on his hired interpreter, trader Antoine Baronet Vasquez, and, second, on the tracings of a map recently prepared in Mexico City for the Spanish government by a famed German scientist, Alexander von Humboldt. Humboldt, who had never visited the northern provinces, had drawn his data from such sparse frontier sources as were available in the archives, and there was some doubt about his accuracy. It was comforting, therefore, now that the Americans had passed beyond the area of Vasquez's knowledge, to be able to follow Melgares's tracks back to the Arkansas and then on west into an increasingly cold and unfriendly land.

On November 23, 1806, the shivering explorers reached the site now occupied by the city of Pueblo, Colorado, near the eastern foothills of the Rockies. For several days they had been eyeing a tall, round-topped peak to the northwest. (Their lieutenant called it Grand Peak; later explorers changed the name to Pikes Peak.) In the hope of obtaining a comprehensive view of the country ahead, Pike, Robinson, and two soldiers tried to climb it. Snow and altitude defeated them. After a four-day struggle they fell back for guidance on the tracks of Melgares's little army.

Diverted by an Indian trace, they ended up lost in the shaggy hills. On finally reaching a frozen river amid snow-heaped mountains, they followed it downstream on the assumption that it might be a tributary of the Red. Actually it was the Arkansas and brought them back to the Pueblo site they had left weeks before.

What next? Some horses had died and the remainder were incapable of further exertion without a chance to recuperate. But the men could still move, and Pike, casting himself in an intrepid role, determined to find the real Red. According to the Humboldt map, which was his only aid now, its headwaters were close to Santa Fe, Robinson's goal and perhaps Pike's, too, for all we can tell now. In any event, Santa Fe was certainly the closest possible point of succor.

Pike and his men built a shelter for the two soldiers who were delegated to stay with the horses and then struck west on foot, each walker laden with seventy pounds of provisions and arms. The trip turned into a nightmare of snow, exhaustion, and near starvation relieved by the fortuitous killing of an occasional buffalo. Along the way they dropped off in various improvised shelters men whose feet had frozen, promising to return for them as soon as possible. Finally, at the end of the month they reached the San Luis Valley and another river. Surely, Pike thought, this was the Red. In truth it was the Rio Grande.

Because no timber grew where the party intersected the stream, they crossed it and moved five miles up a tributary, the Conejos, to a grove of cottonwoods. There they built a stout stockade. That done, Robinson, who throughout the journey had been the strongest and most dependable of the group, started for Santa Fe. An indication that he and Pike were really lost, which some commentators have doubted, is that he headed *west* up the Conejos, the direction in which the faulty Humboldt map said that Santa Fe lay. Actually the New Mexican capital was about 125 miles due south. Pike meanwhile sent all but five of his soldiers along their back trail to pick up the men who had been left behind.

Robinson probably would have perished of hunger and cold if Ute Indians had not picked him up. They took him to Taos, and from there that ancient of days, Pedro Vial, blazer of the Santa Fe Trail, escorted him to the New Mexican capital. Under questioning the doctor revealed the site of Pike's stockade, whereupon dragoons sallied forth, and in due time Pike and the men with him were in Santa Fe. (Eventually all of the stranded soldiers except for one killed in a quarrel with a fellow trooper were brought to the capital and from there sent back to the United States by various roundabout routes.)

Now that the authorities had their quarry, they did not know how to handle him. The governor of New Mexico first and then the Comandante-general of the Provincias Internas at Chihuahua tried without success to shake his story that he had strayed across the Rio Grande only through inadvertence. As a uniformed officer of a country with which Spain was at peace, he could hardly be imprisoned. In the end the disgruntled officials confiscated his papers but, yielding to his insistence, let his men keep their arms as a point of honor. All (Robinson included, but without Lalande's money) were then escorted across the deserts of Chihuahua to the southeastern border of Texas. There, on June 29, 1807, they were turned loose.

In 1810 Pike published an account of his trips up the Mississippi and across the plains to New Mexico. Because of Meriwether Lewis's death in 1809 and William Clark's involvement in other affairs, his book was, to the author's great satisfaction, the first account of the huge lands west of the Mississippi to reach the general public.

It is an easy book to criticize. The writing is undistinguished and the editing obtuse. In important instances the author let preconceptions get in the way of his judgment. For instance, the Spanish told him that at least one of the major tributaries of the Missouri headed near Santa Fe. That mistake led Pike to declare flatly that from a snowy point near the source of the Arkansas he had seen the headwaters of the Yellowstone, though in fact the Yellowstone rises several hundred miles to the north. As a result of Pike's error, the central part of the Rockies vanished from men's thinking, north-south distances shrank, and fur traders with posts on the upper Missouri were thoroughly bedeviled during the course of the next several years in their efforts to reach "nearby" New Mexico.

Another mistake had to do with the ease of reaching the Pacific. Lewis and Clark had found the crossing of the northern Rockies far more difficult than they had anticipated. It was another satisfaction to Pike, accordingly, to be able to assert confidently on the strength of statements "from Spanish gentlemen of information" that a land carriage of only two hundred miles separated the navigable waters of the Arkansas River from those of the Rio Colorado. As a consequence, *his* route afforded "the best communication on this side of the Isthmus of Darien between the Atlantic and Pacific oceans." Having marched beside the Arkansas for many miles, he should have been more restrained in his definition of "navigable." As for the Colorado, his Spanish gentlemen of information obviously had never read the descriptions of its awesome canyons left by Francisco Garcés and the Domínguez-Escalante party.

But to emphasize such errors is to depreciate unduly the value of Pike's accounts. Once he got his preconceptions out of the way, he observed New Mexico's people, landscape, and scanty resources lucidly and reported them accurately. He noted the high cost of merchandise brought north from Chihuahua, a point certain to be noted by frontier merchants in Missouri. But mostly his book, like the subsequently published journals of Lewis and Clark, was an embodiment of the spirit later known as Manifest Destiny. He helped bring continental awareness to the United States. For years no literate trader, military man, diplomat, or private traveler ventured toward Mexico's northern provinces without a copy of Pike's book in his baggage. With him and his handful of men the conquest of the Far Southwest can be said to have begun.

## Infiltration

In New Spain, meanwhile, alarming upheavals were underway. The earthquakes of self-determinism triggered by the French and American revolutions had reached into Mexico and were releasing discontents that would rock Madrid's colonial empire for a dozen years. The two forces, American expansionism and Mexican revolutionary aspirations, promptly entwined—an unnatural melding destined to have a profound impact on the fortunes of both nations.

At first Mexican independence seemed to promise stability, and that was important to pioneering Americans. Spanish administrators in New Mexico had been worse than unfriendly; they had been capricious. Pike had noticed the ambiguity at once. Although on an official level he had been rigorously questioned and finally expelled, he had been received socially with great warmth. He was entertained by many priests, established a firm friendship with Melgares, and saw his men nursed and pampered by sympathetic commoners. The Mexicans, he wrote for all his countrymen to read, were characterized by "heavenlike qualities of hospitality and kindness." Nor were the pleasurable aspects of his adventure attributable only to his uniform. In 1807, the year Pike returned to the United States, Jacques Clamorgan, an elderly but indefatigable trader from St. Louis—Clamorgan was seventy-four in 1807—rode with three Frenchmen, a Negro slave, and four mule loads of goods to Santa Fe. After selling the merchandise at a handsome profit, they returned contentedly through Chihuahua and Texas.

Alongside those stories there were others of a different nature. Some of the prairie traders who, like Baptiste Lalande, had preceded Pike to New Mexico suffered confiscation of their goods and a technical imprisonment whose expenses they had to meet by plying whatever craft they could. But they were small fry. A more telling case was that of Auguste Pierre Chouteau, a member of an influential French family in St. Louis and for many years one of the West's most successful Indian traders. About 1815 Chouteau took over financial control of a trapping party that had run afoul of the Spaniards on the upper Arkansas River but was willing to return because of the number of beaver the men had found.

Accompanying the revitalized group in the hope that his high lineage would impress the Spanish governor in Santa Fe was Jules De Mun, a fugitive from the ravages of the French Revolution. A scion of French aristocrats who traced their lineage back to the twelfth century, De Mun had married Auguste Chouteau's fifteen-year-old niece. The self-made Chouteaus took pride in the noble connection but disliked supporting the young girl's husband. It was to get those arrogant in-laws off his back that De Mun agreed to embark on this trading adventure for which he had no other aptitude than good looks, fine manners, and fluency in both the French and Spanish languages.

While most of the trappers hovered around the edge of the mountains, De Mun and a small escort made their way to Santa Fe and asked the governor, Alberto Maynez, for permits to hunt beaver on the upper Rio Grande. Maynez was as dazzled by his noble visitor as Chouteau had hoped, but he was also fearful for his job and said that he would have to write to Chihuahua for instructions.

Lulled into hopefulness, the Americans hung around the northern fringes of New Mexico for months. Some trapped, some pursued wild horses, some traveled to St. Louis to replenish supplies. De Mun, it is said, made ten round-trip rides between the Arkansas River and Santa Fe to keep the machinery oiled. To no avail. Late in 1816 a new governor arrived with orders that the intruders be gone. They tried to comply by pushing into the mountains toward the Columbia, which Pike's compression of geography led them to believe was much nearer New Mexico than is the case. When snow and icy winds drove them back, Spanish forces pounced on them.

Goods and furs worth $30,000 were confiscated and the men were jailed for forty-eight days. At their hearing they protested that they had been arrested on American soil. The governor thereupon leaped to his feet and cried out that Spain had never relinquished her lands west of the Mississippi, a statement no more preposterous than some American claims of owning to the Rio Grande. After being terrified by threats of execution, the captives were given one old horse apiece and told to make their way home as best they could. Shaken by the capricious behavior of the Spaniards, Chouteau never again risked traveling to unknown areas.

Another hard-luck but significant adventure was one launched in 1812 by Robert McKnight and James Baird. McKnight was a partner in a prosperous St. Louis mercantile firm, Baird a substantial blacksmith familiar with the beaver trade through making traps for mountain men. The inspiration for their trip was the arrival of news from Mexico that a humble parish priest, Fray Miguel Hidalgo y Costilla, had sparked a savage revolution with his famed *grito* ("shout") for justice and freedom. Spanish forces were reeling under an onslaught from Indians and *mestizos,* and because of the admiration that Hidalgo had for the democratic institutions of the United States, it seemed likely that the new revolutionary regime would welcome Americans all along the border.

Pooling resources, McKnight and Baird purchased $10,000 worth of the kind of dry goods that Pike had said were desirable in New Mexico —silk, muslin, linen, velvet. Hiring half a dozen roustabouts, they headed west by mule train.

In Santa Fe they learned that their news about Hidalgo's success had been premature. A rally by government forces had defeated the insurgents and the priest had been executed. When the Americans appeared in New Mexico they were arrested, and their goods were auctioned off so that the proceeds could be used, at a rate of about nineteen cents a day each, for supporting them in Chihuahua's gloomy jail. There one of the men soon died.

For at least some of the rest the incarceration proved less confining. One man escaped his cell by entering a monastery. Blacksmith James Baird became the servant of a wealthy resident of Durango, some 450 miles south of Chihuahua. McKnight made his way across the mountains to Sonora, where he obtained control of a mine, flourished, took a wife, and fathered a child.

Spain meanwhile had been sorely weakened by the Napoleonic wars, and her New World colonies were vulnerable to attacks of all sorts. In desperation the Spanish minister to Washington, Luis de Onís, sacrificed the Floridas, which he knew could not be defended from the Americans, in exchange for a firm line protecting Texas—up the Sabine River toward its sources, then to the Red and along it to the 100th meridian, the present eastern border of the Texas Panhandle; north along that meridian to the Arkansas; west into the Rockies and then north again through the heart of Colorado to the 42nd parallel, which defined the rest of the border to the Pacific. But by the time the agreement, known as the Adams-Onís Treaty, had been ratified, revolutions had flared again in Mexico and Spain's empire was crumbling.

One symptom of the imminent collapse was Ferdinand VII's acquiescence to a revolutionary demand that he declare a political amnesty that included in its broad sweep all foreigners held prisoner in Mexico. The decree reached the Interior Provinces in September 1820. Most of the survivors of the Baird-McKnight party of 1812 thereupon promptly headed home—but not the leaders. Perhaps because he was not immediately informed of the order, James Baird waited a year before leaving his household job in Durango. As for McKnight, he was content to stay in Sonora.

Those who did hurry east reached Fort Smith, Arkansas, early in 1821. Stagnancy greeted them. Agricultural prices in Arkansas and Missouri were so depressed that farmers had to search for outside income. Merchants had more goods on their shelves than they could sell. Inevitably bold souls among them were eager to hear of whatever opportunities might exist in liberalized New Mexico.

Among the yearners was a tall, energetic, semiliterate, well-liked Missourian named William Becknell. In June 1821 he appealed in a Missouri newspaper for seventy men to join an expedition "destined to the westward for the purpose of trading for Horses & Mules and catching Wild Animals of every description." An organizational meeting was scheduled for August 4 at a farmhouse near Franklin, Missouri. But costs of goods and equipment were high and only seventeen of the hoped-for seventy men appeared. They set September 1 as their departure date. On the appointed day, five, counting Becknell, showed up. Off they went, anyhow, ready to adapt their movements to whatever developed.

Another grasper at hope was Hugh Glenn. Ruined by a bank failure and unprofitable contracts for supplying Indian agencies and army expeditions, he had opened a trading post on a shoestring in what is now eastern Oklahoma. Entrenched competition cut him to bits and he decided to recoup by leading a trapping party of whites, Indians, blacks, and half-bloods into the southern Rockies. Joining him in the venture was a former business associate, fifty-six-year-old Jacob Fowler.

Finally there was pompous "General" Thomas James, who had failed as an Indian trader on the Missouri River and was doing no better as manager of a branch store of the McKnight and Brady dry goods firm of St. Louis. Learning of the Mexican amnesty, James took $10,000 worth of unsold woolens off his shelves and announced to his employers that he would redeem himself by selling the merchandise in Santa Fe. John McKnight thereupon joined the party in the hope of learning why his brother Robert had not come back with the other released prisoners.

All three groups reached the edges of New Mexico. All chanced across either Mexican dragoons or Mexican Indian traders who encouraged them to visit Santa Fe. Mexico, these informants said, was now independent of Spain and the people of the northern province would welcome fellow republicans deliriously.

Becknell's small party arrived first. Although by then they had only a pittance of goods to trade, they reaped well. Excited by the results, Becknell left three of his men to trap in the mountains back of Santa Fe. He himself stuffed a buffalo-hide sack with the small silver coins he had garnered, rode back to Franklin with a single companion, and slit the pouch open in the middle of the town's dusty main street so that the gaping citizens could look at the glittering shower before he used the money to buy a fresh stock of merchandise.

Hugh Glenn meantime won permission for his party to trap the headwaters of the Rio Grande, an adventure that took the men deep into the rugged San Juan Mountains of southwestern Colorado. On returning home, Glenn sold his share of the furs for $5,000, enough to pay off his debts. Satisfied, he was content then to stay nearer home, letting others muse over yet another southwestern promise.

Only Thomas James fared badly. He hadn't been willing to trap, his sobersided woolens did not appeal to the color-loving New Mexicans, and he ended up losing $7,500 of his initial $10,000 investment. He, too, stayed home thereafter.

Becknell, the first of the Americans to reach Santa Fe in the fall of 1821, was the first to return in the spring of 1822. Again he blazed new trails. To save the labor of packing and unpacking several mules each day, he loaded his cargo into three wagons. To avoid the wheel-wrenching Raton Pass trail in Colorado that he had followed on his first journey, he risked a dry shortcut from the Arkansas River in southwestern Kansas across the plains of the Oklahoma Panhandle to the Cimarron River. Thirst almost aborted the experiment. The men survived only by killing a buffalo that had been to water, opening its stomach, and drinking the nauseous liquid it contained. But from their mistakes they learned that the new shortcut—it saved a hundred miles over the Raton route—could be made to work.

A few months behind the wagons came James Baird and Samuel Chambers of the 1812 party. They had with them twenty employees and a pack train of sixty horses and mules. Their trouble was cold, not heat. A furious blizzard drove them for shelter to a wooded island in the Arkansas River. In spite of the trees, most of their stock died and for three months they were pinned to their crude bivouacs. When spring came, they buried their goods in the earth and made their way to Taos for fresh animals. After arriving finally, they initiated a custom that many later Americans would follow. They decided to stay in New Mexico.

Meanwhile John McKnight had used his time tracing his brother Robert to Sonora. Arguing vehemently, he persuaded the exile to return to St. Louis, perhaps by telling him that the United States had agreed, under the Adams-Onís treaty, to meet whatever legitimate claims American citizens held against Spain. Here might be a way for Robert to obtain compensation for the goods taken from him in 1812. Instead, Robert ran into a wall of bureaucratic indifference. Furious, he gave up and returned to Mexico and his wife and child.

And still Becknell pioneered. In 1824 several small entrepreneurs wanted to try their hands at the new commerce. Becknell persuaded them to forget their competitiveness until they had all reached Santa Fe, where he was going, too, and travel for convenience and protection in a single column. Compared to later trains, the one that left Franklin that year did not amount to much. In it were twenty dearborns, which is a kind of light carriage with protective side curtains, two farm wagons, two carts, and one small cannon. It throve remarkably, nevertheless. An initial investment of about $30,000 returned 600 percent gross profit, or $180,000! After that, even though profits would never again reach a comparable scale, there was no stopping the penetration.

## The Trail to Santa Fe

As the edge of settlement advanced westward across Missouri, Franklin was replaced as the starting place for Santa Fe by the rival towns of Independence and Westport, located eight miles apart where the yellow river makes its great bend to the north. Tall-chimneyed, shallow-draft stern-wheel steamers snorted up to the docks; stevedores heaved bales of cargo into transfer wagons that toiled up the hills to the warehouses in the towns. There the merchants checked the bills of lading against the orders they had dispatched east many months before. Most of the items had been chosen to meet practical needs. But some would feed hungry spirits as well. Packed beside rough muslin and work shoes were gay calicoes and silk, dainty slippers, and dress patterns from eastern magazines. There were metal tools for hands that until then had worked mostly with makeshifts of bone and wood. Occasionally there were books and, in 1834, a printing press. Quite unintentionally there were also new ideas about a man's relationship to his God and his government, about land use, the treatment of Indians, social conduct, and even food.

A motley mix of several hundred men accompanied each setting forth. Most noticeable because of the air of authority with which they sat their fine horses were the proprietors. Many were educated and prosperous, pillars of their communities during winters at home. Their favorite dress on the trail was a long-skirted, many-pocketed coat of coarse corduroylike fustian. As hands for doing camp chores and tending to the hundreds of draft animals, they brought along younger members of their families or jean-clad country boys out for adventure. (In 1826 illiterate Kit Carson, aged sixteen, ran away from his apprenticeship to a saddlemaker to join a Santa Fe wagon train.) There were buffalo hunters and fur trappers in leather; a sprinkling of Negro slaves; and Mexican muleteers dressed in dirty serapes and high-crowned sombreros covered with oilcloth. In the later years of the trade there were also many Mexican proprietors, who went east with bars of Chihuahua silver to buy merchandise so they could compete with the foreigners. Some even sent their sons to Missouri to study or work as clerks for the Americans.

As the volume of freight grew, so did the size of the conveyances. Soon every proprietor who could afford to do so was using specially made blue-painted Conestoga wagons from Pennsylvania, with their flaring high sides and their tall wheels rimmed with iron tires three inches broad. Arching over the bed was a double thickness of canvas, often with Mackinaw blankets placed between the layers to add durability and to escape the eyes of the customs officials at Santa Fe.

Different kinds of draft animals called for different modes of travel. A man with oxen—generally a hired hand—walked beside them, guiding them with shouts of "Giddap," "Haw," "Gee," or "Whoa," spiced with uncomplimentary epithets. He kept the lumbering animals on the move by sending the long lash of his bullwhip curling over their backs until at the climax of its reach, the popper snapped with a crack like a rifle shot. Any time he chose, the bullwhacker could draw blood from the tough hides as well as make a noise.

A man driving mules—he, too, was generally hired—sat on the high wagon seat behind the animals, his hands full of reins and the small of his back sore from the constant banging and jouncing of the wheels. He had to be alert. Mules were spooky. As Alphonso Wetmore, a newspaper editor who took a flyer at the trade in 1829, wrote in his journal, "It is one of the foibles of mule teams that, after they have traveled four or five hundred miles, and when it is supposed they are about to tire, to take fright from a profile view of their own shadows, and run like the antelope of the plains," often upsetting the wagon during the wild dash.

Not far from Independence, trees gave way to prairies spangled in the spring with wildflowers. To most forest-bred Anglos so much unrestricted vision was a new experience. Folk-say blossomed: Where else could a man look so far and see so little? What they meant was that there was nothing familiar to look at. No timber for cabins and fences, no streams for floating barges or flatboats. Game could not be stalked as it had been in the forests, and old patterns of fighting Indians, who could pour out more arrows in a minute from horseback than a man could shoot from a muzzle-loader musket, had to be changed entirely. Strangeness—the feeling would ride with them all the way.

For the first 150 miles the merchants generally traveled in individual groups. Then, as the danger from Indians increased, they met at a prearranged rendezvous, most often a place called Council Grove. There they elected a captain whose job it would be to establish routines of travel, camping, hunting, and messing. From then on the train traveled with greater precision, sometimes in a single column, but more often, on that flat terrain, in parallel columns to reduce dust and to increase the speed with which the wagons could be swung into a defensive circle if the need arose.

Gradually the tall prairie grass gave way to short, curly buffalo grass. Sometimes wild thunderstorms lashed the caravan, but most days were dry, windy, and hot. The men marveled at mirages of ponds and forests, at fleet antelope and huge villages of prairie dogs, actually ground squirrels. Rattlesnakes abounded: "I will not say 'thousands,'" wrote Josiah Gregg, the trail's great chronicler, "though this perhaps was nearer the truth—but hundreds were coiled or crawling in every direction. They were no sooner discovered than we were upon them with guns and pistols, determined to let none escape."

In what is now southwestern Kansas, the travelers hitched double teams to each wagon in order to ford the broad, soft-bottomed Arkansas River. After that immersion came the fifty-seven-mile dry *jornada* to the Cimarron "River," where often water could be obtained only by scooping pits into the sandy bottom. Nerves grew taut. This was the land of the Comanches. In 1831 they had lanced to death the greatest of the American mountainmen, Jedediah Smith. Other scattered killings had led both the United States and Mexican governments to send occasional military escorts with the caravans as far as their shared boundary. Most years, however, the traders had to take care of themselves.

It could be a grim experience. During the latter part of the 1829 trip, William Waldo remembered, "We seldom obtained more than three or four hours' sleep out of the twenty-four; men became so worn down with toil by day and watching by night that they would go to sleep and fall from their mules as they rode along. . . . In several instances men seized their knives in their sleep and struck them into the ground, and the men became afraid to sleep together, for fear of killing each other."

Other harassments came from the New Mexican customs officials. Import duties varied according to the state of the territorial treasury and the whim of the governor in power. To deal with the uncertainties, the leading traders left the wagon train several miles outside the first settlements and rode to Santa Fe to make arrangements—that is, to resort to bribery. As a further precaution, the people waiting with the caravan frequently buried part of their goods in the earth, then returned weeks later with pack mules to smuggle the hidden merchandise across mountainous trails to the smaller settlements of Taos and Santa Cruz.

The long trail, to be sure, had bright times as well as dull—the thrill of hunting buffalo, freedom from social restraints, blossoming health, lasting friendships, and finally the triumphal entry into Santa Fe. As that climax neared, the wagoners cleaned their faces, combed their hair, donned their best clothes, and tied loud new poppers to their whips, in order, wrote Josiah Gregg, to impress "the 'fair eyes' of glistening black that were sure to stare at them as they passed."

As the wagons lurched one by one down the juniper-studded hill beyond the town, almost the entire populace streamed into the plaza. "Los Americanos!—Los Carros!" Myths took shape. Because each caravan's arrival late in June or early in July coincided with the breaking of the spring drought, humble Hispanos came to think that the Americans brought rain with them. Feeling superior and expansive, the newcomers set out to look the town over, the hired hands for amusements, their employers for whatever commercial possibilities might already exist or be developed.

## New Mexico and Beyond

To the Americans one unfailing source of disdain, located on the north side of the dusty, manure-filled plaza, was the long, low, flat-roofed Palace of the Governors, fronted by a wooden awning resting on roughly hewn tree trunks. Palace, indeed! And the two other principal downtown buildings were churches—a military chapel that served the soldiers of the presidio and a community church, scrubbed and polished, it was said, by the highest placed ladies of Santa Fe. Like the palace, both churches were constructed of bricks made of dried mud.

Small stores, a dark tavern or two, a few private dwellings—all flat-roofed, all built of adobe—bordered the rest of the square. Narrow streets meandered off among tawny homes surrounded by corn patches and ragged orchards. An occasional ox-drawn cart laden with children and produce crept toward the plaza at snail's pace. The sides of each vehicle were a latticework of sticks; the wheels, formed of round pieces of wood sawn from cottonwood trees, wobbled erratically and shrieked to high heaven on seldom-greased wooden axles. Every now and then along came a donkey, invisible except for fuzzy ears and twinkling hooves under towers of firewood. More dashing were the curvetting horses that bore riders dressed in flat sombreros, tight jackets decorated with needlework, and silver-studded trousers slit from ankles to knees.

In front of the church at the west end of the plaza was the market-place. Women in loose blouses and short red skirts sat beside fiber mats on which were arranged small piles of cheese, loaves of bread baked in outdoor ovens, beans, chili peppers, and corn husks for making the cigarettes that everyone smoked. Slabs of mutton, goat, and dried buffalo meat hung from a line stretched to one of the uprights support-ing the palace's portico. In the winter the flesh might be bear, turkey, or venison. At the southwest entrance to the plaza were neat bundles of grass that one could buy for one's horse or donkey to munch on as it waited in the center of the square for its master to go home again. Beggars droned among the stalls and at the entrances to the public buildings, especially on Saturdays when people congregated for shop-ping. One traveled Anglo thought they gave an Oriental look to the town.

As soon as caravans began arriving annually, wealthy women took to dressing in American style, but eschewed bonnets and continued to cover their heads and shoulders with shawls called *rebosos*. Peasant girls and ladies alike protected their skins from the sun with daubings of dried berry juice and masklike plaster. Everyone gambled, particu-larly at *el monte*, a game of pure chance.

Everyone also danced. Occasions were frequent—celebrations of some saint's day, weddings, homecomings, or no reason at all. Artfully adorned for such occasions, the younger Mexican women struck Ameri-cans as pretty because of their small waists, small feet, and uncorseted bosoms. True, their uninhibited ways could be shocking at first to people from a more puritanical land. Their whirling fandangos struck many as lascivious. The newcomers were taken aback, too, by the fact that women smoked as readily as men. It was considered a great honor for a woman to light a man's hand-rolled cigarette for him and place it between his lips while looking full into his eyes, a byplay that wasn't always mere flirtation. Concerning one New Year's Eve celebration, trapper James Ohio Pattie wrote: "When the ball broke up, it seemed expected of us that we should each escort a lady home, in whose company we passed the night, and we none of us brought charges of severity against our fair companions." When jealous Mexican males tried to break up such goings-on, donnybrooks resulted that added still more spice to the beddings-down that followed.

While the roustabouts were examining social resources, the merchants were studying economic patterns. They quickly learned that most of the cash available to their customers came from the payrolls of the presidial soldiers and government workers. To this had been added, at about the time the commercial invasion began, limited amounts of gold dust from placer mines discovered in 1823 less than thirty miles south of Santa Fe.

The labor involved in obtaining the metal was great. Using the most primitive of tools, workers gouged holes ten, fifteen, sometimes twenty feet deep into the alluvial soil of the desert mountains. They piled the earth to be washed into leather sacks and climbed with the burden on their shoulders up shaky poles into which shallow notches had been cut for their bare feet. In winter they obtained water for separating metal from dross by throwing heated stones into earthen basins filled with snow. According to Josiah Gregg, those crude methods produced, during the life of the placers, about a quarter of a million dollars' worth of gold. The peak period was 1832–35, when production averaged $70,000 a year, less than half the value of the American merchandise brought into New Mexico during the same period. Moreover, heavy export duties were levied on gold and coin leaving the territory. So if commerce was to thrive, the merchants were going to have to trade their goods for other commodities that were readily available in New Mexico and could be easily resold at a profit when taken East.

One item that suggested itself was sheep. Peace with the Indians had allowed a few enterprising Hispanos to build up huge herds—as many as 250,000 head on some *estancias*—that were grazed far and wide under a system of peonage whose harshness varied from ranch to ranch.

The arrangement went roughly like this. A worker bought more supplies from his *patrón* than he could pay for when the bills fell due. As long as the debt endured, he was irrevocably bound to his *patrón* and creditor. If he ran away, he could be brought back by force. He could be punished physically for infractions of the ranch rules at the whim of his employer, and there was little he could say about the hours of work and the living quarters that were inflicted on him.

As many Anglos pointed out, peonage was little different from the slavery that prevailed in the American South, except that a peon could not be sold, at least not legally. Also, the conditions of peonage were often alleviated by personal attachments. On community grants in particular, peons were frequently related to the *patrón*. He helped them in times of trouble and sickness, attended their weddings and funerals, stood as godfather to their children, and advised them how to live so as to escape their terrible shackles of debt. By letting efficient herders run sheep for him on shares, the *patrón* gave some men who otherwise would have been doomed to poverty a chance to rise in the world. True, the *patrón* held the winning cards in the arrangement. At the end of the season he received a specified number of animals and a specified amount of wool. This meant that if storms, animals, or Navajo raiders injured the herd, the loss fell on the sharecropper. But if he was lucky and built up a herd of his own, he then always had a market for his surplus—the *patrón*, who, to be sure, paid mostly in goods at rates favorable to himself.

The *rico* ("rich man") in turn used Chihuahua and Durango as his markets. A caravan went south each fall, as it had been doing for almost a century. By the 1830s, according to lawyer Antonio Barreiro, who had been sent north by the central government to help New Mexico's untutored officials, between 50,000 and 100,000 animals took to the trail each year.

American entrepreneurs quickly experimented with diverting part of the woolly flood to the United States. No luck. The wool the animals yielded was sparse and coarse, and the sheep themselves were smaller and tougher than their counterparts in the Midwest. As a medium of exchange, that resource would not suffice in Missouri, and so the search for a more acceptable item went steadily on.

Mules proved to be part of the answer. They did not reproduce themselves, however, and, like horses, were a temptation even to peaceful Indians. As a consequence, there were never as many mules available on the ranches as there were sheep. But as demand quickened, other sources of supply developed and mules flowed east in such numbers that they helped make Missouri the mule center of the United States, which was no small matter in the days before steam locomotives and gasoline.

One small, colorful group of mule providers were the Comancheros, whose flowering, like that of the sheepherders, came about as a result of Anza's peace with the Comanches. As soon as it had become clear that those Indians meant to keep their bargain, a scattering of Hispanic *mestizos*, Pueblo Indians, and *genízaros* decided to carry trade goods onto the plains rather than wait for the Comanches to resume their trips to Taos.

At best it was a marginal business and drew into its ranks a shabby, illiterate, but persevering mix. Their dress consisted of conical sombreros, striped leather jackets, baggy trousers that reached to the knees, long cotton stockings, and Indian moccasins. For arms they carried bows and arrows, lances decorated with fluttering strips of colored cloth, and an occasional ancient fusil whose barrel was stoppered against the weather with wooden plugs also made gay with tassels of cloth.

They liked to make short trips in June after planting was done, and longer ones after the fall harvest. Their trade goods included a dark hard-crusted bread that the Indians liked to soak in sweetened water, or coffee if it was available, a home-grown tobacco called *punche*, dried vegetables, corn meal, iron lance points, hatchets, hunting knives, and bits of woolen or cotton cloth that had been woven at home. They carried this material along with their camp equipment and food in carts as far as they could, and then switched to pack animals. In time they learned to find their way east across the trackless Llano Estacado to the Wichita Mountains of Oklahoma, south into the Davis Mountains of Texas, where they encountered Apaches, and north as far as the South Platte in Colorado, where they came into contact with Cheyennes and Arapahos. When finally they started home, they took with them, in place of their original articles, dried buffalo meat, hides, horses—and mules, most of which the Indians had stolen from ranches in Texas, Chihuahua, and Durango.

Associated with the Comancheros were *cíboleros* ("buffalo hunters"). They dressed like the Comancheros but traveled shorter distances and with their women and children in larger groups. As soon as a herd was sighted, young lancers galloped wildly into it, selected choice, fat cows, thrust a lance behind a front leg into the heart, wrenched the weapon free, and galloped on. Once several dozen carcasses lay strewn about the plain, the carts came up. The women and children stripped each hide from the body, scraped the fat from its inner side, and tanned it. Wool was plucked out for stuffing mattresses. The meat was sliced into thin strips and dried in the sun. Tallow was rendered into candles. According to Barreiro, the lawyer identified earlier, the *cíboleros* brought back to the settlements as many as 10,000 hides a year, which sounds like another exaggeration. Be that as it may, so many animals were slain that the Indians had to be calmed with presents of merchandise. This led naturally to trade, and so the *cíboleros*, too, came back with mules to swap with the Americans for outrageously overpriced goods.

Anglo trappers had meanwhile discovered that California's huge ranches contained an abundance of mules. It was not one of them, however, but a Mexican, Antonio Armijo, who first tapped the supply. In 1829 Armijo and sixty employees collected a pack-train load of bright serapes and slanted off into what is now the Four Corners country, where New Mexico, Colorado, Utah, and Arizona meet. There they bent west through grim deserts, found a way across the Colorado River, rested briefly at the site of today's Las Vegas, and then pushed on into southern California.

They reaped well, but it was a desperately hard route until American mountain men found how to ease the journey by swinging farther north into Utah. Out of memory of Domínguez and Escalante, who had traveled portions of the route in 1776, the way came to be called The Old Spanish Trail, and it provided the first sustained contact between Mexico's northernmost territories. Fittingly, Mexicans were its most regular users, riding west each year with gay woolens and pouches of jingling Chihuahua silver coins and returning not only with mules but even bales of silk brought from the Orient to California aboard Boston trading ships.

The trail was put to less admirable uses when the beaver trade declined. Rambunctious Americans, joined by a few Mexicans and occasional Ute Indians, turned it into a thieves' highway along which they drove horses, mules, and donkeys stolen from California ranchos and missions. A take of 2,000 head a year was normal. In 1842 it is said to have reached 4,150 animals, many of which fell into the hands of the Santa Fe traders.

A more glamorous item of exchange, though less profitable year in and year out than mules, was beaver fur. Beaver were an ideal wilderness resource. They were numerous. Their pelts were easily transported and, until demand dropped during the late 1830s, were readily marketed. Supplying the men who trapped the animals was a problem, however, especially in the northern Rockies. Settlements did not exist there, and the hunters had to be equipped by means of special caravans traveling from Missouri to prearranged meeting places with the mountain men. Soon the hunters, deep in debt to their suppliers, found themselves operating according to the dictates of the Missouri merchants.

In New Mexico, where only a portion of the annual flow of goods was devoted to keeping trappers at work, matters were different. Trappers could buy from any one of several wagon proprietors. They were able to form their own groups without pressure from outside, and they hunted wherever their fancies dictated. They were "free trappers" and proud of it, though not necessarily prosperous because of their vaunted independence.

For the rendezvous with their suppliers the southern trappers went to the village of Don Fernandez de Taos, which had come into being during the 1790s and stood midway between the Taos Indian pueblo a few miles to the north and the older farming community of Ranchos de Taos to the south. Don Fernandez, as it was generally called in the early 1800s, was the germ of today's city of Taos. A sort of secondary rendezvous site lay far to the southwest at Santa Rita de Cobre, a copper mine whose ores had been revealed by an Apache Indian to a Spanish soldier in 1803 and had been worked intermittently ever since. Inasmuch as it was often possible to get supplies at Santa Rita while one's horses and one's weary body recuperated, trappers gathered there, too, until the increasingly restive Apaches closed the place down.

The men from Taos and Santa Rita handled their work just as their counterparts in the north did. They waded into the icy streams to set their traps, scraped the fat off the inner side of the pelts, and bundled them into smelly packs. They kept a sharp eye on their horses and sometimes went out of their way to expose themselves to grizzly bears, mountain lions, and rattlesnakes, for killing such creatures was a proof of virility. Quick-tempered, they fought several brutal battles with the Indians, particularly in the desert reaches of Arizona. In their constant tracing of stream after stream, they unraveled in two decades more of the Southwest's complex geography than their Spanish and Mexican predecessors had discovered in two centuries.

Their despoiling of the streams without leaving anything behind led the officials in Mexico City to impose increasingly severe licensing restrictions on their activities. No matter. By smuggling furs across the mountains to caravans departing for Missouri; by using a Mexican citizen as a front in obtaining licenses; or by sheltering several men behind one American who somehow managed to obtain a permit and then did the marketing for all of them—by such means the exuberant Americans and the numerous French-Canadians who worked with them made light of the laws. On the rare occasions when an offender was caught and suffered confiscation of his furs, he cried his outrage to heaven. Those treacherous Mexicans!

The trappers produced their share of folk heroes. One was James Ohio Pattie, who during the second half of the 1820s roamed from the Missouri River to California, and from the Yellowstone country into Chihuahua and Sonora. He fought grizzly bears, rescued maidens, survived ambushes, saw his father die in a San Diego dungeon, and acted as a doctor during a virulent epidemic of measles. Shortly after returning home in 1830 he turned out a garbled, ghost-written tale of his adventures that gave the stay-at-home East its first titillating glimpse of the Southwest since the publication of Zebulon Pike's journals.

Another legendary figure was Old Bill Williams, a one-time frontier Baptist preacher who was converted to paganism by the Indians. Skinny, red-haired, and over six feet tall, Williams was fairly well educated, although he let his semiliterate companions believe he possessed no more learning than they did. He shambled when he walked, rode like Ichabod Crane, and was given to disappearing alone for long periods of time, only to return laden with furs whose proceeds he spent in riotous entertainment of his wives (plural) and his friends. He was a good linguist, a fascinating storyteller, and the first American to study the southwestern Indians with at least a rudimentary grasp of comparative anthropology. His last days were anticlimactic. As Frémont's guide on that famed explorer's search for a railroad pass through the Colorado Rockies, he shared in the responsibility for the venture's disastrous outcome. Shortly after the debacle he was killed by Ute Indians. Today a river and a big, round, lonesome mountain—both in Arizona—commemorate his name.

Kit Carson, whose name is also perpetuated by rivers, mountains, towns, and counties, was Williams's antithesis—short, soft-spoken, unschooled. As a teen-ager Kit cooked one winter for master trapper Ewing Young, who later took him to California on one of the early crossings of the continent. He was a teamster in Chihuahua and at the Santa Rita copper mine. He trapped throughout the Rockies and helped supply the work crews at Bent's Fort on the Arkansas River with buffalo meat. Ordinary enough. But unlike Bill Williams he proved to be a capable guide on Frémont's earlier expeditions and came to international notice in the explorer's books. The recognition helped bring him an appointment as Indian agent in Taos. That led in turn to command of a volunteer regiment during the Indian troubles of the 1860s and the brevet rank of brigadier general in the United States Army, though he could scarcely sign his name.

The beaver fur that these men and their peers brought to Taos was light brown in color. At intervals the vagaries of fashion lifted its price a bit, but in the main it was not as well regarded as the darker, glossier northern furs. Moreover, there was not much of it, relatively speaking. So even when it was added to New Mexico's dab of coins, gold dust, and mules, the total failed to absorb the quantities of merchandise the caravans brought west each spring. Accordingly the traveling merchants, both Americans and Mexicans, had to search for additional outlets in Chihuahua and Durango, where they competed with sellers working out of Vera Cruz on the Gulf of Mexico and Guaymas on the Gulf of California.

The merchants generally followed the same procedure. Their caravans reached Santa Fe late in May or early in June, whereupon they rented stores in which to display their offerings throughout the summer. New Mexicans, both wholesalers and ordinary purchasers, flocked in and shopped assiduously for the "crazy bargains" (in Antonio Barreiro's words) that the competition made available. Mingling with them were Anglo traders who had spent the preceding winter in Chihuahua and Sonora and who were either on their way back to the United States with their profits or had come to Santa Fe to replenish their stock.

By August New Mexico had been bled of its transportable resources. Merchants with material left on their hands either hired agents to keep store for them during the winter or made plans to join the century-old Chihuahua caravan that started south each October with its herds of sheep and its pack trains loaded with buffalo and deer hides, home-woven woolens, piñon nuts, and salt.

The others sold the empty wagons they no longer needed and with the remainder creaked back across the plains with their beaver pelts, mules, and the miscellany of Mexican coins that helped keep Missouri solvent during the bleak depression of the 1830s. All told, it was mutually beneficial commerce for both Mexico and the United States, but unhappily there was not enough of it to dispel the shadows that the upheavals in Texas were simultaneously casting across the entire Southwest.

## Tumults

Racial antipathies have long existed between the Anglo-Saxon peoples of the United States and the Latins to the south. Part of the trouble springs from ancient folk wariness of races that seem different and therefore unpredictable: blond tribes whose subconscious memories run back to the humid forests of the British Isles and northwestern Europe confronting an olive-skinned people whose homes were the dry, sun-washed peninsulas bordering the Mediterranean Sea. On top of those instincts lay more conscious hatred born of war. For centuries England had fought Spain. More recently England's erstwhile colonists had skirmished with their Spanish counterparts along the lower Mississippi and in the Floridas. In the 1840s those scars were still fresh.

Inevitably the antipathies hardened into stereotypes. To Americans, all Mexicans were greasers; to Mexicans, as mentioned before, all Anglos were *gringos,* a derogatory term derived from *griego,* a Greek, a slinky outsider. Mexico's liberal constitution of 1824 declared that every resident of the nation, no matter what his blood lines, held equal rights of citizenship. To the Americans in the Southwest no law could alter the fact that Mexicans were, in their minds, a mongrel race inherently promiscuous, superstitious, priest-ridden, cowardly, lazy and cruel, obsequious in trouble, arrogant in power. Yes, the younger women were pretty and made good housekeepers. Yes, New Mexicans were good customers. But still . . .

The vision of the Hispanos was just as narrow. They could not understand the apparent callousness with which Anglo-Americans cut family ties, which were a Hispano's main comfort in life, in order to move imperiously on toward illusory higher horizons. Americans were godless, grasping, boisterous, bold, brutal, and lawless. Small matter that some of the storekeepers who married and settled in New Mexico turned out to be pleasant, productive citizens. They were forever searching for personal advantage, no matter what the cost might be.

Affairs in Texas brought these animosities into fresh focus. Newly independent Mexico had hoped to forestall Yankee rapaciousness by diverting it to its own ends. Anglo *empresarios* ("colonizing agents") who promised to bring in settlers willing to become Roman Catholic Mexican citizens were given huge grants of land that they could parcel out among their followers, at a profit to themselves, of course. The idea was that these new citizens would want to defend their holdings against both Indians and Yankee imperialists. Texas would thus become the buffer that Spain had long sought to create in the north.

Texas land was good and settlers came by the thousands. When changing citizenship, however, they did not change their natures. They scorned the constant political turmoil in Mexico City and blandly disobeyed whichever of the shifting laws they disliked. They wanted more autonomy than the central government was disposed to give them, and by the middle 1830s their growing impatience was manifesting itself in a series of armed clashes with governmental authorities. The turbulence drew into Texas a number of professional adventurers eager to batten on the confusion.

Determined to quell the *gringos* before they got out of hand, General Antonio López de Santa Anna marched against a hard core of 187 recalcitrants, only twenty of them bona fide citizens of Texas, who had holed up in a place called the Alamo, an abandoned mission just outside San Antonio. The siege began on February 23, 1836. Before it was over a convention of settlers met in the raw new town of Washington some distance away and on March 2 proclaimed Texas an independent republic. Sam Houston was named commander in chief of the army. It is not likely that the men (and a handful of women) besieged in the Alamo knew of the development.

On March 6 Santa Anna launched his attack. The carnage was dreadful and ended in the annihilation of the outnumbered defenders. Another three hundred volunteers were destroyed by General José Urrea near Goliad. Houston meanwhile assembled about 780 men at a place called San Jacinto. There he caught the pursuing Santa Anna napping and in less than twenty minutes completely defeated the Mexican army and captured its general.

The victors claimed that they released Santa Anna upon his promise to work in Mexico City for the recognition of Texan independence. The general, they added, also agreed that Texas was to reach as far west as the Rio Grande—a bit of geographic leapfrogging that put Taos, Santa Cruz, Santa Fe, and several other towns under Texas jurisdiction whether they wanted it or not.

As soon as Santa Anna was back in Mexico City he repudiated everything he supposedly promised on the grounds of duress. Mexico most certainly would *not* recognize the independence of Texas, he said, aiming the remark at the United States as much as at the self-proclaimed republic.

To the astonishment of most Texans, the United States declined to annex them on the spot. The northeast was in the grip of a severe economic depression and in no mood to finance a war that, in their opinion, was being generated to further the interest of the slave-holding South. Texas then had no choice but to embark alone on the stormy seas of national bankruptcy, Comanche troubles, local factionalism, and the constant threat that if Mexico succeeded in putting its own chaotic house in order, it would attempt to reconquer the lost province.

One harebrained program for economic salvation, dreamed up by Mirabeau Buonoparte Lamar, Houston's successor as president of the republic, was an invasion of New Mexico. Lamar's primary motive was the development of a trade route from New Orleans through Texas to Santa Fe. He hoped to find profit for Texas in taking commerce away from Missouri, and also envisioned that the adventure might help distract his disgruntled citizens and strengthen Texas's shadowy claim of reaching to the Rio Grande. He fully expected, on the basis of reports from agents in the west, that his invaders would be enthusiastically received by the New Mexicans.

In June 1841, off went approximately 320 men of all ages, from striplings to grandfathers. They took twenty-three wagons with them, fourteen loaded with merchandise, each pulled by six to seven yoke of oxen. Their orders from Lamar said to go in peace; if perchance the New Mexicans proved hostile, the adventurers were to accept the insult and withdraw.

Few expeditions have been less prepared for reality. Their late departure guaranteed them miseries from thirst. They were undisciplined and untrained. They had no guides and no knowledge of the country other than a vague awareness that the Red River lay in the north and reputedly would lead them to their goal. They wasted food prodigiously, ending up so starved that they fell ravenously on whatever skunks, lizards, and other small varmints they could find. They lost their way again and again in heavy timber and ravines; they carelessly set grass fires that destroyed part of their own equipment. Lurking Indians picked off scouts who went out in search of trails or famished men who broke away from the main group in the hope of finding game and water. Eventually the party frayed into two groups, the stronger of which was sent ahead with the best horses to bring back succor from the New Mexican settlements.

The territory's governor at the time was opportunistic Manuel Armijo of Albuquerque, who had been in and out of office in Santa Fe almost as many times as Santa Anna had been in Mexico City. The situation, when he learned of it, looked like easy glory for him. Drums beat in the plazas; the militia, commanded by sadistic Damasio Salazar, poured forth with bows, arrows, lances, and antiquated muskets. Although this ragged army greatly outnumbered the emaciated and divided Texans, Salazar took no chances. He subverted W. S. Lewis, one of the emissaries the Texans had sent ahead to calm the authorities, and with his aid persuaded both groups of Texans to lay down their arms. Then the militia pounced, chained the lot, and marched them by slow, arduous stages to Mexico City; a dreadful ordeal that was relieved somewhat by outpourings of sympathy from the humble folk of the towns through which the captives limped. *Pobrecitos* ("poor things!"). "Nothing," wrote George Wilkins Kendall, a New Orleans reporter who had joined the expedition in search of a story, "can be more touchingly sweet than the pronunciation of this word by a Spanish or Mexican woman."

The unfortunate episode generated violent reactions. In Mexico City the captives were jeered, execrated, and put to hard labor before their release was finally obtained. In Santa Fe and Taos mobs attacked several Americans suspected of being in league with the invaders. Land pirates from Texas, operating under government commissions, sought revenge by largely unsuccessful raids against Mexican wagons in the Santa Fe caravans and remote Mexican villages on the eastern slope of the Sangre de Cristo Mountains. More potent was the two-volume story of the Texas–Santa Fe expedition that George Kendall published in 1844. The book enflamed public opinion in the United States to such an extent that it has been called the *Uncle Tom's Cabin* of the Mexican War.

America's mood was shifting dramatically. In 1837 the country had refused to absorb newly independent Texas lest the action precipitate war with Mexico. By 1844, however, war was being actively courted by a large part of the population. Knowing full well what the consequences of his action might be, James Knox Polk campaigned for and narrowly won the presidency on a platform of naked expansionism. In quick response to his triumph, Congress passed—and President Tyler, Polk's predecessor in office, signed—a joint resolution authorizing the annexation of the Lone Star Republic.

Mexico protested, vowing to go to war rather than surrender territory it still considered its own. Westward-looking America paid scant heed. Both France and England were meddling in Texas and California and had to be forestalled. For it was the country's "manifest destiny" (the dynamic phrase was coined by a New York newspaper editor in 1845) "to overspread and to possess the whole of the continent which Providence has given us for the development of the great experiment of liberty. . . ."

The whole of the continent! Obviously the concept included California and the great harbors that faced toward the commerce of the Orient, a fact not overlooked by northeastern mercantile interests. Obviously, too, possessing Texas and California without also possessing the intervening land would violate the logic of geography. That realization in turn raised questions of strategy. Had a quarter of a century of penetration by American commercial interests disposed the people of New Mexico, long neglected by their government, to a change in sovereignty? Or would there be significant resistance if an army sought to invade the Southwest?

## The Patriotic Padre

As it turned out, there *were* pockets of resistance, and the man who gave
them such coherence as they had was a charismatic, controversial priest
of Taos named Antonio José Martínez. As has often been pointed out in
New Mexico, Willa Cather in her novel of the Southwest, *Death Comes
for the Archbishop*, traduced Martínez by making him the leader of the
forces of darkness in their stand against the sunshine of progress. Out
of dramatic necessity she clad him in vice. Actually he was a patriot, and
a glance at his career not only adjusts balances but also gives a picture
of New Mexico's desolation during the time of the Anglo advance.

The offspring of relatively wealthy parents, Antonio Martínez was
born on January 16, 1793, in remote Abiquiú beside the Chama River but
grew up in Taos, where he was educated by private tutors. In 1812, aged
nineteen, he married, only to lose his wife a year later during childbirth.
The baby, a girl, survived. When the child was four Martínez entrusted
her to relatives, rode south, and entered the Tridentine Seminary in
Durango. There he became imbued with the revolutionary ideals then
shaking the country. In 1822 he was ordained. After serving first in
Tomé, a *genízaro* town below Albuquerque, he was transferred to
Abiquiú and then, in 1826, to Taos. Less than a year before he returned
to his home town his daughter died.

He was a zealot now, determined to aid the long-enduring people of
his native land as best he could. He established a school in his Taos home,
searched out able boys and girls, and, largely out of his own pocket,
hired teachers to help him educate them. About 1835 he acquired a small
press, which he used for printing the textbooks his scholars needed. He
urged youths who showed exceptional promise to enter the priesthood.

The devout Catholics of New Mexico needed religious help. For two
hundred years their spiritual welfare had been only an incidental responsibility of the Franciscan missionaries assigned to the Indian pueblos.
Then, during the years that straddled the opening of the nineteenth
century, the missions were secularized and religious affairs passed into
the hands of normal parish priests. There was not the improvement the
local people had hoped for. Few ecclesiastics were willing to cut themselves off from civilization to serve in so poor a land—yet tithes continued to be imposed with ruthless regularity, to the enrichment of a few
professional tax collectors. Sacraments, if obtainable, remained costly.
As a result, Martínez wrote angrily, the humble people of New Mexico
"buried their dead without proper ceremonies, neglected to have their

children baptized by the priests, and many couples lived together without being married because they had no money with which to pay for the wedding."

In their despair the people tried to lift themselves toward salvation by their own efforts. Memory helped: Back in the days when the Franciscan friars had attended to the needs of both Indian and Hispanic congregations, they had been assisted by local branches of a worldwide lay group known as the Third Order of St. Francis. After the departure of the missionaries, the order in New Mexico had disintegrated. To replace it there came into being imitative confraternities known as The Brotherhood of Light and The Brotherhood of Blood—Hermanos de Luz and Hermanos de Sangre. Their purpose was to care for the churches even when there was no curate, to read prayers, celebrate holy days, foster good behavior, dig graves, and perform services for the dead that could not await the arrival of a priest from a distant parish.

The *hermanos'* own fervor found release during Holy Week. They hoped to cleanse their souls of guilt through harsh rituals duplicating Christ's final sufferings—an ordeal that brought the brotherhoods their popular name of Penitentes. The rituals reached their climax on Good Friday. While awed throngs watched and flutes wailed in the cold dawn air, members of the orders stumbled barefooted up a stony trail to a hilltop near the village. Some scourged themselves with whips of leather or even of cactus; others were bent beneath heavy wooden crosses. After they had reached the top of the hill, the *hermano mayor* recited the story of the passion, and one of the number, arms outspread, was tied with thongs to a great cross and heaved upright, to hang until he fainted.

When the bishop of Durango made a rare visit to New Mexico in 1833 and learned of the practice, he ordered it stopped. The Penitentes replied by going underground, meeting in remote, windowless *moradas* (humble chapels) and intensifying their self-mortification until to Protestant Anglos the very name Penitente was a scandal. Not until 1942, when the brothers promised to abandon the more grisly of their practices, were the confraternities readmitted to the Church.

No evidence has been found to indicate that Padre Martínez ever participated in Penitente rituals, and yet his name is revered in the surviving *moradas.* He understood the yearnings that had brought the brotherhoods into being and he appreciated the needs they fulfilled. But his own road to filling the gaps was different. In addition to urging students to become priests in their homeland, he struck hard at the financial burdens that were imposed on the people and for which they received so little in return. At his urgings the national Congress ordered, in 1833, that formal tithings no longer be collected in poverty-stricken New Mexico.

Another ordeal that wracked the area during Martínez's lifetime was an upsurge in Indian raiding. The immediate cause was Spain's discontinuance, during Mexico's struggle for independence, of gifts of food and trinkets to whatever Apaches settled in peace on reservations near the presidios. Free Mexico had declined to reinstate the program, and the disgruntled Indians, after rejoining their untamed relatives in the wilderness, had resumed raiding as a means of staying alive. Again small villages were being depopulated, ranches and mines abandoned. In despair the governor of Sonora in 1835, and then his counterpart in Chihuahua in 1838, offered to pay bounties for scalps. Rates varied. For a time in Chihuahua they ran from 100 pesos for the hair of an Apache warrior down to 50 for that of a squaw and 25 for a child's.

Head hunting became a profession. One early-day entrepreneur was wiry, hard-eyed, redheaded James Kirker, who welded together a merciless gang of Mexican *vaqueros,* Anglo trappers, and eastern Indians led by a notorious Shawnee warrior named Spiebuck. Kirker called his trade "barbering" and was not above passing off as Apache scalps the black hair of unoffending Indians and even of Mexican *mestizos.*

Bounty hunting did not stem the raiding, however. During the 1840s thousands of livestock were driven over remote trails to be sold to members of other tribes or to unscrupulous ranchers in neighboring provinces. The success of the ventures inspired other tribes to imitation. The on-again, off-again vendetta between Navajos and Hispanos flared up, each side doing its share to heighten the animosity by capturing, in addition to animals, women and children, who were held as slaves. The Utes of the north joined in, and the profound fatalism of New Mexico's poor about life's ultimate hopelessness grew ever deeper.

Martínez believed that the Indians could not be subdued primarily because of several Anglo trading posts that dotted the High Plains of Colorado north of the Arkansas River. These posts, he charged, sold arms to the Indians, plied them with alcohol to keep their favor, and purchased their stolen stock. Finally, on November 8, 1843, the padre used his press to print a ten-page "exposition" of the evil. He distributed the pamphlet throughout New Mexico and forwarded copies to President Santa Anna. The main thrust of his argument was a plea that the government devote funds and energy to the old ideal of civilizing the Indians. If they could learn to sustain themselves through farming and craft work, they would cease their stealing. They would also, in Martínez's opinion, cease trafficking with Anglo trading posts whose owners urged them to slaughter buffalo for the sake of the creatures' hides alone, a practice that could lead only to the disappearance of the herds and the destitution of all Indians who knew no other means of livelihood. An unspoken corollary followed: deprived of hides and stolen stock, the disruptive trading posts would wither away.

Readers knew well enough what posts Martínez meant—massive Bent's Fort on the north bank of the Arkansas River and its satellites (and their rivals) northward on the South Platte and in the Texas Panhandle to the southeast. This adobe empire, as it has been called, was the creation of five tough, shrewd, capable men from St. Louis—the four Bent brothers and their partner, Ceran St. Vrain.

The eldest of the Bents, Charles, was small, dark-haired, decisive, and strongly opinionated. Rendered bankrupt by the competitive fur trade of the northern Rockies, he had shifted to the Santa Fe commerce in 1829 and had been the captain of several caravans. In New Mexico he had formed a partnership with Ceran St. Vrain, who had worked in the area since 1825 as a trapper and supplier of goods to trappers. St. Vrain took charge of the company's stores in Taos and Santa Fe while Charles traveled the trail with the caravans. His home between trips was in Taos, which made him a neighbor of Padre Martínez, whom he despised.

Charles's brother, William Bent, husband of a Cheyenne Indian woman, was the one who persuaded the group (by then it also included younger brothers George and Robert) to start trading in buffalo robes. Construction of their Arkansas River post took place in 1834–35, coinciding with the rise of the revolutionary fever in Texas. Mexican officials watched suspiciously, for nothing of equal power existed south of the Arkansas. The fort's great double gate opened into an earthen plaza large enough to contain several score men. Lining the court, their backs butting up to thick adobe walls eighteen feet high, were dwelling rooms, warehouses, and shops. Opposite the gate was a big second-story chamber reached by ladder, as in Indian pueblos. There important visitors, many of them American military men, could sip Kentucky bourbon, glance across the river into Mexico, and discuss strategic considerations. Most noticeable of the many guests was Colonel Stephen Watts Kearny, who in 1845, immediately after the American annexation of Texas, led a contingent of dragoons westward to look over the plains country.

With nerves tightening on both sides of the border, it was not well for New Mexico to be burdened also with Indian troubles. When Utes stole 8,000 sheep and 400 cattle in the Taos area, many of them from a ranch owned by Padre Martínez and his brothers, the priest did his best to prove that inspiration and ammunition had come from the Americans and so stir up government action against them. Charles Bent denied the charge, mocked the Padre's efforts, and gratuitously accused him of drunkenness: "I think he is more sinsearly devoted to Baccus than any of the other gods." Considering the source, the remark does not necessarily bear out Willa Cather's estimate of Martínez's morality.

Another bone of contention was the staggering amount of land that fell during the early 1840s into the hands of what Martínez labeled the American party, a tight little coterie of Anglos and Mexicans living in Taos. Times were ripe for speculation in real estate. New Mexico's population was growing—by roughly 10,000 persons between 1835 and 1845 —and the best land along the upper Rio Grande and its tributaries was already blanketed with grants. Holders of colonizing land grants could anticipate winning enough followers to please the government and bring profit to themselves by holding out to New Mexico's poor a promise of fertile new fields and protection from the Indians. And if the United States took over northern New Mexico, which had loomed as a possibility ever since the Texas revolution, the prospects of gain would be even brighter.

With such considerations in mind, the nucleus of the American party requested from the Mexican government four grants totaling roughly 7.2 million acres in northern New Mexico and what is now southern Colorado. The political and legal manipulations that accompanied the request are too complex to be followed here. The significant point to recall, because of the importance it would assume during the conquest, is the identity of the nine persons involved. The Anglos (a term that here covers two natives of French Canada) were Charles Bent; Ceran St. Vrain; Charles Beaubien, a Taos storekeeper; Beaubien's thirteen-year-old son, Narciso, obviously a front for his father; Stephen Louis Lee, a Taos distiller; and Eugene Leitensdorfer, a prominent Santa Fe trader. Their Mexican associates were Guadalupe Miranda, northern New Mexico's collector of customs; Cornelio Vigil, prefect of the Taos administrative district and an uncle of Charles Bent's Mexican wife; and Donaciano Vigil, another New Mexican official.

Eight men and a boy—7.2 million acres! Not even California, where land speculation was also rife during the early 1840s, could boast of greater ambitions than that.

The decision about the four grants rested in the hands of Governor Manuel Armijo. Tall, fat, clever, industrious, and given to plumed helmets and flashy uniforms, Armijo owned property near Albuquerque and had invested heavily in the Santa Fe trade. If he awarded the grants, his ostensible reason would be the strengthening of New Mexico economically and militarily. The settlers whom the grantees placed on the land, so the argument ran, would be devoted enough to their homes to join their *patrones* in fighting off attacks by Indians or invading Anglos. To make sure that Armijo understood these advantages, he was given a one-sixth interest in two of the larger grants. Their area totalled about 5.7 million acres, of which Armijo's share would be almost 1 million.

Padre Martínez reacted furiously. His particular target was the Beaubien-Miranda grant (later famed as the Maxwell Grant) of 1.7 million acres that lay to the east and northeast of Taos. His arguments, set forth in long letters to President Santa Anna, were powerful. Poor farmers who needed land and Taos Indians who had long hunted game and grazed sheep and horses in the area would be shut out by this brazen grab—unless, of course, the Hispanos consented to become settlers subject to the will of the grantees. The nature of the enterprise, he went on, could be deduced from the fact that the owner of a one-sixth interest in it was Charles Bent—the very Bent who, unlike his Anglo associates, had never bothered to take out Mexican citizenship and whose traders sold guns to Indians, debased them with whiskey, encouraged attacks on Mexican ranches, and then purchased the stolen stock.

(It should perhaps be noted that during this same period several of Martínez's relatives were seeking 2 million or so acres of their own in the north—the Tierra Amarilla grant, of which more later, on the upper Chama River and the Conejos grant on the eastern slope of Colorado's San Juan Mountains. Although Martínez may not have had a direct financial interest in the two grants, the possibility that his relatives were competing with the American party for settlers may have lent sharpness to his plaints.)

Because of Martínez's agitation, Armijo was removed from office and the grant title was suspended. Conceivably, speculates land historian Harold H. Dunham, these actions were mere window dressing designed to calm local opposition. Certainly the "dispossessed" grantees went right on bringing settlers to the new ranches on the east side of the Sangre de Cristo Mountains, and within little more than a year Armijo was back in office.

Local resentment was not calmed. An election early in 1846 for a judgeship in Taos precipitated an ugly political contest between the rival factions. The winner was Martínez's candidate—and brother. Gloomily Charles Bent wrote to the United States consul in Santa Fe, Spanish-born Manuel Álvarez, "Thare may be verry shortly orders heare to expell us, or doe worse, we should be prepaired and on guard."

They were not wary enough. On Sunday, May 3, 1846, Charles's brother George and Francis P. Blair, Jr., a friend from Missouri, had more to drink than they should have, exchanged insults with some Mexicans lounging in Taos's rain-muddied plaza, and were beaten almost to death before they could be rescued. All that night mobs howled outside the homes of the Anglos. "Thare is no doubt," Charles wrote Álvarez, "but the Priest and brothers ware the prime movers."

The sordid little tantrums were symptomatic. They sprang from indigenous difficulties that for decades would plague American efforts to come to terms with the Southwest—religious differences, Indian control, and land-grant manipulations. Nor was timing an irrelevant factor. Animosities throughout the borderland were getting out of hand. Eight days after the beatings (and with no knowledge of them), President Polk, on learning of a more serious clash between United States and Mexican troops on the Texas side of the lower Rio Grande, asked Congress to declare war on his country's southern neighbor.

## Attack

One element in the war strategy of the United States was a drive from Fort Leavenworth, Kansas, to Santa Fe by Stephen Watts Kearny, the lean, tough, capable, and headstrong colonel of the army's First Dragoons. As soon as New Mexico had fallen—if it did—Kearny was to improvise as the situation seemed to warrant. The hope was that he would be able to send part of his troops south to Chihuahua to join a nutcracker squeeze being prepared for the Mexican states lying just south of Texas. With the remaining troops he himself was to march to California and join the battles there. The policing of New Mexico would be turned over to reinforcements that would follow Kearny to New Mexico as soon as possible.

Setting up headquarters at Fort Leavenworth, the colonel, who would soon be commissioned a brigadier general, worked at breakneck speed to form the spearhead of what was named the Army of the West. Its core was six companies of his dragoons, whose bulk was provided by a thousand or so raw, enthusiastic frontier volunteers. These were both cavalry and infantry men, most of them commanded by a colonel of their own choosing—big, hard-knuckled Alexander Doniphan, a lawyer from Liberty, Missouri. The addition of buffalo hunters and topographical engineers raised the total figure of men to almost 1,700. The sweating quartermasters had to requisition tents, ammunition, boots, blankets and food, produce more than 1,000 wagons for carrying the equipment, and round up close to 20,000 animals: beef cattle for eating, horses for riding, and draft animals for pulling the wagons and the expedition's field artillery.

Just before the army marched, Kearny was visited by Charles Bent and Ceran St. Vrain, who had ridden east to meet the annual caravan of traders. The train was unusually large that year—some 400 high-bodied wagons loaded with close to $2 million worth of merchandise. Many of the vehicles were owned by Mexicans, so it was not advisable that they reach Santa Fe ahead of the army with information about its strength. Kearny told Bent and St. Vrain that he wanted the caravan and troops to come together in a huge rendezvous at Bent's Fort. Although the requisition would thoroughly upset the post's trade, the owners agreed. As will become evident, they almost surely were led to expect suitable rewards.

Reaching the fort proved an ordeal for everyone because of the oppressive heat, steaming thunderstorms followed by desiccating winds, insects, rattlesnakes, and insufficient food cooked over hundreds of buffalo chip fires. To the amazement of all, the infantry outperformed the cavalry. Before the end of July the whole confused, complaining, but hardening army was camped with the impatient caravan traders in a long line beside the river near Bent's Fort. William Bent and a party of scouts were engaged to guide the column across Raton Pass into New Mexico.

In Santa Fe, Governor Armijo vacillated painfully. He was not without strength. Shortly before receiving news of the Americans' approach he had been preparing for a major campaign against the Navajos. Word that a stronger enemy was on the way brought the militiamen he had been gathering and many citizen volunteers—4,000 men altogether—pouring with their arms into Santa Fe. Few were trained for anything more than Indian skirmishes, however, and most of their equipment was archaic. By pointing out these drawbacks to the governor while exaggerating Kearny's strength, several emissaries—Consul Álvarez among them—sought to convince Armijo that resistance would only result in carnage.

To cap these efforts a wealthy trader named James Magoffin, joined by Major Philip St. George Cooke, rode under a flag of truce from Bent's Fort to Santa Fe to interview the governor. What transpired is unknown. Tales of bribery have never been discredited—or proved. Neither have suspicions that Armijo was reluctant to fight lest he lose his sixth interest, nearly a million acres, in the land grants that the enemy army would almost surely overrun.

Whatever the facts, Armijo rode with his presidial troops, regular militia, and citizen irregulars to a canyon near the abandoned Indian pueblo of Pecos (its last seventeen inhabitants had moved away in 1838) and began building fortifications. Then as the vanguard of the Army of the West drew near, he fled toward Chihuahua. Dazed by the desertion, his troops melted away, and on August 18 the invaders entered Santa Fe unopposed.

Eager to reach California before the fighting there was over, Kearny plunged straightway into preparing New Mexico for its transition to a new form of government. By his own lights he was thorough. He kept his exuberant soldiers under control, went out of his way to be agreeable to influential citizens, carried a candle in a church procession, attended Mass, and toured the nearby settlements to let the inhabitants see that his troopers had no horns. He made reckless promises about ending the Indian menace (the tribes, however, could not understand why the Americans wanted them to stop slaying the common enemy) and sent detachments west and northwest to awe the recalcitrants. Meanwhile the lawyers in his command improvised the statutes, known as the Kearny Code, under which New Mexico was to be governed.

In hindsight his assumptions of authority seem astonishing. New Mexico could not legally be considered a part of the United States until declared so by international treaty. If and when the territory did pass under American jurisdiction, the formation of its civil (as distinct from military) government was the responsibility of Congress. Perhaps because of poor instructions from his superiors, Kearny ignored these legal niceties, declared that a civil government did exist, and named its slate of officers.

His choices were also astonishing. Of the eight men (and the boy) who were claiming 7.2 million acres of grant land in the north, four received top offices in the new administration. Charles Bent was named governor. Donaciano Vigil, whose office was given the responsibility of recording land-grant titles, became territorial secretary. Charles Beaubien was tapped as a justice of the Supreme Court, and Eugene Leitensdorfer as auditor of public accounts. Bent's hand was visible in other appointments as well. Stephen L. Lee, the claimant, along with Narciso Beaubien, of the million-acre Sangre de Cristo grant in the San Luis Valley of Colorado, became sheriff of Taos County. Twenty-five-year-old Francis Blair, who, with George Bent, had been sorely beaten in Taos the preceding May, was named attorney general. It was not a slate designed to draw approval from Padre Martínez, whose power should have been recognized.

Having spent five weeks at this kind of tedious work, Kearny realigned his forces for the future. Colonel Doniphan of the Missouri volunteers was given the bulk of the men. His first job was to put more muscle into Indian pacification. That done, he was to move south into Chihuahua with the impatient traders. Kearny would lead 300 dragoons and a few ponderous freight wagons to California over the shortest possible route —down the Rio Grande to the now-vanished settlement of Valverde, roughly halfway between Albuquerque and El Paso, and then west to the headwaters of the Gila, a stream he would follow to its junction with the Colorado. Policing of New Mexico would be turned over to Colonel Sterling Price, currently marching over the dry Cimarron Cutoff of the Santa Fe Trail with a second regiment of volunteers from Missouri.

In leaving early and choosing the route he did, Kearny was cutting himself away from an auxiliary column, the famed Mormon Battalion, which had been recruited in Iowa to accompany him west. Its members, part of the extraordinary exodus of Saints then preparing for 1847's migration to Utah, had joined the army so that their clothing allotments and pay, whose total came to about $50,000, could be used for their brethren's trip. Their assignment had been to carry supplies for Kearny while blazing a wagon road to the coast.

On October 2, as Kearny was on his way down the Rio Grande, an express overtook him with word that the battalion was nearing Santa Fe but that its commander had died. Kearny sent Philip St. George Cooke back to take command and continued on his way. On October 6, at a point a little short of Valverde, he met dispatch carriers under Kit Carson hurrying east with word that California had fallen.

This news, together with Carson's insistence that wagons could not travel the route Kearny proposed to follow, brought about a readjustment in plans. To complete the linkage of the two conquered territories, the general decided to use only 100 men, guided by the reluctant Carson. The other 200 and the oversized wagons went back to Doniphan. Cooke and the Mormon Battalion would have to blaze a road on their own by swinging farther south in search of easier ways across the Continental Divide.

Both marches turned into masterfully executed journeys through a land whose thorny growths, toothed peaks, and desolate plains amazed the troopers. "It surprised me," Kearny wrote his wife after reaching San Diego, "to see so much land that can never be of any use to man or beast." But of man's struggles with the desert he saw little. Though he passed within three days' march of Tucson, where he knew a Mexican garrison was stationed, he left its conquest to Cooke.

On October 19 that acerbic, long-whiskered major started down the

Rio Grande with something over 400 men, the stubborn wives of two captains and three sergeants, and twenty wagons pulled by emaciated mules. (All of the good draft stock in the territory had been snapped up by traders and other army units.) A detour around the southern prongs of the Mimbres Mountains took the battalion a few miles south of the present international border.

As the grumbling column cut back north into the valley of the San Pedro, it passed the ruins of huge ranches that had been abandoned because of Apache depredations. Cattle that had gone wild dotted the swales and wormed through the thorny mesquite. On occasion a maddened bull or two would charge out of the brush, upset a wagon, gore a mule, and scatter the troopers in the vicinity like leaves. There was recompense, however. By pumping bullets into the resilient beasts, the hungry men obtained enough stringy meat for several feasts.

It was a tragic land, already defeated by neglect, fear, drought, and famine. In 1842 the Franciscans, despairing of getting further support from the government, had withdrawn the last of their friars from the area. The splendid churches at Tumacácori and San Xavier del Bac were crumbling amid the huts of a few Christian Indians who lingered on because these were the only homes they knew.

The commander of the Tucson presidio refused to surrender to Cooke, but did withdraw from the town and let the Americans enter without challenge. Most of the residents had fled; those who remained came timidly out with offers to sell flour, tobacco, and fruit. The weary conquerors rested awhile, complaining as soldiers do, and then dragged on into the terrible sand dunes beyond the Colorado River. By the time they reached San Diego they were utterly exhausted and had only five vehicles left. But they had found the first usable wagon way across Arizona, as thousands of stampeders would learn during the gold rush of 1849.

Behind them Doniphan completed treaties with several Indian chiefs and then, not realizing how little the scratched X's on the paper meant to Indians who felt no allegiance to the signers, marched south with the traders. His men, unkempt, undisciplined, and cantankerous, slouched along in disorderly bunches, grousing about the cold December weather. An overconfident Mexican force rode out of El Paso to meet them at a place called El Brazito. The 500 Americans in the vanguard dropped to the ground, held their fire until each bullet would count, and broke the attack with close-up volleys. The way cleared, they swaggered on to El Paso, waited impatiently for artillery from the north to catch up with them, and then marched on, still in apparent chaos, to another victory in Chihuahua.

Back in Santa Fe fortune continued to run against the Mexicans. An incipient rebellion was discovered and crushed. Thinking all was well, Governor Charles Bent, in January 1847, rode to Taos, hoping to quiet the restive people there. It was a fatal mistake. On the night of the nineteenth, rioting erupted. Although Padre Martínez has been blamed for inciting the trouble (he had been involved in the aborted Santa Fe revolt), he probably did not do so—at least not directly. Yet certainly his years of fulminating bore bitter fruit that night. A mob, many of its members fired to frenzy with liquor, broke into Bent's home, poured bullets and arrows into him, and ripped off his scalp. Among the others who died horribly that night were Stephen Lee, recently appointed sheriff of the town, Narciso Beaubien, fellow owner of the huge Sangre de Cristo grant, and Prefect Cornelio Vigil, another of the nine grant claimants. The next day the rebels, now more than a thousand strong, overran a group of Americans fortified in a distillery at nearby Arroyo Hondo and then swarmed across the mountains to attack the ranches that Bent and his associates had established on their new Beaubien–Miranda grant.

Retribution was swift. Troops stationed at the New Mexican village of Las Vegas broke the disorganized rebels on the eastern side of the mountains. Colonel Sterling Price marched north from Santa Fe with 400 troops reinforced by 65 incensed trappers under Ceran St. Vrain. They brushed aside a rebel army that tried to stop them and cornered several hundred Indians and Mexicans in the old mission church at the Taos pueblo. Sappers set the roof afire, breached the walls, and tossed in grenades. At least 150 of the defenders died before the terrified survivors surrendered. At a trial presided over by Carlos Beaubien, father of one of the victims, fifteen of the ringleaders of the affray were found guilty and ordered hanged.

All told, it was an inauspicious start toward the Americanization of an alien and deeply suspicious people.

# 5

---

# WHOSE SOUTHWEST?

*The Size of the Prize*

By forcing Mexico to abandon her claim to the already lost province of Texas and by annexing the rest of the Mexican north through the Treaty of Guadalupe Hidalgo (February 2, 1848) and the Gadsden Purchase (December 30, 1853), the United States increased its area by more than one third—and shrank Mexico's by two fifths. Call the roll: Texas, New Mexico, Arizona, California, Nevada, Utah, half of Colorado, bits of Wyoming, Kansas, and Oklahoma—an imperial domain of more than one million square miles.

American costs came to approximately 13,000 military lives, most of which were lost to disease, $97 million in war expenses, and $28.25 million paid to Mexico. The payments included $15 million for the lands acquired through the Treaty of Guadalupe Hidalgo, $10 million for the 30,000 square miles gotten through the Gadsden Purchase, and $3.25 million for claims held by United States citizens against Mexico—claims that Washington agreed to meet.

Financially, the territorial gain was a bargain. In just two years, 1850 and 1851, California alone produced as much in gold as the entire area cost in dollars. Politically, however, the new lands increased the likelihood of national disaster. For on August 8, 1846, a few days before Kearny's Army of the West entered Santa Fe, Congressman David Wilmot of Pennsylvania offered as an amendment to a war appropriation bill a proviso stating that slavery should never exist in any territory acquired from Mexico.

The stipulation released furious debate in both houses of Congress before being defeated in the Senate. It was defeated again two years later when antislavery forces tried to make it a part of the Treaty of Guadalupe Hidalgo. Decision by ballot, however, did not quell moral passions, and it was under the cloud of those swelling hatreds that the Hispanic people of the Southwest had to start preparing themselves for their new destiny.

## Lost History

In 1940 a Mexican-American scholar, George I. Sanchez, wrote an account of his neighbors entitled *Forgotten People: A Study of New Mexicans*. His thesis was that as soon as Anglos took over the Southwest, they also took over the writing of its history. As a consequence, an adequate telling of the Hispanos' struggle to maintain their ways against alien intruders does not exist. The lack turns out to be all the more glaring when one recalls how few outsiders, relatively speaking, settled in the area during the early decades of American rule.

The Southwest, exclusive of California, repelled the conquerors. From accounts written by fur trappers and Santa Fe traders, from Texans, and from the natural antipathies engendered by war, most potential emigrants had absorbed virulent anti-Mexican prejudices. They believed, as a matter of Anglo-Saxon faith, that the dark-skinned people were ignorant, violent, untrustworthy, and constantly plotting rebellion —definitely not the sort one wanted as neighbors. The Mexicans, moreover, were Catholics, and during the 1850s the United States was swept by anti-Catholic demonstrations led by the nativist American party. Finally, most of the land occupied by the Papists of the Mexican cession was said to be worthless and overrun by hostile Indians. So why go?

About the only people who did were outlaws, government appointees, soldiers, and merchants. The exile, as many regarded it, did not improve their opinion of the land. Wrote John Greiner, New Mexico's Acting Superintendent of Indian Affairs in October 1851, "If I succeed in getting safely back again among my friends under Providence I shall consider myself a highly favored man! Between the savage Indians, the treacherous Mexicans, and the outlawed Americans a man has to run the gauntlet in this country." Yet Americans wrote the history, feeling no doubt that the Mexicans, who outnumbered them by roughly sixty to one, had nothing important to say.

For the conquered the main consideration was, as it had been for centuries, sheer survival. Though American rule brought increased opportunities to a few *ricos,* most of the poor continued to live in remote, isolated villages, subject to the vagaries of the weather and raiding Indians. Under the circumstances what did the guarantees incorporated into the Treaty of Guadalupe Hidalgo for the protection of their civil liberties mean to them?

Voting? They and the Pueblo Indians had possessed a franchise of sorts during the Mexican regime. (The problem of Pueblo citizenship bothered the Americans. They were not in the habit of letting Indians vote, and Pueblo ballots created contention in election after election.) Generally the peons had voted as their *patrones* or perhaps the *hermano mayor* of the local Penitentes order recommended, and none of it had seemed to make much difference to their lives. Why should American elections be different?

Sanctity of property? They hungered for land because of the needs of their growing number of heirs. But most land, especially in the north, was in the hands of wealthy grantees, and it was this land that drew the bulk of the Hispanos during the 1850s. They paid in produce for house lots and farm plots around the plaza the *patrón* established and grazed their animals and cut their wood on the commons without hindrance. As for proving the validity of titles, that was a problem to be worked out between the grant claimant and the U.S. surveyor, who was sent to New Mexico in 1854 to unravel the situation. As we shall see, it was not until after the Civil War, when Anglo sharpers—both private individuals and government representatives—began engrossing great amounts of land and ejecting the hereditary users, that the problem became acute. Meanwhile one went on as always, working off debts to the *patrón* at a rate of from $3.00 to $5.00 a month, and at death, if accounts still were not clear, passing the burden on to the children. What visible connection, really, did Anglo-style civil rights have to do with that?

Book learning? One did not need it on the mountain farms or in the meadows with the sheep. According to the census of 1850, New Mexico had a population of 61,549, but only 466 children were in school (parochial schools). Among the adult population were 25,089 who could not read or write their names. Anglos were shocked: How could an illiterate people exercise the franchise that had been given them? Governor after governor urged the territorial legislature to make provisions for public education, but when a bill to support public schools by means of a property tax was submitted to the electorate in 1856, it was defeated by 5,015 to 37.

To be sure, other reasons than the relevancy of school were involved. Parents feared that public, Anglo-directed education would be worldly education, detrimental to the teachings of the Church. Even more acutely, they feared direct taxation, which they did not understand. During the Mexican regime most public revenues had come from customs duties. When a governor from outside of New Mexico, Albino Perez, had sought in 1837, under orders from Mexico City, to impose direct taxes, he had been killed and his head used for a football by rebellious northerners. So those things weighed in the balloting on the measure to support schools through property taxes. But mostly it was a matter of the Hispanos measuring values differently from the Anglos.

Religious problems struck closer. The cutting away of the northern provinces from the homeland had also cut the New Mexican clergy away from their bishop in Durango. The Church met the problem by creating a new vicarate apostolic for the lands lying between Texas and California and appointing French-born Jean Baptiste Lamy (the Father Latour of Willa Cather's *Death Comes for the Archibishop*) as its spiritual head. Lamy knew scarcely a word of Spanish.

Devout, able, ambitious, and undiplomatic, he was appalled by the conditions he found. Many of the handful of priests in his diocese struck him as corrupt and immoral. The Penitentes were, in his mind, an abomination, and the lack of compulsory tithing—because of Padre Martínez's agitation some years earlier—made the building of an inspirational new cathedral in Santa Fe impossible. He was offended, too, by the gaunt wooden *santos* and *Cristos* carved in stark, cruel strokes to convey the agonies suffered by the subjects, that were often the only decoration in many small homes.

Straightway Lamy set about cleaning house. Tithing was restored, and those who declined to pay were threatened with a denial of the sacraments. The Penitentes were banned again, and told that they too would be deprived of the sacraments until they renounced membership in the brotherhood. Wagonloads of doll-like religious figurines and prettified lithographs arrived to take the place of the deeply revered *santos*. French priests and nuns were imported to run parochial schools and, in the case of the priests, to act as curates. Apostolic letters thundered out against the people's addiction to gambling and against, as Lamy saw it, the lasciviousness of the native dances. No matter how deeply such practices were ingrained in the Hispanic character, they must be extirpated.

To the local clergy it was like being conquered all over again. Two resigned; others were dismissed from their posts. (One was promptly elected delegate to Congress in Washington.) Martínez fought back and in 1857 was excommunicated. Inevitably Lamy won. Many of the reforms he instituted had been badly needed, and the power of the Church was behind him. He built his cathedral, became archbishop, attracted able biographers, and is remembered. But in the mountain villages the Penitentes' flutes still wailed; the *Cristos,* splashed with gouts of red paint to represent the blood of suffering, still hung on the tawny walls. That persistent clinging to an ancient culture was part of what the Anglos left out of their history books, even though they must have known that the people they claimed to control remained fundamentally Hispanic in outlook.

## Borrowed Prosperity

Although culture remained Hispanic, the Southwest's economic cast quickly mirrored the bent of the conquerors. Few though they were, the Anglos arrived filled with the euphoria of victory and excited by the challenge of innovation. They analyzed prospects shrewdly and worked hard to utilize in American fashion the best of the monetary opportunities they saw. Like Bishop Lamy they left voluminous records, and so it is their history that has become synonymous with southwestern progress during the last half of the nineteenth century.

Their first innovations were commercial. Whereas prewar merchants had personally supervised the hauling of their goods over the Santa Fe and Chihuahua trails, the new breed turned that burden over to transportation firms that sprang into being primarily to handle army freight. They put branch stores in hamlets the earlier traders had ignored, financed wandering peddlers, and ordered carefully and in greater volume. They made crafty alliances with native entrepreneurs already familiar with Anglo ways. Though by origin most of the new merchants were German Jews bearing such names as Ilfeld, Spiegelberg, and Seligman, their associates—sometimes partners, sometimes competitors—were named Otero, Manzanares, Ochoa. By means of chains of credit reaching from the smallest towns back to the mercantile centers of the East they began drawing commercial New Mexico slowly but relentlessly into the homogenizing maze of American merchandising.

Even more visible was the army. It scattered protective forts at wide intervals along the Santa Fe Trail and down the Rio Grande Valley to the new town of Franklin, across the river from Mexican El Paso. (Soon the name El Paso would be appropriated by the Americans and attached to Franklin; the Mexican city then became Ciudad Juárez.) Other posts guarded the hot, rough road to the Coast, and a few more were built near concentrations of Indian population—Fort Defiance in Navajo country, for instance, and Fort Stanton beside the eastern flank of New Mexico's Sacramento Mountains, where the Mescalero Apaches ranged.

Most of the posts were miserable compounds of adobe brick grouped around the hard-baked earth of a central square. The common soldiers tended to be underpaid derelicts, often foreign-born, who could find work nowhere else and yet somehow had been molded by discipline and long habit into persistent, frequently effective fighters. Too often the officers were martinets, harsh on the men, contemptuous of the Mexicans, and overly fond of the bottle. Still, the posts did help local economy by providing an outlet for Hispanic and Pueblo produce and such intermittent jobs as making adobe bricks, cutting wood, and herding horses.

Through its Corps of Topographical Engineers, the army was also responsible for gathering reliable geographic and natural history data about the newly won land. Throughout the 1850s survey parties crisscrossed the entire Southwest, including the dread Llano Estacado, examining ancient Indian ruins, mapping stream courses, commenting on soil and climate, and watching for wagon ways and potential railroad passes.

The prime stimulator of economic activity, however, was the California goldfields. During the summer of 1848 knowledge of the fabulous strikes filtered across northern Mexico (hundreds of Sonora miners struck out immediately across Anza's old trail into the golden land) and from there leaped like wildfire into Texas and the lower Mississippi Valley. By spring a gigantic westward rush was disrupting the nation. In their hurry for a quick fortune a considerable number of the wayfarers chose to cross the Southwest rather than take the central route through Wyoming. The trails were hazardous, but for Texans and other southerners they were shorter, and a mild climate allowed an early start in the spring.

Vociferous peddlers at the takeoff points did their best to lure clients southward. Storekeepers in Austin commissioned two rugged Texas Rangers, Colonel Robert S. Neighbors and Dr. John (Rip) Ford, to find a way via the Horsehead Crossing of the Pecos River to El Paso and then north to little Doña Ana, gathering point for travelers aiming across the desolate Deming Plain to the Gila. Topographical engineers simultaneously worked out a more southerly road to El Paso from Austin's swaggering rival, San Antonio.

Farther north, the town of Fort Smith, Arkansas, put on an intense publicity campaign to attrack migrants, and by arranging for a military escort under Captain Randolph B. Marcy managed to gather together a throng of 2,000 hopefuls, all with money to spend. Following a route pioneered along the Canadian River in 1839–40 by Santa Fe trader Josiah Gregg, Marcy's soldiers were able to herd their greenhorns across 800 miles of wilderness to Santa Fe in eighty-five days. At that point some of the adventurers headed north to tap the central route in Wyoming; more swung south to swell the throngs at Doña Ana.

Herds of livestock also flowed toward hungry California—gaunt longhorns from Texas, sheep from New Mexico. Most of the latter were handled by one-time mountain men—Kit Carson, Lucien Maxwell, Uncle Dick Wootton, Francis Aubry—who knew the land and had contact with Hispanic ranchers. They either bought the animals for as little as fifty cents a head or took them on consignment, hired Indian and Hispanic herders, cut north through Colorado to the main trail, and on reaching the mines sold the footsore creatures for as much, in the early days, as $16.00 each. Soon prices dropped to $3.00 to $5.00 depending on supplies, but even so California was a better outlet than the traditional one in Chihuahua. Between 1852 and 1861 an estimated 550,000 woollies made the long journey.

The boom exacted its price. Anglo opportunists and the New Mexican feudal *patrones* allied with them skimmed off the cream; the poor too often could participate only by attaching themselves like leeches to their more prosperous fellows. Swarms of beggars infested the larger towns. Prostitution was open and scandalous—just what you'd expect from dusky females of ardent temperament, sniffed one observer, unaware that he was witnessing the consequences that so often occur when poverty comes into sudden contact with overwhelming affluence. The moral disruptions caused economic ills as well. When crusty Colonel Edwin Vose Sumner took command of the Department of New Mexico in 1851 (he was called Bullhead Sumner by his men because a spent musket ball once bounced off his cranium without doing noticeable damage), he found Santa Fe to be such a *"sink of vice and extravagance"* (his emphasis) that he refused to locate New Mexico's major military depot nearby. Instead he moved back up the Santa Fe Trail to the vicinity of today's Watrous. There he built the key bastion of Fort Union, now a national monument, and whatever gains a flourishing installation might have brought to Santa Fe (as huge Fort Bliss has been bringing for more than a century to El Paso) were lost.

But the overriding loss for the Hispanos, again triggered by California, was their being thrust willy-nilly into the victors' impassioned quarrel over Negro slavery (as distinct from peonage and Indian slavery, to which the Anglos paid next to no attention). For the South was determined to tie the Pacific prize to itself by means of a railroad.

Throughout the East, visionaries were eagerly recommending, in floods of print and at a dozen highly vocal conventions, the building of a transcontinental line as the physical capstone of the nation's Manifest Destiny: American technology as well as American democracy triumphant coast to coast. Costs, it was further believed, would be so formidable that only a single road could be built. The monumental project, moreover, although built by private contractors, would have to be subsidized by the federal government.

One line! Whichever section, North or South, gained the eastern terminus would also gain an enormous advantage, for it was widely felt that political persuasion as well as commerce would flow along the rails. As a step toward dominance, each implacable rival hoped to gain control of the governmental structures of the territories through which the proposed railroad would run—a bitter fact of political life brought home to the nation as a whole by Texas's sudden reassertion of its old claim of reaching as far west as the Rio Grande.

## The Texas Crisis

At the close of the war with Mexico, Texas was all but bankrupt, and its principal hope of regaining solvency lay in the sale of land suitable for quick settlement. (Texas was the only state ever to enter the Union with full sovereignty over its public domain.) As a quick means of acquiring readily available acreage, the Lone Star legislature brought into being the County of Santa Fe, Texas, a geographic monstrosity sprawling from the mouth of the Pecos River along the east side of the Rio Grande and then the Continental Divide well into Wyoming. The New Mexican city of Santa Fe was designated the county seat of this "Texan" entity, and a lawyer named Spruce M. Baird was sent west to take charge.

Simultaneously the legislature sought to discharge some of its pressing obligations to veterans of the Mexican War by giving them land warrants that allowed the recipients to take up homesteads in that part of the fertile Mesilla Valley lying along the east side of the Rio Grande between El Paso and the little Hispanic community of Doña Ana, a bit north of present Las Cruces. So many roughnecks moved into the area that its dismayed residents fled across the river onto what they believed was Mexican soil and resettled their families on grants awarded them by the sympathetic government of Chihuahua. The hamlet they founded as a substitute for lost Doña Ana they named Mesilla. A delightful place of low tan houses and tall green cottonwoods, Mesilla is now a New Mexican state monument.

The leading Anglo and Hispanic citizens of New Mexico responded to these moves by assembling in Santa Fe in October 1848, to consider what to do. They elected Padre Martínez as their presiding officer and drew up a memorial to Congress stating their wishes—a civilian government unhampered by the military authorities who had taken over the running of their political lives following Governor Bent's assassination during the Taos rebellion; a ruling against Negro slavery in their territory; and protection against the unlawful ambitions of Texas. Faced with this chill reception, organizer Baird abandoned his organizing efforts and went to Missouri to wait for whatever time produced.

Congress, deadlocked over slavery, did not respond to the convention's appeal. In exasperation New Mexicans decided that the only way to get an effective civil government was to produce it themselves.

The determination unleashed cantankerous internal disputes. Should New Mexico become a territory supported by the federal government or a state with statehood's privileges and responsibilities? While the squabbles raged (the territorial forces won the first round, but Congress refused to seat the delegate they sent to Washington), Texas divided nonexistent Santa Fe County into smaller units and sent out Colonel Robert Neighbors, a more formidable agent than Spruce Baird, to bring the new units to heel. Neighbors reached the town of Santa Fe in April 1850. Baird thereupon scuttled back from Missouri so that he could open court—with himself on the bench—as soon as Neighbors had completed the groundwork. The presence of the two men precipitated a more violent shift in New Mexico politics than either could have anticipated.

Encouraged by representatives sent west by President Zachary Taylor himself, advocates of statehood for New Mexico had called for a constitutional convention to meet on May 15 and draw up the framework for a new government. The President's naive idea was that by writing their convictions about slavery into a state constitution approved by the people, the voters of both California and New Mexico could bypass Congress and let the legitimacy of their actions be determined by the Supreme Court. The nation, the President fondly believed, would accept the decision without fuss and the divisive issue would be settled.

Most Hispanos disliked the idea of Negro servitude. In truth, they disliked blacks and would soon follow the lead of Oregon in trying to ban even free Negroes from the region. Yet more than slavery they disliked

Texans, and a notion was abroad that if they accepted either one, they would have to take both.

The appearance of Neighbors and Baird at this juncture solidified the Hispanos' prejudices. By an astounding vote of 6,371 to 39, the electorate approved a constitution that both outlawed slavery and extended the boundaries of their proposed state east to the 100th meridian, deep in the heart of western Texas. When Baird sought to hold rival elections for officials of Santa Fe County (Texas), troops barred the way to the polls. The rout, in New Mexican eyes, was complete.

Instantly the backwoods scuffle ballooned into a national crisis. Frenzied orators in Texas told equally frenzied mass meetings that New Mexico's action was "an outrage beyond which it is not possible to go." The governor of Texas talked of raising 3,000 volunteers to retake the territory. Abolitionists throughout the nation roared their approval of the New Mexican stand; slave states rallied behind Texas. Millard Fillmore, who had become President following Taylor's unexpected death, called Congress into special session to consider the problem. As tempers heated, the commanding general of the United States Army, Winfield Scott, sent 750 additional troops to Santa Fe for meeting, in Scott's words, any "painful contingency that might arise," whereupon Alexander Stephens of Georgia thundered at Congress that if a single federal soldier fired on a single Texan, freemen from the Delaware to the Rio Grande would rally to the rescue.

Clearly the situation was leaping out of hand. Sobered suddenly, more and more Congressmen took to listening to the pacification proposals of Kentucky's Henry Clay. The result, from the ninth through the twentieth of September, was a series of acts afterward lumped together in history books as the Compromise of 1850. Some bills dealt with slavery problems; others with the western lands. California, which had preceded New Mexico in drawing up a constitution without Congressional authorization, was admitted to the Union as a free state. New Mexico and Utah, both of which extended west to California, were organized as territories without reference to slavery; presumably they could eventually decide the matter for themselves. Texas was given $10 million for abandoning its Rio Grande claims—enough to settle its debts. And the boundary between the contentious units was set at approximately Meridian 103—"approximately" because the surveyors who ran the line bungled their job and Texas ended up getting, through no effort of its own, many more thousands of acres than it should have.

By 1851, then, New Mexico was firmly bounded on the east and west. But not so on the north or south. Those lines, too, became matters of contention with neighboring governments, and again slavery operated as a paramount consideration during the resolution of the turmoils.

The Adams-Onís Treaty of 1819 had established the Arkansas River as New Mexico's northeastern boundary. During the realignments following the Compromise of 1850, the Americans, always fond of precise rectilinear lines, changed that boundary and made the 38th parallel serve as the northern border as far west as the Continental Divide. There the line dropped south to the 37th parallel and followed this the rest of the way to California (until Nevada took out a bite in 1861).

That one degree of extra latitude between the 38th and 37th parallels east of the Continental Divide covered most of the huge land grants that Armijo had given to his Taos cronies just before the war. The battles finished, the grantees who remained alive went diligently about populating their holdings. Sheep and cattle ranged the upper Purgatory Creek sections of the Las Animas grant (once the Vigil–St. Vrain grant); livestock ranches, farming plazas, and small irrigation ditches dotted the lower part of the Sangre de Cristo and Conejos grants in the southern part of the San Luis Valley. The Penitentes provided the principal religious outlet. Stalwart *patrones* like Lafayette Head, erstwhile Indian agent married to a Mexican wife, helped furnish stability. Recognizing its duty to protect colonists from the temperamental Utes, in 1852 the army built Fort Massachusetts at the strategic western end of La Veta Pass through the Sangre de Cristo Mountains. New Mexico, in short, had every reason to assume that the area was permanently its own—until the Colorado gold rush of 1859 led to demands for the formation of another territory in the mountain West.

During the agitation speculative Anglos glanced pensively at the New Mexico Notch, as they called it. There was good land south of the line, and the mountains might contain precious mineral. Besides, the Notch was an affront to symmetry. After all, the southern boundary of Kansas was the 37th parallel, and west of the Continental Divide the same parallel formed New Mexico's northern boundary. Would it not be logical to eliminate the protrusion east of the divide by redrawing the boundary at Parallel 37?

The Hispanos in the area—estimates of their numbers in 1860 range from 2,000 to 7,000—protested. Family, cultural, linguistic, and historic ties bound them to New Mexico. They did not want to become a submerged minority in the raucous Anglo frontier mining society that was developing in Colorado. Santa Fe supported them, but no one outside New Mexico listened. Abraham Lincoln had just been elected President, and the South was bristling. As a conciliatory gesture, the lame duck Congress of the winter of 1860–61 formed Colorado Territory (and Nevada and Dakota) without reference to slavery. Then, to placate Colorado, most of whose voters had wanted a strong antislavery pronouncement, the new territory was given the New Mexico Notch, roughly 17,000 square miles in extent. And so, as a side issue of the slavery dispute, one more group of Hispanos became a neglected people, their history remade by Anglos indifferent to their interests.

The situation was not unprecedented. Earlier, during the drawing of the boundary with Mexico, the Hispanic settlers of the Mesilla Valley had also become pawns in a struggle for territory, but in their case the dispute had been potentially more explosive because it involved land deemed necessary for the building of the transcontinental railroad so eagerly desired by the South.

## The Mesilla Crisis

About the time that the survey of the new international boundary had been completed eastward from the California coast to the Colorado River, the administration in Washington changed. The spoils system prevailing at the time dictated that the Democrat in charge of the work, John B. Weller of Ohio, should be replaced by a Whig. The choice fell on John Russell Bartlett.

Bartlett knew no more about surveying than Weller had. He was a good artist and part owner of a popular bookstore located in New York City's Astor Hotel. He got the job as Commissioner of the U.S. Boundary Survey because several influential Whigs were in the habit of stopping by his store to exchange literary chitchat. His own motive for going to the Southwest was to gather material for a travel book that he could illustrate himself. Let it be said here that the two volumes he produced were, unlike his survey, very good indeed.

The man charged with overseeing the actual surveying was Andrew B. Gray of Texas. Lazy and possessed of no more than mediocre talents, Gray was less interested in the boundary than in finding a satisfactory railroad route to California for a group of southern capitalists whom he represented. The backbone of the surveying party, as well as its guardians, were carefully trained, drill-toughened members of the Army Corps of Topographical Engineers. They made little effort to hide the scorn and jealousy they felt for the civilians to whose authority they had to bow. The first assignment given this ill-mixed group was to survey, in conjunction with their Mexican counterparts, the international line between the Rio Grande and the Colorado River.

During the closing months of 1850 Bartlett's party, minus surveyor Andrew Gray, who was ill, moved in pandemonium across Texas from the Gulf port of Indianola to El Paso. Bartlett hired too many men for the labor involved and let his brother, who was in charge of the commissary department, indulge in free-swinging graft while purchasing more supplies than were necessary. Weary of the confusion and eager for material for his book, the commissioner went off ahead of the group. Discipline among the civilians thereupon collapsed; drunkenness enlivened by constant theft prevailed, and there were one suicide and three murders.

In the town of Socorro twenty miles downstream from El Paso, teamsters celebrating the end of their march killed the son of a Rhode Island senator whom Bartlett had let come along for a lark. At that the commissioner pulled himself together, arrested the principals, and had them tried. The description of the incident he later penned for the titillation of his eastern readers suggests his metier: "There sat the judge, with pistol lying before him; the clerks and attorneys wore revolvers at their sides; and the jurors were either armed with similar weapons, or carried with them the unerring rifle. . . ." Found guilty, the accused were promptly taken outside into the Socorro plaza and hanged in front of the church.

Less easily handled were the ambiguities concerning the boundary which were written into the Treaty of Guadalupe Hidalgo. In defining the line the negotiators had relied on the so-called Disturnell map, a plagiarism of earlier works filled with inaccuracies, yet the only chart available.

According to the treaty, the boundary was to follow the center of the deepest channel of the Rio Grande from the Gulf on "north of the town called Paso" as far as the old Mexican line separating Chihuahua from New Mexico. Unfortunately no official in either province had ever stated exactly where, in his opinion, the Mexican line lay. Thus a proper interpretation of the Disturnell map became crucial.

There were two ways of reading the map. If the surveyors followed its scale, the boundary would lie eight miles north of Mexican El Paso —today's Ciudad Juárez. If they followed its coordinates (there is not much use explaining the distinction here), the boundary would lie forty-two miles north of El Paso.

The topography of the mountains just north of El Paso suggested a natural division at the eight-mile point. Historical precedent, however, favored the forty-two-mile point. Trader Josiah Gregg had declared in his classic, *Commerce of the Prairies*, that Chihuahua's commercial jurisdiction extended at least that far. The governor of Chihuahua must have thought so, too, when he handed out land grants to the Mexican citizens of the Mesilla Valley who had fled from one side of the river to the other in order to escape encroaching Texans.

Quite naturally the Mexican Boundary Commission, headed by suave, able General García Condé, former military governor of Chihuahua, favored the forty-two-mile line, for it would protect the citizens of Mesilla as well as give his country more territory. After talking to the Mexicans in the area, who emphatically did not wish to be returned to American jurisdiction, Bartlett—as kindly as he was incompetent—let Condé have his way. In return the American received minor concessions about the point where the west-running boundary would turn north to meet the Gila River, which was to form the rest of the line to the Colorado.

Happily scribbling notes as he went, Bartlett then set up a base camp at the Santa Rita copper mines near today's Silver City, New Mexico. There, head surveyor Andrew Gray joined the group on July 19, 1851, and explosively refused to approve the Bartlett-Condé agreement. The bumbling commissioner, he fumed in letters to Washington, had given away the one strip of territory through which it would be possible to build a southern railroad between the East and gold-rich California.

Several of the topographical engineers backed Gray's stand, but months would pass before replies could be received from the East. Until then—and perhaps longer if friends rallied to his defense—Bartlett would remain in charge. Blandly he ordered the workers to continue the line according to the terms of his compromise with Condé. As for himself, he would travel with a small escort on a buying trip into Mexico and send the supplies he obtained to a rendezvous on the Gila.

He meant to rejoin his party at the rendezvous, but the literary treasures he was unearthing proved irresistible. On and on he went until he reached Mazatlan, a thousand miles south of the Gila. From Mazatlan he took a steamer to San Diego, met some of his hungry surveyors there, but left them cooling their heels while he wandered north to see the sights around San Francisco Bay.

Needless to say, he was fired—as was surveyor Gray—for insubordination to Bartlett! Congress repudiated the Condé agreement, and the survey was turned over to urbane, competent Major William H. Emory of the Army Corps of Topographical Engineers.

But what about Mesilla? While awaiting instructions, Emory kept his men busy taking observations along the Rio Grande south of El Paso. To bellicose Anglos in New Mexico such caution in the face of Mexican "aggression" was unendurable. Leading the fire breathers was the territory's governor, William Carr Lane, who had previously served eight terms as the mayor of St. Louis and had come west to forget, if he could, the terrible grief caused him by the death of a beloved son. After issuing a call for volunteer troops, Lane hurried south to Fort Fillmore, the U.S. Army post closest to the critical area. There, on March 13, 1853, he declared by proclamation, "I, William Carr Lane . . . (upon my own official responsibility, and without orders from the cabinet in Washington) do hereby . . . re-take possession of the said disputed territory, to be held provisionally for the U.S., until the question of the Boundary shall be determined."

Predictably the action stirred violent excitement among the Mexicans of the Mesilla Valley. Fearful that his volunteers might not be able to handle the situation, Lane called on Colonel Sumner to supply him with 350 regular troops as reinforcements. Sumner refused. In outrage Lane fumed that while Mexicans "trampled on the rights of the citisens of the U.S.," troops only five miles away "fold their arms in frigid Tranquility & thereby sustain the enemies of their country."

Outraged in turn and perhaps trying to bluff the United States government into a more immediately profitable arrangement than the Bartlett-Condé compromise, President Santa Anna of Mexico ordered the governor of Chihuahua to march north with 800 men. At that point (and perhaps by coincidence only), Governor Lane developed a hankering to see the East again. Resigning his governorship, he sought election as New Mexico's territorial delegate to Congress. That contest, too, ended in a dispute, but eventually he lost his seat to José Gallegos, an Albuquerque priest who had been defrocked by Bishop Lamy.

Fortunately no one in either El Paso or Mesilla pulled a trigger, but dispatches to Washington about the situation made the possibility of that seem uncomfortably close. The dispute, moreover, was becoming entangled with the growing crisis about the location of the rail line to the coast. Was a southern route really the best one? Northerners did not think so.

Hoping to break the deadlock, Jefferson Davis of Mississippi, Secretary of War under President Pierce, sought a compromise. Let all the proposed routes be surveyed so that the final decision could be based on cold engineering facts. The South would be handicapped in the contest, however, unless the Bartlett-Condé line was eliminated and land more suitable for rails was acquired below the Gila River.

The man chosen to negotiate with Mexico's chronically bankrupt president, Antonio López de Santa Anna, was a railroad tycoon from South Carolina, James Gadsden. He worked effectively, and a treaty granting the United States the minimum amount of territory that President Pierce asked for was signed on December 30, 1853. Northerners howled in outrage at what seemed another slaveholders' plot, but after forcing certain modifications and beating down Santa Anna's price from $15 million to $10 million, the Senate ratified the agreement on June 29, 1854. The resultant boundary between El Paso and the Colorado River is the one that appears on maps today.

The maneuver apparently solved nothing. The Pacific Railroad surveys launched by Jefferson Davis showed that several routes, some far in the North, were possible. The Mississippian nevertheless recommended building through Gadsden's acquisition. The mountains, he argued, were lower and fewer there than in the North. Snow would not be a problem. Administrative difficulties would be lessened because the way lay through areas already organized into states and territories. Wasted breath. The infamous Kansas-Nebraska bill of 1854 had split the country asunder, and no hope remained that either North or South would agree to a railroad through the other's sphere of influence. As far as transcontinental trains were concerned, California would have to stay isolated.

Swallowing their disappointment, the frustrated westerners began crying out for improved wagon roads. This time Congress listened. The residents of the far coast, who were continually threatening to form a separate republic, deserved a sop of some sort; and, besides, everyone clearly understood that wagon roads would serve as useful pilot projects for a rail line when one was finally built. Early in 1857, accordingly, appropriation bills were passed authorizing four wagon ways, two to originate in the North and two in the South. Of the last pair, one was to begin at Fort Defiance in New Mexico and run to Fort Mohave on the Colorado River a few miles above present Needles—the so-called 35th parallel route. The other, the 32nd parallel route, was to span the deserts and mountains lying between Franklin (El Paso), Texas, and Fort Yuma, California. None of the roads was to enter a state, for prevailing constitutional theory held that the states themselves, and not the federal government, should pay for internal improvements within their borders.

Normal muddling confused the bill. Supervision of the work was transferred from the War Department (because army engineers were deemed to be unduly interested in esoteric science—and were also southern in their leanings) to the more "practical" Department of the Interior. Clumsy wording, however, left the construction of the wagon way from

Fort Defiance to the Colorado River in the hands of the army. The supervisor of the job was one of the West's more dashing adventurers, Edward Fitzgerald Beale, and though he performed competently, the episode is remembered today primarily as the occasion when the nation first extensively used imported camels for desert work.

Beale was enamored of the beasts: "The harder the test they are put to the more fully they seem to justify all that can be said of them. They pack water for others for days under the hot sun and never get a drop; they pack heavy burdens of corn and oats for months and never get a grain. . . . They are [he added at the end of his assignment] the salt of the party and the noblest brute alive." American mule skinners never agreed, however, and after Beale had moved on to other affairs, his experiment was abandoned, and the camels, turned loose to fend for themselves, gradually died out. Not so the road. By and large the route Beale laid out is followed today by both the Atchison, Topeka & Santa Fe Railroad and Interstate Highway 40.

Southward, the Department of the Interior pushed work on the El Paso–Fort Yuma road less expeditiously. Top jobs were awarded on the basis of personal friendships, party politics, and sectional leanings. The hundred-plus men of the group used most of the year 1857 to gather together their equipment and crawl in segments across Texas to the starting point of their project at Mesilla. Once launched on the actual labor of hewing out a passage eighteen feet wide on straight stretches and twenty-five feet wide on curves, the rank and file performed well. Harassed by sun and wind, they dug wells, built little reservoirs, cut off side hills, made fills, rolled boulders out of the way, chopped mesquite, and eventually emerged with a bed suitable for both stagecoaches and heavy Conestoga freight wagons. Less can be said of the supervisors, two of whom were indicted for conspiring to defraud the government while purchasing supplies. Because the outbreak of the Civil War made the gathering of witnesses from remote places almost impossible, neither was brought to trial.

A far greater conspiracy, in the minds of many northerners, was connected with a post office appropriations bill authorizing overland mail service between the Missouri River and San Francisco. Passed shortly after the wagon road bill became law, the act allowed the Postmaster General to let contracts for the service under certain specifications. Supposedly the winning bidder was to choose the route he preferred, but preferences obviously would be swayed by the Postmaster General's wishes.

In September 1857, a consortium of eastern stage and mail line

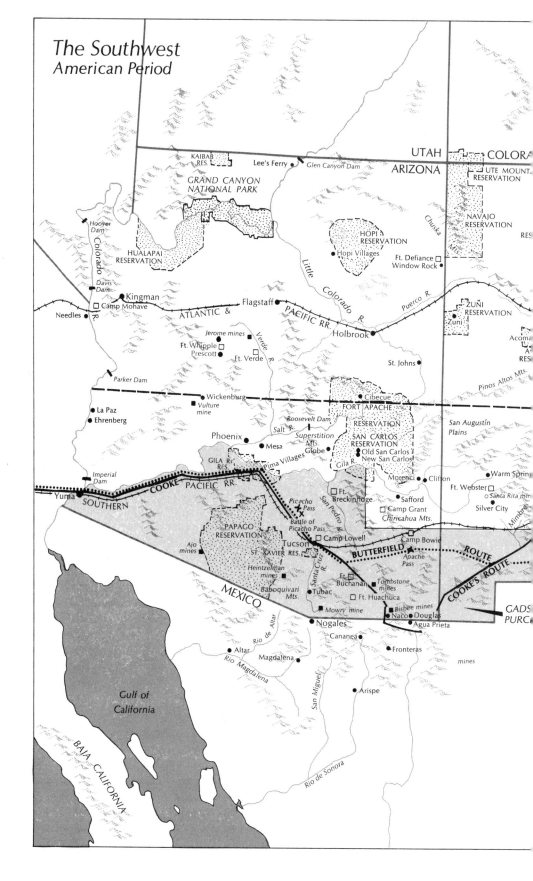

# The Southwest
## American Period

UTAH · COLORA
ARIZONA

KAIBAB RES.
Lee's Ferry · Glen Canyon Dam

UTE MOUNT. RESERVATION

GRAND CANYON NATIONAL PARK

NAVAJO RESERVATION

RES

HOPI RESERVATION
Hopi Villages

Chuska Mts.

Ft. Defiance · Window Rock

Hoover Dam

Colorado R.

HUALAPAI RESERVATION

Little Colorado R.

Puerco R.

ZUÑI RESERVATION
Zuñi

Davis Dam
Kingman
Camp Mohave
Needles
Colorado R.

ATLANTIC & Flagstaff PACIFIC RR.

Holbrook

Acoma
A RES

Jerome mines
Ft. Whipple
Prescott
Ft. Verde

Verde R.

St. Johns

Pinos Altos Mts.

Parker Dam
Wickenburg
Vulture mine

La Paz
Ehrenberg

Cibecue

FORT APACHE RESERVATION

San Augustín Plains

Phoenix
Mesa
Salt R.
Superstition Mts.
Globe
Roosevelt Dam

SAN CARLOS RESERVATION
Old San Carlos
New San Carlos
Gila R.

Morenci · Clifton
Ft. Webster
Santa Rita min
Silver City
Warm Spring

Imperial Dam
Yuma
COOKE PACIFIC RR.
SOUTHERN
GILA RI RES.
Pima Villages

Ft. Breckinridge
Safford
Camp Grant
Chiricahua Mts.

Picacho Pass
Battle of Picacho Pass

San Pedro

PAPAGO RESERVATION
Ajo mines
ST. XAVIER RES.

Camp Lowell
Tucson

Camp Bowie
BUTTERFIELD ROUTE
Apache Pass

COOKE'S ROUTE

GADS
PURC

Heintzelman mines

Santa Cruz R.

Ft. Buchanan
Tombstone mines
Tubac
Ft. Huachuca

Baboquivari Mts.

Mowry mine
Bisbee mines
Naco · Douglas
Agua Prieta

MEXICO

Nogales
Cananea
Fronteras
mines

Rio de Altar
Altar
Magdalena
Rio Magdalena

San Miguel R.

Arispe

Gulf of California

Rio de Sonora

BAJA CALIFORNIA

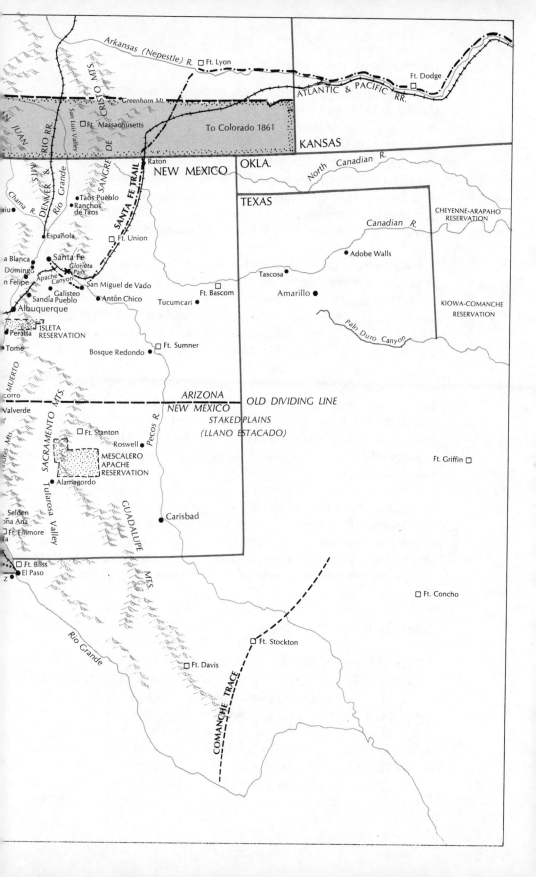

Arkansas (Nepestle) R. □ Ft. Lyon

Ft. Dodge □

ATLANTIC & PACIFIC RR.

SANGRE DE CRISTO MTS.

SAN JUAN

DENVER & RIO RR.

•Greenhorn Mt.

San Luis Valley

□ Ft. Massachusetts

To Colorado 1861

KANSAS

Raton

OKLA.

North Canadian R.

NEW MEXICO

SANTA FE TRAIL

TEXAS

Canadian R.

CHEYENNE-ARAPAHO
RESERVATION

•Taos Pueblo
•Ranchos
de Taos

Rio Grande

Chama R.

•Española

□ Ft. Union

•Adobe Walls

a Blanca

Domingo

n Felipe

Santa Fe
Glorieta
Pass

Apache
Canyon

•San Miguel de Vado

•Antón Chico

Tascosa

Amarillo •

KIOWA-COMANCHE
RESERVATION

Galisteo

Sandía Pueblo

Albuquerque

Tucumcari •

□ Ft. Bascom

Palo Duro Canyon

□ISLETA
RESERVATION

•Peralta

•Tome

Bosque Redondo •

□ Ft. Sumner

corro

Valverde

ARIZONA
NEW MEXICO

OLD DIVIDING LINE

STAKED PLAINS
(LLANO ESTACADO)

SACRAMENTO MTS.

MUERTO

Pecos R.

□ Ft. Stanton

Roswell •

MESCALERO
APACHE
RESERVATION

•Alamagordo

Ft. Griffin □

Tularosa Valley

•Selden
oña Ana

□Ft. Fillmore

Carisbad •

GUADALUPE MTS.

□ Ft. Bliss

• El Paso

z •

Ft. Concho □

Rio Grande

□ Ft. Stockton

COMANCHE TRACE

□ Ft. Davis

operators headed by dynamic John Butterfield landed the lucrative assignment—$600,000 a year for twice-a-week service, both east and west, each run to be completed in twenty-five days or less. They wanted to use the central route through Wyoming but bowed to directions issued by Postmaster General Aaron Brown of Tennessee. Though the way was 600 miles longer, they were to go "from St. Louis, Missouri, and Memphis, Tennessee, converging at Little Rock, Arkansas . . . and along the new road being opened and constructed under the direction of the Secretary of the Interior to Fort Yuma, California; thence . . . to San Francisco."

Again more favorable climate and lower mountain chains were cited as reasons for the long oxbow loop to the south. Northern newspapers refused to accept the explanation. "One of the greatest swindles ever perpetrated upon the country by the slave-holders," charged the Chicago *Tribune*. To the uproar Butterfield paid no heed. He was allowed only one year in which to get his 2,800-mile line operating. Amazingly, he collected enough livestock, coaches, and workers, and built enough relay stations, corrals, and blacksmith shops, and hauled in enough hay, grain, and equipment to do the job. The miseries travelers endured were so manifold that most dropped out en route to rest a few days before continuing on the next coach, but those who stuck it out arrived, on the average, several hours and sometimes a day or two sooner than the time schedule stated.

If such success was truly prophetic of a railroad along the same route (and today the Southern Pacific does follow it in the main), then the Gadsden Purchase and the subsequent maneuverings in Congress relating to western development had indeed been a gain for the South —one that might even be worth shedding blood for when the approaching conflict between the sections at last erupted into violence.

## Southwestern Skirmishes

With all his might, Sam Houston, sixty-seven years old and once again governor of Texas, opposed the secession from the Union of the state he had done so much to bring into being. The effort failed. Early in February 1861, a special convention declared for withdrawal, submitted the proposal to a popular referendum (Texas was the only Confederate state in which such a plebiscite was held), and saw it carried by a vote of 46,129 to 14,697. This action led General David E. Twiggs of Georgia, commander of the military department of Texas, to turn over to the Confederates

2,700 federal troops and military property worth $1.5 million.

Much of the surrendered materiel was stored in Fort Bliss near Franklin, and the Texans were eager to lay hold of it before Union forces anticipated them. First, however, troops had to be raised and organized, a job undertaken by John R. Baylor under the supervision of General Earl Van Dorn. Baylor was a remarkable if not altogether savory person. He had a high, balding dome, staring, glassy eyes, and a forked beard of jet black. He had been a special Indian agent, a farmer, a backwoods lawyer, a member of the Texas legislature, and above all an Indian fighter. He generally wore a revolver stuffed butt forward under a thick belt whose buckle was made from the silver hair ornament of a Comanche chief he had killed with his own hands.

His 400 volunteers took Fort Bliss without opposition on July 1. That was as much as he had been ordered to do, but he needed a fight to keep his edgy men occupied. Unwittingly the Union provided the opportunity. The federal troops scattered throughout the southern part of New Mexico, which then reached west to California, were ordered to destroy their posts and gather at Fort Fillmore, located on the east side of the Rio Grande near the base of the steeply pitching Organ Mountains. The rendezvous completed, the united groups were to move 150 miles upstream to Fort Craig, where the new commander of the Department of New Mexico, Colonel E.R.S. Canby, had determined to make a stand against any Texans who might appear.

Fort Fillmore was garrisoned by three companies of infantrymen. Four more companies had appeared on June 16 from Fort McLane, the nearest of the western posts. On their arrival, their ranking officer—tall, immaculate, silver-bearded Major Isaac Lynde, had assumed command of the combined groups. Lynde did not like Fillmore. The closest water for the post's livestock was the river, nearly a mile and a half away. Nearer at hand was a mesquite-covered hill from whose top he could easily be bombarded. Although he grumbled about these demerits in his letters to Colonel Canby, he did nothing to remedy them, for he expected to move on as soon as the troops from forts Breckenridge and Buchanan in the Gadsden Purchase joined him.

On learning from southern sympathizers of Fillmore's vulnerability, Baylor decided to exceed his orders and strike before the reinforcements arrived. Because he could muster only 300 or so effectives for attacking twice that many fort-protected men (many of his volunteers were sick), he counted on surprise to carry the day. But the plan went awry and, on realizing he had been detected, he crossed the river, bypassed the fort, and on June 25 occupied the town of Mesilla, four miles to the north.

In 1861, Mesilla, population 2,500, was the second largest, and perhaps the busiest, town in New Mexico. Much of its prosperity derived from its position astride two of the Southwest's principal roads. One of these roads ran north to Santa Fe; Major Lynde would have to follow it when moving from Fort Fillmore to Fort Craig. The other led west to California; the federal troops marching in from that direction would have to follow it to their rendezvous at Fillmore. Baylor thus was in a position to cause problems—or suffer them if caught between converging forces.

Mesilla's energetic Anglos, most of whom hailed from Texas, welcomed the troops enthusiastically. They had long resented what they considered Santa Fe's neglect of their interests, a sentiment fully shared by another hundred or so Anglo merchants, miners, freighters, and floaters in the Tucson area nearly 300 miles to the west. On at least ten occasions during the late 1850s the residents of the two regions, sometimes acting in conjunction and sometimes separately, had tried to break away from New Mexico and form a territory called variously Arizona and Arizuma. This entity they conceived of as taking in the full southern half of New Mexico from the Rio Grande to the Colorado River.

Congress ignored their pleas. A new approach came with secession. A convention meeting at Mesilla in March 1861 declared Arizona to be divorced from New Mexico, forbade participation by Hispanos in the new government, roared defiance at Abraham Lincoln's Black Republicans, and sent delegates to Richmond to apply for admission to the Confederacy as a territory. By the time of Baylor's arrival, no reply had been received from Jefferson Davis's beset government, but the silence in no way muted the welcome the invader received.

Stung into action, Lynde marched out of Fort Fillmore with 380 men and three small cannons. Baylor placed his defenders strategically: some in the dense cornfields that surrounded the town; others behind the roof parapets of the low adobe houses; more in the shelter of the fence corners of the numerous corrals. The thickly growing corn and the hot sand dragging at the wheels of the Union guns kept Lynde's men from forming a coordinated skirmish line. When a sharp burst of fire killed three of them and wounded six more, the rest of the federal troops, unable to see what was happening amid the rustling green stalks, gave way to panic and fled back across the river to their fort.

There fear fed on itself. Without consulting his staff, Lynde determined to destroy his ample store of supplies, abandon what he believed to be an untenable post, and strike by way of difficult San Augustin Pass across the Organ Mountains to Fort Stanton, 150 miles to the northeast. He dared not head for Fort Craig as ordered because Mesilla stood in the way.

The retreat began before dawn on July 27. Folklore says that as the soldiers were smashing the fort's stores, they salvaged a few barrels of whiskey of which they partook liberally before filling their canteens with additional spirits, though the next water was many miles away in the mountains. The truth seems to be that there was no whiskey and that the canteens were empty because the men had no opportunity to go to the river, a mile and a half away, to fill them. In any event, as the desert sun rose ahead of them and the blistering heat smashed back from the pale walls of the pass, they withered with thirst. Baylor's pursuing Texans, outnumbered two to one, had no trouble sweeping them up and forcing an unconditional surrender from the demoralized Lynde.

Returning to Mesilla, the victor declared on August 1 that Arizona Territory really did exist and that he was its military governor. Learning from spies what had happened, the federal troops that had been marching east to join Lynde dodged off through the mountains and reached Fort Craig undisturbed. With them gone, the way to California was open, but until reinforcements arrived, Baylor did not have enough men available to take advantage of the opportunity he himself had created.

Although he had no way of knowing it then, reinforcements were already being gathered by Louisiana-born Henry Hopkins Sibley, a notable self-promoter, a brand-new Confederate general, and brother-in-law of Colonel Canby, commander of the Union forces in New Mexico. Because Sibley had campaigned extensively in the Southwest before resigning his commission as a Union major in order to join the Confederates, he was well aware of New Mexico's weaknesses. He knew that recent Indian wars had sorely reduced available means of transport. He surmised correctly that the desertion of many officers to the South had increased the uncertainties of the enlisted men, whose morale had already been sapped when their pay failed to come in on time over the Santa Fe Trail. (Raiding Indians had made off with one wagonload of coin.) It may also be that Sibley was contemptuous of his brother-in-law, a hesitant and conservative commander.

On leaving New Mexico, Sibley hurried to Richmond, Virginia, to see Jefferson Davis. His recommendation was that he, Henry Hopkins Sibley, recruit a strong force in Texas, invade New Mexico, secure his flanks, send part of his men against the Colorado gold mines if circumstances warranted, and use the rest for striking at California.

Davis was intrigued. Although Confederate strategy called for a massive effort to take Washington, D.C., as quickly as possible, he was not blind to California's lures. Possession of the mines would strengthen the South's credit; Pacific ports would help circumvent Union naval blockades; and a wide band of territory reaching from coast to coast might help the Confederacy win recognition and perhaps active help from European nations. And now here was a man who said he could do the job. Davis commissioned him a brigadier general (Sibley now outranked his unenterprising brother-in-law, Colonel Canby) and authorized him to raise a brigade of dragoons and a battery of howitzers—a total of roughly 3,500 men.

By the time the brigade arrived at El Paso in mid-December 1861, Sibley's fortune seemed less bright. Pneumonia and smallpox had cut strength by approximately 25 percent. Supplies were dangerously short. Sibley had counted on being able to requisition what he needed in New Mexico, but the Hispanic farmers disliked Texans and distrusted Confederate paper money. So the invaders had been forced to seize much of what they needed. This led the Hispanos to conceal their resources, and soon it was evident that if the Confederate brigade was to survive intact, it would have to capture New Mexico's principal supply base, Fort Union.

By taking over Baylor's command (to soothe that vainglorious trailblazer's feelings, Sibley let him stay on as military governor of Arizona), the general was able to send a company of mounted riflemen under Sherod Hunter west to occupy Tucson and scout the trails to California. With about 2,500 men he himself started up the Rio Grande. On February 21, 1862, he was challenged by his brother-in-law at Valverde Crossing, a little above Fort Craig. Canby's force numbered roughly 2,200 men, many of them Hispanic volunteers under Kit Carson.

Although Canby liked Carson well enough, he distrusted the Mexicans, damning them as cowards by nature. Whether they bore out his opinion during the battle or whether the regular troops initiated the panic by breaking under the Texans' artillery fire is a matter of historical dispute. Anyway, the line caved in and there was a wild splashing as cavalrymen and infantrymen fled back across the river to the protection of Fort Craig. Casualties were numbered officially at 263—68 dead, 160 wounded, 35 missing. Sibley's were considerably lighter.

Lacking supplies to lay siege to Fort Craig, Sibley next took a calculated risk and without securing his rear lines marched toward Albuquerque and Santa Fe. Both towns succumbed easily, but much of the materiel they had once contained had either been destroyed or removed. Capturing Fort Union thus became more necessary than ever.

Late in March Sibley sent the bulk of the men along the Santa Fe Trail toward the prize. He himself stayed comfortably in Santa Fe, drinking excessively, as was his wont, and expecting to catch up with the marchers before battle was joined. What he did not know was that shortly after his arrival at El Paso, cautious Canby had hurried a message to the governor of Colorado, asking for reinforcements whose timely arrival might help keep the enemy out of the Rocky Mountain gold fields.

Revelation came March 26, less than thirty miles out of Santa Fe. Equally matched advance guards of the opposing Union and Confederate forces collided in Apache Canyon, the dry western approach to the sandstone cliffs of Glorieta Pass. The opponents grappled fiercely—hungry Texans on one side, and on the other a mix of New Mexican volunteers, federal regulars, and a hard core of Colorado miners under Major John Chivington, a one-time Methodist preacher who was a towering six and a half feet tall. No decision developed, and at sundown the battlers broke off the engagement and dropped back on either side of the pass to camp in meadows containing water.

The next day was spent in bringing up the main forces and sending spies out through the gritty-soiled mountains in search of information. On learning where the Confederates were camped, Colonel John P. Slough, a Colorado lawyer in command of the Union force, decided to try to throw the enemy off balance with a series of harassing probes. As a part of the improvised plan, preacher Chivington and 430 picked men, mostly Coloradoans, were delegated to follow a Mexican guide through the mountains to the enemies' rear.

While Chivington's group was working a way across the steeply pitching ridges, the Confederates, rising early, caught Slough by surprise near a place called Pigeon's Ranch. A confused battle followed, in which the disorganized men fought dozens of separate engagements among the boulders and dark juniper trees. The Confederates were slowly gaining the upper hand when horsemen dashed among them shouting that Canby's army was coming up behind.

What had happened was this. As Chivington was creeping cautiously toward the camp the Texans had left hours before, he had seen below him at a place called Rock Corral the enemy's lightly guarded supply column of 80 laden wagons and 500 to 600 horses and mules. What a tempting prize! Stealthily the men—some with the aid of ropes —slid down the timbered slope and fell yelling on the startled guards.

Three Confederates were killed and several captured, but a few managed to break loose to ride pell-mell over the pass to the battlefield, gasping out a natural misassumption—that Canby was on them. Meanwhile Chivington's troops methodically burned every wagon and with grisly thoroughness bayoneted the animals to death.

The false alarm broke the Confederates' momentum. Rallying without supplies proved impossible, and Sibley began a disastrous withdrawal down the Rio Grande toward El Paso. Canby appeared then, but except for skirmishing lightly at Albuquerque and Peralta, a town twenty miles farther south, did not attack, preferring to let the desert break the enemy without cost to himself. It did, relentlessly. Men dropped out by the score, famished, exhausted, beaten. Harassed by delighted Mexicans, Sibley returned to Texas with less than half his original force.

New Mexicans like to call the battle at Glorieta Pass the Gettysburg of the West. It was hardly that decisive. Even if the Confederates had captured Fort Union, they would have found fewer supplies than they anticipated. And where would they have gone from there? Colorado would have resisted furiously. Several thousand Missourians could have been sent against them along the Santa Fe Trail. More significantly, a strong column of Californians under Colonel (later General) James Henry Carleton was marching east to join Canby and smash at the invaders from the rear. So it can even be argued that the Glorieta action saved Sibley, for if he had not been forced to turn back when he did, he might have run into real trouble.

## The Californians

James Henry Carleton was destined to leave a stronger imprint on the Southwest than any other military man since Juan Bautista de Anza. Ramrod straight, given to standing with his arms folded imperiously across his chest, hard-jawed and steely-eyed, he looked like the martinet he was. "Have your command in fighting order all the time, night and day," he ordered one subordinate. ". . . Drill, drill, drill until your men become perfect as soldiers, as skirmishers, as marksmen." His men did not like it and fell short of perfection, but at least they were sure that their commander, unlike many gentler men, had each situation under control.

A native of Maine, Carleton had developed a taste for the army while serving in the state militia and had transferred to the United

States Cavalry in 1838. He was decorated for meritorious service at the battle of Buena Vista in the Mexican War (his book on that campaign is still a standard source) and then spent much of the 1850s chasing Utes and Jicarilla Apaches throughout northern New Mexico and southern Colorado, with Kit Carson as his favorite scout. At the outbreak of the Civil War he was in California. Although most federal troops in the golden state were summoned east to join the federal forces there, Carleton remained behind to whip a regiment of local volunteers into shape for guarding the central overland route, to which the Butterfield mail had been shifted when the southern states seceded.

Almost immediately the belligerent activities of Confederate sympathizers in southern California changed the assignment, and he was sent there to awe them into quiescence. That job completed, new orders came: March to New Mexico and help Canby fight off the Texans.

The first leg of Carleton's movement east during the fall of 1861 was a model of military planning. Advance units cleaned out and deepened the wells along the abandoned Butterfield mail route. Carleton issued bulletins about edible desert plants and ways of constructing temporary bake ovens out of adobe. Each morning the barley destined for horse feed that night was moistened with water so that the thirsty animals would not be further tormented by dry, dusty fodder. The men themselves (there were 1,500 of them) moved in small, compact, carefully coordinated units in order not to overload the limited water supply at any one camp.

At Fort Yuma on the California bank of the Colorado River he halted to regroup. Before he could move again, the unprecedented rains of early 1862 turned the region into a morass. His supply wagons bogged down, and he had to curb his impatience as best he could while waiting for better weather. Meanwhile he hired local Mexicans and Yuma Indians to learn what they could about Confederate activities farther east. Simultaneously he sent out commissary officers to store hay and grain at Butterfield's abandoned stage stations and stockpile food at the villages of the friendly, agricultural Pima Indians, located beside the Gila River eighty-five miles southwest of Tucson. The key man in the latter assignment was Ammi White, who a few years earlier had built a grist mill beside the stream for grinding the Indians' wheat into flour. Until Carleton's agents commandeered his services, White had made his living selling flour and pork from his adjacent pig farm to passing emigrants.

During this period of preparation the mounted riflemen whom Sibley had sent west under Captain Sherod Hunter performed more capably than the Union advance guard. After raising a Confederate flag over

Tucson on February 28, 1862, they probed cautiously toward California. They made a prisoner of Ammi White, distributed among the Indians the 1,500 sacks of grain and the slabs of pork he had accumulated (the Confederates lacked enough wagons to haul the goods away), burned some of the stage stations, and captured a Union patrol that blundered by. When a rescue group tried to retrieve the prisoners, seventeen Confederates under Lieutenant Jack Swilling clashed with them near Picacho Pass forty-five miles out of Tucson, killing three, wounding four, and sending the rest scampering.

A moral victory. But that was all. The sun was beating down again, caking the earth, and Carleton's California column was on the move. An ordeal. The friable ground turned to powder under boots and hooves, sending up stifling clouds of dust. "Blinding white sand," wrote a newspaper man traveling with the troops, ". . . reflects the rays of the sun with terrible lustre. . . . Men, mules, and horses sink under its power."

They did not stay sunken. On May 20, 1862, a contingent under Colonel Joseph West occupied Tucson, from which Hunter's men had long since retreated, and on June 7 Carleton followed. He proclaimed Arizona, still a long east-west strip reaching from the Rio Grande to the Colorado River, a federal territory and, as Baylor had done a year earlier, named himself military governor.

While the weary troopers found what rest they could in the crushing heat, Carleton set about bringing order to the notoriously lawless community. He imposed martial law, levied heavy taxes on saloons and gaming houses, and cracked down on the town's many Confederate sympathizers.

Among the General's more resourceful victims was an ex–army officer, Sylvester Mowry, a notorious rake who during the late 1850s had commanded the United States garrison at Fort Yuma. After resigning from the service, Mowry had acquired a struggling lead-silver mine near the Mexican border. Concurrently, he plunged into politics, his main platform being separate territorial status for Arizona. An active southern sympathizer, he got in touch with eastern Confederates as soon as the war broke out. Suspecting that the man would eagerly abet any southern strike at California and unsure at the time of what might be developing farther east, Carleton arrested him, sent him as a prisoner to Fort Yuma, and appointed public receivers to operate his mine.

During his short imprisonment, Mowry was allowed what amounted to free run of Fort Yuma, and his marginal mine was handled with due regard for laws concerning the property of suspected enemies. The promoter, however, managed to make a horror story out of the experience and topped it off by hurling a $10 million lawsuit at his tormentor. The case never went to court, but the prospects enabled Mowry to sell more mine stock and borrow more money than he had been able to raise on the property itself. Carleton meantime endured years of legal harassment. Sometimes it is hard to tell who really does win wars.

All this was in the future, however. New Mexico was where Carleton's main assignment lay. On July 23 he started for Santa Fe, to replace E. R. S. Canby as commander of the Department of New Mexico. Meanwhile prospectors exploring the mountains in the vicinity of today's Prescott unearthed enough placer gold to start a small rush. Bemused by the activity, Congress, in February 1863, reorganized Arizona under a civilian territorial government and gave it the boundaries it has today.

The Union's conquest of the Southwest was complete—except for the Indians, who still considered the land theirs and would need a great deal of relentless convincing, much of it administered by James Henry Carleton, before they admitted otherwise.

# 6

## THE ANVIL OF AMERICAN INDIAN POLICY

*Promises to Keep*

On Saturday morning, August 15, 1846, General Stephen Watts Kearny of the Army of the West ascended a ladder to the roof of an adobe house fronting the dusty plaza of Las Vegas, New Mexico. There, his bony features craggy in the slanting sunlight, he delivered to the huddle of brown faces below him a promise whose fulfillment would cost the United States hundreds of lives and millions of dollars.

"From the Mexican government," he intoned, "you have never received protection. The Apaches and the Navajoes come down from the mountains and carry off your sheep, and even your women, whenever they please. My government will correct all this . . ."

Sixteen years and several military commanders later, it became General James Henry Carleton's turn to try to meet that pledge. He started, as one would expect, with monumental self-assurance, only to end up being all but drummed out of the territory by its dissatisfied citizens.

One of the ironies of his failure lies in the fact that most of the Indians under his thumb were peaceful. The Pueblos, secure in land titles deriving from grants made them by the king of Spain, were so quiet during the turbulent years of Carleton's administration that the records scarcely mention them. The *rancheria* people of the western part of the Gadsden Purchase—the Pimas and Papagos—furnished supplies to immigrants bound for California, labored in exchange for wheat on the Anglo ranches that were beginning to dot the area, and helped blunt the force of Apache raids. Even the Hokan-speaking tribes of western Arizona—Yumans, Mohaves, Walapais, Yavapais—were not considered a threat in spite of their occasional harassment of wagon trains and surveying parties. What Anglos and Hispanos meant when they spoke, with sweeping hatred, of the "Indian menace," as though it embraced all Indians, was a handful of tribes—the Apaches and Navajos who dwelt in the heart of the Southwest, and the Utes, Comanches, and Kiowas who ringed its edges.

Unique circumstances in the lifeways of those nomadic Indians gave warfare with them its bitter cast. Foremost was their dependence on plunder. Stolen animals supplemented the game they hunted, the plants they gathered, and, in the case of the Navajos and Apaches, the crops and livestock they raised. If their raiding brought them animals beyond their needs, they traded the surplus in distant provinces for arms and ammunition. Some of the women and children they stole could also be swapped for merchandise. After painful apprenticeships, the rest of the captives were absorbed into the tribe as a means of maintaining strength —the women as workers, the male children as potential warriors.

Plundering was a young man's road to wealth, prestige, perhaps even to a chieftainship. Nor was plundering any less prevalent among the Indians' enemies. When John Greiner, United States Indian agent for New Mexico, scolded a Navajo leader in 1852 for his people's depredations, the man retorted, "I have lost my grandfather and two other members of my family, who were all killed by Mexicans," by which he meant New Mexico's Hispanic residents. As for kidnapping: "more than two hundred of our children have been carried off and we do not know where they are. . . ." The only available balm was retaliation, and so raids of revenge became as common as raids for booty.

The Indians' need for booty grew as the surge of people across the Southwest increased. Explorers, surveyors, road builders, freighters, prospectors, cattle drovers, and soldiers either hunted or were accompanied by hunters. The game they did not kill retreated deeper into the mountains, where it was hard to find. At the same time compensatory targets, ranging from stagecoaches to cattle ranches, became more numerous, more tempting. So, too, did the number of illegal traders willing to buy whatever the Indians offered.

Formal protests from U.S. government officials and Indian agents offended the tribesmen. The United States might have conquered Mexico, but it had not conquered them. The war of the Comanches against the Texans and the Mexicans, and of the Apaches and Navajos against the Hispanos of both Old and New Mexico went back for generations, and they saw no reason to stop it at the behest of outsiders. When the meddling persisted, war spread to the meddlers.

The government's response was reminiscent of policies that had failed the Indian departments of both Spain and Mexico. Cordons of forts running across Texas from northeast to southwest sought to separate Comanche country from the areas of white settlement. Other posts dotted the trails leading across New Mexico and Arizona. Additional bastions, and these were the ones the Indians resented most, were set down like rocks in the heart of their homelands: Fort Massachusetts among the Colorado Utes; Fort Stanton in the rolling foothills of the Sacramento Mountains, the range of the Mescalero Apaches; on-again off-again Fort Webster (it became Fort McLane) near the Santa Rita copper mines in territory claimed by the Mimbreño Apaches; and Fort Defiance in lovely Canyon Bonito, favored by the Navajos.

Bored patrols tried to guard the gaps between the forts, but the Indians, who knew the country much better than the whites, generally slipped through without trouble. As depredations escalated, territorial politicians grew shrill. Punitive expeditions, often called "scouts," were then launched to augment the patrols. If they could not come to grips with the Indians, and the tribesmen tried to avoid direct confrontation with the better-armed columns, the soldiers consoled themselves by destroying whatever gardens and equipment they could find and methodically killing or driving away livestock.

Sometimes the belabored Indians would sue for peace. At other times they gathered at designated spots in answer to calls for parleys sent them by the Anglo agents and superintendents who had been appointed to represent their interests. The conferences were made as alluring as possible with gifts of cloth and food for those who attended, but in spite of the sociability no one ever forgot that the velvet glove holding out treaties for the Indians' headmen to sign hid an iron fist.

The simplest kind of document presented to the Indians was a peace treaty calling for an end to raiding. In return the whites promised to repair the Indian economy with an annual distribution of stated amounts of food and merchandise defined as annuities. The whites also agreed to station agents at central spots, generally forts, to listen to Indian grievances and, with the help of dedicated teachers, to instruct the Indians in what the Anglos called "the arts of civilization": farming, blacksmithing, craft work. After long harangues, punctuated at times by scuffles and even, on rare occasions, by shootings, the Indian headmen scratched their X's on the rustling documents and the gathering dispersed. Tantalizations and frustrations then began.

The Anglos were teased by the existence in each of the harried tribes of a tiny peace party whose members felt that wisdom lay in complying with the treaty's terms. The small handfuls gathered wistfully at their agencies (who knows what wrenchings the departure from familiar ways cost them?) and waited patiently for what they had been promised. Miraculously, it seems, because the era was otherwise noted for fraud, they were greeted by sterling men—Kit Carson among the Utes; Lorenzo Labadie among the Mescalero Apaches; hot-tempered Michael Steck among the Mimbreño Apaches; and Henry N. Dodge, former cavalry officer, among the Navajos. Struggling constantly with the disruptions caused by bootleggers of rotgut whiskey, most of them Hispanos, these selfless men buoyed their hard lives with hope: here were the seeds of the future. Let scoffers note what could be done.

What scoffers mostly noted, however, was the refusal of the bulk of the Indians to pay the least attention to the treaties their chiefs had accepted. Their disdain resulted not from inherent mendacity, however, but from another fundamental of Indian social organization.

No political suprastructure united the scattered members of what Anglo treaty makers persisted in calling nations. Their only bonds were language, myth, ceremony, and intricate clan relationships. These bonds helped create in the related groups a strong sense of superiority over outsiders, as shown by the name each tribe gave itself. In their own language the Navajos were *Diné;* the Apaches, *T'nde;* the Comanches, *Nermernuh.* Each name translates into English as "The People" or "True Human Beings." But feelings of shared superiority could not hold a tribe together against the imperatives of geography. They broke into groups and groups into bands according to the interrelationships of valleys, mountains, and available food.

Most bands consisted of no more than a few extended families. Each had its headman, but his authority was limited even among his own people. Young braves could form raiding parties—invariably small because of the need for stealth—with only casual consultation with their chiefs. When war parties were pulled together for the sake of revenge, the groups were larger; clansmen from neighboring bands joined in, and for as long as the adventure lasted a war chief, chosen because of proved ability, held broad jurisdiction. As soon as the strike was over, however, the force broke apart again.

This apparent lack of community among Indians was a continual exasperation to whites, who soon found that the chief of one band had no authority to speak for the people of another, though both might belong to the same tribal group. Even when many chiefs were prevailed on to sign their X's to some promissory document (one Navajo treaty contained fifty-four signatures), they blandly excused later infractions by insisting that they could not control their young men.

The Indians found the Anglos equally unpredictable. No agent or military commander could compel the United States Senate to ratify a treaty he had entered into with his wards, and when annuities were not forthcoming as promised, the official's attempted explanations sounded lame to the Indians. White citizens did not feel any more bound by a distant agent's treaties than did young warriors. Few Anglo officials could—or would—force contractors to heed stipulations about the quality and quantity of the annuity goods they delivered across atrocious roads to the distribution points.

The upshot, in time, was cynicism. The Indians often signed treaties as a means of gaining surcease to recuperate for fresh raids. White negotiators often proferred treaties for no other reason than to impress their superiors, quiet the criticisms of local newspapers, or share in the annuity profits that resulted. Soon the raids began again, citizens wailed, dragoons marched, and the Indians melted away into the shaggy landscape.

Discouraged by the constant bafflements of short-lived peace treaties, Anglos proposed that the nomads be forced onto isolated reservations and kept there. It was a hoary idea justified by social philosophies and historical precedents reaching back a hundred years.

The laws of evolution, the moral argument ran, dictated that land should belong to those who put it to the best use. A relatively small number of "squalid savages" (in Theodore Roosevelt's words) simply had no right to shut a superior race away from soils and minerals that it alone was capable of utilizing to the full.

As for history, as long ago as 1763 England had tried to separate white settlements from Indian country by drawing a line along the crest of the Allegheny Mountains. The rapid growth of the colonies had upset the experiment, but it had not been forgotten. To Thomas Jefferson one merit of the Louisiana Purchase had been the possibility that its semiarid reaches, which Zebulon Pike and other explorers had declared unfit for white agriculture, could serve as a home for the dwindling, hard-pressed tribes of the East.

Speculators who saw in the proposal an opportunity to lay hold of the last Indian lands in the East and South boomed the idea. Calhoun agreed; Andrew Jackson pressed; and in 1830 the land between the western borders of Missouri and Arkansas and the Rocky Mountains was declared to be Indian Territory forever and forever. The tribes already living along the eastern edges of the area were placated with promises and presents, and the enforced removal of the eastern and southern Indians along the notorious "Trail of Tears" to their new homes followed.

Again rapid growth caught up with the Indians. The formation of Kansas and Nebraska territories in 1854 forced some of the tribes that had been located there to move once again, this time into what is now Oklahoma, already crowded with Indians from the South. But the *idea* of reservations, it was thought, still remained sound, for only by separation of the races could frictions be avoided. Only in isolation could Indians be ministered unto by devoted missionaries and teachers and thus learn white virtues rather than vices and be absorbed into American society. The Indians might object, of course, to this form of extermination, but obviously they did not realize what was best for them.

The men responsible for subduing the Indians of the Southwest argued long and earnestly in favor of an extension of the reservation program to their areas. In spite of the proddings, however, the government moved slowly. The War Department, which was responsible for controlling the Indians, and the Department of the Interior, which was responsible for their well-being, feuded constantly, paralyzing action. And always there was hesitation about removing, for the sake of Indians, large blocks of land from the public domain—land that might turn out later to hold resources of value to whites.

Still, a few tentative steps were taken—disastrously. In 1855 the state of Texas was prevailed on to set aside two small reservations, one for the sedentary tribes of east Texas and the other, located not far from Fort Worth, for the southern group of Comanches called Penatekas. The Penateka reserve contained 17,500 acres, which was totally inadequate to support the hunting economy on which some 1,500 Indians depended. Nevertheless, about a third of the Penatekas consented to settle on the land, and when raids continued, victimized Texans suddenly decided (mistakenly, it seems) that the reservation provided a haven for the scoundrels. In 1858, John Baylor, later the self-proclaimed governor of Confederate Arizona, marched out with 250 angry frontiersmen to storm the place.

Texas's superintendent of Indian affairs, Robert S. Neighbors, whom we met when he was trying to extend his state's dominion across eastern New Mexico, managed to break up the fighting. Hoping to prevent a repetition of the attacks, he then moved his charges out of Texas into Indian Territory (present Oklahoma). On his return he was killed by a vigilante who accused him of protecting guilty savages. As for the Comanches as a whole, the new propinquity among the bands crowded into the north increased their sense of tribal unity. This in turn led to stronger raids on the Texas settlements and placed unaccustomed pressures on New Mexico as hunters roamed westward across the Llano Estacado in search of buffalo.

The Navajos' first experience with restrictive boundaries was no more salutary. In 1855 smooth-tongued Governor David Meriwether summoned several headmen to a conference and offered them a treaty that would confine the tribe to lands west of a line parallel to and near today's New Mexico–Arizona border. "If we have a dividing line," he cooed persuasively, "so that we know what each other's country is, it will keep us at peace."

But it didn't. New Mexican sheepmen pressed eagerly into the newly opened lands, only to have Meriwether's agreement nullified by the failure of the United States Senate to ratify the treaty. Conflicts developed on what was legally still Indian land, troops marched, and in the closing, icy days of 1858, a new treaty and a new line were forced on the Indians.

More turmoil followed, including an unprecedented but ultimately fruitless attack on Fort Defiance by a thousand Indians. But though they could not reduce a fort, they could kill people, destroy lonesome ranches, and capture livestock—300 murders and a $1.5 million worth of vandalized property within half a year, a Santa Fe newspaper railed, undoubtedly with exaggeration, on November 10, 1860. Back in Washington, New Mexico's delegate to Congress, Manuel A. Otero, stormed that if the United States Army could not take care of the situation, the people of New Mexico would form irregular guerrilla units and do the job themselves.

Otero's suggestion was enough. Eager for child slaves and Navajo sheep, roughneck Anglos, Hispanos, Utes, and Pueblos drummed themselves into a regiment and asked Colonel Thomas Fauntleroy, in command at Fort Union, for guns and cartridges. Stung by the implication that his army was incompetent, Fauntleroy refused. Undeterred, the volunteers thundered raggedly ahead with whatever weapons they had at hand, raiding and destroying for as long as their ammunition lasted.

The Navajos fought back with stealthy retaliatory raids. As the carnage mounted, Colonel (later General) E. R. S. Canby was sent to Fort Defiance to prepare for a major campaign. Alarmed by the gathering of troops, which contained several companies of New Mexico volunteers, the Indians requested peace and consented to a severe reduction in their territory. Perhaps their amiability was designed to gain yet another breathing spell, but there is no way of being sure. The Civil War began, and Fort Defiance, like most of the outlying posts, was abandoned as federal troops were drawn east. The Navajos looked at each other in wonder, just as Indians elsewhere in the region were doing. Had they won, after all?

Their hope was fired still higher by the Confederate invasion. The whites were at each other's throats, and while they fought, the Indians could perhaps regain momentum. Exuberantly, the Navajos resumed their old, wild ways, on one occasion sweeping up a mule herd within eight miles of Santa Fe itself. They stayed defiant even after the Confederates retreated and Canby resumed preparations for his interrupted expedition.

He had no chance to launch the attack. Carleton appeared on the scene with his trigger-happy California Column and on September 18, 1862, took over full command of the Department of New Mexico from his cautious predecessor. Now to keep Kearny's sixteen-year-old promise that the Americans would protect New Mexico from Indian raids! As a first step, and using Canby's plans as his starting point, Carleton ordered a series of coordinated sweeps throughout New Mexico and into the eastern fringes of what would become, less than half a year later, Arizona Territory. (The Utes were not included; the formation of Colorado Territory had taken most of them out of Carleton's jurisdiction.)

Although his strategy was of a piece, the campaigns were separate, a division that became more pronounced when Arizona was removed from Carleton's jurisdiction in 1865 and placed within the Department of the Pacific. Thus for ease in following the maneuvers it is well to break the story into appropriate segments.

## The Experiment at Bosque Redondo

Carleton's nature bristled with contradictions. Greedy for wealth, power, and fame, he was convinced that goldfields as extensive as those in California existed elsewhere in the Southwest and would be found as soon as the Indians were out of the way. Many of the men in his California Column were prospectors who had enlisted for a free trip to the untested land, and their commander had entered into agreements with some of them that would let him share in whatever they found. As for power, he kept himself on top of the New Mexican heap by maintaining martial law for four years after the last Confederate had retreated. Fame, he thought, would come automatically if he subdued the hostile tribes and placed them on model reservations.

All true. Yet within the limits of his vision he was an idealist. He believed that confining the tribes would not only stimulate enough white immigration to make the Southwest a sturdy part of the Union, but would also save the Indians. He was convinced, furthermore, that he knew the best possible place for an all-embracing, central reservation—1,600 square miles of lonesomeness whose heart was Bosque Redondo, a grove of giant cottonwoods beside the Pecos River in eastern New Mexico. During the 1850s, while stationed at Fort Union, 125 miles to the northeast, he had recommended the Bosque as the site for a cavalry post, but the establishment had not been built and the area remained available for this greater work. Miles of waving grass for Indian livestock, thousands of acres of irrigable land for Indian farms—a man could, if he chose, detect the workings of Providence in the way circumstances were developing.

Carleton's proposal was helped by the continuing threat of the New Mexicans to override the federal government and solve the Indian problem in their own merciless way. Partly to forestall that possibility, Congress authorized the million-acre reserve Carleton wanted. Now to round up the Indians!

As his field commander, Carleton chose Christopher Carson, who had served as his guide a decade earlier during expeditions against the Utes and Jicarilla Apaches. Since then Kit had risen fast. In spite of his inability to read or write anything more than his name, he had been appointed agent for the Indians of northern New Mexico, which then reached well up into future Colorado. His charges liked him, and although he had become internationally famous through Frémont's laudatory reports in the 1840s and DeWitt Peters's biography, published in 1858, he preferred living among them to courting attention in the cities.

He was five feet six inches tall, spare, soft-spoken, with clear, light blue eyes, long blond hair on the nape of his neck, and a firm upper lip that was sometimes smooth shaven or, when he felt like it, adorned with a soup-strainer mustache. He was easily swayed by others into doing what they considered to be his duty.

When the Texas invasion had loomed at the outbreak of the Civil War, he had resigned his agency position to accept a commission as lieutenant colonel under his old fur-trade boss, Ceran St. Vrain, in the hastily formed First Regiment of New Mexico Volunteers. On St. Vrain's resignation he became the regiment's colonel, and it was largely because of the Hispanos' devotion to him that the First performed well (most other regiments did not) during Canby's defeat at Valverde.

The Confederates ejected, he asked to be released. He was fifty-three and unwell. A horse had fallen on him in 1860, producing an aortal aneurysm that he had neglected; it kept swelling slowly until, in 1868, it would kill him. Aware already, in 1862, that more campaigning would be hard on him, he wanted to return to his family in Taos. But General Canby, Henry Connelly, governor of the territory, and Carleton all insisted that he was needed, and because he liked them (there were few men he didn't like), he gave in.

Carleton's strategy was simple and ruthless. Columns of volunteers and regulars were to converge from three directions on the relatively small Mescalero subtribe of Apaches that roamed the slopes of the Sacramento Mountains. After the Mescaleros had been subdued, General Joseph West, who had led the first contingent of the California Column into Tucson, was to press against the Apaches who lived around the headwaters of the Gila River in southwestern New Mexico. Meanwhile Carson was to lead a thousand troops into Navajo country.

No tribe or band was to be allowed to sue for peace in order to gain time. In a frequently quoted order to his commanders, Carleton decreed, "The men are to be slain whenever and wherever they can be found. The women and children may be taken prisoners, but, of course, they are not to be killed." Critics have called this a policy of extermination, and some hardcases, mostly in Arizona, acted as if it indeed gave them total license. Carleton himself, however, included an alternative. If the Indians surrendered and went to Bosque Redondo, they would be cared for.

After Captain William McCleave of the California Column had trounced the main band of the Mescaleros near Alamogordo, the bulk of that tribe caved in. Preferring to surrender to Carson, they fled across the mountains to Fort Stanton, which he had reactivated as his headquarters, and pled for understanding. "You have driven us from our last and best stronghold," said their spokesman, Chief Cadette, "and we have no more heart. Do with us as may seem good to you, but do not forget we are braves and men."

Carson sent the principal warriors and their agent, Lorenzo Labadie, to Carleton. The general told them crisply that their free days were gone; henceforth Bosque Redondo was to be the Mescaleros' home. The ultimatum given, he let the warriors go back into the mountains to spread the word and pick up their families. Throughout the bleak winter of 1862–63 small bands straggled into the reservation until more than four hundred Indians were clustered in miserable brush wickiups on the wind-torn flats beside the alkaline Pecos. It was estimated that no more than a hundred others lurked in tiny groups in remote canyons scattered throughout the Sacramento, Guadalupe, and Davis mountains.

Again Carson asked for his release, but Carleton was hot after the Navajos now. In July 1863, he sent Carson to Fort Wingate, recently erected a little south of present-day Grants, New Mexico, by his second-in-command, Lieutenant Colonel Francisco Chávez, stepson of Governor Connelly. Leaving 326 men at Wingate, Kit and nearly 800 more men continued northwest another ninety miles to red-walled Canyon Bonito. There Carson reopened Fort Defiance as Fort Canby. The new name failed to stick; the bustling Indian town that now occupies the spot is still called Fort Defiance.

From that base Carson began his "scouts"—long, corkscrewing rides through a dry, wind-scoured land. His troopers killed as many Navajo males as they could catch and captured several women and children, but their main effort was devoted to destroying crops and rounding up livestock. A score or so Ute Indians acted as guides and scouts, and at one point Carson suggested that they be allowed to keep the Navajo children they seized. Refusing them this normal form of plunder, he said, would diminish their zeal, and the children would not suffer unduly, for the Utes would sell them to Hispanos, who would give them a Catholic upbringing and incorporate them into New Mexican society as *genízaros*.

Carleton refused. Every Navajo must go to the Bosque Redondo, as fifty-one members of the Navajo peace party already had. They would acquire new values and new goals in life from the kindly teachers there. "The old Indians will die off and carry with them all latent longings for murdering and robbing: the young ones will take their places without these longings: and thus, little by little, they will become a happy and content people." But, Carleton went on, if the Utes—and the troopers—needed incentive, let them be paid $20.00 for each Navajo horse they brought in and $1.00 for each sheep. The army would put the horses to work and the mutton into cooking pots.

On and on, in fatigue and intensifying cold—destroy, capture, kill. The Ute trackers quit and were replaced by Zuñis. So many of the command's horses played out that during the latter part of November all the troopers were afoot in the snow except for Carson and his staff. Wracked with pain, Kit was so weary that he often fell asleep in the saddle. "I will venture to assert," he had his adjutant write Carleton, "that no troops in the United States have been called upon to endure such hardships."

During those arduous weeks his men destroyed an estimated 2 million pounds of Navajo food and an unrecorded number of fruit trees. The Indians' resistance began to crack. While Carson was still in the field in November, 187 Indians, led by a prominent chief named Delgadito, surrendered to Francisco Chávez at Fort Wingate. There they were assured that extermination was not the Anglos' aim—*if* the Indians would move to Bosque Redondo. Delgadito was told to return to the Navajos' secret places and give that message to as many people as he could find.

The episode exhilarated Carleton, who on December 3 answered Kit's request for a leave over Christmas with a steely declaration: "*Now* while the snow is deep is the time to make an impression on the tribe." Obediently Carson prepared to scour the one great stronghold he had not yet attacked, Canyon de Chelly and its principal tributary, Canyon del Muerto, hemmed in by weather-streaked sandstone cliffs that in places towered a thousand feet above the flat canyon floor. Pack trains carried supplies, but the men marched afoot through snow and cold that froze fingers and toes. The mules suffered, too, breaking through the ice of the shallow streams and tumbling down with their loads. According to Captain Albert H. Pfeiffer of the volunteers, one laden animal "split completely open under the exhausting fatigue of the march."

Where the terrain allowed, the Indians tried to crush the attackers by rolling huge boulders from the canyon rims. But, as with the Mescaleros, the heart had gone out of them. Finally sixty of them signaled for a parley. Carson told them what Chávez had told Delgadito: They could save themselves by accepting new homes at Bosque Redondo.

During the early months of 1864 Indians began turning themselves in by the hundreds at both Fort Canby and Fort Wingate. Some, ill and starved, died before they could be moved. The others were herded slowly eastward in widely spaced divisions. Wagons carried baggage, small children, and any other individuals unable to walk. The columns straggled badly. Utes and Hispanos followed like wolves, making off with livestock and occasional children. Overwhelmed by the unexpected size of the deluge, Carleton rushed appeals to the adjutant general of the United States Army for food, clothing, agricultural implements, and qualified supervisors. "For pity's sake, if not moved by any other consideration, let us as a great nation treat the Indian as he deserves to be treated."

The exodus continued fitfully for more than a year. (To speed it up, soldiers returned to Canyon de Chelly in the summer of 1864, destroyed more crops, and chopped down 5,000 peach trees.) Bosque Redondo reached its peak population in January 1865—8,577 Navajos out of the tribe's estimated total of 12,000, plus 465 Mescalero Apaches, and 20 Gila Apaches from the Warm Springs area.

By the time the Navajos reached the reservation, the Mescaleros, with the aid of grumbling soldiers, had created a workable irrigation system and had planted several hundred acres of foodstuffs. Navajos so destitute that they had nothing but hunger to worry about followed suit —also with the aid of troopers and civilian supervisors—and for three years kept on breaking out more and more of the alkaline soil even after successive infestations of insects made mockery of their efforts. Meanwhile Navajo *ricos*—families who had reached Bosque Redondo with appreciable numbers of sheep, goats, and horses—scattered across the reservation's million acres of grazing land, where they excited the jealousy of Hispanic and Anglo ranchers. Now that the countryside was safe, the ranchers would have preferred to see the land turned over to them.

Especially dear to Carleton's heart was the building of an orderly community around Fort Sumner. He sent Kit Carson there in July 1864 to supervise its construction and operation. Though Kit now had his family with him, he found the work more taxing than even his winter campaign had been. No longer an army officer, he became the target of petty men whom he had outranked only weeks before. Simultaneously he discovered how intractable Indians could be when subterranean cultural beliefs were involved. Navajos, for instance, refused to stay in quarters in which someone had died—and deaths at the Bosque were frequent. Persuasion could not change the custom, and in such a situation force was inadmissible. And so Carleton's hope of keeping his Indians domiciled in an adobe pueblo as proof of their changing ways was shattered by an ingrained concept. Baffled by such incidents, Carson again resigned, and this time Carleton let him go—mainly so that Kit could lead a new campaign against the Comanches, of which more in the following section.

In every phase of reservation life, ideals were undercut either by shortages or shortcomings. The lone school that Bishop Lamy was able to found (*one* school for 3,000 children!) was crippled by inadequate funds and by Carleton's running feuds about policy with the priest in charge. When a hospital belatedly opened its doors, 235 of the first 321 persons treated turned out to be afflicted with syphilis. To obtain food, Navajo women, reputedly less restrained sexually than Mescalero women, customarily sold themselves to the soldiers for as little as a pint of cornmeal per night, and then spread the diseases they picked up on throughout their own communities.

The supply system was soft with its own kind of rot. Soldiers filched and sold articles of food and clothing intended for distribution to the

Indians. Bootleggers were almost as numerous as corn worms. Contractors, many of them army officers who had resigned to enter the lucrative field, gouged the government unmercifully, charging up to $22.00 for the same kind of blankets the army bought for $5.85. Although supplying the Bosque's 12,000 Indians, soldiers, and civilian workers was a powerful stimulus to New Mexico's economy, prices rose and disgruntled citizens heaped the blame on Carleton and the helpless Indians.

The fall of 1865 was especially bad—crop failures, sickness, violence. Firewood could be obtained only if the user carried it on his own back from scrawny mesquite groves a dozen miles away. Famished Navajos took to stealing food from the more prosperous fields of the Mescaleros; the latter would rush out to drive the plunderers away, and vicious battles were fought with hoes and shovels among the rattling cornstalks. Deciding finally that any other existence would be better than the one they were enduring, the Mescaleros carefully planned and masterfully executed a break for freedom. On the night of November 3, every mobile member of the tribe vanished—the old and infirm on horses that had been hidden in prearranged places. Once outside the reservation, they broke into small groups and scattered in different, twisting directions to confuse trackers. Pursuing troops caught not a single one.

Carleton became a political issue. His imperious ways, his highhanded maintenance of martial law, and his espousal of General George McClellan against Abraham Lincoln in the presidential election of 1864 made him an appealing target, and every wrong at Bosque Redondo, whether his fault or not, furnished the shooters with buckshot aplenty. By the fall of 1866 even his tough skin could take no more. He asked to be mustered out of the volunteer service and, in April 1867, was allowed to relinquish his command.

During the time of discontent the Navajos had been pleading that they be transferred to a reservation in their old homeland. A delegation of chiefs carried the request to President Johnson in Washington. Ranchers who wanted the reservation land applied pressures on their behalf; and when the costs of maintaining the hated spot were toted up —roughly a million dollars a year—Washington became sympathetic. The Navajos were given 3.5 million acres of their own land in western New Mexico and sent home with promises of sheep and goats and schools.

Escorted by troops and carrying their possessions and their sick in wagons, the Indians, released in segments, began their long walk in June 1868. They took with them an improved knowledge of agriculture and vocational trades, better methods of constructing the hogans in which they lived, and an appreciation of the convenience of wagons. The Navajo women had come to like the full, pleated skirts called squaw dresses that they still wear and first learned about by copying the clothing of the wives of army officers at Fort Sumner. The people as a whole had a fresh, strong sense of tribal unity, and a determination somehow to make their way peacefully in the Anglo world while retaining their own values. It would not be easy; it still isn't. But after a few last sputtering raids against the Mormon communities of southern Utah, they went to war no more.

And so they marched west, eyes yearning, and finally, after climbing the long slope of the Rio Grande Valley beyond Albuquerque, they glimpsed the sacred mountain whites call Mount Taylor. Later Chief Manuelito recalled the time with unforgettable poignancy: ". . . we wondered if it was our mountain and we felt like talking to the ground, we loved it so, and some of the old men and women cried with joy when they reached their homes."

## Comanches, Comancheros, and Buffalo Hunters

Of the many indigenous problems that confronted the civilian governors and military commanders charged with pacifying the tribes of the Southwest, none was more exasperating than the Indian traders called Comancheros. As noted earlier, they were a mixed bag of Hispanos and Pueblo Indians from little towns on the western slope of the Sangre de Cristo Mountains—Trampas, Embudo, Picurís—and *genízaros* from the fringes of settlement; Antón Chico beside the Pecos River was one of their communities. As a group they were endowed with the kind of cunning that devotes itself to survival with gain. They were capable of extraordinary feats of endurance but brave only when there was advantage in it. They would deal in whatever promised profit, be it a crusty loaf of bread, a strip of dried buffalo meat, or valuable mules that their Indian customers, the Comanches and Kiowas, had stolen from *haciendas* deep in Mexico.

After the American occupation of the Southwest, cattle for feeding military garrisons and, later, Indian reservations assumed prominence in their trade. Plenty of animals were available, for the Indians of the Southern Plains had developed a notion that they could halt the advance of the Texas frontier by depriving the settlers of their livestock. They worked with vim. In *The Comanches: Lords of the Southern Plains* Ernest Wallace and E. Adamson Hoebel estimate that between 1853 and

1873 the Indians rustled at least 100,000 longhorns from Texas ranches. A contemporary Texas cowman, Charles Goodnight, shortened the time span to 1860–1867 and raised the figure to 300,000. And the Santa Fe *New Mexican* declared in italics on May 24, 1871: *"In the last three months more than 30,000 head of cattle have been brought to this country from that source* [Comancheros in the Pecos area] *alone."*

Whatever the figure, most of the animals went to the Comancheros in exchange for guns, ammunition, and inflammatory whiskey—articles often furnished the traders on credit by New Mexico and Colorado ranchers holding beef contracts with the United States government. The trading grounds where the peddlers met with the Indians were for the most part located in areas unknown to Anglos—the ragged canyons on the eastern edges of the Llano Estacado. Dickering generally occurred in late summer or early fall. Dances, gambling, and contests in archery, wrestling, and horse racing enlivened the gatherings. To prevent whiskey from fueling fights, the Comancheros often cached their kegs at a distance from the campgrounds and revealed the location only after trading was over.

The authorities did not know how to handle the situation. The Texans of course wanted the trade stopped, but an official ban would have created expensive and difficult policing problems, annoyed the Comanches, and pinched the already lean economy of northern New Mexico. It might also have ended all hope of escape for the captive women and children whom the Comancheros often rescued.

For instance, consider seventeen-year-old Jane Wilson of Texas. Around 1857 a Comanche war party slew her husband and father and made prisoners of her and her two small brothers-in-law. For months they were forced to roam the countryside with their captors, tending camp and, in Jane's case, probably performing other functions as well. For the girl, hope returned one afternoon when she spotted, while gathering firewood, a large, upright hollow stump. While cooking dinner that night she secretly set aside some antelope meat. After the camp—and her small brothers-in-law—were asleep, she crept to the refuge with the food, pulled herself up to its rim, and slid down inside. A knothole provided a view of the camp. She watched the Indians search for her the next day and then ride on.

For weeks she hovered around the stump, supplementing her meat with raw terrapins, frogs, and snakes. In time she grew so weak that she could not climb out of her hiding place, and she would have died there if some Comancheros had not happened by while she still had enough strength to call to them through the knothole. At first they thought they were bewitched. Then, regaining their courage, they investigated, hauled the girl out of the log cavern with a lariat rope, and took her to the New Mexico settlements. There the authorities paid them, according to varying accounts, either $40 or $50 for their pains. Recovering with the resiliency of youth from her ordeal, Jane went back to Texas, where her small brothers-in-law rejoined her after being ransomed from eastern Indians who had bought them from the Comanches.

There were many Janes on the frontier, some of them torn from homes as remote from New Mexico as Chihuahua and Durango. One of the untold heart-rending sagas of the Southwest is that of the bereaved Mexican families who traveled deep into the strange land of the *norteamericanos* in the hope that they might somewhere find word of their loved ones. Thanks to the Comancheros, with their eye for profitable merchandise, the quests occasionally had happy endings.

For such reasons the government compromised on the Comanchero question. Traders were ordered to obtain licenses, at a cost of $10 for Hispanos and nothing for Pueblo Indians. Trade in arms or alcohol was prohibited. Nothing was said about cattle, perhaps because of the stolen animals' importance to New Mexico's economy. The point was academic, anyway. Only a few traders bothered to apply for licenses, and the officials chose to overlook those who did not. It was just not possible for the undermanned law-enforcement agencies to police so much empty ground for so small a cause.

Although the settlements in New Mexico were not mauled like those in Texas, there were depredations. Comanches wandering through eastern New Mexico fed themselves beef and their horses corn from pioneer ranches beside the Pecos and Cimarron rivers. They chased a surveying party out of the Canadian Valley and announced through Mexican emissaries that whites were to stay away from their country. To check the Indians' cockiness, the army in 1856 established a post at Hatch's Ranch near Antón Chico in eastern New Mexico, only to abandon it four years later during the general withdrawal of federal troops to the East.

Worried about the deteriorating condition of Indian affairs on the Great Plains, General James Henry Carleton replugged the eastern approaches to the territory by building Camp Easton, soon renamed Fort Bascom, beside the Canadian River, a little north of today's city of Tucumcari. It was a small, lonesome place and faced troubles of frightening potential. The bloody 1862 outbreak of Santee Sioux in Minnesota had sent shock waves throughout the West. By the summer of 1864 Cheyenne and Arapaho war parties were devastating western Kansas and eastern Colorado. Denver was isolated for weeks at a time, and in

Texas the Comanches drove the line of settlement backward a full hundred miles.

So far the individualistic Indians had not coordinated their attacks, but as intensity mounted stunned officials began alarming themselves with nightmares of a Plains-wide alliance. Already strong affinities existed between Arapahos, Cheyennes, and Sioux, and between Comanches, Kiowas, and Kiowa Apaches. (The latter were not Apaches, but were called by that name because of mistaken identification on the part of early observers.) In 1840, moreover, at a barbarically splendid conference beside the Arkansas River near Bent's Fort, the southern branches of the Cheyenne and Arapaho tribes had ended their long feud with the Comanches and Kiowas. So the prospect of union among the hitherto self-centered bands no longer seemed far-fetched.

To these worries Carleton brought a twist of his own. An alliance of Utes and Jicarilla Apaches with Kiowas and Comanches could spread havoc throughout New Mexico. In addition, Carleton was deeply suspicious of the Comancheros. They had too much influence with the Indians, and they had no love for the Anglos, who had overrun their country less than twenty years before. Suppose they were not only peddling arms to the Indians but were also urging them to unite, then rise up and drive the Anglos out while the invaders were still distracted by the Civil War? What all of them needed, Carleton felt, was a lesson in American might.

He found his justification in a series of strikes made by Comanches and Kiowas during the summer of 1864. The wagon trains they fell upon were creeping through southern Kansas with merchandise that was badly needed in Santa Fe and at Bosque Redondo. Deciding to emulate the winter campaigns that had crushed the Navajos the year before, Carleton called again on Kit Carson, recently released from his frustrating job as supervisor of the Bosque, to lead operations in the field. A new wrinkle in the plan was his order that Carson employ several Utes and Jicarilla Apaches as auxiliaries. Their presence on the battlefield, Carleton reasoned, would so enrage the Comanche-Kiowa groups that any thought they had had of allying themselves with the mountain Indians would evaporate.

Having outlined his strategy, he requested Governor Connelly to call up the territorial militia and asked Michael Steck, the newly appointed Indian agent for New Mexico, to cease issuing licenses for traders to enter Comanche country. To his astonishment, both men defied him, arguing that a random attack to punish unidentified raiders was morally unjustifiable. The bulk of the Comanches, they said, were at peace.

Carleton retorted by calling for volunteers among the recently discharged men of his California Column and on veterans of the Navajo campaign. The plea netted 335 cavalry, including fourteen officers. Carson added 75 mounted Utes and Jicarillas. On November 12 the column started down the Canadian River from Fort Bascom, taking with it two small mountain howitzers. The initial goal, two hundred miles away in what is now Hutchinson County, Texas, was Fort Adobe, an abandoned trading post built originally by the Bent brothers. Carson had risked a trading venture there sixteen years before, only to be driven away by the hostility of the customers. Because the place was centrally located, he thought it would provide an ideal base for the coming campaign.

As events developed, there was no campaign. Two snowstorms chilled the marchers but raised hopes that the Indians would not expect an attack in such weather. First events substantiated the theory. Carson's scouts told him of a big Kiowa camp fifteen miles west of his goal, and he surprised it at dawn on November 25. Then, as he pursued the fleeing occupants, he was surprised in turn by close to a thousand Kiowas, Comanches, Arapahos, and Kiowa Apaches. They had been prepared for the coming attack—though not for its exact timing—by Comancheros who, licensed by Superintendent Steck, had visited them with fresh ammunition not ten days before.

Except for the little howitzers, expertly handled by veterans of the California Column, the outnumbered whites might have been destroyed. But the roar of the cannons and their exploding shells kept the Indians at a distance, and after an all-day fight the whites were able to withdraw. Putting the best possible face on matters, Carson reported that he had destroyed one large Kiowa village and had inflicted at least sixty casualties on the enemy.

Carleton was ecstatic. That would show the Indians—and the doubters in New Mexico! He praised Carson publicly: "This brilliant affair adds another green leaf to the laurels you have so nobly won in the service of your country." For a time Kit went along with the adulation, but then honesty got the best of him and he admitted that he had been lucky to extricate his men. The fault, he said, lay with Steck for having licensed the Comancheros before the column marched. The agent had known full well, he said, "that the Mexicans would take what they could sell best, which was powder and lead and caps," to be used against Steck's own people.

Steck lost his job but not his tongue. Declaring that the campaign against the Indians had been unwarranted and would simply provoke them, he and his supporters carried the issue into New Mexican politics, further eroding Carleton's dwindling strength. As we have seen, by the spring of 1867, the general, too, was out.

In the East meanwhile, outrage over the bloody campaigns in the West resulted in new efforts to bring peace by persuasion. A carefully orchestrated attempt was made in October 1867, under the tall trees, golden with autumn, that line Medicine Lodge Creek in southwestern Kansas. There a peace commission, escorted by 500 cavalrymen, offered the Comanches, Kiowas, Arapahos and southern Cheyennes adjoining reservations in southwestern Oklahoma. They would have to stay within those bounds: No more fighting with the Indians in eastern Oklahoma; no forays against the Santa Fe Trail; no raids into Texas or Mexico. In return, the commissioners promised, they would be supported by their white father until they had learned to care for themselves with farming.

Not a single Kwahadi Comanche—the Antelope People of the Staked Plains—was at Medicine Lodge that October. Of the other bands, fewer than half the members attended. Many of those who were on hand pled against the reservation. Said Ten Bears, a Comanche, "I was born upon the prairies, where the wind blew free and there was nothing to break the light of the sun. I was born where there were no enclosures and everything drew a free breath. I want to die there and not within walls."

Nevertheless, the majority of the headmen who were present signed the treaty offered them. A few complied because they felt that it was the only way to avoid a war they could not win. More acted cynically, for the sake of the presents that accompanied the scrawling of their X's.

The Senate ratified the treaty with unusual dispatch, and it was proclaimed in effect on August 25, 1868. When the Indians proved slow about coming onto the reservation, troops converged on them from Kansas, Colorado, and New Mexico. Colonel George Armstrong Custer devastated a village of Cheyenne Indians beside the Washita River, and if, after that exhibition of raw muscle, the government had kept its promises about annuities and instruction in crafts and agriculture, matters might have improved. But the promises were not kept.

The Indians grew restive. The army, subdued by criticism of the Washita affair, relaxed its pressures. Further incitement, the whites suspected, came from the Comancheros and from the Antelope People, free on the Llano Estacado.

As a result of all this, fewer than half the Kiowas and Comanches settled on the reservation. The others grew so bold that they killed agency beef to feast on and ran off horses and mules from the herds around Fort Sill itself, built in 1869 to keep the tribes under control. The

Kwahadi even sent a message to the post saying that inasmuch as winter was coming, they would cease raiding until spring. "The white people," they jeered, "need not sit trembling in their tents, peering out to see if our warriors are coming. You can now send your horses out to graze, and your men out to chop wood."

Yet at that very time disasters from causes the Indians could not have anticipated were taking shape. One of these was an order in 1872 by General Philip Sheridan, Commander of the Department of the Missouri, concerning the Comancheros. "If hereafter such traders are found at any point east of the eastern line of New Mexico, their goods *will be burned and their stock killed.*" Patrols from forts in Texas jumped to oblige. Meanwhile a vigilante group of ninety Texans under a man named John Hittson roamed the ranches of eastern New Mexico, searching for stolen stock, seizing animals that looked suspicious to them, and roughing up anyone who protested.

Their arrogance culminated in a raid on squalid Loma Parda, an adobe town infamous for providing sex and booze to the soldiers of nearby Fort Union and for purchasing anything the troopers could pilfer from military wagon trains or the fort's well-stocked commissary. Loma Parda was also reputed to be a hangout for Comancheros. So Hittson invaded with a roaring shoot-up of the town's single street, during which the Texans wounded the *alcalde,* killed two Hispanos, and made off with several longhorns. This was too much even for Anglos who sympathized with the Texans. The U.S. district attorney rained down indictments, and the vigilantes departed, taking with them 6,000 cattle before anyone had had the opportunity to determine whether or not they really belonged in Texas.

The Hittson raids brought caution to the buyers of stolen cattle. Constant patrolling inhibited the Comancheros. The result was a reduced flow of supplies to the Indians at a time when they needed all the articles of warfare they could lay hold of.

Unprecedented numbers of buffalo hunters were invading the Texas Panhandle, an area that until then had served as an inviolate game refuge for the Indians. Two technological developments had combined to produce the stampede: the discovery of ways to tan buffalo hides so that the leather could be used for such things as belting in factories, and the arrival in 1873 of the Atchison, Topeka & Santa Fe Railroad at Fort Dodge in southern Kansas, an event that made huge shipments possible. Frantic with excitement over the thought of the profits waiting in the Panhandle—an estimated 2 million buffalo!—Kansas entrepreneurs hired hunters and skinners to risk the area, formed wagon trains to take in supplies and bring out hides on a regular schedule, and began building, out of sod turned up with heavy plows, plains-style company towns, complete with bunkhouses, stores, saloons, and blacksmith shops.

The first of these settlements, located on a small knoll four miles east of the ruins of the Bent brothers' Fort Adobe, was called Adobe Walls. Built in March 1874, it consisted of a straggle of buildings along a street 700 feet long, and was stocked by two competitors—A. C. Myers and Charles Rath—with $70,000 worth of food, clothing, ammunition, and whiskey.

Sensing well enough the threat to the way of life they were trying so hard to maintain, the Indians resented Adobe Walls bitterly. Two men urged an immediate attack. One was the great warrior-chief of the Kwahadi, Quanah, son of a Comanche brave and a captive white woman, Cynthia Ann Parker. The other, Isa-tai, whose name translates variously as Coyote Turds or Wolf's Ass, was a mystic who claimed such supernatural powers as the ability to render bullets powerless. Claims of that kind were common, and commonly believed, during times of Indian desperation, and Isa-tai's eager listeners were no exception. Their hour had come!

At dawn on June 27, 1874, they attacked. Numerically the odds were on their side—300 or so Comanches, Cheyennes, and a few Kiowas against twenty-seven white males and one white woman, Mrs. William Olds, wife of one of the hunters. The defenders were not without resources, however. They managed to distribute themselves among the community's three strongest buildings, the Rath and Myers stores and the sod-roofed saloon. And they were equipped with new, long-range, ultrapowerful buffalo rifles.

Isa-tai's medicine by no means deflected the bullets. No one could say, after the fight, how many casualties the Indians suffered, because they were able to retrieve the bodies of many of their dead and wounded. Not all, however. After the shooting ended late in the afternoon, the whites sallied out and cut the heads off eleven, twelve, or thirteen corpses (depending on who was telling the story), and impaled them on corral posts as clear messages to other ambitious Indians. A more arduous task turned out to be burying the many dead, potentially odorous horses that ringed the place. The defenders' casualties amounted to four killed, including William Olds, who in his excitement after the fight was over accidentally shot himself in the head.

Aching for revenge, the tribes scattered out from the Arkansas to the Pecos, striking at whatever targets offered. New Mexico suffered particularly. Scores of settlers, it was claimed, died in the Cimarron Valley alone.

The whites answered swiftly. Late in the summer of 1874 troops converged on the Panhandle from north, south, east, and west. Following examples inaugurated in the west by General Carleton, they struck as ruthlessly at property as at people. The Comanches alone lost 7,500 horses, 1,400 of them in one swoop to Colonel Ranald Mackenzie's Fourth Cavalry from Fort Concho, Texas. Thousands of tipis and tons of dried buffalo meat were destroyed—and without horses how could that essential material be replaced? Despairing as the winter cold deepened, the Comanches and Kiowas began drifting toward the reservation to surrender. Though there would be sporadic outbreaks during the next few years, the forays sputtered out in hopelessness when the Indians realized, during a hunt they were permitted to make in 1878, that two million buffalo had vanished. Only the white man's way of life remained.

## Ferocity

Apache. So many stereotypes have clustered around the word that it is hard now to recapture the terror it brought a century ago to persons like young Martha Summerhayes, riding, derringer in hand, through the Arizona mountains with her infant son in a light horse-drawn ambulance. Nothing in her experience had prepared her for this. Her genteel Puritan-Quaker upbringing had been topped off by a year abroad in the glittering household of a retired, socially prominent German general. On returning to the United States in 1874, she had married her fiancé, Second Lieutenant John Summerhayes—she called him Jack, of course, and he called her Mattie—and then had moved across the continent to start housekeeping at Camp Apache, Arizona, the fort guarding the White River Reservation. There, her home was one half of a small log cabin with a detached shed for a kitchen. Her "domestic" was an enlisted man; he was devoted but of no great shakes during the arrival of her baby, the first white ever born at the fort. She was still exhausted and depressed when the orders came transferring her husband to a different station.

Their cavalcade was small: two lieutenants, each with a wife and small child, two "ambulances" (light wagons with tops and side curtains) for them to travel in, two freight wagons, a Mexican guide, and six soldiers. After they had traveled too far to turn back, they were told that marauding Apaches had recently attacked other travelers in a strategic pass just ahead.

Martha had been equipped for such contingencies. "I wore a small derringer with a narrow belt filled with cartridges." But she had not truly understood what the little pistol was for until her husband made her and the baby lie down out of sight in the ambulance and then told her, "You have your derringer. . . . *Don't let them get either of you alive"* (her italics).

Lying there, shaken by the roughness of the road, ears straining, she took the weapon from its holster and, she remembered, cocked it, which from this distance seems an injudicious thing to have done in a jouncing wagon. And for unmeasured minutes she watched the baby's "delicate temples, lined with blue veins." Could she?

The test did not come. Safely out in the open beside the Little Colorado River, the travelers halted, and the husbands made the trembling young women swallow warm whiskey diluted with canteen water. "I believe we cried just a little."

One wonders: How would young Apache mothers have described their fears after the following incident, which occurred in 1871? Ulysses S. Grant had become President two years before and had inaugurated his famed peace policy for dealing with the Indians. The commanding general of the Department of Arizona was given orders henceforth to treat the Apaches with "moral suasion and kindness, looking toward their Christianization," and to set up "feeding stations" where the Indians could come for rations while awaiting the establishment of permanent reservations.

This official policy was very much in the mind of Lieutenant Royal Emerson Whitman when he reached Camp Grant beside the San Pedro River late in 1870. Not long after his arrival, five elderly, half-starved Apache women came into the post seeking information about the son of one of them who had been taken prisoner. Whitman was unable to provide the information, but he could give kindness and food. The word spread and more Indians drifted in until there were perhaps five hundred on hand. About sixty were warriors.

Whitman established an unofficial reservation for them, passed out food every two or three days, and found employment for both men and women cutting hay at the post and on nearby ranches. Results were so salutary that when the group asked permission to move to a traditional campground five miles away in Aravaipa Canyon, he complied.

Certain citizens of Tucson watched the coddling, as they called it, with rage. One was William Oury, a fire-breathing Virginian who had gone to Texas with Moses Austin, had fought at San Jacinto under Sam Houston, had ridden with the Texas Rangers during the tumultuous forties, and in 1849 had joined the gold stampede to California. After moving to Tucson in 1856 he had served as town mayor and county sheriff, the latter a job that afforded him an opportunity for a bit of embezzlement revolving around the sale of county guns to the Mexican state of Sonora. He was quick to believe—or at least to say—that two Apache raids that hit southern Arizona during the spring of 1871 were the work of the band sheltered at Camp Grant.

Operating in conjunction with Jesús Elías, one of Tucson's representatives in the territorial legislature, Oury assembled a task force whose composition guaranteed ferocity. Ninety-four of its members were Papago Indians; forty-eight were Tucson Hispanos. The heritage of hatred that both groups held for Apaches ran back through the centuries. Six members of the expedition, including Oury, were Anglos. Why so few Americans joined in for the sport is unknown. However, the adjutant general of the territory, who was an Anglo, did furnish guns, ammunition, food, and a wagon in which to carry the supplies.

The "memorable and glorious morning of April 30, 1871," as Oury later described it, began with a dawn attack on the sleeping camp in Aravaipa Canyon. Most of the Apache men were away on a hunting trip. In a matter of minutes Oury's avengers had clubbed, knifed, stabbed, shot, and chopped an unknown number of Indians to death. Several women were raped. Oury put the death toll at 144. The stunned Whitman, who hurried up with medical help as soon as he heard of the assault, estimated the number of corpses at 125. Other reports reduced the total to 85. Whatever the figure, only 8 of the dead were men; the rest were women and children. Another 29 children were seized and dragged away to be sold into slavery. At President Grant's insistence, the perpetrators were tried for murder. After deliberating nineteen minutes, a Tucson jury found them not guilty.

Derringers, anyone?

During the decade following the Mexican War, American relations with the Apaches, though by no means unruffled, had been more amiable than those with the Navajos and Comanches. The desert Indians felt a kinship with the Anglos: Both fought Mexicans. Even after the Americans insisted the war was over, the Apaches stayed relatively quiet and offered no serious objection to the cattle ranchers and prospectors who flowed into the Gadsden Purchase lands after 1855. As was noted earlier, some Apaches took to farming under Anglo tutelage at Fort Webster in New Mexico, and they agreed not to molest the stagecoaches of the Butterfield Line when they began running through their hunting grounds in 1859. Indeed, Cochise, a chief of the Chiricahua band that roamed the jagged hills of Arizona's southeastern corner, even held a contract to supply the stage station in Apache Pass near the New Mexican border with firewood. (Chiricahua, incidentally, is pronounced Cheer-ee-CAH-wah, which Anglos soon twisted into Cherrycow.)

Yet conflict was bound to come in time. Frontier America had marched west with a centuries-old policy of getting inconvenient Indians out of the way by whatever means opportunity and the government's loose check reins allowed. The Apaches on their part had held Spaniards and Mexicans at bay for just as long and were supremely confident that they could handle these new intruders just as efficiently.

The most serious of the early conflicts revolved around chief Cochise of the Chiricahuas and his father-in-law, Mangas Coloradas ("Red Sleeves"). Some Anglos, heads tilted back, swore that Mangas towered six and a half feet tall, a phenomenal height among the short-statured Apaches. He was the headman of the Mimbreños, a band that lived around the upper reaches of the Mimbres River in western New Mexico and was closely allied with the Chiricahuas.

In the spring of 1860, gold discoveries at Pinos Altos, on the crest of the Continental Divide six miles north of present-day Silver City, New Mexico, drew several miners into the region. Hoping to get rid of them, Mangas Coloradas rode into their camp with false rumors of a better gold area some distance away. Divining his motives and hungry to break the monotony of their digging, the whites seized the chief, bound and flogged him. Most of southern New Mexico suffered from the retaliatory raids that followed.

Not long thereafter, in February 1861, Cochise had a confrontation of his own with soldiers under Lieutenant George Bascom at the stage station the Apaches supplied with wood. Bascom wanted information about a kidnapped child and believed, mistakenly, that Cochise could provide the data if he would. Each side seized hostages in an effort to force its views on the other. After a few days of shouted long-distance haggling, Cochise killed and mutilated the Anglos he held. The American soldiers retorted by hanging their Apache hostages, many of whom were related to Cochise. Meanwhile, lumbermen working some distance away in the mountains behind Tucson helped a delegation of Mexican ranchers from Sonora ambush a party of Apaches driving three hundred stolen horses and mules. For this the lumbermen received half the stolen animals. Again spirals of revenge flared up.

The furies intensified with the withdrawal of federal troops at the beginning of the Civil War. The former Spanish presidial town of Tubac south of Tucson was besieged. Mines were devastated, ranches abandoned. Cried one excited reporter: "The horribly mutilated bodies of men, women, and children marked nearly every mile of the road to the Rio Grande. The blaze from many a comfortable home, and the agonizing shrieks of the victims, and the fiendish yells of the red demons, were the sights and sounds throughout the Gadsden Purchase."

The approach of Carleton's troops from California in no wise awed the Apaches. Putting together an exceptionally large force of 700 warriors in June 1862, Mangas Coloradas and Cochise ambushed an advanced detachment of 126 soldiers escorting 22 wagons through Apache Pass, where the slaying of the hostages had occurred sixteen months before. Fortunately for themselves, the Californians, like Kit Carson's New Mexico volunteers at Adobe Walls, had two mountain howitzers with them. Shells lobbed against the mountainsides by the little cannons killed 63 of the 66 Indians who died in the battle. The whites lost two men.

The unexpected resistance led General Carleton to place Fort Bowie in the pass, to the outrage of the Indians, and to send Brigadier General Joseph West into the mountains that straddle the New Mexico-Arizona border with orders to protect the miners there, about a quarter of whom were soldiers to whom Carleton had granted leaves so that they could prospect the area. To General West protection involved, as a corollary, Carleton's so-called extermination order: Kill the men and imprison the women and children—unless they consent to go to Bosque Redondo with the Mescalero Apaches and the Navajos.

About twenty Mimbreños (also identified in the records as Gila or Warm Springs Apaches) did consent, but for the most part West preferred extermination. He set his sights on Mangas Coloradas. Somehow, and it is not likely that the exact methods will ever be known, he lured the chief to a peace parley and seized him. According to the general's official report, during the night of January 19, 1863, the big old chief ("a murderous Indian," West called him) made a break for freedom and was killed in the ensuing fight, "his life clearly forfeited by all laws either human or divine. The good faith of the U.S. military authorities was in no way compromised."

But Daniel Connor, a prospector who was in the area at the time, and Clark Stocking, a soldier of dubious reliability, told different stories. Although their versions vary in details, both agree that Mangas Coloradas was deliberately goaded into resistance and then shot down while unarmed and helpless. When these charges leaked out, one angry judge from Mesilla, who was a dedicated enemy of Carleton's, railed at the general, "You have taken no steps to call the authors of these crimes to account," with obvious results. "It has prevented the Indians from surrendering themselves [to go to the Bosque] and has led them to revenge."

And on the dreary story went. Daniel Connor's prospecting party—thirty-three miners led by famed mountain man Joseph Reddeford Walker, then sixty-four years old, snow white of hair, and tough as a mesquite root—drifted on west. Entering the mountains just south of present Prescott, Arizona, in the spring of 1863 they found the gold for which they had searched so long. Other strikes followed quickly, notably Henry Wickenburg's bonanza Vulture claim, which he sold for $85,000 to a corporation that took $20 million preinflation dollars from it. A stampede developed and clashes straightway followed with the Tonto Apaches who claimed the area.

Hunting Indians became a local sport. One noted leader of the expeditions (he was officially commended by the first Arizona legislative assembly for his exploits) was thick-bearded King S. Woolsey. Once while tracking stolen cattle in a steep canyon with a posse of Anglos and Maricopa Indians, Woolsey encountered a large band of well-armed Apaches. After a tense confrontation, he persuaded their leaders to meet him halfway between the opposing lines for a parley. As soon as the Apaches' attention was distracted, he signaled for his men to open fire —a swift bit of carnage that netted the Maricopas twenty-four Apache scalps. And it was all justifiable, said Daniel Connor, who was along. The Apaches were contemplating treachery, and the group that struck first was the group that would survive.

Outrage in the East over such attacks, principally the one at Camp Grant, led Washington to call for new directions. One of the country's best Indian fighters, fierce-whiskered, crop-haired Lieutenant Colonel George Crook, was jumped over the head of several dozen jealous colonels to the rank of brigadier general and sent to Arizona to handle the military side of affairs. He assumed command on June 4, 1871. Simultaneously President Grant dispatched an inflexible Quaker humanitarian, Vincent Colyer, secretary of the United States Board of Indian Commissioners, to the same territory to devise a workable system of reservations for the different bands of Apaches. Colyer arrived by way of New Mexico on September 2, 1871, and ordered military operations to pause while he tried his hand.

He was not greeted warmly. Many Arizonans were former Confederates, and during the Civil War, Colyer, a Union supporter and ardent admirer of John Brown, had served as the colonel of a Negro regiment. The Prescott *Miner* recommended throwing him down a mine shaft and piling rocks on him. "A rascal who comes here to thwart the efforts of military and citizens to conquer a peace from our savage foe, deserves to be stoned to death like the black-hearted dog he is." Nevertheless, the Quaker was Grant's personal representative. Crook had to yield to him, and while the citizens fumed, Colyer toured the centers of disturbance and in time outlined four reservations for the different bands of Apaches. The only group he neglected, because he was unable to meet with its leaders, were the Chiricahuas, but the oversight was remedied a few months later by another peace commission representative, one-armed General O. O. Howard.

Thus by early 1872 the Apaches had available five sizable reservations: Camp Verde in central Arizona beside the Verde River; Fort Apache, north of the Salt River in east-central Arizona; San Carlos, due south of the Salt; Chiricahua in the southeast corner of the territory; and Warm Springs in west-central New Mexico for the Mimbreños. And by 1872 the Mescaleros of eastern New Mexico who had fled from Bosque Redondo had also been granted a reservation on the slopes of the Sacramento Mountains.

Few people in Arizona (Crook among them) believed that the Apaches, no matter what they had told Colyer, would voluntarily submit to being penned. Accordingly, the general had employed his time during the peace negotiations to studying the rugged terrain of his command. Having thoroughly learned the area, he set up a supply system of mule trains in place of wagons and inaugurated the practice of employing Apache scouts (like most tribes the Apaches were riven by factionalism) to aid the troops in tracking down the enemy. When the outrages he expected occurred, he was ready. A remorseless, masterful campaign crushed the Tonto Basin groups and so sobered most of the other bands that by the end of 1873 roughly 5,000 Apaches had straggled into the different reserves, saying that they were willing to submit.

At that point John P. Clum, aged twenty-two and one of the extraordinary whites in the history of American-Indian relations, appeared on the scene. He obtained his job largely through default. The board of religious leaders responsible under President Grant's peace policy for appointing honest, devout agents at minimal salaries to supervise the country's Indian reservations was having a hard time enlisting qualified candidates. Clum, however, was eager, confident, and faintly familiar with the Southwest after a brief stay in Santa Fe. Under the circumstances his youth could be overlooked, and he was put in charge of San Carlos, the largest of the five Apache reservations. He arrived there in

August 1873, brimful of ideas certain to enrage the people with whom he would have to work.

Legally the agents had complete control of civil affairs on the reservations, and the army appeared only when called on to handle military matters. In practice, however, the troops ran affairs to suit themselves. Their control allowed a nefarious union to develop between lesser officers, willing noncoms, and a grafting group of civilian supply contractors known as the Tucson Ring. An effective agent would upset this merry-go-round, and effective is just what Clum turned out to be. The stripling not only declined to call on the army for any kind of cooperation, but announced—as jaws dropped dumbfounded all over Arizona—that he would run his San Carlos agency with no other help than that furnished by the Indians themselves.

He thoroughly enjoyed his situation. Perhaps in compensation for his slight stature (he was five feet six inches and thin as a splinter), he strutted around in fringed buckskin shirts, a heavy cartridge belt, and whatever odd headgear he could locate. But if he was impudent, he was also daring and original. He gave the San Carlos Apaches an opportunity to speak their minds through representatives they elected to an advisory council he instituted. He established an Apache police force and had the Indian malefactors they arrested tried in a court presided over by himself and an associated Apache judge. He pressed farm work successfully and made happy social occasions out of the issuing of rations. His wards became devoted to him.

Unhappily for his program, efficiency experts in Washington decided that expenses could be pared if the Apaches were concentrated on a single reservation rather than spread out over five. Hot, dusty San Carlos was the reservation chosen. General Crook, who was on the point of leaving Arizona now that peace had apparently been achieved, predicted disaster. Under the new plan Indians who had worked hard to create farms on their original reserves would have to exchange them for uncleared land in a less propitious environment. Moreover, the different bands of Apaches were not always friendly, and the crowded situation on the new reservation would almost surely awaken frictions.

The concentration went ahead, nevertheless. Clum labored diligently to further it, using his Apache police rather than the military to escort the confused, unhappy tribesmen to their new home. Personal ambition was involved. After successfully bringing to San Carlos 450 rebellious Mimbreños from the Warm Springs agency in New Mexico, along with a few renegade Chiricahuas under Geronimo, the young agent notified the commissioner of Indian affairs, "If your department will increase my salary sufficiently and equip two more companies of Indian police, I will volunteer to take care of all Apaches—and the troops can be removed." By that time, June 1877, he was twenty-five years old and had 4,200 Indians under his control.

Neither the army, nor the merchants associated with the army, nor the citizens who were still terrified of the Apaches wanted the troops to leave. A great howl went up. Clum's offer was ignored, and he resigned. The degeneration of relations with the Apaches that followed was hastened by the discovery of gold and silver in the outlying parts of the reservation. The Indians' territory was nibbled away and given to the whites. Goods intended for the reservation were diverted to the miners. The rations the natives did receive were almost inedible and insufficient for maintaining health. Epidemics sapped the Indians' morale as well as their strength, and white contractors, eager to keep the Indians from achieving any semblance of self-sufficiency, reputedly hired thugs to destroy the pathetic crops before they could be harvested.

What followed should have been predictable. Bold leaders, most of them Mimbreños and Chiricahuas, took to breaking out of the reservation. With their followers—men, women, and children—they resumed their raiding in a despairing effort to stay alive with dignity, as they saw dignity. The whites went into a frenzy, the Tucson press crying out for unremitting war "until every valley and crest and crag and fastness shall send to high heaven the grateful incense of festering and rotting Chiricahuas."

Victorio, Nana (who was seventy-three), Juh (pronounced Ho), Nachez, Geronimo—their names have become part of western fable, and with reason. Every bit of craft they had went into this last effort of theirs. They could ride a hundred miles a day, carrying their water in thirty-foot tubes of animal intestines coiled around the body of a pack horse. The bigger cavalry horses of the pursuing Americans could not keep up with them in the rough country they chose as refuge. When crowded hard, they killed and ate their horses and slipped away afoot until they could steal new mounts. They fouled the water holes on which their pursuers had to depend with feces and decaying animal corpses.

Victorio, who never had more than 300 people with him—including women and children—killed close to 400 Americans and Mexicans before he was finally cornered in the mountains of Chihuahua and killed, along with more than 80 of his followers, by Mexican forces. Aged Nana broke free during the battle and with 30 warriors and their families cut a bloody, thousand-mile swath northward into the United States, slaying upward of 30 pursuers before attrition forced him to go to San Carlos and surrender to General Crook, who had been recalled to handle the situation.

As the outbreaks continued, 5,000 soldiers—almost one quarter of the United States Army—were concentrated in southern Arizona and southern New Mexico. Apache scouts, many of them former members of John Clum's Indian police force, were employed to do the tracking the whites could not handle and proved as hot as tigers on the trails of their own people. Permission was gained from Mexico to carry pursuit across the border when necessary. General Nelson Miles replaced Crook, who was considered too lenient for this final thrust. Under the new commander's distant and somewhat vainglorious direction, picked troops invaded the Indians' hitherto untouched stronghold in Sonora during the spring of 1886 and brought the last holdouts to bay—two dozen starved men, women, and children under Geronimo.

Most white residents of Arizona wanted the prisoners tried in the territorial courts for murder, with the outcome a foregone conclusion. The government was more compassionate—by a hair. All Mimbreños and Chiricahuas, even peaceful ones, even some of the scouts who had helped run Geronimo down, were exiled to Florida. There and, later, in Alabama, in climates completely debilitating to them, they led a miserable existence until 1894, when those still alive were transferred to Fort Sill, Oklahoma. Some, Geronimo among them, spent the rest of their days there. In 1913, 107 others, a figure that includes descendants of the original exiles, were permitted to go to the Mescalero reservation in New Mexico. Officially, though in some cases not actually, that was as close to their old homes as they ever got.

## The Cultural Conflict

While the last rebellious Apaches were still being driven from their mountain strongholds, the government in Washington decided that if Indians in general were to be assimilated into white society (and no one at the time seriously questioned that they should be), they would have to be pitched headfirst into the American mainstream and learn to swim by swimming.

The logic went like this. What factors gave America its Americanness? One essential, it was widely agreed, was the ownership of property. Landholders took care of their acreage, were stable, industrious, responsible, and civic-minded. Another factor was the spreading system of public education, its curricula designed to bring home to every student the values that sustained the dominant culture. A third was Christianity, preferably, during the nineteenth century, the Protestant version. Once the Indians had become educated Christian propertyholders, it was believed, tribal solidarity would dissolve, leaving each red individual free to enter into the American way of life.

In 1887 this theory became the basis for a national law known as the General Allotment Act. To oversimplify its complexities, the act provided that reservations would be terminated and each tribal member given a piece of land. The size of the plot (the maximum was 160 acres) would vary according to use, whether farming or grazing, and according to the age of the recipient. (Children received smaller pieces than adults, but everyone got something.) The government would hold this land in trust for twenty-five years, during which period the owner would presumably learn to manage his acreage without being cheated of it by eager speculators. At the end of the trust period he would be granted not just an unencumbered patent to the land but also the privileges of full citizenship in the United States.

The small size of the plots guaranteed that at the end of the division a considerable amount of reservation land would remain unassigned. This "surplus," as it was called, was to be sold to white bidders, a provision that ensured widespread support for the bill. Proceeds from the sales were to be deposited at 3 percent interest in the United States Treasury and the increment used for the benefit of the tribes concerned. The government had the sole power of deciding what constituted a benefit.

Like most of the reservations in Indian Territory (soon to become Oklahoma), the Comanche-Kiowa reserve was eliminated by the General Allotment Act. Elsewhere in the Southwest, Indian lands either held so little attraction for speculators or, in the case of the Pueblos, were so well protected by Spanish grants that only about 3 percent of the holdings were alienated. Indeed, while the rest of the country was losing reservations, the Southwest gained them. The Papagos were granted 2.77 million acres in 1916, and the original Navajo reserve of 3.5 million acres kept expanding until it now embraces 15 million acres in New Mexico, Arizona, and southern Utah.

Still, it is not beside the point to mention the kind of disruptive impact the Allotment Act exerted where it was applied. For example, the Hopis. Desirous of luring them off their overcrowded mesas, the government during the early 1890s promised to build new houses for those who moved onto allotted land. But the Hopi clans were accustomed to working communally and to moving their fields from place to place as circumtances suggested. One group that wanted to plant land assigned to certain individuals near the villages of Oraibi and Moenkopi tore up the survey stakes marking the plots and drove the "owners" away. Informed of the difficulty, the Hopi agent arrived with troops, arrested nineteen of the "aggressors," and had them imprisoned for seven months on Alcatraz Island in far-off San Francisco Bay. For such reasons, land allotments languished in the Southwest, reservations remained largely intact, and no white holdings speckled the Indian lands like measles.

But if land allotments in the Southwest were minimal, the rest of the government's Americanization program went ahead full steam. As in Spanish times, native religious celebrations and healing ceremonies were so scorned and harassed, that they survived only by going underground. The Apaches' favorite home-brew, *tiswin*, was ruthlessly prohibited. Some Anglo supervisors grew almost paranoid about long hair as a symbol of Indian intransigence. One Mescalero agent bribed his Indian police with extra rations to trim their locks and then sent them out to force compliance from the others. Hard labor awaited those who resisted. Results, the agent reported, were worth severity: "The task of moving them upwards [i.e., civilizing them] has been perceptibly easier from the time scissors clipped off their wildness."

Health measures could be disruptive. At one point whites believed that lice were spreading disease through the Hopi town of Hotavila. Men, women, and children were forcibly rounded up, taken to an earthen vat filled with sheep-dip, and ordered to strip and immerse themselves in the stuff while their clothing was boiled. The women resisted with what the agent described as "pure unadulterated fanatical perversity" and had to be forced, by agency males, into the vat with physical violence. The program was a success, nevertheless, "the only objectionable feature [being] the obscene and revolting vituperations the Indian women hurled at the employees."

Schools were especially detested. Because roads were bad and distances great, children were often required to board at the institution they attended. Boarding also removed them from the baleful influence of their families. It was easier then to force the boys into trousers, the girls into coarse uniforms, to cut the boys' hair, and order everyone to speak only English, even on the playgrounds. The Indian children may have found some vocational classes in sewing, woodworking, and the like helpful to them, but they learned the academic subjects by rote from textbooks that had been prepared for white children and had little relevance to their life on the reservation, where, heaven knows, the tribe were already bewildered enough.

When the opening of the school year neared, parents who needed the children's help at home and who believed that white education served only to erode cherished values often tried to hide the young ones. Soon the absences were noticed. The agent then marched on the offending village with troops, pried out information by seizing hostages, conducted slam-bang searches, and forced traumatic separations. Adult male obstructionists were often punished by being put to work on road gangs.

As soon as the children were away from home they were led to believe that their Indianness was an offense. Inevitably they ended up being torn between two worlds; this was particularly true of the students who by one means or another were persuaded to attend Indian schools and colleges at such distant places as Riverside, California, and Carlisle, Pennsylvania. When they returned home with short hair and in Anglo clothing, they were derided by their peers. Those who had been converted to white religions were sometimes reluctant to join native ceremonies. According to Walter Minge, historian of the pueblo, a Acoma holdouts were horsewhipped until they did participate. For such young people, where was home?

As far as the Indians were concerned, the center of white dominance was the headquarters compound of the agent (later called the superintendent) who ran reservation affairs according to rules sent him from on high. It was a miniature satrapy. To it came huge freight wagons laden with food, clothing, and equipment that eventually would be doled out to the subservient people. Here were the agency police station, sometimes a military barracks, a hospital, the Christian church, the boarding school. Here, too, were the living quarters and workshops of the agency farmer, blacksmith, carpenter, and home economics matron, all of them charged with teaching white crafts by force of example.

More appealing to the Indians was the store of the agency trader which was crowded to the rafters with groceries, bolts of cloth, lanterns, tools, cutlery, harnesses, and saddles. Trading posts were also located in outlying districts. The Indians gathered in the stores to sip coffee, gossip, and dicker. After buying candy out of glass-topped display cases for the children and perhaps tobacco for themselves, they pointed wordlessly with their chins toward whatever item they could afford and then studied it with tedious care after the trader had moved it from its shelf to the counter. Often a good trader exerted more influence than either the superintendent or missionary. By extending credit to his Indian customers (his security for loans consisted of silver and turquoise jew elry that he called "pawn"), he tided them over recurrent economic emergencies until they could pay their debts by bringing him their limited output of raw wool, woven blankets, pottery, and even piñon nuts. By teaching the Indians to adapt their crafts to the desires of the growing number of tourists in the Southwest, he not only expanded the market for Indian goods but also brought to both red men and whites a broader understanding of each other's cultures.

Dishonest traders existed, but generally not for long; without the trust of the Indians they could not succeed. Agents, however, were appointed by the federal government on the basis of political pull, not ability. By dispensing the jobs within their control to complaisant men, they created their own little machines. Some were crooked in picayune ways, but that flaw was flaccid compared to the rigor mortis of their imaginations. Even agents who were devoted to their charges, as many were, found no gain in being innovative or farsighted, or in questioning the policies they were directed to enforce. They ordered; the Indians obeyed. Inevitably so inflexible a program debilitated native leadership and turned initiative and self-respect into sullenness and apathy.

The stagnation could not last. The trigger that helped end it was the increasingly brazen manipulation of the General Allotment Act by hungry land grabbers. Between 1887 and the early 1920s they had scooped up about 90 million acres of former reservation holdings throughout the United States. In the Southwest, the ingenuity of the speculators was epitomized by Albert B. Fall, wealthy New Mexico rancher, United States senator and, during the early 1920s, President Harding's Secretary of the Interior, a position that gave him control of Indian affairs. Fall sought to invade the Mescalero Apache Reservation by using as an opening wedge a bill that would turn part of the area into a National Park, with the edges going—well, such things could be arranged. Fall's shadow was also visible behind Congress's notorious Bursum bill, which, had it passed, would have given outright title to several squatters on Pueblo Indian land. But the action that really shook Santa Fe's artistic and intellectual community was the secretary's acquiescence in a missionary-supported bill designed, through government directive, to phase out Indian religious dances.

Angry protests from New Mexico swelled the national complaints about mismanagement already emanating from such organizations as the Indian Welfare League under May Adams. In 1924, partly to reward their participation in World War I and partly to assure their religious freedom (including their right to perform religious dances), the country conferred full citizenship on the Indians, whether they owned land or not. (Backward Mexico had granted citizenship to all Indians exactly one century earlier.) This major step was followed by sweeping investigations of the country's Indian programs. The proposals that resulted were quickly adopted by the social experimenters of Franklin Roosevelt's New Deal.

The chief legal instrument used in establishing the new order was the Indian Reorganization Act of 1934. It abolished land allotments, but more importantly it opened the way to tribal self-government based on written constitutions. These constitutions, prepared with the advice of Anglo administrators, were modeled on the Constitution of the United States and empowered the enfranchised adults of the tribes concerned to elect representatives to governing councils. Henceforth the councils would play leading parts in formulating and administering tribal policy.

It is difficult for Anglos to imagine how drastically the step cut across Indian cultural patterns. Though variations existed between the many tribes, it is generally true that government had been a function of the different bands, not of the tribe as a whole. Decision, furthermore, was based on consensus, not on majority rule. If a consensus could not be reached, dissidents split away from the main band to form new units of their own. Several Hopi villages, for instance, were created within the present century by just such atomization.

Even so, by the second decade of the twentieth century, Indians were beginning to realize the advantages of tribal political unity. When oil was discovered on the Navajo reservation in 1921, the Secretary of the Interior ruled that the money obtained from leasing drilling rights to outside corporations should be used for the benefit of every Navajo. This decree led the reservation superintendent to appoint delegates from each major district on the reserve to a deliberative council, and although this body met only at his call, it was a move toward political unification. So, too, was the ad hoc All-Pueblo Council formed in 1922 to fight the Bursum bill mentioned above. Nevertheless, the idea of representative government remained largely incomprehensible to the people whom it would affect.

Being alien, the idea was also suspect. When the proposal was offered to the Hopis in 1935, the traditionalists among them rejected it out of hand as another devious attempt by Anglos to assert dominance over their daily lives. When the issue was voted on, they boycotted the polls. As a result the measure passed, but since it was without their consent, there are some Hopis who to this day insist that the tribal council has no right to speak for them.

Alone among the nearly fifty southwestern tribes (this count considers each New Mexican pueblo as a separate entity), the Navajos voted down the constitution proffered them. Timing was partly responsible. Without consulting the women of the tribe (though in Navajoland they are the owners of livestock), New Deal soil conservationists ordered a sharp reduction in the number of sheep and horses herded on the badly overgrazed range. Sensing the Indians' resistance, the conservationists belatedly tried to explain the reason for the program in the seventy-four chapter houses that in 1927 had been scattered across the reservation to aid in the dissemination of information—another force, incidentally, pointing toward unity. But this time it wasn't the kind of unity the advisers wanted. Their pride and pocketbooks hurt by the livestock reduction, the Navajos found revenge, when the government's constitution was presented to them in the same chapter houses, by resoundingly defeating it. Then, drawing legitimacy from the 1868 treaty that had ended the Bosque Redondo experiment, they shrewdly formed their own governing council. Though it operates much as all the others do, it is *theirs*, and because the authority for it reaches back to what the Anglos themselves had said, in the preamble to the treaty, was an agreement between sovereign powers, the newly unified tribe proudly claimed to be uniquely a Nation within a Nation, part of the United States, yet separate and distinct, with full rights of self-determination. So do chickens come home to roost.

Actually, through their constitutions and councils, all the tribes exercise sovereign powers roughly comparable to those of the major municipalities and states of the union. Their courts hold jurisdiction over civil matters on the reservations and over criminal affairs not specifically reserved to the federal government. They can sue the federal government over inequities in the taking of their lands during bygone times and have done so with ardor, collecting heavy damages. They have powers of taxation over tribal members (they also determine who is a tribal member, an important point because of frequent intermarriages through the years), and they are able to contract with outsiders for a multitude of services, most especially those relating to Indian education off the reservations.

More than half the young Indians of the Southwest now attend public schools supervised by state and county entities, but financed in part by the tribes whose children use the facilities. The rest attend on-reservation missionary schools and day and boarding schools that are run either by the Bureau of Indian Affairs or by the tribes themselves. At Tsaile, Arizona, the Navajos have founded America's first Indian-owned college on an Indian reservation, with an architecturally unique campus dominated by a six-story, six-sided tower of pink glass. Instead of ignoring Indian culture, most of these schools now emphasize it. Earnest attempts are being made to train and recruit Indian teachers. Both the Bureau of Indian Affairs and the tribal governments support extensive scholarship programs that send students to outside colleges, and although the recipients of the aid are urged to bring the expertise they acquire back to the reservations, there is no requirement that they do so.

Next to education the most important phase of a tribal council's work is the stimulation of economic activity. Barter has been almost entirely replaced by a money economy, yet there are not many job opportunities on the reservations. For years young people have been drifting away to nearby towns or sometimes distant cities in search of employment. The trend was quickened by the national manpower shortage during World War II and, later, by the federal government's "relocation" program, which helped finance Indians seeking jobs off the reservation.

Can the dichotomy be partly healed by creating jobs at home? The hurdles are manifold. The Indians are starting from substandard bases. Unemployment among them far exceeds the national averages. In spite of yeoman work by the U.S. Public Health Service, health standards are low. School dropout figures are high. There is no backlog of experience to guide Indians who would like to start businesses of their own. All tribal lands, moreover, are held in trust by the federal government. Consequently a would-be entrepreneur must lease the property on which he wishes to build his filling station, store, trailer park, or whatever. This means reviews by the local community, the tribe, and the federal government, resulting in delays that sometimes stretch out across three or four years and entail paperwork often beyond the capabilities of the applicant to handle.

The result has been the formation, in this land of free, individualistic enterprise, of several cooperative and communally run ventures. Arts and craft guilds push native handiwork in attractive, tribally financed stores. The Apache tribe, rather than Apache individuals, maintains elaborate inns, hunting lodges, and ski resorts for white recreationists. The Apache and Navajo governments keep lumber mills humming. Apaches and Papagos operate communally owned cattle herds. The most populous tribe in the United States (with an estimated 150,000 persons in 1978 and a tribal budget of scores of millions of dollars), the Navajos have their own newspaper, utility corporation, highway department, and, currently, one of the most ambitious agribusiness programs ever

ndertaken by any people anywhere. Using an ultrasophisticated irriga-
on system and housing their workers in specially built towns, they are
ying to put into production within ten years, 110,000 acres of raw
agebrush land in northwestern New Mexico.

Income from established projects is plowed back into those still
nder development, as are royalty payments from coal, oil, and ura-
ium leases. Still more money comes as donations and loans from
everal agencies of the United States government. Not all the track
cords have been impressive—and in this connection it is well to
ote that top managerial posts have generally gone to hired Anglo
xperts. Some years ago, for instance, the Mescalero Apaches bor-
owed money from the U.S. government to finance the building of a
ush resort for Anglo vacationists in the pine-scented Sacramento
ountains above Ruidoso, New Mexico. By 1978 the project was said
be $12 million in debt. The accuracy of the figure, however, cannot
determined. The Mescaleros will not let government auditors in-
ect the inn's books, saying that even though Washington put up
uch of the original money, operational details are solely Apache
usiness. Concurrently, outside inspectors were reporting that the
nancial affairs of the parent corporation of the gargantuan Navajo
rigation project were in disarray.

Supporters of the Indian efforts refuse to take alarm. These are
ootstrap operations, they say, and the Indians, like Anglos who have
umbled, will learn from trial and error. And at least the slips will be
eirs instead of a repetition of gross errors inflicted on them over the
enturies by outsiders.

Red ink is not the heart of the problem, anyway. A profound cultural
ruggle is involved. Many Indians think that the threat to their tribal
tegrity is much greater now than during the days when Anglo-
ominated individuals were forced to cut their hair and speak only En-
lish on the playgrounds. They say that their dependence on the govern-
ent for financing of all kinds is as great and as degrading as when they
sed to line up for handouts of food. They see their tribal constitutions
d councils as transitional devices to get them used to Anglo-style
overnment. And the business operations, however communally run,
ey regard as thinly disguised ploys to woo them into the alien world
Anglo economic procedures. Meanwhile they are very aware of the
lls continually being presented in Congress to terminate the reserva-
ons; give them, as the high-sounding phrase has it, "the privileges and
sponsibilities common to all other Americans"; and then turn them
ose in a society whose competitive goals and nature-conquering atti-

tudes they do not like and are not prepared by temperament, trainin or background to meet.

To this dark view other Indians retort that only by adaptation rath than surrender to the dominant society can they achieve true self-go ernment and the economic independence to make that government wor Then, and then only, can they remain Indians—true to their heritag without sacrificing their claims to the future.

Are the proponents of compromise right? Can the adaptations wor without destroying what they are designed to save? Is the risk worth tl social disruptions it entails? At this point no Anglo, and possibly ı Indian, can offer a realistic prediction.

# 7

## A SAMPLING OF ROGUES

*Background to Violence*

In 1878 President Rutherford B. Hayes of the United States sent a special agent, Judge Frank Warner Angel, to New Mexico to investigate a reputed reign of terror. Angel was so agitated by what he found that his rhetoric suffered.

"It is seldom," he wrote in his preliminary report of October 3, "that history states more corruption, fraud, mismanagement, plots and murders than New Mexico has been the theater under the administration of Governor Axtell."

Nor was New Mexico alone in receiving presidential attention. In 1882 Chester Arthur issued a special proclamation ordering Arizonans to give over their evil ways. And so questions arise. What factors underlay the eruptions of violence in the Southwest following the Civil War? Why were local authorities so helpless in dealing with the criminal element?

A variety of explanations have been offered. One theory relates casual murder to a lethal combination of readily available, cheap whiskey and improved pistols that did not misfire during brawls. Others have found antipathy toward the law to be a natural result of the callousness, bitterness, and alienation created by the long sequence of domestic wars: the troubles in Texas, the conflict with Mexico, the Civil War, and the furious struggles to dispossess the Indians. Still others cite the attraction of like for like: Wherever some outlaws flourish, more are sure to congregate.

Sheer space was an element. During the years of greatest violence in New Mexico, Lincoln County embraced 17,280,000 acres, an area more than half that of Pennsylvania. Days were required for persons in the outlying sections to go to the county seat at Lincoln town (originally La Placita del Rio Bonito) to do business or attend court. Though no other county was equally bloated, several were extensive enough to be split by waterless deserts and towering mountains. In all of them population was scanty, travel hazardous. Law enforcement agencies were widely scattered and sorely understaffed because of the insistence of vested interests that property taxes stay low. It was often difficult to assemble posses big enough to run down outlaw gangs. If the gangs were caught, it was even more difficult to assemble the witnesses and jurors necessary for a legal trial.

Feeling vulnerable in an ill-policed land, witnesses, jurors, and prosecutors could often be intimidated or bribed. Naturally thugs and gentlemanly thieves alike used these advantages to their own gain. When their machinations grew exasperating enough, vigilante groups formed almost spontaneously. Seven suspected criminals were executed by mobs in Tucson and Phoenix in 1873; twelve in Socorro and Las Vegas, New Mexico, during the early 1880s. Necessary though proponents said the housecleanings were, they did little to enhance the area's reputation in the nation's eyes.

Nor was the nation itself blameless. Civic immorality was endemic during the last part of the nineteenth century. It was the era when the "Indian Ring" in Washington became a national scandal; when railroads bought up state legislatures; when steel, oil, sugar, tobacco, and meat trusts indulged in merciless competition, using as justification the pseudo-Darwinian argument that only the strong have a right to survive. Frontiersmen, who by nature admired self-reliance and rugged individualism, admired that philosophy, too, and emulated it by stealing so much public land throughout the West that a reform-minded President, Grover Cleveland, appointed a special commissioner, W. A. J. Sparks, to clean up the situation—only to have Sparks so beset by outraged pioneer thieves that he resigned.

The national political spoils system aided territorial schemers in their drive for power. Because New Mexico and Arizona were not considered choice patronage plums, the party hacks who were sent there to reap their meager rewards as governors, judges, territorial secretaries, and federal marshals often had less than outstanding ability. It would be absurd to claim that all of them were dishonest as well. Still, until the day came when occasional native-born residents received appointments, the majority were outsiders with no other attachment than greed to the territories they were supposed to serve. Inevitably they were quick to identify their ambitions with the desires of the local politicians and businessmen who monopolized or sought to monopolize the land's resources.

The alliances that resulted were regularly challenged by other greedy men, and it was out of those challenges—whether for the control of a town police force or mastery of millions of acres of rangeland—that much of the Southwest's violence arose. But can it be said that the disorders were worse than those that prevailed elsewhere in the West during the same period—say, for example, Montana during the reign of the Plummer gang or Wyoming when cattlemen and nesters were fighting what came to be called the Johnson County War?

For a partial answer, consider this political measurement. The American nation as a whole believed that aspiring states should be admitted to the union only after serving apprenticeships as territories. (California and Texas were the only exceptions.) Now, notice how long a trial period was demanded of some of the Southwest's neighbors. Wyoming languished under federally appointed territorial officers for thirty-one years; Colorado for fifteen; Nevada for three. Even Utah, wracked by disputes over Mormon polygamy, cracked the barrier and became a state in less than half a century. Arizona, however, kept its inferior status as a territory for fifty-nine years and New Mexico (of which Arizona originally had been a part) for sixty-four.

National and local politics played roles in the delay. So, too, did doubts about the dependability, as citizens, of the large Hispanic element in both territories. But equally damning was a belief held by many of the nation's policymakers that both regions were the haunt not of civilized people but of murderous Indians, fiery Mexican bandits, cattle thieves, professional gunmen, drunken miners, conniving businessmen, sly speculators, and corrupt politicians. How could such places dare to claim, as they often did, that they were ready to shake off the yoke of federal supervision?

Examining the sources of that belief is the burden of the rest of this section. Altogether it is a story not without relevance to some of the darker aspects of the American character today.

## A Glorification of Thugs

Let us start with a story of raw small-time corruption and of the patina of romance that the great American polishing machine has spread over it—the feud between the five Earp brothers (actually only three—Milton, Virgil, and Wyatt—figured prominently in the feud) and old man Clanton, aided by his sons Ike, Phineas, and Bill. Each group had its satellites. A principal one for the Earps was a consumptive gambler, Doc Holliday, who had gained his nickname from his early forays into free-lance dentistry. Chief supporters of the Clantons were the brothers Frank and Tom McLaury.

The prize for which these stalwarts contended was political control, for different purposes, of the silver mining town of Tombstone, Arizona. Discovered in 1878 and named with grisly humor by prospector Ed Schieffelin, the area had been a haunt of Apaches who at the time were breaking out of their hated San Carlos Reservation to the north. The prospector had been told that if he ventured into so dangerous a region the only thing he would find would be his tomb. Hence the name.

The Clantons and McLaurys reached Tombstone ahead of the Earps. Their headquarters were neighboring ranches in the San Pedro Valley a few miles from the raucous town. They were not above ordinary banditry both north and south of the international border, but their main source of income came from stolen cattle. They hid these animals on their ranches and then passed them on in small, steady dribbles (lack of refrigeration made the storage of beef for any length of time impossible) to unquestioning butcher shops, restaurants, mine boarding houses, and hotels. To keep the law from making inconvenient visits to their base of operations, they entered into understandings, at a price, with whatever deputy sheriffs were assigned to that far end of huge Pinal County, whose seat was at Tucson, eighty miles northwest over rough and dangerous roads.

Enter, in 1880, the Earp brothers and Doc Holliday. Their last stands of any duration had been, in succession, the cattle shipping towns of Wichita and Dodge City, Kansas. Morgan Earp had worked on and off as a deputy sheriff, Wyatt as an ordinary policeman. They had performed their jobs with reasonable efficiency (at times Wyatt busied himself repairing wooden sidewalks, which was one of the duties of a policeman in Wichita), but the main part of the family income came from gambling and pimping.

On arriving at Tombstone, Wyatt parlayed his Kansas experiences into a job as deputy sheriff for the east end of Pinal County. Almost immediately, however, he was replaced by lanky John Henry Behan, an old-time Prescott miner who had been in Arizona since 1864 and had sat for two terms in the territorial legislature. Exactly what caused Behan's star to rise over Wyatt's is unknown, but a fair guess would center on the machinations of the Clantons. In any event, Wyatt brooded. When

Cochise County was formed in the early days of 1881 out of the east end of Pinal County, he asked the governor to appoint him sheriff. Instead the job went again to Behan. This was a blow to pocketbook as well as to pride. In those days sheriffs functioned as tax collectors, keeping a percentage of their gleanings as pay for their work.

Not all was lost, however. Tombstone was being wracked by municipal disorders. Angry citizens formed a Law and Order party, which the Earps joined, and elected as reform mayor the Republican editor of the Tombstone *Epitaph,* John P. Clum, whom we last encountered as the dynamic Indian agent of the San Carlos Apache Reservation. Clum liked the Earps and, in June 1881, appointed Virgil city marshal. Virgil promptly named brothers Wyatt and Morgan and friend Doc Holliday as his policemen.

Clum's action split Tombstone into factions, as he must have known it would. Because the town was the seat of the new county, it served as Sheriff Behan's base. Behan was ardently supported by the *Epitaph*'s bitter rival, the Democratic *Nugget.* Finances were involved in the split. The *Nugget* received all contracts for county printing, the *Epitaph* those for city printing (Clum, remember, was mayor). If one or the other of the papers could monopolize all the presswork, it would have a bonanza.

It was a peculiar setup. Behan, or at least some of his deputies, wanted to keep the Clantons' meat business flourishing and feared that if the Earps waxed strong they would cause ripples. The Earps' ambitions, however, lay in another direction—the profits they could harvest by shaking down Tombstone's tenderloin. They wanted no interference from the sheriff's department. The rivalry gained still more sharpness when Wyatt Earp charmed Behan's big-busted mistress away from him.

The Clantons brought the tensions to a breaking point when brother Ike offered evidence purporting to show that Wyatt Earp had planned, and Doc Holliday had attempted, a stagecoach robbery near the town. The bungled effort produced no loot but resulted in the death of the driver and one of his passengers.

In a not very original stab at retaliation, Wyatt a little later, on September 8, 1881, blamed yet another stage robbery on two deputy sheriffs who, he said, were also members of the Clanton gang, which, incidentally, went by the name of The Cowboys.

By this time old man Clanton was no longer alive. Mexican outlaws had just killed him and five other Cowboys in revenge for their having robbed a caravan of smugglers a little south of the border. Conceivably the surviving Cowboys would have preferred a moment's quiet for catching their breath and regrouping.

They had no chance. Recriminations over the various holdup charges led, on October 26, 1881, to some street fights in which the Earps were the aggressors, and then to the famous shootout near—not at—the OK Corral. The Clanton contingent had numerical superiority—five to four—but some weren't armed and so firepower was on the side of the Earps. They made it count, killing both McLaury brothers and young Billy Clanton, aged nineteen. Virgil and Morgan Earp were wounded; Doc Holliday was nicked; Wyatt was unscathed.

The size of the turnout for the McLaury-Clanton funerals gave clear indication of where the town's sympathies lay. Even so, the Earps tried to tough out their unpopularity—until assassins firing shotguns from ambush crippled Virgil for life. A little later assailants killed Morgan and just missed Wyatt by shooting through the windows of a billiard parlor. The surviving Earps and Holliday thereupon hunted down and killed two of the men they suspected of being Morgan's slayers. Indicted for the murders, they split up and headed for other parts.

Apprised of the carryings-on, President Chester A. Arthur on May 3, 1882, belatedly issued a proclamation threatening to bring the United States Army into the field unless the "insurgents . . . disperse and retire peaceably to their respective abodes within a limited time." Significantly, many Arizona newspapers objected to Arthur's interference. They said, and perhaps believed, that Arizona was capable of cleaning its own stables. In addition, fumed the new editor of the *Epitaph* (Clum had fled the territory out of fear for his life), such a declaration from on high was likely, through the negative image it created, to "deter the investment of capital in the territory."

Actually time brought Tombstone a profitable image. Romancers turned frontier marshals into steady-eyed symbols of the forces that tamed the West. Taking advantage of the trend, Wyatt Earp, helped by uncritical biographers, sought with some success to present himself as the epitome of all brave marshals. Tombstone meanwhile was saved from normal mining-camp decrepitude by being reconstructed according to its imagined 1880 pattern, and began a new career mining tourists. Thus are heroes made to stand on feet of clay.

## The Baron of Arizona

At the very time the Earps were laying the groundwork for their dubious immortality, a far more imaginative man, originally from Missouri, was reaching out yearning hands toward the one tangible resource that the slowly developing Southwest possessed in abundance—land. The schemer's name was James Addison Reavis. His plots were as luxurious as the twin sideburns that rippled down to his collarbones. Alas, however, his birth had not placed him where he could realize his potentials, and he had spent his early adult years humbly as a Confederate soldier, clothing salesman, peddler of real estate, and conductor on a horse-drawn streetcar in St. Louis.

The dreary routines changed when he met in St. Louis a visiting Arizona miner named George Willing. Willing told an unlikely tale about being the owner of an old Spanish land grant, which had remained undeveloped because of Apache dangers. This huge piece of property had come to him, in return for favors rendered in the past, from the dying, poverty-stricken owner of the grant's title papers, Miguel de Peralta. But Willing did not know how to go about presenting his newly acquired claim. Would Reavis, who was familiar with the real estate business, lend advice for a share in whatever developed?

Though well aware that the whole claim was phony, Reavis agreed, and now luck struck. Willing died in Prescott, Reavis laid hold of the papers, forged a deed conveying them to him, and at last was free to soar as high as his imagination would allow. As a starter he invented an illustrious Spanish military officer, Don Nemecio Silva de Peralta de la Cordobá, who, he said, had lived in the middle of the eighteenth century. This worthy, Reavis's concoction continued, collected for his sovereign, with great difficulty, long overdue revenues from Mexico. As a reward for the service, Peralta received from the king the title Baron de los Colorados and an estate to match, the Peralta grant. Seventy-five miles wide, this spurious gift reputedly stretched from the Continental Divide in New Mexico to a point west of Phoenix—eleven million acres all told.

Now come the touches of genius. With infinite patience, Reavis set about making his story believable. After mastering Spanish, he learned Spanish law and colonial history. He prowled tirelessly through the dusty governmental archives in Mexico, noted what deeds looked like, how they were inscribed, the details of seals, the swirls of rubrics. Realizing that a family as illustrious as the Peraltas would leave traces, he learned to manufacture wills, property transfers, birth and death records, army commissions, and whatnot. He wrote Spanish poetry extolling the noble line, collected obscure paintings that he could pass off as being likenesses of family members, drew complex genealogical charts, and surreptitiously planted his creations in various depositories. He then gained official permission to make copies of the documents he had "discovered" in the archives, had the copies notarized as authentic, and in 1883 presented them to Arizona's astounded surveyor general in Tucson.

So far Reavis had only a claim. Title would not accrue until the surveyor general recommended that Congress pass a routine law confirming the grant—and the surveyor showed no disposition to hurry. Reavis nevertheless set about suggesting to trespassers on "his" property that they protect themselves by buying quitclaim deeds from him. It was a breathless stroke, for by then a dozen towns, many mines, hundreds of prosperous farms and ranches, and a sizable part of the Southern Pacific Railroad had appeared on "his" eleven million acres.

After the railroad's attorneys had inspected the documents and advised compliance, the Southern Pacific handed over $50,000. A noted mine added $25,000. Those examples frightened smaller fry into listening to the collectors Reavis sent among them, and, rumor says, he was soon collecting $100,000 a year.

He must have been nervous, however, for he decided to strengthen the claim by introducing a reputedly real Peralta. His choice settled on a pretty, round-faced orphan who looked Spanish to him but was actually the offspring of an Indian mother and an undistinguished Anglo later identified as John Treadway. Reavis named the girl Sofia Loreto Micaela Maso y Peralta de la Cordobá. He coached her in the ways befitting her station (he now often used the titles Baron and Baroness of Arizona as well as de los Colorados), married her, took her to Spain, and introduced her in court. He also found time to place more documents in the archives in Madrid and Seville.

In 1890, seven years after the introduction of the claim, the surveyor general of Arizona threw it out as fraudulent. Reavis countered by suing the United States for $10 million, the value of *his* property that he said the government had illegally given away over the years to homesteaders, prospectors, railroads, and town promoters. In the end, that bravado proved his undoing, for the suit brought into action several crack investigators of the State Department. They combed the archives. Discrepancies and anachronisms appeared—for instance, type faces and kinds of paper not in use when the documents were dated. Tried on charges of conspiracy to defraud, Reavis was convicted and sentenced to six years in prison. He served two before being paroled.

## Legal and Illegal Theft

Fraud as naked as Reavis's did not appeal to most engrossers of land. They preferred to acquire a foothold legally, though not always ethically, and then, by manipulation, to stretch their original takings—be they Hispanic grants, railroad lands, or acquisitions from the American public domain—as far as brazenness allowed. It is a reflection on our love of legalisms that these affairs—"I'll stand on my rights!"—produced far more violence than did simple cheating. Reavis never pulled a gun. Many of his more righteous contemporaries did, either directly or through the employment of conscienceless men.

Arizona's most notorious example, rendered so in part by a deadly feud loosely associated with it, revolved around railroad land. Its timing coincided with Reavis's operations. Its trigger was the hope of certain Eastern and British capitalists that they could earn a 20 percent return on money invested in cattle, as some ranchers were doing. A necessary part of the operation was cheap land to use for grazing. The device for obtaining it that these men hit on was almost as slick as Reavis's.

The backbone of their plan was the land grants earned by the Atlantic and Pacific Railroad as it thrust across Arizona toward California. Chartered by the federal government in 1867 to build west along the so-called 35th parallel route, the A&P had been promised forty sections of 640 acres each for every mile of track completed. To keep monopolists from swooping up solid chunks of desirable land close to the line, the government required that as the grant lands were earned they be divided into square-mile sections and be scattered in checkerboard fashion throughout a broad strip on either side of the railroad. By selling off its grant in small pieces to numerous farmers, the railroad supposedly could recover the costs of construction.

Interspersed among the railroad holdings was another checkerboard, this one made up of public domain land. These public sections were open to homesteading or preemption by small farmers who could not obtain or did not wish to pay for railroad land. Theoretically everyone —the general public and the providers of transportation—benefited from the admixture. Actually, the aridity of the West spoiled the prospect. The land as a whole simply was not suited to one-family farms like those prevalent in the humid East. This truth was often mentioned to

Congress but went unheeded; the lawmakers were too enthralled by the apparent democracy of the federal land-grant system to see its flaws.

After a hesitant start in western Missouri, the Atlantic and Pacific had fallen under the joint control of two other railroads with transcontinental ambitions but without land grants. One was the St. Louis and San Francisco, generally called the Frisco, and the Atchison, Topeka, and Santa Fe, now known as the Santa Fe. To forestall a possible revocation of the A&P land grant, the parent companies maintained a fiction that the captured railroad was still a separate entity, managing its own operations, finances, and construction program. Interlocking boards of directors, however, allowed the controlling lines to dictate policy.

By 1884 the finances of the A&P were in parlous shape. Most immediate of the crises was an interest payment due January 1, 1885, on some of the road's bonded indebtedness. The directors of the Santa Fe and its bankers, the Seligman brothers of New York, were of course aware of the A&P's needs. To take advantage of the situation, some of the Santa Fe directors and the Seligman brothers formed with certain Texas cattlemen a corporation called the Aztec Land and Cattle Company. Blandly they forced the A&P in its desperation to sell to the new firm, for 50 cents an acre, 1,059,560 acres between Holbrook and Flagstaff. They then imported from New Mexico upward of 40,000 cattle. Because of the shape of the brand burned onto the sides of those animals, the Aztec Land and Cattle Company was known locally as the Hashknife.

The beauty of all this was that by purchasing one million acres, the Hashknife gained control of two million, for its checkerboard of railroad land surrounded every alternate section of public domain land. To make certain that no one crossed Hashknife holdings to reach public domain land, the cattle company hired a patrol of roughneck Texas cowboys.

Bully boy of the crew was hard-drinking, ugly-tempered John Payne, sometimes spelled Paine. He had two principal targets—sheepmen who wandered through the region on the assumption that the public parts of the range were open to them, and Mormons, who, in 1871, had begun moving south out of Utah to form colonies along the upper tributaries of the Little Colorado River. Because the area where they settled had not yet been surveyed, these migrants, like other pioneers throughout the West, simply squatted on whatever land appealed to them, hoping to perfect title later on. By the time the Hashknife had appeared with its adverse claims stemming from the railroad grant, the colonists had created several small towns surrounded by irrigated farms. (As a matter of incidental information, one of the towns, eventually the seat of the Apache County, was named Snowflake, not for the weather but for two leading Mormon colonizers, Apostle Erastus Snow and land agent William Flake.)

The policy Payne followed in dealing with transient sheepherders, many of them Hispanos working under *partido* (sharecropping) arrangements with their backers, was first to warn them away with scowls and a gesturing of guns, and if that did not work, to resort to harassment. A favorite stunt was for a considerable force of riders to wait until dark and then gallop through the sheep camp upsetting wagons, filling cooking pots and water barrel with bullet holes (how then could the two or three frightened men in the camp cook their next meal?), and stampeding the herd. If the herders still stayed around, the next step was to kill as many of their animals as was convenient with fire, clubs, guns, or by driving them over cliffs or into quicksand. To a *partidero* who was bound by contract to return 20 percent of his "borrowed" herd each year to his backers, such attacks could be devastating. On occasion the herders fought back, but it was a losing battle since invariably they were outnumbered and the law was in the hands of the big cattle ranches.

Comparable tactics were used against Mormons who had inadvertently settled on land claimed by Aztec. Occupants were driven away and their places taken by hired claim jumpers. One elderly farmer later testified during a government hearing that Payne threatened to kill and scalp him if he lingered on his own farm long enough to salvage his potato crop. Another settler was horsewhipped for rounding up his own stock on company land. The law? It was an uncertain remedy for Mormons in those days. Polygamists were being hunted down and persecuted. So many men had gone into hiding or were in jail that the settlements were defenseless, and, in addition, the county courts were not inclined to aid people in such bad odor with the territorial and federal governments. Matters grew so hopeless that the Mormons actually abandoned two towns that the Hashknife insisted were on its land.

In the end the terrorists became so obnoxious that vigilantes stepped in, hanged three men, and forced four others, Payne among them, to flee south across the mountains. Investigators for the federal government's General Land Office warned Aztec to clean its hands. Violence subsided, but harassment, according to Charles Peterson, historian of the Little Colorado River communities, did not. The cattle company switched to legal threats: either trespassers buy, at company prices, the land they were using or face a series of civil lawsuits whose expenses the company could afford but the settlers could not. Years passed before the federal government finally moved in to help untie the tangles for which it was partly responsible.

Meanwhile, across the mountains from the Hashknife ranges, Arizona's most dreadful feud was gathering momentum. The scene was the Pleasant Valley section of Tonto Basin, a grassy delight shaded by tall ponderosa pines and watered by cool creeks draining into the Salt River. The chief actors were members of the Graham and Tewksbury families, friends once but afterwards bitter enemies because of clashes that developed when Tewksbury hands working for the Grahams had protested the latter's rustling, first from the Mormons and later from ranchers within the valley itself. Thus the seeds were planted. The Grahams wanted to get rid of the inconvenient Tewksburys and their neighbors, and the Tewksbury faction declined to be driven from ranches it cherished and had worked hard to build into paying operations.

The Grahams expanded rapidly. Pickings were easy. The livestock boom had resulted in the crowding of more animals into all parts of the Southwest than could efficiently be handled. Outlaws swept up freight horses from the Mormons along the Little Colorado, cow ponies from Sonora, and cattle from everywhere. Sales outlets were developed in Mexico and southern Colorado. The Aztec's bully boy, John Payne, and some of his cowboys were certainly involved with the thieves, and when the vigilantes began breathing down their necks it was to the Graham stronghold in Pleasant Valley that they fled.

The death Payne thought he had escaped on the Little Colorado caught up with him in Pleasant Valley. On August 9, 1887, he, two other ex-Hashknife cowboys, and two local Graham partisans tangled with four Tewksbury people who were forted up in a cabin. Two of the attackers died—Payne was one of them—and the other three were wounded. Afterward the sheriff rode in with five deputies, decided he could do nothing useful with so small a party, and departed, leaving behind a legal vacuum.

More men died, with the Grahams suffering the most. Infuriated, they attacked the Tewksbury cabin at sunrise on September 7, 1887, less than four weeks after the Payne affair. They killed John Tewksbury and a friend, William Jacobs, as the pair were saddling their horses outside the house and then laid siege to the survivors in the cabin while the corpses lay outside for three days, crawling with flies and partially eaten by wandering hogs. By the time the attackers had withdrawn and the county coroner had been summoned, the task of burying the bodies was, in the words of one participant, "disagreeable. . . . All we did was to dig two very shallow graves and roll the swollen, mutilated bodies into them with our shovels."

The reaction was as bad as the murders. Eight valley ranchers formed a committee of vigilance that hanged four suspected rustlers, roughed up people riding through who had no satisfactory explanation for their presence, and perhaps were responsible for various mysterious disappearances. Tales of horror, impossible to authenticate even by indefatigable Clara T. Woody, the most recent student of the affair, and her assistant, Milton Schwartz, flashed from household to household. One murdered man, it was said, was hidden inside a gutted cow and left to decompose with the maggot-infested beef.

More certainty attends the demise of most of the Blevins family, Graham supporters who fled Pleasant Valley to take refuge, as they hoped, in a shack close to the railroad tracks in Holbrook. Discovering their whereabouts, the county sheriff, truly named Commodore Perry Owens, a tall man given to big hats and batwing chaps, picked up a rifle, went to the shack, and knocked on the door. When Eva Blevins, wife of one of the fugitives, opened it, holding a baby in her arms, Owens stepped inside and without warning began to shoot. Four bullets killed three of the male occupants, one of whom was twelve years old, and wounded the fourth. One of the dying men toppled against Eva. The gush of blood, she told Clara Woody years later, "saturated my baby and me."

And still the feud continued until 1892, when Ed Tewksbury killed the last Graham, brother Tom, from ambush beside a road near Tempe —and, with the aid of good lawyers, created enough doubt in the minds of the jurors who heard the case so that he was acquitted. Some summaries say that twenty-six Graham supporters and five Tewksburys died during the war. Woody and Schwartz are more restrained. They list twelve Grahams and three Tewksburys as dead, with no count available on woundings and disappearances. Apparently, legal retribution brushed across only one of the feudists, John Blevins, wounded during the shootout at the Holbrook shack. A jury found him guilty of interfering with officer Owens during the performance of his duty and then signed a petition recommending that he be pardoned. He was.

## Rings of Rascals

James Addison Reavis worked at his land scheme alone. The Grahams and Tewksburys fought their own battles, not someone else's. In New Mexico, however, frauds and feuds were more tangled. There the dominant factor in the local "wars" (war in Western terminology being any confrontation between antagonistic groups during which guns are fired in anger) was a manipulative agency so shadowy that some observers have denied its existence. Most historians, however, recognize it as the Santa Fe Ring, a southwestern imitation of a social phenomenon widespread throughout the United States during the last part of the nineteenth century.

*Bouviers's Law Dictionary* defines "ring" as "a combination of persons usually for the attainment of a selfish aim or purpose; especially a clique formed for controlling a market or local or state politics." Such goals, the University of Chicago's *Dictionary of Americanisms* adds, "are not in the public interest."

Reduced to print, the charges seem grave, and yet no nineteenth-century ringmaster would have considered himself immoral. He and his fellows were simply getting along in a nation buffeted by change—Reconstruction and its grim aftermaths in the South, labor strife in the industrializing East, and unnerving economic fluctuations everywhere. In the West violent disruptions came from Indian wars, wild mining rushes, and a parade of carpetbagging governors, judges, military officers, government contractors, surveyors, and other opportunists intent on feathering their little nests as downily as they could before being replaced by a new set of main chancers.

In that kind of milieu a ring produced stability. True, it had no legal life, no charter, no bylaws, no membership rules. It could not be haled as an entity before any court of law. It was simply an amorphous, shifting association of lawyers, businessmen, speculators, and local officials who stayed in place while the federal appointees who supposedly ruled their region's destiny were constantly changing.

Politics was the glue that held the associates together. In New Mexico most ring members were Republicans. This allowed them to share in the patronage plums dispensed from Washington, where Republicans controlled nearly all national administrations between the Civil and first world wars. As Republicans, they formed alliances with their temporary federal officials by promising suitable rewards in return for favorable responses in times of crisis. Meanwhile they maintianed a precarious hold on the faction-ridden territorial legislature by supporting the strongest available county leaders, who did not need to be Republicans. What the ring wanted was the kind of predictability that would lead, if all went well, to economic gain.

Although the personnel of the Santa Fe Ring varied according to the demands of expediency, two men stood out over the years as its most effective leaders. Both bore the same middle name: Stephen Benton Elkins, born in Ohio and educated in Missouri, and Thomas Benton

Catron, born in Missouri but unrelated to the other Benton. Inevitably Catron was nicknamed Tomcat. Elkins was known to both friends and enemies as Smooth Steve.

The two men graduated together from the University of Missouri in 1860. After studying law briefly in different offices, both were swept up by the Civil War, Elkins going into the Union Army, Catron into the Confederate. Mustered out in 1863, Elkins reached New Mexico in 1864. Within months he was admitted to the territorial bar and elected to the legislature. Pleased with his headlong rise, he let his classmate know that New Mexico's political climate was favorable to Republicans who could speak Spanish.

Easily shedding his Democratic allegiance, Catron bought enough flour to fill two wagons, joined a Santa Fe caravan at Independence, Missouri, and creaked west with his nose buried in a Spanish grammar. On reaching Santa Fe in July 1866, he sold his cargo, oxen, and wagons for more than enough to cover expenses and then, to perfect his Spanish, lived for a time in the little Hispanic plaza of Alcalde, halfway between Santa Fe and Taos.

Elkins meanwhile was pulling strings. On February 22, 1867, Catron was appointed district attorney of New Mexico's third judicial district, with headquarters at Mesilla in the southern part of the territory. The next year he was elected to the legislature. In 1869 he was appointed U.S. district attorney for all New Mexico and moved from Mesilla to Santa Fe, where Smooth Steve, now attorney general for the territory, was already in residence. There they slipped easily into the embryonic Santa Fe Ring, which was just then being welded into shape for masterminding a conflict over a piece of real estate that would help keep New Mexico in turmoil for the next quarter of a century. To understand the reasons for the struggle, it is necessary to turn back to the close of the war with Mexico.

## The Colfax County War

Mention has already been made of the method by which the Spanish and Mexican governments placed land within the hands of their citizens—the *merced*, the ruler's mercy, operating through designated officials, who gave grants of varying sizes to Indian pueblos, to Hispanic settlers desirous of forming new towns, to partners who agreed to colonize frontier tracts as buffers against wild Indians and encroaching Anglos, and to individuals who had performed other meritorious public services.

By the time of the American conquest, the best farmland and pastoral ranges in New Mexico and southern Arizona had been blanketed by such grants, and it seemed that small American freeholders who risked venturing into the Southwest were going to be blocked from carrying forward their country's traditional patterns of land occupation.

Congress found the prospect objectionable. In 1854, six years after the Treaty of Guadalupe Hidalgo became operative, the legislators sought to stimulate the settlement of New Mexico (of which Arizona was then a part) by passing a liberal donation land law modeled after programs already in effect in Oregon and Washington. This act promised 160 acres of public domain land free of charge (government land elsewhere sold then at $1.25 an acre) to any citizen who would occupy and work the piece of ground he wanted for four years.

Obviously donation lands could not be carved out of legitimately held Spanish or Mexican grants. It therefore became necessary for the General Land Office to determine what part of the Southwest was privately held and what part lay within the American public domain. This onerous job, along with the title surveyor general of New Mexico, was assigned to an industrious, fair-minded Texan named William Pelham. If Pelham decided after examining all available records that a grant's papers were in order, he was to recommend approval to Congress. If Congress agreed with his estimate, the legislators would pass a special law confirming title. An American-type survey would then be run to determine the exact boundaries of the holding, and a patent of title would be issued to the claimants.

On reaching Santa Fe, Pelham discovered that very few title papers were in order. Eventually (and without Pelham ever participating in the illegalities), the situation opened the doors wide to fraud and enabled many a bargain-hunting speculator—*and also the United States government*—to wrest land on technicalities from the conquered Hispanos. The harm resulting from those grabs has lasted until our own time and will be noted at the end of this section. Right now, however, we are concerned with a grant whose papers were in order but whose uncertain size launched a bloody twenty-five-year struggle between its promoters, backed by the Santa Fe Ring, and hundreds of small Anglo farmers who had come into the area in hopes of getting free land.

The grant involved was the one that Governor Manuel Armijo had awarded early in the 1840s, over the protests of Padre Antonio José Martínez, to Charles Beaubien and Guadalupe Miranda, with Charles Bent as silent partner. This grant, which blanketed most of New Mexico's Colfax County when that county was formed, was approved by

Pelham and accepted by Congress in 1860. A survey should have followed, but because of the Civil War did not. Meantime Beaubien bought out Miranda's interests. After Beaubien's death, his son-in-law, former mountain man Lucien Maxwell, who had been helping establish settlements on the property and who during the war made considerable money selling beef and grain to the army, acquired the interest of all the other claimants, including those of Charles Bent's heirs, for about $43,000.

Though it was a considerable sum of money for the time and place, Maxwell found that he had acquired a bargain. He grazed, legend avers, 1,000 horses, 10,000 cattle, and 40,000 sheep on . . . who knew how many acres? There were 500 men on his payroll; an indeterminate number of Hispanic settlers scattered across the holding paid him rent in the form of produce. He built a fine house under the cottonwoods beside Cimarron Creek, and because there were no banks in New Mexico kept up to $25,000 in ready cash in a bureau drawer in his bedroom.

In 1867 gold was discovered in the mountains along the western edge of the grant. Elizabethtown, commonly called E'town, boomed into life. In addition to acquiring mines of his own, Maxwell tried to levy royalties and rents on the miners, businessmen, timber cutters, ditch builders, and farmers who rushed into the region. Some paid; some didn't. An easygoing, generous soul, Lucien made no great fuss about the delinquencies.

Nor was that the end. Two railroads were eyeing the grant. One was the Kansas Pacific, which in the 1860s had notions of cutting across Maxwell's lands on its way to the West Coast. (In 1870 it settled for a terminus in Denver instead.) The other was the Denver & Rio Grande, which planned to build to Mexico City on a route through the grant.

The impact that the arrival of either railroad would have on property values was not lost on Jerome B. Chaffee, a wealthy Colorado mine owner and all-around promoter. Chaffee formed a syndicate to buy the grant. Involved with the coterie, not as investors but as expediters (in 1869 they were still relative newcomers to New Mexico and could not command the necessary amounts of money) were Smooth Steve Elkins and Tomcat Catron.

The purchasers had no intention of operating the grant themselves. Their hope was to sell it immediately in London, where they had gilt-edged contacts, for $1.3 million, half going to Maxwell as owner and half to themselves as promoters. The sum was predicated on the assumption that when the grant was surveyed, it would be found to contain about two million acres. Thus the offering price worked out to sixty-five cents an acre, an attractive price even for sparsely watered grazing land. In that same year, however, 1869, the Secretary of the Interior, Jacob Cox, ruled that the grant's size would be limited to the amount allowed by a Mexican colonizing law of 1824: eleven square leagues (about 48,500 acres) per person, or twenty-two leagues (97,000 acres) for a partnership, which the original Beaubien-Miranda grant had been. If this limitation prevailed, a sale price of $1.3 million would boost the price to $13.40 an acre, which was not attractive.

Maxwell was indignant. He insisted that the 1824 colonizing law had applied to foreigners entering Texas and not to citizens of New Mexico. He contended further that the only mention of size in the grantees' original papers had been in connection with "metes and bounds," that is, boundaries determined by the natural landmarks—creeks, trees, and mountain crests—specified in Beaubien's and Miranda's application to Governor Armijo.

Confident that Maxwell's contention was correct, the syndicate hired a deputy surveyor of the territory, W. W. Griffin, to determine the grant's size according to metes and bounds. (Pelham had long since given way to a politically appointed surveyor general who was subservient to the wishes of the coalescing ring.) Griffin reported as expected—2 million acres, not 97,000. The English buyers accepted the figures without waiting for Interior's response, perhaps because they had already prevailed on a group of Dutch investors to buy the $5 million worth of debentures they had issued against the property—property Maxwell had acquired for $43,000. It's something to remember when complaining about the current inflation of property values.

Miners and farmers who had settled on what they believed from the secretary's ruling was public domain land were outraged. There were riots in E'town and meetings of protest in various farmhouses. After reviewing the situation, the Department of the Interior again declared, in 1871, that the 97,000-acre limitation would be upheld. The Dutch company, which had invested its $5 million in good faith, appealed in the United States courts and also demanded that the sellers meet their original representations.

As one move toward gaining enough clout to reverse the secretary's decision, Stephen Elkins, who by this time had become president of the Maxwell Land Grant and Railroad Company, ran for Congress in 1872 and again in 1874. (Jerome Chaffee was already in Washington, having been elected Colorado's delegate in 1870 and again in 1872.) Although noisy charges of corruption at the polls surrounded Elkins's campaign, he was elected and seated.

Again the company acted precipitately. Without waiting for final court decisions on its title, it started levying rents. Opposition swelled, much of it led by a Methodist circuit rider, the Reverend T. J. Tolby. In his sermons and at settlers' meetings, Tolby excoriated the Santa Fe Ring not only for its greed in connection with the grant but also for every other alleged wrongdoing laid at its doors throughout the territory. Accordingly, when he was murdered on a lonely road the night of September 14, 1875, most of New Mexico jumped to the conclusion that the ring had hired the killing done.

A vigilante group loosened one suspect's tongue by tightening a rope around his neck. After the terrified victim had sought to save himself by naming another man as the culprit, the vigilantes hanged him anyhow, just in case he was lying. They then rode down the person he had accused and shook three more names out of him. The revelation confirmed widespread suspicion: The trio were the ring's principal Colfax County agents. Suddenly uncomfortable, the Santa Fe clique demanded help from New Mexico's newly installed governor, Samuel Beach Axtell.

A one-time California congressman, Axtell had been appointed governor of Utah early in 1875. There he had become so embroiled in local political strife that within four months the President transferred him to New Mexico. Wild rumors followed: Axtell had been converted to Mormonism by Brigham Young and then foisted off onto New Mexico to prepare the way for an influx of Mormon colonists. Though the charges were baseless, other complaints about Axtell's unduly swift accommodation with the ring were not, and soon he was in very bad odor throughout the Southwest.

He responded to the ring's demand for help by attaching Colfax County to Taos County for judicial purposes. This act allowed the three suspects to be taken out of the unfriendly atmosphere of Colfax County to the more obliging courts in Taos. It also forced witnesses against them to endure a long ride across the mountains if they wished to testify. One witness who did undertake the journey to appear against the first of the accused was killed from ambush as he approached the courtroom. In spite of that, the trial continued, and the accused was acquitted on the basis of insufficient evidence. The cases against the others were then dropped.

Disorders swept Colfax County. One attorney unfriendly to the ring publicly declared that he could prove that Governor Axtell was involved in a plot to bring about his death. Finally troops restored tranquillity, but soon a new episode brought on yet more violent outbursts.

In 1876 the Supreme Court of the United States upheld the contention of a Colorado grant company that its area should be determined by metes and bounds and not by the square leagues specified in Mexico's 1824 colonizing laws. On the basis of that decision a new Secretary of the Interior said reluctantly that his department would also accept as the Maxwell grant's boundaries whatever line was laid down by a new, official survey of its metes and bounds.

At once the ring exerted its pressures on Henry M. Atkinson, most corrupt of the many surveyor generals who had been inflicted on New Mexico since Pelham's time. Obligingly, Atkinson contracted the measuring job to a surveying firm headed by Smooth Steve Elkins's brother John. Within the eyebrow-raising time of twenty-two days, Elkins's surveyors turned in their maps: The Maxwell grant contained 1,714,764 acres.

The announcement fired antagonisms in Colfax County to new heights. An estimated 2,500 farmers, miners, and timber cutters whose homes were contained within the newly confirmed lines refused to pay rent to the company. They gained control of the county offices at the next election and filed suit, demanding that the Elkins survey be set aside on the grounds of fraud. When the company went stubbornly ahead asserting its rights, more rioting followed. Between November 1877 and November 1878, declared grant historian Jim Pearson, the bitter conflict resulted in two score deaths. Even if one swallows the figure with a large grain of salt, the turmoil, sensationally covered by the nation's press, did little to brighten the Southwest's reputation among outside readers.

Other damaging publicity soon followed. Land-grant cases, the press discovered, moved with glacial slowness toward adjudication. Between 1854 and 1880 the surveyor general of the territory had submitted to Congress 136 cases out of a possible thousand or more. Congress had acted on forty-six. The uproar over the Maxwell case then paralyzed action completely, and after 1879 the legislators acted on none at all. Title to millions of acres of property remained in abeyance, resulting in a scandal of such proportions that when Grover Cleveland's Democrats assumed power in 1885 they sent a reform surveyor general, George Washington Julian, to New Mexico to repair as much of the damage as possible.

Julian, a crusty seventy-year-old former congressman from Indiana, was appalled by the conditions he unearthed. In an angry article in the *North American Review,* he declared that 90 percent of all homestead entries in New Mexico had gone not to bona fide settlers but to dummy entrymen employed by large landowners. Illegal operations in grant lands, he continued, had deprived the United States, and hence its small yeomen, of 9 million acres of public domain land. Most of these wrongs he attributed to members of the Santa Fe Ring. "They have hovered over the territory like a pestilence. To a fearful extent they have dominated governors, judges, district attorneys, legislators, and surveyor-generals —they have . . . subordinated everything to the greed for land."

Unhappily, Julian overplayed his hand, and like his superior, Andrew Jackson Sparks, head of the General Land Office, he was soon out of office. But something had to be done with the cases that were piling up in the southwestern land jam. Finally, in 1891, Congress appointed a five-man Court of Private Land Claims. After thirteen years of hearings involving nearly 35 million acres in New Mexico, Arizona, and Colorado, the court brought the books to a close.

Meanwhile, in 1887, the Supreme Court decided that no fraud had been proved in connection with the Elkins survey of the Maxwell grant and let the 1.7 million acres stand as measured. Although occasional flare-ups continued to trouble northeastern New Mexico almost until the opening of the twentieth century, the main struggle was over. Sensibly, the company now played fair with its discouraged antagonists. It paid those who were legally trespassers full market value for their buildings and livestock, though not for the land they occupied, and thus persuaded many to move away. As peace returned, it developed mines and cement plants, lumber mills and livestock operations. It sold land for summer homes and during the 1950s broke its huge holding into smaller but still sizable ranches, which it passed on to a variety of investors. One large, lovely piece called Philmont (and there must be some irony in this somewhere) is now the property of the Boy Scouts of America.

## The Lincoln County War

When reformer George Washington Julian declared that the Santa Fe Ring dominated New Mexican politics to a fearful extent, he neglected to mention one of the primary factors that made the domination possible. That was loyalty. In order to avoid challenges to its established political order in Santa Fe, the ring maintained throughout the territory a web of alliances designed to put amenable men in office. When the web was challenged at any point, the ring then had to give back the same kind of support that it asked for at election time. This involvement could be strenuous—and it was never more so than during the late 1870s in vast Lincoln County, sprawling across the southeastern quarter of the territory.

The political and economic leader of the county was the mercantile firm of L. G. Murphy & Company, commonly called The House of Murphy or, simply, The House. Thomas Catron of the Santa Fe Ring knew it well. He had met its partners, Major Lawrence G. Murphy and Colonel Emil Fritz, during the two years he had served as district attorney for New Mexico's third judicial district, with headquarters in Mesilla beside the Rio Grande. After moving to Santa Fe, he let Murphy and Fritz invest money for him in southeastern New Mexico. Later he advanced funds to the firm and its successors and eventually became the company's owner.

The founders of the firm had been born and educated abroad—Murphy in Ireland, Fritz in Germany. After traveling different paths to the Southwest, both had enlisted in the New Mexico Volunteers during the Civil War. They had served with distinction in Kit Carson's Indian campaigns and had been mustered out as commissioned officers in 1866, Murphy as a major, Fritz a colonel. Joining forces, they became post traders at Fort Stanton on the Rio Bonito a dozen miles above the Hispanic plaza that was destined to become Lincoln town, seat of Lincoln County when it was created in 1869. They were also traders for the Mescalero Indian Reservation, a day's horseback ride to the south. Associated with them were two other Irish-born army veterans, James J. Dolan and John G. Riley. On separate occasions both Dolan and Riley had killed civilians but had escaped trial by pleading due provocation.

The firm's commercial misdeeds led to its being banned from Fort Stanton in 1873. Small matter. By then Murphy and Fritz had become the local representatives of a pair of potent Santa Fe businessmen—William Rosenthal, one of the largest beef contractors in the Southwest, and A. A. Staab, who dealt primarily in flour. On winning contracts to supply Fort Stanton and the Indian reservation with beef and flour, Rosenthal and Staab called on The House to help them meet the commitments. Moving their headquarters to Lincoln town, the partners continued expanding with more vigor than scruple.

Lincoln was a Hispanic-style string village of thirty or forty adobe houses on the south side of Rio Bonito, a small creek winding between timbered hills. It had neither newspaper nor bank. Criminals departed from its makeshift jail with ease, and the courthouse was a decrepit building where itinerant judges held sessions in April and October.

The county deserved such a seat. Outlaws driven from Texas on the east and the mining communities to the west enjoyed a haven there, for the underfinanced county law enforcement agencies could not cover the area. Apache Indians roamed at will, stealing horses and having horses wrested from them in retaliation. Soldiers, most of them blacks, rode about on desultory patrols. Hispanic settlers formed tiny plazas beside the most easily diverted streams. Anglos hoping to sell hay, grain, and vegetables to the fort and reservation moved in beside them and quarreled bitterly over water. Other settlers and small cattlemen were beginning to dot widely separated sections of the broad Pecos Valley farther east. There they came into contact with Texas ranchers being crowded off their former ranges by the westward advance of the farmers' frontier. Rustling was widespread. That, too, brought on violence, as did the antipathies that had long existed between Texans and Mexicans.

The situation suited The House of Murphy. No one else in the county could import as much merchandise as it did. No one else could afford to extend as much credit and then wait for livestock to be sold and crops to be harvested before calling in the debts. The partners abused the monopoly. They charged high for what they sold, paid little for what they received. Customers who objected were tormented with lawsuits, writs of attachment, and threats of violence. Unable to afford redress, some victims left the country. The House then seized their real estate and, though title was questionable, sold or leased it to newcomers. They were suspected, moreover, of buying stolen cattle at bargain rates and of holding the animals on a ranch owned by their clerks, Dolan and Riley, near present-day Carlsbad in the Pecos Valley, until needed for meeting their Rosenthal commitments.

Political domination strengthened The House's economic grip. Once Murphy stormed into a nominating convention that was not going as he liked, overturned the recorder's table, tore up his papers, and bellowed at the audience, "You might as well try to stop the waves of the ocean with a fork as to try and oppose me." He was about right. According to one enemy "L. G. Murphy & Co. were absolute monarchs of Lincoln County and ruled their subjects with an oppressive iron heel."

All was not well within this seemingly invincible institution, however. Murphy was drinking himself to death, Fritz was incapacitated by tuberculosis, and finances were in a greater muddle than outsiders realized. When Fritz, a bachelor, died in 1874, a $10,000 insurance policy on his life assumed major importance. Although the policy's beneficiaries were Fritz's brother and sister, who lived in Lincoln County, Murphy sought to claim the proceeds on the grounds that his erstwhile partner had owed the firm several thousand dollars. The insurance company proving dilatory about payment, he hired the county's first lawyer, newly arrived Alexander A. McSween, to apply pressure.

Canadian-born Alex McSween had begun his practice of law in Kansas, where he had also acquired a vivacious, red-haired wife. Civic-minded and religious (reputedly, he had once studied for the Presbyterian ministry), he did not drink or carry weapons. He had bushy hair and a drooping mustache whose ends dangled below his jaw line. His courage was of the sort that comes from excessive stubbornness. Because he suffered from asthma, he sought relief in the high, dry climate of New Mexico. He chose Lincoln town as his home because of its mountainous surroundings and lack of lawyers. Two months after he arrived, he accepted Murphy's commission and traveled east to interview the insurance company.

Rebuffed by the firm, which claimed insolvency, he turned the matter over to a collection agency and went back to Lincoln. There he acquired a new client, John Chisum, one of the legendary cattle kings of the Southwest.* Like McSween, Chisum did not wear a revolver, though he sometimes rode with one nestled in a holster hung from his saddle horn. He was of medium height, his lean features adorned with a spike-ended mustache and small goatee. He was poker-faced, canny, sarcastic, humorous, and tough. Even at home he preferred sleeping on the floor to resting in bed. Unmarried, he had come out of Texas with his brothers during the late 1860s and had laid claim, through the bald right of occupancy, to about two hundred miles of the Pecos Valley.

By the time the river reached that section of New Mexico, it was so laden with alkali that it gave miserable scours, as diarrhea was often called, to man and beast; cowboys carried canned tomatoes with them rather than drink from it. The few tributaries that reached it from the west (none flowed into it from the Llano Estacado on the east) were like heaven, and it was beside one of these—a short, crystal gush of artesian water called South Spring River—that Chisum established his adobe headquarters.

Estimates of the number of cattle he owned ranged from 40,000 to 80,000. They were longhorns, not choice stock, but salable to Indian reservations in New Mexico and Arizona and to would-be ranchers throughout the High Plains. Managing the different herds required the labor of a hundred cowboys, many of them hardcase wanderers hired for lack of better applicants. Thieving Indians and rustling Anglos who resented Chisum's claims to so much range were a constant irritation, and by 1875 the rancher had decided that he would be just as prosperous

*John Chisum should not be confused, as he often is, with Jesse Chisholm, a half-breed trader to the Cherokee Indians of Oklahoma, whose wagon trace through Indian Territory eventually became the famed Chisholm trail linking north Texas to the railroad shipping towns of Kansas. As far as is known, Jesse Chisholm never drove a cow over the trail named for him.

and considerably more at ease if he cut back on quantity and concentrated on quality. Accordingly, he sold all but the South Spring River part of the outfit to a St. Louis cattle brokerage firm for a quarter of a million uninflated, untaxed dollars.

It was understood that two or three years would pass before the herds could be gathered and transferred to the buyers' ranches in Kansas. Meanwhile Chisum was to fill their beef contracts with Indian reservations in Arizona and open new contacts, if he could, with the Mescaleros of New Mexico. The arrangement put him on collision course with contractor William Rosenthal of Santa Fe, and through Rosenthal with Tom Catron and The House of Murphy. Rustlers meanwhile used the sale as an excuse to prey more heavily than ever on herds that now belonged to absentee owners. Chief among the suspects was the Jesse Evans gang, which allegedly used the Dolan–Riley cow camp as a hideout.

As a representative both of Murphy and Chisum, McSween stood in the middle of the developing tensions. He chose to side with Chisum. Precipitator of the decision was a twenty-three-year-old Englishman, John G. Tunstall. Son of a wealthy London merchant with a subsidiary store in Victoria, young Tunstall had clerked for a while in the British Columbia capital, found the work boring, and persuaded his father to back him in ranching. He reached Lincoln County during his search for a site in November 1876, and was about to buy property from Murphy when McSween warned him that the title was defective. So he went south about sixty miles and acquired two small ranches, one on the Rio Peñasco, and the other north of it on the Rio Feliz. McSween then helped him pick up, at a sheriff's sale, some cattle on which The House of Murphy had had its eye. Nor was that the end of effrontery. Tunstall, Chisum, and McSween decided to build a store in Lincoln that would compete with The House and to open a bank. McSween's contribution (he was perennially short of cash) was mostly in the form of services. Although he was promised a partnership in Tunstall's growing little empire, it was not to take effect until a specified time in the future.

Meanwhile Lawrence Murphy had grown so unwell that in April 1877 he sold his interests, including his Rosenthal beef contracts, to clerks Dolan and Riley and retired to his ranch. The high cost of the purchase and Tunstall's unexpected competition soon had the new owners floundering, and they were electrified on learning that the eastern collection agency employed by McSween had collected Fritz's insurance money and, after deducting expenses, had remitted over $7,000 to the lawyer. The storekeepers demanded the money on the worn ground that it was owed the firm by Fritz's estate.

McSween refused to surrender the funds either to them or to Fritz's heirs. His grounds: the Dolan–Riley claim was fraudulent, yet they would use it to cheat the heirs of the money if McSween turned it over to them. Therefore he would act as trustee until the matter was settled. Perhaps he was being honest—he had just prevailed on a Presbyterian minister to come to heathen Lincoln—but it is also well to remember that he, too, had little money and had recently embarked on expensive ventures.

McSween's refusal triggered what Texas historian J. Evetts Haley has called, in *George W. Littlefield, Texan,* "the bloodiest southwestern saga ever sung by 30-30 bullets and .45 slugs." The first shots, however, were legal and fired outside Lincoln County by beef contractor William Rosenthal, assisted by United States District Attorney Tom Catron. The motives were clear. Rosenthal did not want Chisum, who was financing the new competition, to upset his beef-gathering arrangements with J. J. Dolan & Company, as the old House of Murphy was now legally known. And Catron, who had just loaned J. J. Dolan & Company money, did not want to see them put to the wall by these upstarts.

They attacked cleverly. McSween, his wife, and Chisum left Lincoln shortly before Christmas of 1877, on a combined business and vacation trip to the East. As their stagecoach was rattling north from Las Vegas, New Mexico, a sheriff's posse swooped down and hustled them roughly back to Las Vegas for legal examination.

As U.S. district attorney, Catron had issued a warrant charging McSween with the criminal embezzlement of the Fritz insurance money and of conspiring to flee from the territory. As Rosenthal's attorney, Catron declared that his client held certain notes of indebtedness against John Chisum and that according to New Mexican law the rancher could not leave the territory without proving to the satisfaction of the authorities that he was able to meet the obligation.

Chisum fell into the trap. According to him, the notes that Rosenthal held had been signed illegally years before in Texas and even if they had been actionable once, which he denied, they no longer were because of the statute of limitations. Rosenthal had bought up the paper simply to harass him. To hell with them.

His refusal to make out a schedule of his property gave Rosenthal and Catron an excuse to hold him under surveillance in a Las Vegas hotel for eight weeks. Presumably they hoped that he would dislike the experience enough so that he would disassociate himself from Tunstall and McSween.

McSween's situation was serious. A Las Vegas deputy, A. P. Barrier, was ordered to take him to Mesilla for arraignment before Judge Warren Bristol of the third judicial district. Bristol and District Attorney William Rynerson, both of them creatures of the ring, tongue-lashed him severely, refused to accept the sureties he offered for bond, and told Barrier to turn him over to Sheriff William Brady in Lincoln.

In Lincoln The House rejoiced publicly. Chisum was out of circulation; McSween was all but in prison. Now for Tunstall. They attacked recklessly. At their prodding the Fritz heirs filed a civil suit in Mesilla against McSween for the insurance money and obtained from Judge Bristol a writ allowing them to attach enough of the lawyer's property to make the $7,000 good in the event they won the case.

This writ was turned over to Sheriff Brady. At Dolan's behest he moved to attach Tunstall's property as well as McSween's on the ground that the two were partners. The move was illegal. The partnership had not yet gone into effect, and, in addition, the value of the property Dolan wanted to confiscate far exceeded the amount of the insurance policy. Brady certainly knew this but filled Tunstall's store with deputies, nevertheless. He then sent a posse containing in its ranks the notorious Jesse Evans to the Englishman's ranch to attach his livestock. Learning that their quarry and five employees (a youth known as Billy the Kid was among them) were on the trail with a small herd of horses, part of the posse galloped after them. It was February 18, 1878.

By chance the lawmen came onto Tunstall just after his men, unaware of any pursuit, had scattered out to shoot some wild turkeys they had seen. Later the posse insisted that Tunstall began firing at them as they approached, an unlikely development in view of the odds involved. Anyway, they gunned him down. Awed by the size of the group, the five employees stayed out of sight, and the posse rode proudly back to Lincoln with the attached horses.

McSween was not in jail. He had convinced Deputy Barrier that he was the victim of unlawful harassment, and instead of turning him over to Brady as ordered, Barrier let the lawyer go to his own home. On learning of Tunstall's death, McSween rushed to the local justice of the peace, John B. Wilson, and obtained warrants for the arrest of the murdering possemen. The warrants were given to Constable Atanacio Martínez for serving. Accompanied by Billy the Kid and another Tunstall employee, Martínez went to Dolan's store, where some of the men named in the warrants were known to be. Sheriff Brady blocked the way, saying that legally appointed possemen were immune from arrest. He then locked the would-be servers in jail for several hours to show them the error of their ways.

By that injudicious move Brady created an American legend. Until then Billy had been an amiable lad whose brushes with the law had not been unduly serious by southwestern standards. Born Henry McCarty, probably in Missouri in 1855, he was bright and reasonably well-educated. He bobbed up in New Mexico when, at the age of eighteen, he attended the wedding of his mother and her longtime lover, William Antrim. Two years later he was arrested in the mining town of Silver City for helping a friend hide some clothing stolen from a Chinese laundry. Rather than face his stepfather's wrath, Billy wriggled out of jail by way of the chimney, fled to Arizona, and got a job as a teamster at a sawmill near Camp Grant. There, aged twenty-two, he killed a blacksmith who was abusing him and fled to Lincoln County.

He traveled under the alias of William Bonney or, more simply, The Kid. He was slender and of average height. One frequently printed photograph shows him draped with firearms and dressed in ill-fitting clothes topped by a battered black hat. A slight deformation given his face by his protuberant front teeth makes him look simple-minded. He was not, and it was Brady's misfortune that he failed to sense this.

Realizing that Tunstall's death would not be avenged legally, Billy and other supporters formed a vigilante group called the Regulators and set out to settle the score with the slayers. Their prompt killing of two suspects, along with a third House ally who happened to get in the way, brought increased demands from throughout the territory, already shocked by Tunstall's murder, that Governor Axtell intervene.

Yielding to the pressure, Axtell went to the strife-torn town and stayed there for three hours, during which time James Dolan never left his side. His sole official action consisted in removing from office the justice of the peace who had dared issue warrants against Brady's possemen and then arranging for the discharge of a deputy United States marshal who had been an employee of Tunstall's and was now making a nuisance of himself.

Obviously peace did not return. On the morning of April 1, 1878, Billy the Kid and five other Regulators hid behind an adobe wall abutting on Tunstall's store and shot down Sheriff Brady and a principal deputy, George Hindman, as they were walking along the street in broad daylight. Four days later, at a nearby lumber mill, Billy and company killed another suspect, losing in the process the leader of the Regulators, husky Dick Brewer. Counting Tunstall, the number of deaths now stood at eight.

When the grand jury met shortly thereafter, it issued about two hundred indictments. Billy the Kid was among those charged with murder. McSween came off unscathed. In spite of Judge Bristol's highly prejudicial instructions, the jury refused to indict him for embezzlement. McSween was so afraid for his life, however, that he, his wife, and the Regulators hid out, sometimes in the hills and sometimes at Chisum's South Spring home, to which the rancher had recently returned from Las Vegas. From him they received groceries and ammunition. The help was needed. Although the Lincoln County commissioners had named a relatively impartial man to be acting sheriff in Brady's place, Governor Axtell annulled the appointment and gave the job to George Peppin, a longtime House supporter. McSween, in short, could expect to be hounded to death.

By this time the Lincoln County scandals had come to the attention of the British embassy, which demanded a satisfactory explanation of Tunstall's death. Perturbed at last, President Hayes sent a special representative, Frank Warner Angel, to New Mexico to winnow the charges.

Angel arrived in New Mexico in June 1878. Officials were chilly; the ring's newspaper, the Santa Fe *New Mexican,* derided him; Dolan supporters in Lincoln were surly and uncommunicative. McSween's people, however, who stood to gain from the examination, gave him bales of affidavits under oath. Those collected, Angel went to Las Vegas to investigate the Maxwell land-grant scandals. While he was there, Lincoln erupted again.

Emboldened by Angel's visit, McSween decided to risk a showdown and on July 14 rode into Lincoln town with fifty or sixty men. Dividing the force into three parts, he occupied his own home and two other buildings, put up barricades, and awaited reactions.

They came fast. Rounding up an army of deputies, Sheriff Peppin laid siege. He also sent an appeal to Colonel N.A.M. Dudley, in command of Fort Stanton, for help. In spite of a federal law forbidding troops to serve as possemen in civilian disputes, Dudley, who was under obligations to Tom Catron, found an excuse for marching a company of soldiers into town. The campsite on which he chose to place the troops cut communications between McSween's house and the other buildings occupied by the Regulators.

Deciding during the night that McSween's quixotic attack was doomed, the men in the two outer forts melted away through the darkness. By dawn on the nineteenth the lawyer knew he was thoroughly outnumbered.

That morning Peppin's deputies managed to set fire to the far wing of McSween's U-shaped house. Extinguishing the blaze consumed all of the defenders' available water. When more tendrils of flame curled up later in the day, the remaining Regulators had to retreat grudgingly into the farthest of the back rooms. After examining the scattered outbuildings separating the house from the willows lining the creek several dozen yards away, Billy the Kid proposed that he and a few volunteers dash at dusk through the back door. While attention was on them, McSween and the others could flee past the chicken house to the creek.

To redheaded Susan McSween the plan looked suicidal. Defying her husband, she rushed outside and, counting on her skirts to protect her, ran up to Dudley, demanding that he stop the fighting. He refused, saying that the conflict was none of his business; he was there just to protect uninvolved women and children. In tears she returned to her smoldering home.

At dusk the Kid's diversionary dash took place as scheduled. One of his group was killed; the rest escaped into the brush beside the creek. Unhappily, McSween delayed his own start a moment too long. A roar of guns met his party. Four dropped lifeless, McSween with five bullets in his body. The women, children, and those who had chosen to stay in the house with the wounded surrendered as smoke began to overpower them.

Chaos followed. Throughout the county frightened settlers loaded their household goods into wagons and abandoned their homes. John Chisum started the best of the cattle he had retained from the sale of his ranch toward new range in the Texas Panhandle. Men who had been on the winning side in the battle, or who pretended to have been, rewarded themselves by looting the buildings and stealing the cattle of their former enemies. The embittered losers were no better. But worst of all were the criminals who flocked in, burning, thieving and—rare in range conflicts—raping. Appalled, Colonel Dudley, with no apparent realization of his own contributions to the breakdown, wrote his superiors: "I respectfully ask in the name of God and humanity that I may be allowed to use the forces of my command to drive these murderers, horse thieves, and escaped convicts out of the county." Local officials and ordinary citizens also begged for troops.

The President of the United States, who had been slowly digesting investigator Angel's reports, finally responded. He removed Axtell from office and allowed suggestions to reach U.S. District Attorney Catron,

New Mexico's attorney general, William Breeden, W. L. Rynerson of the third judicial district, and Frederick Godfrey of the Mescalero Reservation that it would be well if they resigned. They did. Strangely, Angel's files on Catron have since disappeared from the national archives.

Axtell's successor, who took office on October 1, was Civil War General Lew Wallace, currently engaged in writing his novel *Ben Hur*, which he finished during sleepless nights in the Palace of the Governors at Santa Fe. Sensing instantly the hostility of the ring, and startled to learn that the criminal docket at Lincoln was clogged with more cases than could be heard during the October session, the new governor moved circumspectly. The strategy he finally decided on in November was to declare a broad amnesty and under its umbrella to try to bring the warring factions together.

To an extent the program worked. Wallace, however, could not restrain Susan McSween. Hiring a lawyer as intemperate as she was—Houston Chapman of Las Vegas—she hurled at her dead husband's opponents every kind of actionable charge she could think of, reserving the greater part of her acerbity for Colonel Dudley. In the end Chapman was the one who suffered most from her actions. By chance he reached Lincoln on a visit during the bitterly cold evening of February 18, 1880. Leaders of the contending factions (Dolan was a principal negotiator on one side, Billy the Kid on the other) had just concluded a peace meeting in Dolan's erstwhile store, which was now the property, through foreclosure, of Tomcat Catron. The new pals sealed their bargain with more drinks than were wise, then staggered into the street, and bumped against Chapman, who was unarmed. Sharp words were followed by two shots—one almost certainly fired by James Dolan. Chapman crumpled. Some of the group, it is said, soaked his clothing in whiskey and set it afire. Or perhaps powder flashes from a gun pressed against his side started the blaze. Be that as it may, the charred corpse lay in the street until eleven-thirty the next night, when soldiers from Fort Stanton, fearing new outbreaks of violence, arrived to take charge.

Aroused, Wallace formed a county militia unit composed mostly of Mexican Americans and swept up as many persons associated with recent killings as he could find. Nobody suffered much. Many managed to flee in time. Some, Dolan included, had their indictments quashed and were released. Others were found innocent by their trial juries or were convicted, through plea bargaining, of minor charges. Dudley easily survived a military court of inquiry. Catron oozed back into public life; at the ring's behest, another President appointed Axtell chief justice of the New Mexico Supreme Court.

Billy the Kid, still under indictment for Brady's murder, sought immunity by offering to testify against Chapman's killers. When circumstances made him feel that Wallace was not treating him fairly, he broke jail and began the spectacular career of banditry that did not end until Pat Garrett, elected sheriff of Lincoln County on a stern law-and-order platform, attained his own bit of immortality by tracking Billy to a ranch bedroom at Fort Sumner and there, on the night of July 31, 1881, killing him in the darkness.

## *The Assassins*

Southern New Mexico learned little from the Lincoln County debacle. New feuds, nourished as usual by unquestioning courage and stiff-necked refusals to compromise, broke out on the western slopes of the Sacramento Mountains, in Lincoln's neighbor, Doña Ana County, where swift little streams dance down through grass-covered foothills to obliteration in the gritty wastes of the Tularosa Valley.

Again the story involves the obstinacy of an established figure being challenged by an ambitious newcomer. In this case the old-timer was one of the West's extraordinary soldiers of fortune, Colonel Albert Jennings Fountain. If Fountain's own stories are to be believed, he spent his late teens sailing the seven seas with other reckless youths. He was mixed up with Chinese smugglers and with William Walker's filibuster in Nicaragua. Still only twenty-four, he came to New Mexico with Carleton's California Column, fought with the wagon train that Mangas Coloradas and Cochise ambushed in Apache Pass, married a fourteen-year-old Mexican beauty, and on being mustered out settled in Franklin, Texas, predecessor of American El Paso.

He served briefly in the Texas legislature as a radical Reconstruction Republican, which did not endear him to the defeated Confederates. After surviving a wild daytime shoot-out in an El Paso street, during which his opponent was killed and he was severely wounded, he moved to Mesilla. Contentious always, he founded (as he described it) a crusading law-and-order newspaper, dived deep into Republican politics, became a lawyer (he represented Billy the Kid as long as that young man consented to stay in jail), and, as a sideline, formed a guerrilla troop, mostly Hispanos, devoted to chasing down cattle thieves and fending off Apaches who raided the area during breakouts from their reservation. But he had gentler yearnings, too, and in order to temper the rawness of his home town put together what contemporaries considered to be a highly competent theatrical group. Naturally Fountain played most of the leading roles.

His challenger, Albert B. Fall, was twenty-three years younger. Fall had farmed, taught school, and read a little law in his native Kentucky before moving to Texas for his health. There he married and in between more bouts of reading law worked as a ranch cook and cowboy. Becoming infected with the prospecting virus, he roamed the hills of both Old and New Mexico in search of the pot of gold he never found. He wanted a more stable life for his family and settled, in 1887, in burgeoning Las Cruces, New Mexico, across the Rio Grande from Mesilla. Financed by his brother-in-law, he founded a rival newspaper to Fountain's, opened a law office, and dived deep into Democratic politics.

Conflicts between the two men were fierce, especially at the polls, which at times had to be guarded by the militia. Both served on occasion in the territorial legislature and both were appointed to important posts, with the lion's share going to Fall. Meanwhile a crippling drought followed by the Panic of 1893 were playing havoc with the ranchers and farmers of southern New Mexico. Short of grass, large ranchers crowded onto land claimed by "nesters." Short of cash, the nesters and small cattlemen took to raiding the herds of their larger neighbors. To protect themselves, the big ranchers formed the Southeastern New Mexico Livestock Association and hired Fountain as their lawyer. Fall became the representative of the small operators, whose leader was tough, black-eyed Oliver Lee, formerly of Texas.

Arrests, shootings, and trials muddied with charges of bribery kept tempers at fiery pitch. During a street battle in the autumn of 1895, Fall and his brother-in-law wounded a Fountain adherent without serious injury to themselves. After that, Fountain pressed the association's attack on Oliver Lee more grimly than ever. Because some of the offenses for which he wanted indictments had been committed in Lincoln County, the lawyer traveled by buggy to the county seat in January 1896, to obtain them. With him he took his youngest son, aged nine, evidently on the assumption that his opponents would not harm a child.

He was wrong. Later reconstructions indicated that during Fountain's return journey three riders dogged the buggy for many miles and then attacked in the Chalk Hills section of the gaunt San Andreas Mountains. In time the buggy was found twelve miles off the road, but no trace of Fountain or his son was ever discovered.

The murders were a western sensation. Fearing that no lawman in southern New Mexico was impartial enough to handle the case, the governor of New Mexico bribed the sheriff of Doña Ana County to resign and then appointed Pat Garrett, slayer of Billy the Kid, to fill the vacancy. The going was slow. Not until April 1898 did Garrett collect sufficient evidence, as he saw it, to obtain warrants for the arrest of Oliver Lee and two rancher accomplices. The attempt he and four deputies then made to capture the trio led to the lawmen losing one of their number and being driven off in confusion.

During this time Albert Fall, commissioned captain of a group of New Mexico volunteers, was sweating out the Spanish-American War at a training camp in Georgia. Discharged, he returned to New Mexico and persuaded the Lee trio to stand trial for the alleged murders.

Thomas B. Catron was chosen to head the prosecution. Tomcat had become familiar during the years with assassination—that is, murder with political overtones. At a legislative meeting on the night of February 5, 1891, he had happened to change seats with another man after a moment of stretching and shifting around. Instants later a shotgun blast intended for him hit the person in his erstwhile seat. Although the state offered a $20,000 reward for the apprehension of the killers, no arrests were made, because of the persuasiveness, whispers said, of certain high-placed Democrats.

Soon the Democrats suffered in their turn, though not, as far as can be shown, as a consequence of the attempt on Catron. One Santa Fe stalwart, Francisco Chàvez, was slain in 1892; his friend, Sylvestre Gallegos, was murdered in 1893. Five Hispanos led by the Republican Borrego brothers were brought to trial for the murders. While conducting their defense, Catron resorted to such reprehensible tactics that he was threatened with disbarment. Though he carried the case to the Supreme Court of the United States, he lost, and his clients were executed in March 1897.

Now he was being pitted, as Lee's prosecutor, against another rising Democrat in a murder case that many people believed was politically inspired. Some even gossiped (without, as far as is known, any direct evidence to support their assumption) that Fall himself had prevailed on Oliver Lee to kill Fountain. Then Fountain's son had been slain lest he identify the assailants.

The trial began on May 26, 1899. County lines were redrawn to obtain jurisdictions favorable to the accused. Telegraph companies ran special lines to the tiny mining town of Hillsboro, where, under a change of venue, the confrontation took place. After a trial filled with sulfurous rhetoric, the jury retired and in less than a quarter of an hour found Lee and his associates not guilty.

The deadly feuds seemed to have no end. After a stint as U.S.

collector of customs in El Paso, Garrett returned to Doña Ana County and became involved in a complex land dispute with a rancher named Cox. On February 29, 1908, while in the company of two Cox cowboys, Wayne Bazel and Carl Adamson, who had reason to fear him, the ex-sheriff stepped out of his carriage to urinate. While in that vulnerable position, he was shot in the back of the head. Legal suspicion fell on Wayne Bazel, who may or may not have been acting on the orders of his employer. In any event, Fall leaped to Bazel's defense and won his acquittal.

This was in the twentieth century, and still New Mexico's "long and painful journey" into maturity, as Marc Simmons has described the state's trials, was not ended. As Tom Catron had done half a century before, Albert Fall switched political allegiance from Democratic to Republican and on the territory's admission to the union as a state in 1912 became one of its first two senators. Nine years later Warren Harding picked him to be Secretary of the Interior, in which position his Teapot Dome dealings made him the Republicans' scapegoat when scandal was threatening to shake the administration apart. He was the first United States Cabinet member ever to be imprisoned for malfeasance in office.

Tom Catron's life faded out more pleasantly. Having, through his land-grant dealings, made himself the wealthiest man in New Mexico, he became Fall's fellow senator in Washington and eventually died in apparent peace. But, as the next section will show, the agonies he helped bring to the Hispanic people of New Mexico have persisted until our own time, the culminating legacy of the refusal of a coterie of willful men to abide by their own country's laws and international promises.

## No Place to Go

When Surveyor General Julian denounced land fraud in New Mexico, his primary concern was with the acreage that artificially enlarged grants abstracted from the public domain of the United States. Before a grant could be enlarged, however, title to it had to be obtained from its original owners, most of them native Hispanos. In this area, too, indefensible practices were often involved. Julian gave less heed to that point, though as time would show, such losses were of potentially greater harm to northern New Mexico than was the deprivation brought to the public domain. For the New Mexican loss was an ultimate violence—not just the taking of land or even life, but the erosion of cherished patterns of living.

The Hispanos themselves inadvertently prepared the way for the Anglo assault on their holdings. When the first surveyor general of New Mexico, William Pelham, reached Santa Fe, he found 168,000 documents jumbled together with wanton carelessness in the archives. It took him and his small staff months to separate land-grant papers from the rest of the bureaucratic droppings, and as the pile slowly grew, unfortunate gaps appeared.

Most were attributable to the province's remoteness. No Spanish or Mexican overseer was likely to check on whether or not every applicant for a grant followed every step prescribed by law—any more than the men in charge of American land offices checked on the details of every homesteader's statements. As a result some steps had not been taken. Essential documents had not been properly filed or had been lost. Because instrument surveys had often been impossible to make, grant boundaries were vaguely located and frequently overlapped. Many heirs of the original grantees, it also developed, had lost their papers, too, and had only the fuzziest notion of what their legal, as distinct from their traditional, rights really were. These flaws, of scant consequence during the Mexican regime, became crucial after the American conquest.

The Treaty of Guadalupe Hidalgo that closed the war pledged the victors to respect the property of former Mexicans as amply "as if the same belonged to citizens of the United States." As Senator Thomas Hart Benton of Missouri and others pointed out, the fairest way of meeting that promise would have been to assume that all land titles in the conquered area were sound and to have required challengers, the government included, to demonstrate otherwise. Congress, however, chose to consider claimants guilty until *they* proved their innocence. In consequence every grant owner had to gather up such papers as he could resurrect, find witnesses, make the long, expensive journey to Santa Fe, present his case in a foreign language to a suspicious surveyor, and endure an indefinite period of waiting for a decision. If the outcome was favorable, then came the necessity of winning final approval from the American Congress in a far-off, mysterious place called Washington, D.C.

So laborious a process, coupled with the inadequacies of the Hispanic records, made New Mexico a paradise for lawyers. One of every ten Anglos in the territory during the early decades of American rule, it has been said, was a barrister. And since these lawyers' land-grant clients had little ready cash, most took as their pay a portion of the grant —up to one half in many instances.

Half of how much? It was generally at this point that those swellings of which Julian complained so bitterly occurred. The Maxwell grant's mete-and-bounds survey for 1.7 million acres has already been noted. Another notorious case among many was the Tierra Amarilla ("Yellow Earth") grant located on the watershed of the upper Chama River in New Mexico and Colorado. Under the transits of surveyor H. M. Atkinson it expanded to 600,000 acres and landed in the capacious pockets of Thomas Benton Catron. A few aggressive and cooperative Hispanos, it should be mentioned, also learned to take advantage of these elastic qualities in grant surveying.

Once a lawyer (or the company he represented) had acquired a portion of a grant, he could generally find ways of absorbing the rest. One favorite device was an American law that allowed any individual among the multiple owners of a grant to demand a partitioning of the whole. After the pie had been sliced and the integrity of an essentially communal unit destroyed, the petitioner then set about persuading his neighbors to sell to him. The jingle of relatively small amounts of cash in that barter-oriented, largely uneducated society would always win over some, and then the holdouts would be less able than ever to resist the pressures that followed—a large herd of sheep crowding their animals out of a traditional grazing ground, say, or the unexpected failure of water to run through a ditch at a crucial time.

Another path to full ownership was through tax titles. Neither Spain nor Mexico had imposed levies on real estate, nor did the territory of New Mexico do so until well after the Civil War. When the system finally engulfed the Hispanos, they did not understand it. More often than not they were unaware of the date when their payments were due and, in any event, frequently lacked funds with which to meet the levies. Alert Anglos needed only to appear early at regularly scheduled tax sales in order to acquire thousands of expandable acres at a fraction of their true value.

By far the largest area of any grant was its *ejido* ("commons"), where the people of the grant ran their livestock, cut firewood and roof beams, and fished and hunted game for their tables. The existence of these *ejidos* faced American judges with a knotty problem. American law does not recognize communally held land. Although exceptions developed with time, title to a piece of the public domain within the United States was first established by someone actually living on the property and working it. This property, moreover, was supposed to be rectangular in order to fit the American grid system of surveying.

The Hispanos, by contrast, did not live on the land they farmed but clustered in villages. The only real estate to which the ordinary dweller had title was his house lot and a long, narrow field for farming, its shape determined by the way the community irrigation ditch ran. The commons lay out beyond the village and was not divided. It was there for the use of anyone and everyone who lived on the grant—and after a few generations the total might come to several hundred persons. What was to be done with them?

Some lawyer discovered that perhaps the rights of those who used certain *ejidos* could be challenged. Fuzzy precedents in antique Spanish law seemed to say that although the king might permit villages to use a designated stretch of land in common, title remained with the sovereign. Thus in acquiring the Southwest from Mexico, the argument ran, the United States had also acquired title to the *ejidos* and could place them in the public domain, where they would be subject to homesteading by any American citizen, whether native or naturalized.

There were two exceptions. One said that if a grant's original deed specifically gave an *ejido* to a town, the king's right expired and the town held title. Even today there remain in New Mexico nineteen small communities that own their *ejidos* and manage them through an elected board of trustees.

Not many villages could cite specific references to their *ejidos* in their grant papers, however. Accordingly, after the turn of the century, the U.S. Forest Service was able to sweep up 600,000 acres of timberland that had once been used communally by Hispanos in north-central New Mexico, and by calling it public domain land incorporate it into the Santa Fe and Carson national forests. Later, in the 1930s, the Bureau of Land Management extended its sway over parts of certain *ejidos* that were suited primarily to grazing. This thrust the Hispanos into an unfamiliar economic system. They had to compete with Anglo ranchers to obtain, at a cost, permits for grazing stock and cutting wood on the forests they had always assumed were theirs. They were told that they must participate in the erection of costly drift fences and that they could hunt and fish only if they procured licenses, again at a cost.

The other exception to retained sovereignty dealt with grants given to individuals who promised to colonize them. In such a case the grantee held the *ejido*. Invariably, however, he allowed the colonists he attracted to his grant to use the land around their villages in the traditional way, or else they would not have followed him to the holding. But when aliens acquired the grant, they either levied rents against anyone who used the land, as the owners of the Maxwell grant did, or else closed it off entirely so that their herds could range it undisturbed. When this happened, the dwellers on private grants were in no better shape than villagers whose *ejidos* had been declared part of the public domain. Both groups were confined to the little farm plots they owned beside the pueblos. The severity of the situation is suggested by the extent of *ejido* losses suffered by the Hispanos of northern New Mexico after the American occupation—about 3.7 million acres of *ejido* land.

Nor was this the end of the pinch. During the middle of the nineteenth century, Hispanic New Mexico experienced a mild population boom. Families searching for new land moved up the Rio Grande into Colorado and across the Sangre de Cristo Mountains to its eastern slopes. (Some of the migrants were Penitentes searching for freedom from religious persecution.) Sheepmen went still farther—down the Canadian River onto the Texas Panhandle and southeast into the then-open stretches of what became Lincoln County.

About 1880 this slow drift was brought to an abrupt halt by pioneering Anglos—farmers in the San Luis Valley and along the upper reaches of southern Colorado's Purgatory River, and Texas cattlemen in the Canadian and Pecos valleys. During times of violence, as in Lincoln County, racial prejudices became entangled with the main issues, and the Hispanos suffered from that, too. Meanwhile lands that they might have used in the west and north had become part of the Navajo, Ute, and Jicarilla Apache reservations.

Boxed in, the Hispanos retreated to their old homes. But these could give them only the scantiest subsistence, for they had been divided again and again among many heirs. After the arrival of the displaced Hispanos, plots became as small as ten, even six acres. Inevitably they were overfarmed and overgrazed. Silt clogged the little streams. The evidences of poverty kept pace—plaster peeling off the adobe walls of the houses, sagging fences, litter in the yards. Infant mortality soared. Children who lived had such decayed teeth and swollen tonsils that they could only eat with difficulty.

Desperate for jobs, entire families became migrant workers, shearing sheep throughout the mountain states or thinning sugar beets with backbreaking, short-handled hoes as far north as the Canadian border. Others sought work in the cities, but because of their lack of education and training could find only unskilled jobs at minimum wages. Yet always, if they possibly could, they retained the family home back in the red hills. It was a refuge, the source of their lives, a symbol of continuity. Or as the New Mexico State Planning Office put the matter in its *Land Title Study* of 1971, "The land providing a living for the family has always been as much a part of the family as the home or the children. To sell it was, and is, equivalent to selling a family member."

Wrath over lost *ejidos* sometimes exploded. During the 1870s and 1880s a Hispanic vigilante group calling itself Gorras Blancas ("White Caps") roamed San Miguel County, cutting the fences being erected by new grant owners, killing livestock, burning barns. About 1912 a group called Manos Negras ("Black Hands") used similar tactics when fencing first appeared on the Tierra Amarilla grant in Rio Arriba County. But there was no systematic effort to give cohesion to the protests until the advent, during the 1960s of Reies Tijerina, sometimes called El Tigre ("The Tiger").

Although no one has ever denied Tijerina's charisma, strong differences of opinion exist, even among Spanish Americans, as to whether he is a dangerous mountebank or a selfless idealist. He was born in west Texas in September 1926 to a family of migrant workers. He says that during the depression he ate from garbage cans and added to the family income by collecting and selling rags. Converted to Protestantism, he went to a fundamentalist Bible school in Isleta, Texas, a few miles down the Rio Grande from El Paso, and became a fiery, ever-roaming evangelical preacher. He is of medium height, powerfully muscled, with nervously mobile features, green eyes, and coarse black hair.

His attempt to found a commune in Arizona brought on clashes with neighbors and warrants for his arrest on charges of theft, which were trumped up, he insists. He fled to New Mexico, and as he roamed among the Hispanos who were clinging to the remnants of their old lives, a conviction came to him like an epiphany: "I saw the land question as the hope of the Southwest." To increase his hold on those who flocked to hear him, he joined the Catholic Church. He played up the Indian blood of his audiences, called them a new breed, and shouted over and over, "They took your land away and gave you powdered milk [a hated symbol of welfare condescension throughout the Southwest]. They took your trees and grazing away from you and gave you Smokey the Bear. . . . They took your manhood away and asked you to lie down and be" —his wide mouth flexed savagely—"a Good Mexican."

Such talk and the recommendations for violence that accompanied it repelled middle-class Hispanos who, adapting to the American system, had created small businesses or had found places in the professions or politics. The poor, however, cheered and many, though there is no way of knowing how many, became members of Tijerina's Alianza Federal de Mercedes, ("Federal Alliance of Land Grants"), which he later renamed the Confederación de Pueblos Libres (the Confederation of Free City-States).

The volatile 1960s were a propitious time for Reies Tijerina. New ranchers had purchased parts of the former Tierra Amarilla grant that had not been occupied for some time and were closing it off to the local people who had resumed using it. The Forest Service tightened its regulations on grazing and began paying more attention, the mountain folk believed, to the wants of outside hunters and fishermen than to the region's hungry workers.

Elsewhere other minorities were demanding justice. Tremendously excited by the Watts riots in Los Angeles, Tijerina repeatedly held up to his followers the example of the militant blacks. Indian tribes, he pointed out, had been and were suing the United States over the injustices involved in the taking of their lands, and they were winning settlements. At that very time, the mid-1960s, the inhabitants of Taos Pueblo were demanding that the Forest Service return their sacred Blue Lake area in the Sangre de Cristo Mountains. Could the Indio-Hispanos, as Tijerina liked to call his followers, be satisfied with less?*

New violence struck the mountains, particularly in Rio Arriba County, whose seat, dilapidated Tierra Amarilla, had once been the principal pueblo of the Tierra Amarilla grant. Long stretches of wire fence were cut to pieces; haystacks, barns, even ranch houses went up in flames. Tijerina was suspected, but insisted that he had been in Mexico studying land-grant law. Perhaps so. Anyway, he struck out on a new tack, insisting that the old land-grant villages had in effect been free city-states (an argument that Myra Ellen Jenkins, State Archivist of New Mexico, says is without merit), that their charters had never been abrogated, and that the taking of Hispanos' communal lands had been a breach of international law.

When petitions bearing these assertions brought either evasive responses or none at all from the President of the United States, his Cabinet members, and the governor of New Mexico, Tijerina decided on a daring stroke to call attention to his pleas. On October 22, 1966, he led a hundred carloads of followers onto a Forest Service campground at Echo Amphitheater, where a huge, overhanging sandstone cliff beside U.S. Highway 84 repeats even whispers that are uttered in front of it.

Echo Amphitheater stands on land once claimed by the San Joaquín del Rio de Chama Land grant in the southern part of Rio Arriba County. Toward the end of the last century the cattle company that had acquired ownership of the grant submitted to the Court of Private Land Claims a request that it confirm the owner's deed to a questionably large 472,-737 acres. The court rejected all but 1,422 acres. The rest, at least part

*In 1970 Congress did pass, and the President did sign, a bill returning the Blue Lake area—48,000 acres—to Taos Pueblo.

of which had been the *ejido* of the heirs of grantee Francisco Salazar, was placed in the public domain. Later the Forest Service appropriated part of it.

Tijerina now took it back. He and his lieutenants ran up a crude banner, proclaimed the existence of the Free City State of San Joaquín del Rio de Chama, arrested two startled forest rangers for trespassing, and temporarily appropriated their pickup trucks. The grant, Tijerina thundered, once again belonged to the people.

After the occupation forces had disbanded, the state responded with arraignments of its own, accusing several Alianza members of seizing government property and interfering with the work of legally designated officials. This triggered a winter-long round of protest marches, interviews with the governor, inflammatory rhetoric, and the like. When the dry spring came, forest fires of suspicious origin erupted throughout the northern mountains. Tijerina then announced that the Alianza would hold its annual convention on June 3, 1967, at the little adobe town of Coyote in southern Rio Arriba County. Word leaked that this time the Alianza would take over the old San Joaquín de Chama grant for good. Tijerina even invited a Chicano radical of Denver, Corky Gonzales, founder of the Crusade for Justice, to come south and watch them do it.

District Attorney Alfonso Sanchez, whose jurisdiction covered Santa Fe, Los Alamos, and Rio Arriba counties, promptly overreacted. He announced through statewide media that the proposed assembly was illegal and that anyone attending it would be subject to arrest. Roadblocks were set up, cars halted and searched, and several Alianza members detained on a variety of charges. The principal target, Reies Tijerina, eluded the net, however.

A preliminary hearing for those arrested at Coyote was set for June 5 in the Tierra Amarilla courthouse, a high-windowed, dejected old building whose paint was peeling and whose façade of pseudo-Roman pillars leaned askew. Supposing that District Attorney Sanchez would be present at the arraignments, about twenty Alianza members decided to subject him to a citizen's arrest for (as they said) his illegal breaking up of their convention.

Although citizen's arrests for due cause are legal in New Mexico, the methods used by the vengeful Alianza posse probably were not. They charged, heavily armed, into the courthouse, and when a startled deputy seemed to be reaching for his gun, fired wildly. Two officers were badly wounded; another was beaten across the head with a pistol barrel. The presiding judge fled into the nearest toilet and locked the door. Sanchez, it developed, was not in the courthouse. Although Tijerina appeared after the assault, the question of whether or not he actually participated in the shooting became a matter of tragic controversy.

After whooping triumphantly through the courthouse for an hour and a half, the victors decided to disperse. Some took with them, as hostages, a deputy sheriff and a newspaper reporter. It was an injudicious move since it rendered them liable to charges of kidnapping, a crime then punishable in New Mexico, under certain circumstances, by death.

This time it was the state's lieutenant governor who, in the governor's absence, overreacted. Revolution! Out came five hundred militiamen supported by two tanks, some cannons, jeeps, and helicopters. This formidable array captured about two score villagers, and incarcerated them overnight in a sheep pen, presumably in the hope that alarm over the well-being of the prisoners would draw the fugitives out of the hills. The tactic failed and the militia were recalled. During the next few weeks routine procedures succeeded in rounding up the fugitives, some of whom were declared subject to two trials, one for the Echo Amphitheater episode, the other for the courthouse raid.

The first confrontation resulted in a relatively minor sentence for Tijerina. The second, potentially far more dangerous to him, revolved around his whereabouts during the shooting. He said he had been visiting in a nearby house and had not left it until he heard the gunfire; after that he had tried to restore peace. The principal witness contradicting this alibi was jailer Eulogio Salazar, one of the two men wounded during the shooting. Less than a month before Tijerina's preliminary hearing in Santa Fe, Salazar was brutally beaten to death in his own car on a snowy road outside Tierra Amarilla. All Alianza leaders were rounded up for questioning, but all offered unshakable alibis, and the murder has never been solved.

Tijerina conducted his own defense in Santa Fe. Roaring theatrics. Impassioned pleas that his people receive justice. He made his point to the nation's press, but was bound over for full trial, to be held in Albuquerque in November 1968. There the prosecution proved inept and the identification by witnesses, in the absence of Salazar, hesitant. The jury deliberated only four hours before finding El Tigre innocent.

To militant America, Reies Tijerina was, for a brief time, a national hero. He was a speaker on college campuses and at Indian conventions. He led the Chicano branch of the Poor People's March in Washington, D.C., and discussed strategy with Martin Luther King and Cesar Chavez. But the heady excitement did not last. Once he had departed from the land-grant issue he lost his effectiveness. Young Chicanos grew impatient with him, factions split the Alianza, and the declining radicalism of the 1970s eroded much of his support.

His maneuvers grew wild. After the United Nations ignored his plea that it investigate the failure of the United States to meet its pledges in the Treaty of Guadalupe Hidalgo, he turned on Mexico. That nation, too, was guilty, he charged, for it should have made sure that the treaty obligations were fulfilled. Since it had not, it was bound to pay claimants for their losses, a sum he set at between $40 million and $200 million.

Thousands of wistful heirs and pretended heirs in California, Arizona, New Mexico, Texas, and Florida paid Tijerina $22 each to process their records. In January 1978, two thousand of them poured into the border town of Edinburg, Texas, to hear him outline his strategy. To their outrage they were charged ten dollars to attend the meeting. Again factions split the gathering, and when the claims were at last forwarded to Mexico, President Lopez Portillo said, "Mexico cannot pay Mr. Tijerina his millions of dollars, nor should she." To which an aide added, concerning the claimants, "They're nuts."

Possibly. But however impractical the appeal seemed in Mexico City, to the Hispanos it had been a last desperate attempt to hang on to crumbling lifeways. For most of them public welfare had become the bounds of their horizons. The extended family was shrinking in on itself. Schools were bringing incomprehensible new values to their children. The Catholic Church and the fiestas and ceremonies that had once provided a core for their daily living had lost its hold. Only the enduring land remained.

You can still see the symbols of the desperation at Tierra Amarilla and the other Hispanic towns of Rio Arriba: gaunt old adobe houses, doors and windows boarded up, roof lines sagging—not abandoned, just waiting for the people to come back. Of course they're nuts. But there has to be some kind of hope.

Currently there seems to be only this: Someday, perhaps, its conscience touched, the nation will establish a trial board like the one that reviewed Indian claims to hear the Hispanos' story. But can monetary recompense, if it ever comes, reestablish the things that are slipping away but that Tijerina, whatever his motives may be, has promised to bring back?

# 8

## GROPING TOWARD STABILITY

### Dreams and Realities

And now to account for the name Arizona, which has nothing to do with "arid zone," logical though that derivation may seem.

Let us begin with Thomas Butler King, one of the first Americans to believe in and urge the building of a railroad from the interior of the continent to the Pacific. A five-term Georgia congressman, King had resigned from his seat in 1849 to go to California as President Taylor's personal representative during that region's statehood agitations. He hoped to become a senator from the Golden State but was defeated and had to settle for a sinecure position as head of the San Francisco customhouse. Railroading remained his paramount interest, however, and in 1852 he returned to the South to become vice-president of the Texas Western, a San Diego-bound line being promoted by his friend Robert J. Walker, Secretary of the Treasury during the Polk administration.

The enormous handicap deterring investment in such a line was dearth of population. What would generate traffic?

A part of the optimistic answer revolved around the mines presumed to lie in the strip of territory south of the Gila River that James Gadsden, another railroad man, was authorized, in 1853, to buy from Mexico. Surely those 30,000 square miles embraced enough deposits of gold, silver, and copper (ancient Spanish records actually named some of them) to keep enterprising Anglos busy for years to come. What the Texas Western needed to do, in order to impress potential investors, was to pinpoint some of those mines as quickly as possible.

Enter Charles Debrille Poston, a clerk in the San Francisco customhouse. He was crop-bearded, black-haired, glib and nimble. He knew

King and, presumably, was aware of the Texas Western's plans. He had done considerable reading, much of it in Spanish, about the resources of the Southwest.

When news reached San Francisco late in January 1854 that the Gadsden Purchase had been completed, Poston recruited a party of prospectors that included a skilled, footloose German mining engineer, Herman Ehrenberg, for whom the Colorado River town of Ehrenberg would later be named. Whatever the motives of the others may have been, it seems fairly certain that Charles Poston's hope was to discover mines that would help bolster the sagging stock of the Texas Western.

The quickest way to reach the newly discovered territory, he decided, was to sail aboard the British bark *Zoraida* to Guaymas, a small port beside the Gulf of California on Mexico's west coast. From there the party could strike overland to Tucson.

If the prospectors covered as much ground as Poston later claimed in his sometimes contradictory reminiscences, they wore seven-league boots. The *Zoraida* wrecked on an island in the Gulf that fortunately contained a spring of sweet water and a herd of wild cattle. Living well on "our [salvaged] sea-bread, roast beef, and the honey and wild fruits of the island," the castaways knocked together a small craft in which they reached the mainland. On horseback they struck north. En route they were held for a time as suspected members of a filibustering party that had followed William Walker of California (no relation to railroader Robert Walker) south in a knuckleheaded attempt to wrest Baja California and Sonora from Mexico.

Eventually, after an ill-considered, nightmare side trip to the sun-blasted delta of the Colorado River, the party reached Tubac and from there fanned out east and west through the gaunt mountains. They came back loaded with samples of silver, gold, and copper ore, most of it probably acquired from Anglo and Mexican miners already in the area. Now to promote the "discoveries"! Poston and Ehrenberg headed overland for San Francisco, pausing long enough on the way to survey and lay claim to the town site that later grew into Yuma, Arizona.

In San Francisco Poston distributed enough copper samples to spark what was called the Arizona Mining and Trading Company—more about that choice of name in a moment. Then off to the East he went via Panama, to push his silver. By that time the Texas Western was in dire straits, and the promoters were maneuvering so close to the edges of the law that Sam Houston himself declared it might not be amiss "if a respectable number of citizens of Texas were to take these fellows out and administer a decent number of lashes, accompanied by a coat of tar and feathers." Most definitely a gleam of hope from the West was needed.

After several rebuffs, Poston managed, in March 1856, to put together in Cincinnati the Sonora Exploration and Mining Company, capitalized for $2 million. By selling stock at 10 percent of its face value, he raised enough money to begin operations. His journey west led him through Texas and Mesilla. And there, in Mesilla, we at last come back to the name Arizona.

Agitation to split New Mexico in half by a line running east and west had already begun. The proposed southern section, whose capital was to be Mesilla, of course needed a name. Some of the schemers were suggesting Pimería; some, Cibola. Poston shook his head. No romance. Arizona would be better.

To show why, he dug out a history of Sonora written by José Francisco Velasco and published in Mexico City in 1850. It was not a very good book, but it had served him well. Because of it, the name Arizona had been attached to the Arizona Mining and Trading Company recently founded in San Francisco, and it had been one of his mainstays in persuading his Cincinnati backers to part with their funds.

Arizona: just listen! Way back in the 1720s Don Gabriel de Prudhom, a great believer in minerals as the hope of Sonora, had become *alcalde mayor* of the province. In 1730 showings of metal near the site of present-day Nogales, Mexico, led him to establish a *real de minas* there, a mining concession whose title, like all those in New Spain, derived from the king. The *real* had to have a name, and Prudhom chose Arizonac, after a local spring of good water that the Papago Indians called, approximately, *ali shonak*. On the tongues of the Spanish prospectors in the region, *ali shonak* became Arizonac.

For a while Arizonac did not amount to much. But in 1735 a Yaqui Indian stumbled across a great lump of almost pure horn silver. A rush unearthed scores more. Teams of oxen could not budge one silver boulder, whose weight was estimated at 3,750 pounds. A poor black ingeniously attached pulleys to convenient tree branches to raise another chunk, weighing 425 pounds, high enough so that he could lead his pack mule underneath it.

How could the phenomenon of this silver be explained? Was it buried treasure left behind by the predecessors of the Aztecs? Or a *criadero*, literally a growing place of metal?

Actually, horn silver, or cerargyrite—which is a form of silver chloride—is fairly common in the upper reaches of ore bodies in arid regions, but generally it occurs in thin seams, not as ingots. *Bolas de plata* ("balls of silver") the Arizonac prospectors called them in awe, and they broke them up with hammers and carried them off on their pack stock with such speed that the king received only a fraction of the royalties due him. But although the ore vanished, the story did not, and the name Arizonac, often clipped to Arizona, clung to the region. What was more, Velasco intimated in his history, many more comparable discoveries awaited only the quieting of the Apaches.

So. There was a name—Arizona. People would listen to that.

The hope faded. Though the early mines in the Gadsden Purchase area earned small profits by the selective extraction of high-grade ore, they were soon overshadowed by more exciting, if more ephemeral, gold placers discovered on the Gila River and beside the Colorado at scattered spots above Fort Yuma. The Texas Western died, and the approach of the Civil War ended the possibility of luring in another line. For transportation the handful of Anglos and Mexicans in the region had to rely on rough wagon roads winding out of the east, on mule trains toiling north from the inadequate Gulf of California port at Guaymas—or on the Colorado River.

How that river was hated—and yet it was a lifeline for Fort Yuma and the gold camps upstream, for the mining regions around Prescott, and even, during a brief period, for the Mormons' immigrant landing docks and cotton warehouses at Callville, buried now under the waters of Lake Mead. Most of the merchandise destined for those spots was loaded onto schooners (later steamers) at San Francisco and sent around Baja California's long finger into the treacherous waters of the Gulf of California. Buffeted by unpredictable storms, the ships crawled north into the thick red water of the marshy Colorado delta. Split by numerous hard-to-distinguish channels and troubled by huge tides, the delta was crushed during the long summers by indescribable heat. While uncountable waterfowl shrieked overhead, the ocean ships tied up at a variety of desolate landing places. There Indian and Mexican workers transferred bales, bags, and boxes directly from their holds onto the decks of the shallow-draft, sternwheel steamers of the Colorado Steam Navigation Company and to the mud-smeared barges that the steamers towed behind them as they toiled upstream between twisting banks, across shifting sandbars.

"The wind," wrote Martha Summerhayes, who made the trip with her army officer husband in August 1874, "was like a breath from a furnace; it seemed as though the days would never end." Indeed, those dreadful blasts kept their ship immobilized against the river bank for seven days. The only relief at night was stillness and the absence of glare. But nights were short. "Before the crack of dawn . . . came such a clatter with the fires and the high-pressure engine and the sparks . . . that further rest was impossible."

Yet Martha and her husband Jack were traveling in relative comfort aboard the steamer. For enlisted men being sent to inland posts the trip was a passage through inferno. They were packed onto the barges with no shelter from the sun. At night they camped on the low, flat mudbanks, cooking their suppers as best they could in openings in the underbrush, amid the stinking arrowweeds.

After a third soldier had succumbed to the heat, Martha grew disturbed. A hard fate—"to die in that wretched place, to be rolled in a blanket and buried on those desert shores." Jack braced her up. " 'You mustn't cry, Mattie; it's a soldier's life, and when a man enlists he must take his chances. . . . It would not do for the soldiers to be sad when one of them dies. Why, it would demoralize the whole company.' And I began to feel that my tears must be out of place."

## Cramped Patterns

Transportation costs and the unpredictability of the future held life for the Southwest's workaday citizens to small, erratic swirls. Suppose, for instance, that you wanted to build a modest house in Tombstone. Bringing in nails, no matter by what route, cost between 15 and 20 cents a pound for freight alone—and an Anglo miner's pay for a ten-hour shift was $3.00. A Mexican's was less.

So you did not buy many nails. Your home out on the edge of town was of the simplest sort of raw plank or adobe construction, spartanly furnished. No plumbing, for who could afford it? Laundry could be a chore—hauling in wood for fires, heating the water, beating the soaked, soiled clothing on corrugated washboards or even rocks, rinsing them, wringing them, and spreading them on fences and bushes to dry. Washday? Generally it was two days.

Suppose, further, that you built your Tombstone house in 1884. The next year underground water flooded the lower levels of the principal mines and started the town on an irreversible decline. Soon your new house was next to worthless, even though the handful of nails in it had cost, by themselves, a day's wages.

A farmer's career was equally unstable. He had to depend on local markets—perhaps selling hay to an army post. But if the nearby Indians unexpectedly signed a peace treaty, the post closed.

Even if markets stayed relatively steady, irrigation was a perennial problem, whether in the Hispanic towns of northern New Mexico or at embryonic Phoenix in central Arizona. Flash floods repeatedly swept out the brush dams that diverted water into the ditches. Or the streams went dry. What was needed were dams big enough and strong enough not only to resist floods but to store their excess water. Seldom, however, could a local group raise the necessary money.

Instability. It helped intensify attitudes all too familiar throughout the American frontier. One face of the coin was the cruel eagerness of men in power to monopolize the few opportunities at hand. The Tucson Ring opposed "pampering" the Indians lest the coterie's members lose government supply contracts that were fattest when fighting was on. The Santa Fe Ring absorbed cheap land; the merchants of Lincoln County fought to the death for economic power; cattlemen warred over grass with sheepmen or with each other. And there was the coin's other face: the average man's carelessness about the future, described somewhat churlishly by Robert Forbes, pioneer Arizona agronomist, as "a shiftless, live-for-today, Texas spirit," hostile to any kind of conservation.

The key, the Southwest fervently believed, was transcontinental railroads. They would cut costs, bring in population, raise property values, increase the demand for services, and spin off locally owned feeder lines linking farms, ranches, and mines to the main stems. Combined, the prospects would lure in the greatest asset of all—capital.

By the time of Tombstone's discovery in the late 1870s such lines were long overdue. But they were on their way, finally—a rush of them. Two were building west from the continent's interior toward the Pacific Coast; one was driving south from Denver; a fourth was pushing east through southern California to halt the first two before they reached the coast.

The nature of the southwestern terrain was such that only a few key mountain passes and river crossings were available for rail lines. Because the completion of successful transcontinental lines depended on controlling those vital spots, titanic struggles were inevitable. No matter. Although the contending lines might hurt each other sorely, the nation's southwest corner was bound to benefit. Or so the people told each other, hugging themselves in suspense as they watched the battle lines take shape.

## Smoke on the Horizon

The first railroad to reach the West Coast was built by two unfriendly partners, the Union Pacific working west up the Platte River Valley of Nebraska and the Central Pacific pushing east across the Sierra Nevada. In the opinion of the principal owners of the Central Pacific—the Big Four of Leland Stanford, Collis Huntington, Mark Hopkins, and Charles Crocker—California did not produce sufficient freight and passenger service to warrant a second line. Whenever a rival appeared in the distance, they set about trying to block its entrance into the state. A principal method was to occupy in advance whatever geographically strategic approaches the contender might be tempted to use. A vital tool in this ungenerous procedure was a once feeble shortline called the Southern Pacific that the Four acquired and built into a giant.

Among their worries were the only two practical sites between the Grand Canyon and the sea where a bridge could be thrown across the treacherous Colorado River into southern California. One site, a little south of today's Needles, California, was a key to the 35th parallel route, so named during the Pacific Railroad surveys of the 1850s. The other, critical to the 32nd parallel route, was the river gap separating Yuma, Arizona, from Fort Yuma, California.

Learning that an eastern concern called the Atlantic & Pacific Railroad Company was trying to raise enough money to lay track west along the 35th parallel, the Big Four obtained a federal charter—plus federal land grants—that allowed the Southern Pacific to build to the California-Arizona border. Their intent was to discourage the Atlantic & Pacific by blocking the Needles bridge site before the eastern road could come anywhere near it. As work was progressing, however, a more formidable rival materialized—the Texas & Pacific, no kin to the Texas Western—headed by Thomas A. Scott, a widely experienced, aggressive, and resourceful railroader. Abruptly the Southern Pacific switched priorities and thrust a branch line toward Fort Yuma, whose edges it reached in the spring of 1877.

There it encountered blockades of its own. One was the military reservation, whose lands closed off the approaches to the bridge site. The other was its charter, which allowed it to build only to the California-Arizona border, a line that wandered down the middle of the Colorado River. The Texas & Pacific, by contrast, though still 1,200 miles away in Texas, held a charter that allowed it to span anything necessary on its way to San Diego.

Well, if legal rights did not exist, reasonable facsimiles would have to be provided. The SP associates won from the Arizona legislature (later it was charged that they used bribery in doing so) a territorial franchise to build an ostensibly separate railroad, the Southern Pacific of Arizona, across the territory from the middle of the river to the New Mexican border. New Mexico added a similar franchise as far as Texas. Those papers firmly in hand, the SP shipped a prefabricated steel bridge to the Yuma site by way of the Gulf of California. Simultaneously Collis Huntington, the SP's blunt, hard-hitting lobbyist in Washington, called on the Secretary of War and asked permission to lay rails across the reservation and the bridge so that the SP could hook up with its friendly counterpart in Arizona.

Suspecting shenanigans, the secretary stalled. Only Congress, he said, could grant a right of way across a military reservation. But he would allow the Southern Pacific to lay a temporary track for construction purposes across the reservation and onto the limit of its franchise at the midpoint of the bridge—no farther. If Congress later denied its permission, the tracks would have to be removed.

The concession was all but meaningless. Tom Scott exerted awesome leverage in Congress and was urging the lawmakers to grant aid to his southern transcontinental as a matter of simple justice to the resurgent South. When a permanent right of way across the reservation was granted, Huntington feared, it would go to the Texas & Pacific.

The only recourse, the associates decided, was a tactic they had used before: Seize first and then let the opposition yelp. Picked crews began laying permanent track across the reservation and grading for additional rail on the Arizona side of the skeletal bridge. Major T. S. Dunn, in command at Fort Yuma, promptly reported the disobedience to Washington. The Secretary of War stiffened and ordered Dunn to halt, at once, all unauthorized work.

Unfortunately for the major, the fort's garrison had just been sent to Idaho to help fight Chief Joseph's Nez Perce Indians; in addition to himself, only a sergeant and two privates had been left behind to garrison the normally untroubled installation. The Southern Pacific engineers on the scene immediately apprised San Francisco of the weakness. Charles Crocker of the associates thereupon put together a special mail and passenger train and sent it chuffing toward Yuma. Under cover of darkness on Saturday night, October 6, 1877, carefully rehearsed crews laid half a mile of track to the bridge, crossed it, and pushed as far into Yuma, Arizona, as Madison Avenue and First Street. Major Dunn and his three-man army slept quietly through it all, not having anticipated such strenuous activity on either a Saturday night or a Sunday morning.

At sunrise on the seventh the work engine rumbled over the still shaky bridge, tolling its bell and blowing blast after blast from its steam whistle. Half-clad citizens rushed out of their homes just in time to see the special train from San Francisco glide into the center of town, its locomotive bedecked with American flags. They went wild with joy. The world had come to the Southwest!

In San Francisco the newspaper *Alta California* told the story under the headline "THE IRON HORSE HAS SNORTED IN THE EAR OF NATIONAL AUTHORITY," and then asked in delight, "Now what are you going to do about it, Uncle Samuel? . . . Will you set us back to the days of Forty-Nine, when we crossed the river in a basket covered with the skin of a dead mule? . . . Uncle, what will you do?"

Uncle did nothing. Blandly, Collis Huntington visited, one after another, four Cabinet members and then the President of the United States. They were cross at first, he wrote his associates, and threatened punitive action, "but I soon got [them] out of that idea." He held the tracks, the bridge, and franchises from the territories of Arizona and New Mexico. If the federal government would extend his charter over the same area, he would complete the line across both territories without the aid of federal land grants and join the Texas & Pacific somewhere in Texas. The Southwest would then be connected to both sides of the nation, a feat Scott might never be able to accomplish on his own. According to Huntington's smug letter, President Hayes replied, "Will you do that? If you will, that will suit me first rate."

To Huntington's dismay, his associates refused to budge from Yuma. Their railroads were still feeling the pinch of the financial depression that had begun in the East in 1873, and they felt they had strained their resources far enough. Huntington argued a full year before two unexpected developments came to his rescue. One was the increase in strength that the Texas & Pacific gained from Tom Scott's alliance with Jay Gould, evil genius of American railroading. The other was exciting evidence of a real mineral boom in Arizona. Financing was becoming easier to obtain, and as the purse strings loosened, San Francisco capitalists showed increased interest in the silver properties around Prescott. Nor was that all. The Silver King mine on a rugged tributary of the Gila was turning into a bonanza; there was high-grade copper near New Mexico; and already rumor was buzzing that Tombstone was likely to surpass them all.

Under such circumstances a lone bridge at Yuma no longer seemed formidable enough. A better defense would be to push east, nip Gould somewhere in Texas, and then continue to New Orleans, as Huntington wished. In November 1878, accordingly, grading crews began driving toward Tucson.

Almost simultaneously another formidable rival, the Atchison, Topeka & Santa Fe, which had gained enough control over the Atlantic & Pacific to utilize its 35th parallel charter, appeared in the northeast. Incredible! The long-isolated Southwest was suddenly being overrun by railroads.

## Skulduggery in the Passes

The AT&SF, called the Atchison in Wall Street and the Santa Fe everywhere else, was the child of a shortline—the Atchison & Topeka—that had been formed initially to link a small steamboat landing on the Missouri River to Topeka, capital city of Kansas. The Civil War kept it from laying a rail. Even so, the sight of the wagon freight creaking toward New Mexico to feed General Carleton's California Column and the Indians at Bosque Redondo led its promoters to tack "Santa Fe" onto the original name and apply, successfully, for a land grant that would reward their reaching the Colorado border by March 3, 1873.

The war over, the company crept west, living off shipments of buffalo hides and Texas cattle. Having earned its land grant in the barest nick of time, it waited out the depression of the mid-1870s and then crawled on up the Arkansas Valley to the town of Pueblo near the foot of the Rockies. Its arrival there on March 7, 1876, uncorked what the local paper called "the biggest drunk of the present century."

Going into Pueblo was like going into a box. To the west lay the front range of the Rockies, penetrable by rails in two places only—the great abyss later called the Royal Gorge of the Arkansas River and, farther south, a saddle more than 9,000 feet above sea level known as La Veta Pass. Due south, a long spur of shaggy hills thrust out from the Rockies along the Colorado–New Mexico border. The only feasible opening in that direction was a gap called Raton Pass, nearly 8,000 feet high. Breaking out of the Pueblo box by any of those three gaps would call for skilled engineering studies and expensive construction work.

At Pueblo, the Atchison, Topeka & Santa Fe found another railroad eyeing the gaps. This was the Denver & Rio Grande, incorporated in 1870 with high hopes of reaching Santa Fe, El Paso, and eventually Mexico. The D&RG was a narrow-gauge line (3 feet between rails rather than 4 feet, 8 1/2 inches) and hence could lay track in the mountains much more cheaply than could the broad-gauge Santa Fe. The D&RG also connected in Denver with the Kansas Pacific, which ran east across the central part of Kansas.

There was little coal in Kansas. But from Pueblo south across Raton Pass to the tawny foothills of Colfax County, New Mexico, were almost immeasurable black beds filled with what local boosters declared was the hottest, longest-burning coal west of the anthracite fields of Pennsylvania. Hauling that fine product to market in Kansas would be the making of a railroad. Plus this: prospectors at a place called Leadville up near the headwaters of the Arkansas River had discovered showings of silver as fine as anything in Arizona. Silver ore would either have to come down the river to Pueblo for smelting, or coal would have to go to Leadville.

Mountains of freight—some day! Financed by that traffic, the railroad that controlled the gaps out of the Pueblo box could probably spin on as far west or south as it wished. But as 1877 opened, coal traffic was not yet moving in significant volume, and neither line was able to tackle those rugged passes. So they marked time, breaking each other's telegraphic codes and watching each other's division officials like hawks, knowing that the first company that filed survey plats with the proper officials and afterward occupied the desired territory with work crews would win the route.

The Santa Fe had one advantage in a civil engineer named William Raymond Morley. A Civil War veteran and dropout of Iowa State College, Morley had worked for both the Kansas Pacific and the Denver & Rio Grande before becoming, at the age of twenty-six in 1872, manager of the Maxwell Land Grant. Disgusted by the carryings-on there, he had resigned four years later to join the Santa Fe. Because he knew the area well, he was able to disguise himself as a sheepherder and survey Raton Pass without arousing the suspicion of the D&RG spies. The survey in hand and promises of Boston money in his pocket, the general manager of the Santa Fe, William Strong, went to the New Mexico capital with an influential Hispano, Miguel A. Otero, and, in February 1878, won from the legislature a territorial charter for building in New Mexico.

At that the D&RG officials woke up. Their last chance to control Raton Pass was to put track into it ahead of the Santa Fe. A grading crew was ordered to move south from the D&RG railhead at El Moro as fast as possible. Though the men traveled most of the night, they were too late. Apprised of what was happening, Morley had hitched up a buggy and had raced ahead of the enemy along a toll wagon road built through the gap years earlier by his friend Uncle Dick Wootton, former mountain man. Wootton helped him round up and provide with shovels a bunch of hangers-on who were lounging and yarning in a tavern. When the D&RG crew arrived on the scene the next morning, a miscellaneous gang of bleary-eyed men were scattering dirt out of a ragged scrape in the hillside that Morley solemnly swore was the beginning of a legitimate railroad grade.

Defeated at Raton, the D&GR was determined to hang on to the Royal Gorge. Again there was a wild midnight race, Morley this time astride his famous black stallion, William. Maybe he won; maybe he didn't. Details have long since been lost under legends heaped up by a partisan local press too delighted by the affray to waste time on accuracy. Anyway, both companies rushed men, some of them armed, into the canyon. The crews built rock forts, gesticulated fiercely at each other, but never got around to shooting. Courts were called on for injunctions, suits were filed, exhibits amassed. Jay Gould stirred the seething pot; the AT&SF leased the entire Denver & Rio Grande system, only to have the disgruntled enemy find excuses for breaking the agreement and for sending out gangs of roughnecks to reoccupy its properties at greater speed than the Santa Fe relished. Two men died in the scuffling.

The upshot, in 1880, was the "treaty of Boston." The Santa Fe agreed not to build north to Denver or west to the Colorado mining camps. The Denver & Rio Grande promised not to build east into Kansas or south of the 36th parallel in New Mexico. It promptly did go as far as permitted, however, twisting rails across La Veta Pass into the San Luis Valley and then following the Rio Grande to Española, where a theoretically independent company took over and finished the line to Santa Fe.

The AT&SF meanwhile was sharpening its claws for the Southern Pacific. As rapidly as financing allowed, it drilled a tunnel under the crest of Raton Pass and then veered across Glorieta Pass to Albuquerque. It skimmed past Santa Fe, declining because of difficult terrain to build eighteen miles into the city from which it had drawn part of its name. Santa Fe's outraged citizens had to approve a $150,000 bond issue for underwriting a stub line to connect their town with the main stem at a junction named Lamy, after the archbishop of the same name.

Just south of Albuquerque the Santa Fe tracks forked. Working through the Atlantic & Pacific, which it now controlled, the company sent one branch west close to the 35th parallel (Morley surveyed that line, too) to challenge the Southern Pacific at the Needles crossing of the Colorado River. Simultaneously, and this time working under its own name, the AT&SF strung more rail down the east side of the Rio Grande to the hamlet of Rincon. There another forking took place. One set of tracks went to El Paso. The other slanted southwest and, in December 1880, hooked up with the eastward-building Southern Pacific at the bleak, dusty town of Deming.

The Deming connection put New Mexico and Arizona into direct rail contact with both the Pacific Coast and Kansas City. The ties, moreover, soon extended to New Orleans. The SP brought Gould's Texas & Pacific to a jarring halt at Sierra Blanca, gateway to the difficult mountains of west Texas, and in 1883, working through a combination of subsidiaries, reached the Mississippi.

Challenging so formidable a system (the Big Four also controlled the western part of the central transcontinental between Ogden, Utah, and San Francisco and was reaching north into Oregon) took considerable brashness, but that was what the Santa Fe proposed. The heart of the plan was a colossal bluff.

In the fall of 1879, a year before the hookup with the Southern Pacific, the Santa Fe had ordered Raymond Morley to survey a line from Deming southwest through Mexico to the port of Guaymas on the Gulf of California. This was an adaptation of an old dream. Before the Civil War, promoters of southern Arizona had urged the United States to acquire Sonora so that a railroad could be built from their mines to schooner docks at Guaymas. While still employed by the Kansas Pacific, General William Palmer (later head of the Denver & Rio Grande) had contemplated extending the KP to the same port. Financial difficulties, the uncertainties of railroad operations in politically unstable Sonora, and the inadequacies of the Guaymas harbor had deterred him. For the sake of the stakes involved, however—and with the thought in the back of their corporate minds that the United States might yet annex Sonora —the directors of the Santa Fe were willing to risk the hazards. For the SP could not block them from the Gulf, and after they had gained that goal, they could run steamships to San Diego, Los Angeles, and San Francisco as well as to the Orient. Faced with such competition, the Big Four might agree to cooperative arrangements.

Finding no crossing of the Continental Divide in Mexico that suited him, Morley left Deming behind and routed the projected line from Benson in southern Arizona through the twin border towns of Nogales to the Mexican coast. President Porfirio Díaz granted a charter and promised government aid, never wholly fulfilled, to a subsidiary named the Sonora Railroad Company. Under pressure, the Southern Pacific allowed the Santa Fe to use its tracks between Deming and Benson.

Construction from Benson southward to Nogales and from Guaymas north to the same point began during the summer heat of 1881. Morley, in charge of the Mexican section of the work, reached Nogales one year later. His wife, Ada, from whom his work kept him separated for long periods, came from New Mexico to tap the traditional silver spike that signified the completion of the two segments. American Nogales named its main street Morley Avenue, and everyone was very happy—for a while. Six months later, still surveying in Old Mexico, Raymond Morley, aged thirty-six, was killed by an accidental gunshot.

Once again, however, he had helped open a gateway for the Santa Fe. In 1883 the Atlantic & Pacific—that is to say, the AT&SF—staggered into Needles. By then the rival lines were both badly overextended and in need of breathing time. To forestall cutthroat competition, the SP did as the Santa Fe had hoped; grudgingly it took over the Guaymas line and in exchange allowed the Santa Fe to enter California at Needles. The Southwest could now boast that although it had never been, of itself, the destination of a major railroad, it was at last crossed by a pair of them. Surely the spinoffs that resulted could not help but broaden and stabilize the economy of what until then had been one of the poorest, most strife-torn regions in the nation.

## The View from the Caboose

In hindsight it is clear that the completion of the Santa Fe and Southern Pacific railroads benefited California far more than New Mexico or Arizona. Their tracks were scarcely laid when a wild rush of midwestern farmers seeking retirement in lotus land sped through the southwest corner to buy house lots in Los Angeles and San Diego in one of the most frenzied episodes of land speculation in the nation's history. Los Angeles's population jumped from 11,183 in 1880 to more than 100,000 in 1890—almost as many as lived that same year in the entire territory of Arizona. Ten years later, as the twentieth century approached, San Francisco alone housed 343,000 persons, while New Mexico and Arizona together could produce only 315,000 inhabitants.

In some ways the railroads were a burden. Rather than spend their own money building branch lines through the sparsely populated territories, they encouraged local firms to do the work with local aid. One result was that the federal government eventually had to donate to each territory 3 million acres of public land that it could sell for redeeming recklessly issued county railroad bonds. The railroads meanwhile were maintaining lobbies to keep taxes low and fend off unwelcome regulations.

Some unintended side effects also proved harmful. Until the railroads offered new markets for livestock, much grazing land was scarcely touched. One wild-eyed Arizona booster estimated that the tall sacaton grass in his territory's southern valleys, the various grama and mesquite grasses in the foothills, the brome and wheat grasses on the plateaus could feed at least 7.5 million cattle. By 1890, however, a few more than two million head had denuded Arizona and New Mexico besides. The regions' hard flash floods turned cattle trails into arroyos, slashed raw wounds through once softly winding stream channels, and swept incalculable tons of topsoil off the rocky hillsides into reservoirs that farmers farther downstream were struggling to build. As beneficial forage disappeared, unwelcome sagebrush, greasewood, and mesquite advanced into the barren spots.

To complete the damage, drought shriveled the land during the early 1890s. Hundreds of thousands of cattle had to be shipped out of the area. Those that remained were kept alive on a costly new crop, alfalfa, just then appearing in the irrigated valleys. Still, the parching wind did blow some good. Breeds were improved so that fewer cattle produced more pounds of beef (more wool in the case of sheep), and the fattening of livestock in feedlots before shipping became a major industry. Government intervention through the National Forest Service and the Bureau of Land Management has brought howls of resistance from the individualistic stockmen but has helped restore some of the grasslands. For the ranchers who had to make these adaptations during the depressions of the 1890s and 1930s it was a painful time.

The railroads changed the appearance of many towns. Location engineers seldom went right into a village, but built depots and switching yards on the outskirts, hoping to attract businessmen to nearby land the railroad owned. Results emphasized the Southwest's racial duality. Anglos who clustered near the railroad built brick business houses like those lining the main streets of any small midwestern town and erected, in the new residential areas, homes ornate with Victorian cupolas and gingerbread trim. From this new center a dusty road led to Old Town (still called that, as tourist attractions, in Albuquerque and Tucson), with its sleepy plaza surrounded by flat-roofed adobes shaded by verandahs supported on thin wooden pillars. Yet even the timeless Hispanic dwellings felt such new influences as corrugated iron for roofs, toppings of brick on the adobe walls, larger windows, carvings on corbels, and more iron hinges and steel nails than the residents had been able to afford during the era of wagon freight.

In prerailroad days, most local capital for ranching and mining had been provided by combinations of merchants and freighters whose credit connections in the East enabled them to act also as bankers and promoters. By diluting their dominance, the railroad allowed more specialized trades and services to develop. When the Santa Fe arrived in New Mexico in 1879, there had been two banks in the territory; in 1900 there were more than fifty. Even tourism assumed importance as writer Charles Lummis pointed out the charms of Hispanic Santa Fe and Taos, and archaeologist Adolph Bandelier began unraveling the secrets of ancient Anasazi culture. And as Lummis drove home his theme, "See America First," the Grand Canyon of the Colorado, served by a branch line of the Santa Fe, became a top tourist attraction for travelers in the West.

Though all these developments were stimulating, the main contribution of the railraods was the ending of what has been called the tyranny of distance. Virgin land located where growing seasons were long was now within reach of America's westward-pushing farmers, an agricultural bonanza—if sufficient water could be developed. Also within reach was a new world of copper ore, necessary for feeding the nation's lustily growing electric industry. That might be an even greater bonanza—if complex mining procedures and metallurgical problems could be solved. Inevitably, where lures were so bright, there were new Coronados willing to explore.

## Copper Country

Arizona's plunge into copper began while the Santa Fe Railroad was still hundreds of miles away in Kansas. The unlikely pioneers were the brothers Charles and Henry Lesinsky, Jewish wholesalers of Las Cruces, New Mexico, who distributed merchandise throughout the southwestern part of the territory. One profitable market was the boom town of Silver City, nestled against the eastern side of the Continental Divide. At this listening post the brothers heard, early in the 1870s, that local prospectors had made good strikes of silver and copper beyond the Divide beside Chase Creek, just inside the Arizona border.

Chase Creek flowed through a rusty canyon of burned-looking rocks into the San Francisco River, a principal tributary of the upper Gila. It was a dangerous place to work, especially with the Apaches on the prowl. In 1872, however, the Indians agreed to settle on reservations (no one knew how short-lived the agreement would prove to be), and the Lesinskys reevaluated the situation. Copper was selling at twenty cents a pound. The ores in Chase Creek were a high-grade copper oxide that could be handled by cheap Mexican labor in primitive adobe smelting furnaces. Wages, moreover, could be paid in the form of chits redeemable in the company store the brothers intended to build. Finally, the Lesinskys could use their own wagons for hauling in supplies and freighting out the partially refined matte to the railhead for shipment east for additional treatment.

Excited by those favorable factors, the brothers purchased for a song a group of copper claims on Chase Creek five miles above its junction with the San Francisco River. These became the basis of what they called the Longfellow Copper Mining Company. Miners extracted the material through an adit high on the hill above the creek and sent it down a steep incline to mule-drawn ore cars running on rails only twenty inches apart. The cars transported the muck down Chase Creek to the San Francisco River, where Mexican workers had put together a string of adobe huts named Clifton, after one of the region's early prospectors. At Clifton the ore was loaded into baskets and carried to the blast furnaces. Heat for smelting came from mesquite wood grubbed out of the surrounding hills by Mexican woodchoppers. In the early days, before compressors were available, Mexicans pumping on hand bellows provided the air stream needed in the reduction process. A handful of Anglos acted as supervisors and as timbermen, blacksmiths, carpenters —crafts that supposedly required more skill than the Mexicans could muster.

Troubles were constant—mechanical breakdowns; Indian attacks on teamsters, woodcutters, and once on the town itself; and a gradual decline in the richness of the ore. Even so, other companies moved into the area and erected additional smelters at or near the jumble of shacks crawling up the thorny hillside above Clifton. The hamlets of Morenci and Metcalf took scabrous shape nearer the mines. Axmen and fumes peeled vegetation from the hills, and the bald ground they left behind was soon wigged with dumps of waste rock and slag.

To speed transportation between mines and smelters and also to discourage Apaches looking for mules, the Lesinskys ordered a diminutive, woodburning locomotive from Philadelphia and hauled it, in pieces, to Clifton. The drop in costs wrought by the engine—Arizona's first— beguiled a group of Scottish capitalists into offering the brothers two million dollars for their holdings. The Longfellow Copper Mining Company was then transformed into the Arizona Copper Company, managed by a thin, trim-bearded engineer with a thick burr in his voice, James Colquhoun.

The Lesinskys bailed out at the right time. The huge mines at Butte, Montana, were pouring out new streams of copper and prices were slumping. Almost from the moment of his arrival, Colquhoun was faced with what became, and to an extent still remains, a prime headache of the copper country: how to increase volume economically enough to maintain profits in the face of dwindling returns.

His first step, in 1882, was to build, largely on borrowed money, a seventy-five-mile railroad to connect with the Southern Pacific at Lordsburg, New Mexico. This met the problem until the percentage of copper in the ore grew too small for direct smelting. So, beginning in 1892, Colquhoun tried a fresh approach based on his knowledge that copper could be dissolved out of its oxides with diluted sulfuric acid and then recovered in almost pure form by precipitation on iron. Short of money, he built on a slag dump a makeshift plant of old mine timbers, discarded engines, and locally forged fittings. The scarecrow worked, the first successful copper leaching plant in the country. Within three years Colquhoun had raised production by 40 percent while cutting costs by two cents a pound.

And still the price of copper declined. Mining engineers at Clifton and at other mines springing up throughout the copper belt experimented with dangerous underground caving methods that could break loose greater volumes of rock than conventional stoping could. Metallurgists crouched over jigs, jerking tables, settling tanks, thickeners, flotation cells, and various other contrivances designed to separate heavy mineral from lighter waste rock—concentrating the product, as they said, so that it would be amenable to smelting in increasingly sophisticated furnaces that burned coke hauled in by rail from coalfields hundreds of miles away.

This earnest quest for high volume at low cost proved to be the undoing of even knowledgeable people. The most notorious example concerned ancient mines located near the three sunblasted little peaks of Ajo, 42 miles south of the Southern Pacific line at Gila Bend and 132 wagon miles west of Tucson. Spanish prospectors from the old *real de minas* at Arizonac probably found the deposits first but abandoned the site because of distance. A hundred years later Anglos reopened the workings and in 1855 sent the first ore out of the Gadsden Purchase—selected high grade that they packed on mules to the Colorado River and shipped to the British Isles for smelting. The feat turned out to be more newsworthy than lucrative.

Toward the close of the nineteenth century a promoter named A. J. Shotwell obtained an option on the claims from the half-starved ranchers who owned them but who made their living, with the help of their Papago Indian wives, running scrawny cattle among the creosote bushes and across the smelly little garlic plants, *ajos*, that gave the district its name. Carrying his option to St. Louis in 1900, Shotwell caught the attention of a highly regarded distributor of wholesale clothing named J. R. Boddie. Boddie knew nothing of mining. Neither did the other merchants to whom he introduced Shotwell. Nevertheless the promoter persuaded them to come west and look at the Big Water Melon, as he jovially called the Ajo property. They trusted Shotwell enough that they didn't even take an engineer with them, and after two days of looking over prearranged exhibits, they bought the claims for $19,500 in cash and several thousand shares of stock in what they named the Cornelia Copper Company.

Because the new owners had solid reputations, they were able to sell enough Cornelia stock back in Missouri and Arkansas to start operations. Shotwell rode their coattails by setting up another company on an adjoining claim and letting the value of their stock rub off on his. Annual balance sheets soon left nothing to rub, however. Like James Colquhoun of the Arizona Copper Company, the new operators needed some economical way to concentrate their low-grade ore, but unlike Colquhoun they hadn't the foggiest notion of what to do about it—until a sparkling-eyed little Irishman named Fred McGahan appeared on the scene.

McGahan told the desperate owners he had invented a vacuum smelting furnace that would work on any kind of ore, however lean. It was a marvelous metal cylinder, twenty-five feet high, surrounded by pumps, valves, and tanks for oxygen and hydrogen. Its principal adornment was a line of spigots placed vertically like buttons. Once a charge of ore and flux was seething away inside the vacuum, McGahan said, molten gold would sink to the bottom spigot for removal. Above it, in sequence, came spigots for silver, copper, calcium, and so on.

How many times can the same people be burned? Without investigating either McGahan or the scientific principles behind his alleged discovery (McGahan, incidentally, had already swindled two St. Louis chemical companies with other magical processes), the owners of the Cornelia Mining Company bought the North American rights to McGahan's creation and told him to start work. After they had paid him $34,000—and it is a pleasure to report that Shotwell was among those bilked—the truth slowly trickled down to them. There was no way under heaven that the machine could be made to work. They sued McGahan for obtaining money under false pretenses. He retorted with a bigger suit for libel: Call him crooked, would they? Realizing that little could come from the conflict other than injury to their—and their company's—image, the victims let the case drop and closed the mines. But they were still convinced that they were sitting on a lot of copper if they could just get at it.

A succession of engineers looked the mines over and rejected them as hopeless. Shotwell disappeared. Then, in 1911, John C. Greenway, able general manager of the huge Calumet and Arizona Copper Company, wandered in for a personal look. After checking the ground like a dog hunting rabbits, Greenway formed the New Cornelia Copper Company, obtained an option on the property for enough stock that it eventually made millionaires of Boddie and his loyal friends, and launched a staggering program. He developed water at a depth of 1,250 feet under the desert soil, built a railroad to Gila Bend, erected around a green central plaza dotted with oleanders a tawny, porticoed, Spanish-style company town that eventually housed 8,000 workers. Aided by metallurgists L. D. Rickets and Ira Joralemon, he capped the work with a leaching plant not greatly different from Colquhoun's pioneering setup at Clifton—except that the first Clifton plant had been capable of handling 1,000 tons of ore a year whereas the New Cornelia's could treat 5,000 tons *a day*.

Mining enough ore to keep mills of such size busy was copper's other great challenge. The problem arose because of the peculiar nature of ore deposits in arid regions. Most were horizontal masses of porphyry rock dusted throughout with infinitesimal specks of copper sulfides. There were few veins of concentrated high-grade ore for miners to follow, a factor that precluded selective mining. (Selective vein mining of exceptional ores had accounted for the success of the early bonanzas.) Accordingly, it occurred to engineers Daniel C. Jackling and Robert Gemmell in 1907 as they contemplated a huge block of disseminated ore in Bingham Canyon, Utah, that the only answer was to scoop up the whole lot and run it through their concentrators as it was, even though an entire ton of such rock contained no more than twenty or thirty pounds of copper.

The machine that made the idea feasible was the steam shovel, which until then had been used only for digging railroad cuts and gravel pits. While skeptics clucked, Jackling and Gemmell formed the Utah Copper Company and produced enough persuasive figures to obtain financing from the Guggenheims. They then built a railroad just to haul away and discard the overburden that covered the Bingham ore body. The stripping completed, they set about removing the ore itself from what became a gargantuan open pit along whose terraces whole railroad trains crawled like little caterpillars. From Bingham the process was carried to Arizona (of the nation's top twenty-five mines, sixteen are in Arizona, and most use open-pit mining) and then spilled over into Santa Rita in New Mexico and Cananea in Sonora.

It's an eye-popping business. Man-made canyons, often highly colored, pock the land. Mills capable of handling from 50,000 to 100,000 tons of ore every twenty-four hours grind and rattle. Tall smelter chimneys emit plumes of smoke visible for scores of miles. The enormous costs involved in building such plants have led to mergers of firms, so that today a very few companies (Phelps Dodge is at the top of the Arizona list) control the industry in the Southwest.

Without question, these highly potent companies have helped stabilize what for a long time was a very shaky economy. They have taken hitherto valueless land out of the public domain and put it on the tax rolls. They and their support industries provided tens of thousands of jobs. Their constant research and exploration have kept the manageable reserves of ore expanding so extensively that copper mining, unlike the ephemeral gold and silver quests of pioneer times, has come as close to being permanent as an extractive industry can be.

There is, of course, another side. Environmentalists protest the destruction of the landscape. Sociologists complain of absentee ownership, of sterile company towns, of dividends distributed afar, with little gain to Arizona. Mexican workers have objected, sometimes violently as we shall see, to racial attitudes that have led to their being pushed steadily down to the bottom of the job ladder. Reformers charge company lobbyists with being far too ready to corrupt the political process in order to achieve legislative preference.

Somewhere between the two views is a balance that probably will not become fully apparent for as long as copper remains a primary determinant of Arizona's economy. Yet this much is certain. Historically, only one other southwestern resource—ordinary water—has drawn from the residents of the area comparable expenditures of ingenuity, energy, and money, or has elicited equal controversy.

## More Stately Dams

One colonizing strategy developed during the 1870s by the Church of Latter-Day Saints (the Mormons) in Utah was an expansion southward into Mexico. Such a movement, it was argued, would open up ocean ports to converts coming from overseas, make available hothouse climates for agriculture, and through the redemption of wastelands help prepare the way for Christ's second coming, which Church officials firmly believed was imminent.

So that the migration might move ahead in orderly fashion, advance columns were ordered to establish permanent way stations along the route. Because of the harsh nature of the land, some of the trailside havens might be difficult to form. No matter. This was the Lord's work. And so colonists called at random for furthering the great mission sold whatever they could not carry, loaded the rest into their wagons, and moved in small parties south across the canyoned Colorado River, a movement destined to continue for more than a decade.

Some colonists were assigned to that section of the Little Colorado River lying between what became the town of Holbrook, Arizona, and the stream's headwaters in the White Mountains near the New Mexico border. Others were told to continue across the mountains to the Salt River Valley a little east of Phoenix. The Little Colorado people are the ones we will notice in fullest detail, for their experiences provide a grim lesson about the heartbreak involved in trying to develop marginal water with inadequate resources.

As soon as a group arrived at one of the scattered sites marked out as community centers, the family members removed the covered wagon boxes from the vehicles' running gears and lived out of the jumble of goods and utensils while clearing fields and building crude, dirt-roofed cabins. In the case of groups operating under the aegis of a church communal organization called the United Order, the dwellings were joined one to another in the shape of a rectangle that also served as a fort against Apache Indians. There were bastions at opposite corners of the enclosure, and in the center stood a boxlike communal hall where meals were prepared cooperatively by the women and eaten together by everyone at a long table, often to the tune of the leader's fervent sermons.

The United Order ventures did not last. The Indian menace dwindled, and like other individualistic Americans the Mormons preferred to expend their labor on their own fields, not their neighbors', and to enjoy family privacy in their own homes. Even after moving into separate dwellings, however, they stayed clannish. They sought to monopolize the best lands in the area and thus aroused the antagonism of non-Mormons who had settled nearby. They set up cooperative marketing and buying agencies and, under Mormon leaders, took extensive contracts for cutting ties and grading the track bed of the Atlantic & Pacific Railroad as it advanced into their area. Their timber and sheep camps offered havens to Utah polygamists fleeing federal marshals—and some of their own people had to flee in turn to refuge in Mexico.

Unity gave them a strength out of proportion to their numbers and raised fears in some breasts that they and their coreligionists in the Salt River Valley planned to dominate the territory politically. During the middle of the 1880s a movement to deny them voting rights was a red-hot territorial issue. Some alarmists would have gone farther. In May 1884, the publisher of the *Apache* [County] *Chief* cried out in his paper, "The Mormon disease is a desperate one and the rope and gun is the only cure. . . . Don't let them settle on any more of our lands. . . . Down with them. Grind out their very existence."

A far greater threat to existence than such vituperation was the capriciousness of the Little Colorado River and its principal tributary, Silver Creek. Late in the year the stream flows only trickles. Sometimes it dries completely—until cloudbursts strike. Then, wrote the wife of an early-day settler, it becomes within minutes "dirty, muddy, gurgling, seething, belching, vicious, demon-like, bringing havoc, destruction, and death. . . . [Yet] without it that part of Arizona could not have been settled."

The labor expended to "develop" the river, as the jargon of the times went, was endless. Using only hand tools and horse-drawn scrapers, the settlers built what seemed to them massive barricades, up to 180 feet long and 60 feet wide, the centers packed with sand, earth, sticks, and rocks, the surfaces fortified with logs and facings of stone. The upstream sides were sloped gently in the hope that high water would roll in harmless waves over the top. The aprons on the downstream sides were paved with rock and asphalt to check back-cutting.

Sooner or later, however, a flood came that whisked the dams away as casually as one would swat a fly. Some communities eventually disappeared because of the repeated shatterings. Others survived only by dint of remarkable persistence. Between 1877 and 1919, the thirty or so families comprising the hamlet of Woodruff a little south of Holbrook rebuilt their dam thirteen times before completing one that would hold. The slightly larger settlement of St. Johns farther upstream did not obtain a permanent reservoir until 1927, by which time the Church's plans for an organized southward thrust had long since been abandoned.

Today some 27,000 acres are under irrigation (not all of it by Mormons) in the entire Little Colorado drainage area of 26,000 square miles —which is about .06 percent of the land available. Has the achievement been worthwhile? The descendants of the pioneers, looking over their neat homes and pleasant fields with pride, probably think so. An outsider, mentally reviewing the other places to which the firstcomers might have gone if a compelling sense of mission had not brought them here, is inclined to wonder.

If the floods of the Little Colorado, demonlike though they seemed to the early settlers, had been bigger and if the growing season on those wind-swept highlands had been longer, the battered colonists would have been bailed out of their troubles by a smiling genie with a bagful of gold—the United States Reclamation Service, known today as the Bureau of Reclamation. But the Service lives by cost-benefit ratios, and so its restorative magic fell on likelier areas.

In some ways the situation was paradoxical. When Congress brought the Service into being in 1902 by passing the Newlands Act (named for Representative Francis Newlands of Nevada and not for the new lands that might be reclaimed from the desert), the intent was to create additional homesteads for small farmers, *not* to rescue existing agricultural operations. But what point was there in letting old farms perish from thirst while fostering new ones practically next door? Almost from its inception, therefore, the Reclamation Service found itself refloating projects that were in danger of foundering on the rocks of their promoters' ambitions. How this worked and why the new Moses of the deserts, the Reclamation Service, was infinitely more popular three quarters of a century ago than it is today becomes apparent in the history of two early southwestern salvage operations, one in the Pecos Valley of southeastern New Mexico, the other in the Salt River Valley of central Arizona.

The visionary who first contemplated an integrated irrigation system for the Pecos Valley was Patrick Floyd James Garrett, the six-and-a-half-foot-tall, cigar-chomping sheriff who had catapulted himself to fame by killing Billy the Kid. Pat owned a ranch beside the Hondo River, near its confluence with the Pecos. The nearest town was Roswell.

As Pat was pondering how to bring water to his dry acres, once grazed by some of John Chisum's multitudes of cattle, it occurred to him (this was in the mid-1880s and Chisum had just died of a malignant tumor) that whatever steps he took could be applied on a larger scale to almost the entire valley from north of Roswell south across the border to the Texas town of Pecos, a whistle stop on the Texas & Pacific Railroad. Although the project would require far more money than Pat could raise, he knew two wealthy easterners who might help. They were the Eddy brothers and had been lured to the Pecos by the romance of the cattle trade.

They agreed. The older brother—redheaded, taciturn J. A. Eddy— confined his cooperation mostly to financial affairs. The younger— Charles B. Eddy, dark, nervous, constantly drinking coffee when it was available—became chief promoter, assisted by a Santa Fe newspaper- man, Charles Greene. They set up a corporation called the Pecos Valley Irrigation and Investment Company, issued stock, bought out the few small ditch companies that were scratching away in the area, and began work.

No one thereabouts had ever before seen such ditching machines— oversized wagon frames on huge wheels, with plows bolted underneath on either side. Each contraption was pulled by teams of from fourteen to twenty horses, depending on the nature of the ground. As the plow- shares turned the sod, the dry earth fell onto what one newspaperman called "endless bands of gum elastics" and was carried off to the side. Meanwhile homesteaders flocked in and took up farms, intending to buy their water from the company as fast as its canals were finished.

High times! The company carved the town site of Eddy—its name since changed to Carlsbad, gateway to Carlsbad National Park—out of thick mesquite brush swarming with cottontail rabbits, rattlesnakes, and chorusing coyotes. The humming village's main lodging house was a huge cube divided into small rooms by partitions that did not reach the ceiling. Beds were homemade cots whose fabric sometimes split under heavy or restless sleepers and dumped them onto the floor. Their vocal reactions to the rude awakening, mimicked loudly at breakfast the next morning, were the town's staple amusement.

Francis Tracy, a young New York friend of the Eddys who came west for adventure, graphically captured in his reminiscences the essen- tial incongruity of such places. The immense sweep of the land, its pervading silence and solitude, the exhilaration of the crystal air, and the star-glitter at night brought him a sense of unbounded personal freedom in a limitless world. But the near scene was hard, resistant, dirty, and enslaving. Sand-laden winds filled ditches, buried vines, tore roofs off tar-paper shacks. Although posts hewn from cottonwood trees would take root simply by being set into the ditch banks, they could not reach maturity unless sheaths of thorny ocotillo wands were used during the early years to fend gnawing livestock away from the trunks.

The ambitious program quickly exhausted the resources of the Pecos Valley Irrigation and Investment Company. Searching for new funds, Charles Eddy made contact with frosty James J. Hagerman, who, after making a fortune in Great Lakes timber and iron, had gone to Colorado Springs for his health. In Colorado he had heaped up more money by building a mountain railroad and investing in silver mines at Aspen. In 1890 (by then Pat Garrett had been eased out of the company he had inspired) Hagerman agreed to take over the ailing project. He plunged in with vim, laying out more dams, extending canals, and building a railroad from Pecos, Texas, to Roswell. He bought as his residence Chisum's old South Spring Creek ranch and turned it into a quiet oasis of luxury in what recently had been the outlaw wilderness of Lincoln County.

But even Hagerman's pockets could not meet the challenge of the Southwest. The Panic of 1893 dried up capital. Floods tore apart key portions of the irrigation system. By instituting his own welfare system, Hagerman persuaded many settlers to hang on even after the company had gone into receivership.

Except for its greater magnitude, the disaster was much like the one on the Little Colorado. Timber, iron, silver, and railroads notwithstanding, James Hagerman had tried to do too much with too little. Only the federal Reclamation Service could save the dream—and it did, pouring enough money into the sand and mesquite to finish the dams and green the area.

Far to the west, in Arizona's desolate Salt River Valley, a Georgia-born soldier of fortune, John Swilling, had, in 1867, a vision much like Pat Garrett's, and one that over the years spun as far out of his control. It's a remarkable parallel: two men, unacquainted with each other, living much by violence, yet launching the same kind of constructive program for the ultimate benefit of hundreds of thousands of people.

Although not quite as big as Garrett, Swilling was a striking man, six feet tall and lithe. He wore a soup-strainer mustache and long black hair to his shoulders. His temper was unpredictable. A search for relief from the pain of a severe head wound suffered during a brawl had left him partially dependent on the drugs morphine and laudanum, and on alcohol. Stoned, he was apt to shoot things up just for the hell of it.

He was working in El Paso for the Butterfield Overland Mail when the Civil War broke out. Enlisting with Henry Sibley's Confederates, he was appointed a lieutenant and sent into Arizona with Captain Sherod Hunter's guerrillas to prowl the road to California. He was one of sixteen southerners who scuffled with Carleton's advance guard of Unionists at Picacho Pass, the westernmost official battle of the Civil War. When the Confederates fled back to Texas, Swilling stayed behind and hired out as a guide and dispatch carrier for Carleton's advancing Unionists. Forsaking that job to join Joseph Reddeford Walker's gold hunters when they drifted west toward Arizona, he played a leading role in the treacherous capture of the Apache chief Mangas Coloradas, who was promptly murdered by Union soldiers.

Although Swilling found gold near Prescott (that ever-sanguine promoter, General James Carleton, sent two nuggets from his claim to Washington for presentation to President Lincoln), his disposition to wander soon left him ripe for new adventures. A possibility struck him when he saw Mexican hay cutters employed by the sutler at Fort McDowell scything down the lush grass that grew in a long, linear depression near the Salt River in the vicinity of present-day Phoenix.

There were other troughlike depressions in the area, and apparently Swilling had picked up enough local lore to recognize them for what they were—remnants of an irrigation system built a thousand years before by the vanished Hohokam Indians. Suddenly other factors came together. The richness of the growth in the dips where rainwater collected indicated fertile soil; the military hay camp proved that markets were available (the miners around Prescott would also be customers); and following the lines of the ancient canals would make ditch digging easy, for workers would need only to clean windblown soil out of the troughs.

Swilling carried the idea to Henry Wickenburg and other Prescott adventurers who had made rich gold finds. Founding a joint-stock company capitalized at $10,000, they hired a gang of Mexicans, went down to the valley in 1868, preempted a few thousand acres of sand and creosote bushes, and began experimenting until they had diverted as much water from the river as they thought they would need. They then sold off their land at auction, luring customers by promising that everyone who bought a 160-acre field would also receive water rights in the Swilling Irrigation and Canal Company.

The first season produced so many fine pumpkins that the settlers clustered along the ditch wanted to call their nascent town Pumpkinville. More sophisticated residents demurred. Someone—possibly Swilling or a freighter named Fred Henry or a wandering Englishman called Darrell Duppa—suggested Phoenix as an alternate. The analogy wasn't exact. After living five hundred years, the phoenix of Egyptian mythology deliberately burned itself on a funeral pyre and was reborn, young and fresh, from the ashes. The settlers hardly considered themselves reincarnated Hohokams. Still, they were creating a new civilization on the site of an old one. Phoenix—close enough. The motion carried.

More settlements sprang up nearby. Swilling gave birth to another with a classical name, Tempe, by building a canal there, too. He married a handsome Mexican girl who bore him four children, but his devils seized him again. He wandered off prospecting and squabbling, and in 1878 was arrested for robbing a stage. It may be he was simply amusing himself and tantalizing his captors when he hinted obliquely that he was indeed the man they wanted—but try to prove it. They never had to. He fell ill and died in his cell, aged forty-seven.

Meanwhile settlers kept drifting into the towns he had launched. Mesa and, to an extent, Tempe became Mormon strongholds. A new county, Maricopa, was formed with Phoenix as its seat. By 1889 the little city had grown strong enough to become the territorial capital, to the disgruntlement of the two communities, Tucson and Prescott, that had held the honor before.

By 1892 a stepladder of brush-and-rock dams not unlike those on the Little Colorado River was diverting water from the Salt River into canals capable of irrigating 120,000 acres. At times, though, it seemed that the new civilization would turn out to be no more permanent than its predecessor. Big floods repeatedly swept out the dams. They were hardly rebuilt when drought caused water companies located on high sections of the river to interfere with the rights of those lower down. During the closing years of the century, affairs grew so bad that nearly a third of the cultivated fields were abandoned and armed riders patrolled the trickles coming to the rest to make sure no one made off with a drop not legitimately his.

As in the Pecos Valley, salvation came from the federal Reclamation Service. A main problem was forming a legal entity capable of entering into a binding contract with the government. Months of mass meetings and newspaper propaganda during 1903 were needed to smooth away enough of the jealousies and suspicions existing among the different districts to open the way for a quasi-public corporation called the Salt River Valley Water Users Association. That done, the association hired the Reclamation Service to build in a tumbled gash of a canyon eighty miles east of Phoenix a huge masonry structure, Roosevelt Dam. Completed in 1912, it was capable of controlling the most vicious floods and storing up to 1.4 million acre-feet of water. The association was to repay the costs in ten years. Actually the debt was not fully liquidated until 1955.

Expenses soared far beyond expectations. More than a hundred miles of access road for huge freight wagons had to be built to the site. A town was created for the workers; the size of the dam's power plants was increased in midflight; transmission wires were webbed out across the desert. To prevent disputes among the original ditch companies, the federal government purchased them, coordinated the system, and ran it until November 1, 1917, at which time full responsibility was turned over to the Water Users Association.

Grown now into a highly complex business organization, the association maintains, through subsidiary corporations, seven dams and hundreds of ground-water wells. It delivers water to close to a quarter of a million acres of farmland and a rapidly growing industrial-residential urban area of 1.3 million persons. Demands for power and light have outstripped hydroelectric generating capacity, which is supplemented by coal-burning plants. Presumably if Jack Swilling's phoenix were to rise again, it would be pleased. But maybe not. One of the things he disliked most was feeling crowded.

## Growing Up

Many of the Anglos lured into the Southwest by its expanding economy soon grew exasperated by their inability to determine their political destinies. Because they lived in federal territories, they could not select their own principal officials. Although they did cast ballots for territorial delegates to Congress, the winner had no vote in Washington and functioned only as an adviser in matters concerning the territory he represented. In the words of territorial Governor Conrad Zulick of Arizona, the situation was "repugnant to the enlightened sense of the American people."

Not all of that repugnance sprang from idealism. Some economically oriented businessmen hoped that the achievement of statehood would be interpreted in California and the East as a signal that the antics of the frontier had ended and that investors could safely loosen their purse strings. Men who had acquired extensive land holdings dreamed of rising property values. Politicians with strong followings eyed the prestige, power, and financial rewards that would come from their being elected to full membership in the United States Senate or House of Representatives.

Comparable mixtures of sincerity and pragmatism motivated the opponents of statehood. Many merchants, mining companies, and small farmers were less concerned about possible increases in investments from the outside than about the rise in taxes that would follow the ending of federal support of the territorial governments. Interstate and local rail companies, it was charged, wanted to perpetuate the territorial system because territorial legislators could be cheaply and easily controlled.

But it was the nation, not the territories, that would have the final say, and the nation, too, was divided. Idealists believed that self-government was the right of every American, and beginning in the 1880s the platforms of both political parties paid at least lip service to statehood for all the western territories—the Dakotas, Montana, Washington, Idaho, Wyoming, Utah, and Oklahoma as well as New Mexico and Arizona. Pragmatists, however, worried that granting statehood to so many sparsely settled regions would give western opinion (often it was a radical opinion) too great a weight in national affairs. Party politicians meanwhile speculated fretfully about whether Democratic or Republican Congressmen would be sent to Washington and what shifts this would bring to their power structures.

As for New Mexico and Arizona, were they really fit for statehood? Frontier lawlessness had not been fully subdued, educational systems were backward, and in New Mexico a largely illiterate, Spanish-speaking, priest-controlled voting majority seemed unaffected by Anglo principles of democracy and the separation of church from state.

In view of the nation's doubts it became incumbent on the Southwest to prove, as the preamble to an abortive Arizona constitution of 1893 expressed the matter, that undesirable, early-day characteristics have "vanished before the intelligent toil, the patient industry, and the high culture of the American bred citizens who have sought the territory for a home." And the most important place for the proof to begin was education.

The curious story of higher education in both New Mexico and Arizona underscores the problem. In 1890, when popular sentiment for statehood was gathering momentum, not a college or publicly supported high school existed in either territory. Nor was grammar-school education very effective, especially in New Mexico. According to the census of 1890, more than one third of that territory's 154,000 residents were illiterate. Of 44,000 school-age children, only 12,000 were enrolled in either public or parochial schools.

This indifference to public education arose from more than the pioneers' usual anti-intellectualism. Hispanic residents were reluctant to pay property taxes of any kind and particularly taxes designed to support an Anglo-type education that they feared would corrode traditional values. On top of that fear was the insistence of Archbishop Lamy and his successors that inasmuch as the great bulk of New Mexico's population was Catholic, the Roman Catholic Church was duty-bound to assume responsibility for its education. The church established as many parochial schools as its resources allowed and, with the power of numbers behind it, won the passage of a bill allowing priests to act as teachers in the few struggling public schools that existed. For years a Jesuit press published all textbooks.

Protestant churches responded by founding a few ill-financed institutions, but not until 1889 did the legislature face up to the problem of education. It then exhibited a sudden ardor. Between that year and 1893 the lawmakers passed bills establishing *six* four-year colleges. In 1891 other bills were passed making school attendance compulsory and bringing the *first* high school into existence. The consequences should have been predictable. To survive, New Mexico's six colleges had to all but eliminate entrance requirements and draw pupils not only from the territory itself but from surrounding states, even from Old Mexico. Years passed before any New Mexican institution of higher learning attained reputable status. Under the circumstances it is hard to avoid cynicism: Did the territory's abrupt interest in public education arise from awakened interest in a long-neglected field or from the desire of statehood advocates to present a skeptical nation with evidence of the high culture of its American-bred citizens?

Except for the Catholic influence, which did not figure strongly there, Arizona's adventure with higher education was similar. In 1885 certain legislative plums were being passed out to the more populous counties. The main one was the state insane asylum, funded by an appropriation of $100,000. Maricopa County, of which Phoenix was the seat, won the prize. Another offering was a state university, to be funded with $25,000.

At the time there were no high schools in Arizona, either, and a university looked pretty useless. No one wanted it, but Tucson was handed it regardless. Raising money enough to meet the requirement that the surrounding county provide the necessary land devolved eventually on two professional gamblers and a saloonkeeper. They succeeded, and, in October 1891, the University of Arizona opened for business. Of the thirty-three students enrolled, twenty-seven were not true college freshmen but were being tutored for that rarefied status in a special school attached to the university. So in fact the college opened with six students only. Increase came slowly. Thirteen years later there were only thirteen high schools in Arizona, and pickings for the university were lean. Still, a college was nice window trimming, in case outsiders asked. And seeds had been planted from which respected institutions did grow.

Steps to quell lawlessness accompanied educational changes. Because land fraud was considered New Mexico's major criminal sore, the establishment of the Court of Private Claims in 1891 was greeted by national observers as a landmark healing operation. Arizona meanwhile tried lifting itself up by its own bootstraps. In 1889 the territorial legislature imitated New Mexico in making train robbery punishable by death. Lesser penalties were imposed for carrying deadly weapons in any town.

In 1891 the Legislative Assembly proposed to deal with widespread cattle rustling by authorizing the formation of a troop of Arizona Rangers modeled after its Texas namesake. Ten years passed before a troop of twelve privates, one sergeant, and a captain came into being. (Later the troop was expanded to include twenty privates and six officers.) The Rangers' headquarters were, in succession, Bisbee, Douglas, and Naco in the rugged southeastern section of Arizona. On paper at least the record was phenomenal. During the fiscal year 1903–04, for example, the riders brought in 1,052 suspects. All the glitter was not golden, however. The rank and file of the Rangers were hired because of exceptional abilities with horses and guns and an intimate knowledge of the countryside. Many had acquired their talents while operating as outlaws themselves. In making arrests they did not heed the niceties of the law, and when they were off duty some of them brawled in saloons and bawdy houses with as little restraint as the undesirable citizens they were pursuing. In 1909, after furious controversy, the troop was disbanded. Again, however, a step had been taken.

During these years the other western territories were being admitted one after the other to the Union. The normal procedure was for Congress to pass an enabling act allowing a territory to call a constitutional convention into session in order to draw up a set of organic laws for the proposed state. The territorial voters then accepted or rejected the document. If Congress was satisfied after reviewing a constitution approved by the electorate, it passed a bill conferring statehood and authorizing elections for state officials.

Territories impatient with congressional procrastination sometimes summoned constitutional conventions without the blessings of an enabling act and then pushed the drive on to success. Not so Arizona or New Mexico. Between them they prepared, without authorization, several constitutions. New Mexican voters rejected one. Others managed to squeak through the House but died in the Senate. By the turn of the century, however, national moods were changing. The free and unlimited coinage of silver, espoused by both territories but anathema in the conservative East, had become a dead issue. The high proportion of southwesterners, including Hispanos, who enlisted in Theodore Roosevelt's Rough Riders during the Spanish-American War reassured the nation about the region's patriotism and attracted favorable comment from people who until then had been uninterested in the distant territories.

The Southwest's two congressional delegates, reinforced by a vocal committee of bigwigs, lobbied hopefully—only to run into their most formidable foe yet, Senator Albert J. Beveridge of Indiana, chairman of the Committee on Territories. Beveridge sincerely doubted the readiness of either New Mexico or Arizona for statehood; he mistrusted their political leanings (he was a Republican); and he suspected, rightly, that outside "special interests" with an eye on the Southwest's natural resources were pouring money into the statehood drives in the hope of being able, later on, to manipulate friendly state governments for their own gain. A whirlwind tour through the area with his committee did nothing to change his mind.

Late in 1905, however, pressure for favorable consideration forced the Indianian to compromise. Arizona and New Mexico would be admitted as a single huge state. Its name would be Arizona (that got rid of the stigma attaching to the word Mexico), but its capital would be Santa Fe (that would placate New Mexicans about the loss of their identity). Entranced by his vision, Beveridge delivered a soaring speech in the Senate: "And what a glorious state this New Arizona would be . . . Arizona, youngest of the Union and fairest; not Arizona the little, but Arizona the great . . . child of the nation's wisdom." Besides, though Beveridge did not say so in his oration, if his creation elected senators from the wrong party, at least there would be only two instead of four.

A hesitant Senate tacked an amendment onto the bill. Its provisions would not become operative until the citizens of the projected unit had voted, in November 1906, on the referendum, Shall Arizona and New Mexico be united to form one state?

Intense campaigning followed. The Santa Fe Ring wanted statehood, and the Hispano *patrones* (and some Penitente leaders) allied with the ring's political machine delivered the vote—26,195 for jointure, 14,-735 opposed. Arizona disagreed. It feared that New Mexico's more numerous population, most of which was agricultural, would hold farm taxes low while increasing levies on mining and industrial properties. Most of all, it objected to being dominated, as several papers put it, by "greasers." Arizona downed the proposal 16,265 to 3,141, enough so that even if the aggregate vote had been the determining factor, it would have won.

So it all had to be done again—and was. Separate enabling acts were passed, separate constitutional conventions summoned, separate documents prepared. New Mexico's constitution, highly conservative though it forbade segregated schools and provided for bilingual education, aroused little opposition in the East. Arizona's liberal one—with its provisions for woman suffrage, the direct election of senators, the initiative, referendum, and recall, including the recall of judges—did. Objecting to what he called a dangerous impairment of judicial independence, President Taft vetoed a congressional bill admitting Arizona, but signed a resolution that would authorize acceptance of the state if the voters removed the objectionable feature. Wearily Arizona did, only to reinsert it as soon as statehood had been achieved.

The long-desired days came at last—for New Mexico on January 6, 1912, and for Arizona on February 14, 1912. After half a century of political inferiority, they were as nearly on their own as it was possible for any state to be in the country's rapidly expanding, rapidly intertwining industrial/federal system.

# 9

## NEW WAYS, OLD PROBLEMS

*The Big Change*

Neither Arizona nor New Mexico was prepared for the surge into modernity that came to them with World War II. During the three decades following the attainment of statehood, their progress had been plodding. More than three quarters of the population remained rural. Such small urban centers as existed were either mining camps or trade distribution points for limited areas. Educational systems were rudimentary, and tourism flourished only in the narrow corridors served by the railroads. The relatively few automobiles that appeared had to contend with frame-shattering roads.

There was some growth, of course; the entire nation was growing. More dams were constructed; for a time Elephant Butte Reservoir on the Rio Grande, completed in 1916, was the largest man-made lake in the world. Drillers stirred small excitements by finding petroleum in the southeastern and northwestern corners of New Mexico. But only mines and smelters, the twin components of the copper industry, achieved out of their need to conjoin water, fuel, and cheap labor the kind of highly integrated economies that marked industry throughout the rest of the nation.

Phelps Dodge can serve as an instance. Dissatisfied with the services and rates offered it by both the Santa Fe and Southern Pacific railroads, the huge copper company built its own line, the El Paso & Southwestern. It stretched from Tucson to the huge smelters at El Paso and from El Paso north through the Tularosa Valley to Phelps Dodge coal mines in northeastern New Mexico. All told, it covered 1,127 miles, including a 70-mile spur south into Old Mexico. Frightened by the possibility that the line might continue spreading into the Midwest on one side and California on the other, the Southern Pacific in 1924 bought it for $28 million in SP stock, $29.5 million in SP bonds, and $6.5 million in cash.

A breathtaking transaction, to be sure, but it seemed so largely because nothing else like it had ever before occurred in the Southwest. Circumstances, however, were changing. With an abruptness that still leaves old-timers shaking their heads, World War II, the conflict with Korea, and the cold war hurtled the region into an urban-industrial economy as sophisticated—and as troublesome—as any in the nation.

The initial impulse came from the government's decision to develop an atomic bomb. One major early problem was finding a site where utmost security could be maintained. While searching for an adequate spot, the Corps of Engineers, which was charged with building the facilities, consulted with one of the country's leading physicists, J. Robert Oppenheimer of the University of California's Lawrence Radiation Laboratory.

The power of accident. The Oppenheimer family owned a summer ranch in the Sangre de Cristo Mountains of New Mexico. Occasionally they took pack trips into the Jemez Mountains on the western side of the Rio Grande Valley and during their excursions sometimes refreshed themselves on Los Alamos Mesa, where a vigorous native of Michigan, Ashley Pond, had established a spartan private school occupied by about forty-five students. Oppenheimer told the investigators from the Corps of Engineers that the isolated school's classrooms, dining hall, and dormitory cabins could serve nicely for housing the small number of scientists originally assigned to the program.

Small! In December 1941 the United States entered World War II. The following month 1,500 construction workers swarmed onto Los Alamos Mesa. By 1946 Los Alamos city—a jumble of trailers, dormitories, laboratories,.and miscellaneous buildings of all types—was housing 10,000 people, all connected in one way or another with the bomb.

Los Alamos was only one phase. Albuquerque deeded its municipal airport to the United States for $1.00. The government transformed the field into Kirkland Air Force Base, where bombers could be modified to serve as carriers for the new weapon and crews could be trained for handling the craft and its load at what were then unprecedented altitudes. The Atomic Energy Commission set up headquarters adjacent to Kirkland and oversaw the development of the huge Sandia military complex, where research and development work were coordinated. A test site called Trinity (no one knows why Oppenheimer picked that name) was selected in the bleakest part of Tularosa Valley.

At Trinity the first massive experimental bomb was attached to the top of a hundred-foot steel tower. Detonation came as dawn was touching the horizon at 5:29:45 A.M. on July 16, 1945. The tower vaporized: the earth leaped. A vast mushroom cloud boiled seven miles into the air above stunned observers huddled under shelters located thousands of yards from the vanished tower. Watchers shivering on a lookout hilltop at Los Alamos, two hundred miles away, gasped at the sight of the distant flare. Oppenheimer murmured a sentence from an ancient Hindu classic, "I am become Death, the destroyer of worlds." For better or for worse, nuclear energy, epitome of modern technology, had received its first test in one of the oldest inhabited sections of the United States.

During those same war years, high prices were stimulating copper mining, cattle raising, wheat and cotton growing—with corresponding drains on limited water supplies. Still other economic boosts came from the military installations that were scattered throughout the region to take advantage of favorable conditions for training aviators and mechanized ground forces.

The slump that followed the end of the war was brought up short by the conflict in Korea and mounting tensions between the United States and the Communist bloc. Fear of missile attacks led to a widespread dispersal of factories as well as of military bases. Although California received the lion's share of the new government contracts, Arizona, New Mexico, and Texas also benefited heavily.

Soldiers who during World War II had trained in the Southwest returned eagerly to new jobs waiting where skies were mostly cloudless, living was casual, and recreational facilities were easily available. Heat was no longer a major problem, for about 1950 the mass production of air conditioning units for buildings and automobiles had brought a comfortable if artificial climate within the reach of almost everyone. Even desolate Yuma, Arizona, the hottest, driest town in the United States, saw its population jump within a decade from 5,000 to 30,000, thanks to a combination of refrigerant cooling units and the development of one of the best varieties of long-staple cotton in existence. Meanwhile extensive federal help in highway construction and the spread of jet airline routes whose schedules were seldom interrupted by bad weather reduced the problems of distance almost to zero.

Other problems, particularly those associated with headlong growth, were not so easily solved. By 1960, the Atomic Energy Commission had expended at Los Alamos and Albuquerque a total of $376 million. Twenty-four thousand workers were directly employed by the interlocked complexes, and perhaps double that many by related services. Between the end of World War II and 1960 Albuquerque's population soared by almost 500 percent—from 50,000 to 225,000. It was not a unique experience. The construction of the half-billion-dollar Glen Canyon Dam on the Colorado River boomed northern Arizona. Defense plants and a burgeoning electronics industry more than tripled the sizes of the Tucson and Phoenix metropolitan areas. Throughout both states universities were rapidly enlarged and rigidly upgraded in order to help supply the talent voraciously demanded by the new economy.

To bring a sense of community to these cities of strangers and to keep growth from slipping out of control, articulate citizens formed activist groups designed to influence the course of civic affairs. Leaders in Albuquerque were the American Association of University Women and the League of Women Voters. Los Alamos created its own county. In Phoenix, 742 concerned citizens formed a Phoenix Growth Committee that split into dozens of aggressive study units, hired consultants, and worked out programs for submission to the city government.

When entrenched local politicians declined to heed the demands, some of the newcomers ran for office and won enough contests to start their programs moving. All the major cities and several small ones passed, after hard fights, expensive bond issues for improving streets, sewage plants, parks, playgrounds, airports, libraries, and the like. In spite of the expenditures, tax loads stayed within reason, thanks to the broadening of the base by continued growth.

This concurrent fact is not irrelevant, however. Phoenix was so concerned with the present that not until 1972, 105 years after the city's beginning, was there a viable local historical society or museum or any other means of preserving a complete set of civic records. Not until the Phoenix History Project was launched that same year, in 1972, had anyone seriously contemplated producing a complete written account of the city's progress. And those who do not learn from the past, it has often been said, are doomed to repeat it.

No southwestern city or state has ever been able to handle, on its own, the region's most persistent problems. Some of the continuing frustrations are intertwined—labor, race relations, international amity. Towering over all is the overwhelming need for adequate supplies of water. Because such problems transcend boundaries, federal intervention is necessary, and yet the political philosophy of the region more and more inclines toward favoring private, or at least local, decisions about issues that are, after all, intensely local in their impact.

To what extent can states' rights of this sort be accommodated within the spreading federal framework? History cannot answer that question, but it can help provide perspective, as the sketchy outlines that follow may indicate.

## The Troubled Border

What American patriots of the Mexican War era called Manifest Destiny looked in Mexico like cupidity. The aftermaths of "peace" did little to change the opinion. Texans supported a revolutionary movement designed to break the state of Tamaulipas away from the mother country. Westward, armed American filibusters sought to seize Baja California and Sonora. James Gadsden was criticized bitterly by expansionists because he did not force Santa Anna, at the time of the Gadsden Purchase, to yield enough land to give Arizona a port on the Gulf of California. Agitation for Anglo annexation of northwestern Mexico continued throughout the rest of the century, and some Arizonans still believe that their state's progress has been irredeemably hampered by the landlocked situation into which it was boxed by a failure of the national will.

These expansionist agitations bred deep distrust among educated Mexicans. Simpler folk were more outraged by personal insults. In innumerable ways along the border they were made to feel inferior, particularly in Texas, where dark skin of any kind was likely to stir prejudice. Rampant banditry and cattle stealing became the backdrop for wanton explosions of racial violence, with both sides contributing to the terrorism that resulted.

The outbreak of the Porfirio Díaz revolution in 1876 twisted tensions still tighter. As a spinoff of the upheaval, the pace of international banditry increased. Angry Texans beefed up their mounted Ranger police force, and President Rutherford B. Hayes said that troops would be allowed to cross the border in hot pursuit of Mexican outlaws. The cavalry had been doing that, on and off, for some years, but Hayes's announcement made the infringement on Mexican sovereignty official, and Mexico reacted indignantly albeit futilely because of the revolution.

Small issues grew into crises, as witness the "Salt War" of west Texas. On desert flats near the slabby prow of the Guadalupe Mountains, a hundred miles east of El Paso, were shallow saline lakes underlain with such pure salt that Mexicans once shoveled the dripping stuff directly into their little two-wheeled *carretas* and hauled it off to market without hindrance.

When an Anglo named Charles Howard tried to assert ownership, by means of Texas land certificates, over a resource that had long been open to everyone, the Mexicans ran him out of the district. Howard retorted by cornering one of their leaders, devious Luís Cardis (actually an Italian), in an El Paso store on October 10, 1877, and blasting him apart with a shotgun. The few Anglos in the region immediately went into a panic and by telegraph appealed to the governor of Texas for a company of Rangers to protect them. Learning of this, the 12,000 or so Mexicans who lived in the little river communities dotting both sides of the Rio Grande for twenty miles below El Paso began gathering in ugly knots.

Howard's acquaintances urged him to get out of the country until tempers cooled. Confident of help from the governor, he refused. In time aid arrived, though not quite in the shape he expected. Because El Paso was so far from the capital at Austin and Apaches were on the prowl, the governor agreed to the recruitment of a special company of Rangers in the troubled area itself. Most of those who signed on were riffraff from the mining camps around Silver City, New Mexico, and trouble hunters who had been floating around the edges of the Lincoln County war. With this choice group, Howard rode downstream to San Elizario, the largest and most inflammable of the river settlements.

Predictably, strife erupted, muscled in large part by Mexicans from the south side of the Rio Grande. American stores on the north bank were looted, men were killed. After being besieged by a mob for several days in an adobe house, the Rangers, Howard, and his Anglo associates surrendered. The lawmen were disarmed and sent packing to the tune of loud jeers, the only company of Texas Rangers ever to be humiliated in such wise. Howard and two Anglo cohorts were put against a wall and executed. Their bodies were then stripped and thrown into a well.

Eventually, after more rioting, looting, and killing, a sheriff's posse from El Paso and troops from the nearest fort in New Mexico restored quiet, not without considerable disorder on their own part. A grand jury assembled and rained indictments. The accused fled into Mexico and were never extradited. Howard's father-in-law was confirmed in the ownership of the salt beds, and thereafter anyone digging up the stuff paid for what he took. Because so many aliens had crossed the border to join the rioting, the United States Army decided to reactivate Fort Bliss, a post at El Paso that had been closed only a few months before. Never shut down since, Bliss played important roles in later border troubles and after the outbreak of the second world war became a prime factor in keeping the heated economies of west Texas and southern New Mexico rolling in high.

Porfirio Díaz meanwhile won his revolution and became a virtual dictator. In a sense he was a patriot, for he sought to strengthen his tormented country by means of taxes on foreign investment. To encourage investments from outside he eliminated banditry by means of the *rurales*, a ruthless police force dressed in dove-gray uniforms buttoned with silver. Shaky finances were shored up, and, as signs of the new order became apparent, foreigners poured fortunes into the country.

Only Mexico's elite benefited greatly, however. All rural land, for example, fell into the hands of a few hundred rich *hacendados* ("ranch owners"), many of them Americans, and half of the populace was reduced to a peonage no better than slavery. New revolutionary plots began to hatch. This time much of the resentment centered on American exploiters, who were looked on as the chief pillars of the oppressive regime—"the capitalist," shouted one incendiary, "who in every way and everywhere has displaced us with his legion of blue-eyed blonds."

Among the Anglos who had decided to take advantage of Díaz's welcome was a gregarious, flamboyant, paunchy, curly-haired Arizona hard-rock miner and rancher named William C. Greene. He was past forty when, in 1896, he and a handful of American and Mexican associates acquired several semimoribund copper claims at Cananea, forty miles south of the Arizona stretch of the international border, and merged them into what became the Cananea Consolidated Copper Company—the Four C's, as Wall Street soon spoke of the holding. The claims turned out to be particularly amenable to the new technologies of copper mining and milling, and Greene proved adept at raising money from investors in the East. To ease his way along the golden path he gave himself the title of colonel, not because of vanity but because he believed the word helped him reach people whose attention he wanted.

The Four C's soared. By 1906, 20,000 people lived in Cananea—some in company houses in the company town, others in the shabby shack slums of nearby Ronquillo. All had to shop at the company store. Workers were paid three pesos ($1.50 American) for a ten-hour shift. It was little enough in God's truth but better than the pay at the other mines in Sonora and on the great *haciendas*. In fact, Díaz ordered Greene to cut his rates because they were unsettling workers elsewhere. But what was most disturbing to the Mexican families in Cananea was the rate commanded by American miners. Greene felt he needed their skills as examples for his Mexicans, but to get them he had to pay American wages, which were three times those allowed south of the border. There was not much use trying to explain such niceties to the Mexican workers, however. They felt they were being belittled, and their pride rebelled.

Egged on by a sticky combination of revolutionary agitators and organizers from the Western Federation of Miners, the men struck at dawn on June 1, 1906, for higher wages and shorter hours. Matters were orderly until about noon, when the intemperate managers of the company lumberyard turned fire hoses on the demonstrators outside their gates. Shootings and burnings erupted then, with casualties on both sides.

As excitement swept through the sprawling works, Greene grew afraid that the strikers might cripple the huge plant and the mines with dynamite. Since the small force of nonstrikers at his command would be helpless to check such sabotage, he telegraphed appeals for aid to Governor Izábel of Sonora and to Colonel Emilio Kosterlitzky, the icy, widely feared, Russian-born head of the Sonora *rurales*. Unhappily for Greene's strategy, however, the headquarters of both officials lay well to the south, whereas the only railroad out of Cananea ran north into the United States. So additional messages chattered off in that direction and produced in Bisbee, Arizona, eight miles north of the border station of Naco, upward of two hundred volunteers willing to take the train to Cananea and teach the greasers not to bother American property.

To keep the march from looking like an armed invasion the leaders resorted to a flimsy subterfuge. At Naco the group disbanded. Declaring that they were private individuals traveling on private business, the men straggled across the border and were promptly inducted into the Mexican army. Their conduct on arriving at Cananea was exemplary. Apparently no one touched a single striker in violence. Nevertheless their presence there where they had no right to be slowed the momentum of the strike, and when Kosterlitzky's *rurales* rode into town on the evening of June 2, the last sparks faded. Bitter resentments remained, however. A Mexican police force and a Mexican governor had come scampering at the call of an American capitalist, and neither had breathed a word of protest against Greene's importation of armed Americans to quell the aspirations of Mexican workers.

The result, as Greene's biographer, C. L. Sonnichsen has shown, was Mexican willingness to believe any anti-American rumor, no matter how extravagant. Educational displays at Mexico City's New Museum of History transformed the untrained civilian volunteers from Bisbee into uniformed United States troops ruthlessly gunning down unarmed Mexican strikers. The blow at Greene became a blow at the hated Díaz regime, and those who died during the opening phases of the strike or suffered imprisonment afterward became martyrs to a gathering revolution.

## *Fever Chart*

The conflict erupted in 1910. For years thereafter Mexico bled. Inevitably the border was involved. El Paso flourished as a center for gun smuggling. During the battles for Ciudad Juárez just across the Rio Grande, residents of the American city climbed to their rooftops with telescopes to watch the fighting. Less entertaining were the skirmishes at the twin towns of Naco, Arizona, and Naco, Sonora, where fifty-four noncombatant Americans were killed or wounded by stray bullets. More deliberate, according to the Mexican government, was the wanton slaying during the course of several months, of 114 Mexican civilians north of the border by rampaging Americans, many of them Texas Rangers.

In Washington Congress wavered over what course to pursue. Interventionists led by Senator Albert B. Fall of New Mexico demanded that the United States invade Mexico if necessary to protect the thousands of Americans and the $1.5 billion of American investments in the war-wracked country. Taft stalled. Wilson professed neutrality (he called it watchful waiting), but ordered American naval units into Veracruz to prevent a shipment of German arms from reaching Victoriano Huerta, temporarily in power after a bloody course of action that had aroused Wilson's deep repugnance. Mexico reacted furiously to the meddling, and war might have followed except for the intervention of Argentina, Brazil, and Chile.

In other ways, too, Wilson's stance of neutrality was slowly eroded. After Huerta toppled, the American State Department recognized the regime of scraggly-bearded, ruddy-faced Venustiano Carranza and cut off aid to one of Carranza's arch rivals, Doroteo Arango, better known by his pseudonym of Francisco Villa and its affectionate diminutive, Pancho. A one-time cattle rustler and mule skinner, colorful Villa has left an ambiguous legacy. One American historian has called him "perhaps the purest revolutionary who ever lived." Others have seen him as a bloodthirsty opportunist who, when faced with defeat, spread destruction throughout the border country merely from spite. Whatever the truth, none of the other feuding warlords is so well remembered in the border country.

His outbursts against the United States began in January 1916, after he had been driven by Carranza's forces back into the mountainous deserts of Chihuahua. The armies that harried him were equipped with American-supplied arms and rode American trains from point to point along the border in their thrusts against him. Either out of revenge or perhaps with a twisted hope that he could lose nothing and might gain much by forcing the United States to invade Mexico, he seized and murdered seventeen American technicians who were traveling into the country at Carranza's invitation to rehabilitate needed mines. He capped that atrocity on the night of March 8/9 with a raid against the border town of Columbus, New Mexico. Because his presence in the nearby area was known, the village had been more heavily garrisoned than he perhaps realized. Though he managed to burn several houses and kill another seventeen people, nine of whom were civilians, he suffered more than a hundred casualties of his own during his precipitous retreat.

If an American invasion was his intent, the strategy worked. Carranza, in apologizing for the raid, made equivocal remarks that the American State Department chose to interpret as granting permission for United States troops to undertake Villa's capture and punishment. Promptly Brigadier General John J. Pershing, who had been sent to Fort Bliss at El Paso some weeks earlier to keep the border situation under surveillance, crossed into Chihuahua with nearly 7,000 men, soon to be followed by almost that many more. Fire breathers exulted. A good beginning, Senator Marcus Smith of Arizona wrote Wilson's Secretary of War, Newton Baker, but what was needed was a full-scale invasion "to give the Mexicans an object lesson in our strength. It will cost money [he made no mention of lives] but it will be worth the price." And to some pugnacious citizens even this was not enough. They wanted more territory to add to that already taken from Mexico by the war of 1846–48.

Villa, however, proved more elusive than the overconfident Americans expected. Pershing, inadequately equipped from his base at Columbus for the job at hand, dispersed the rebel forces but never caught up with the leader. Moreover, the farther he advanced, the more suspicious the Mexicans grew of the hated *gringos'* true intentions. On June 20 a detachment of Mexican regulars clashed at Carrizal, deep inside Chihuahua, with two troops of American cavalry on a scouting mission. Seven Yankees were killed; twenty-three were captured.

American tempers flared. Fifty thousand National Guardsmen were rushed to Brownsville, El Paso, and Nogales, ready for the invasion Marcus Smith and other warmongers had begged for. Rigidity then on either side might have been disastrous. But Carranza, knowing that his country was in no shape for a war against the Colossus of the North, released the captured cavalrymen and promised to take action against bandits who had been raiding the Big Bend country of west Texas. Wilson, wishing to free his attention for the mounting dangers in Europe, responded by pulling Pershing back to what amounted to a holding operation just inside the Mexican border. Diplomats took over, and, in February 1917, the Americans withdrew entirely.

Many consequences flowed from the eleven-month misadventure. Pershing's failures in Mexico, some historians believe, convinced the German high command that the United States was not to be feared. This in turn encouraged Germany to unleash the submarine warfare that led to American participation in World War I. Be that as it may, the Mexican experience did help train a hitherto unprepared nation in mobilization, revealed weaknesses that needed correction, and thus made possible the swift gathering of forces that turned the tide in Europe—the second time, ironically enough, that Mexico has served as an American training ground, for the war of 1846–48 functioned as a school for the Civil War.

Finally, there was a lesson in vulnerability. At about the time that Germany resumed unrestricted submarine warfare, the British secret service learned of and informed the American State Department about the so-called Zimmerman note to Mexico. Emanating from Berlin, the note proposed that if the United States entered the war in Europe, Mexico should ally itself with Germany, receiving in reward a return of Texas, New Mexico, and Arizona when victory came. Publication of the note in the United States gave war sentiment a powerful boost. It also showed, in those days before the advent of missile warfare, that America's two-ocean defenses could be outflanked by attacks mounted through an unfriendly neighbor to the south—a thought made doubly sober by Germany's inclusion of Japan in the Mexican plot.

The Pershing withdrawal also emboldened Mexico to include in its new 1917 constitution a clause asserting Mexican ownership of all mineral and oil resources and limiting future concession to Mexican nationals. That action, along with some actual expropriations of American property, led diehards to demand more sword rattling at the conclusion of the war in Europe. In the 1920s, however, the national mood was pacific. With Herbert Hoover tentatively inaugurating what became Franklin Roosevelt's good-neighbor policy, arbitration and a more patient approach to old irritations began to bring about friendlier relations.

In 1963, little Chamizal, a section of El Paso—or was it part of Ciudad Juárez?—became a symbol of the rapprochement. Back toward the beginning of the century, the Rio Grande, swollen with flood, had chewed out a new channel south of the original bed marking the boundary between the two cities. As a result of the shift, about 600 acres of Juárez's heavily populated Chamizal district had ended up north of the river, where, if treaties were literally followed, it lay within the physical bounds of the United States. The same capricious flood also transferred a small part of El Paso to the Mexican side of the river.

Which nation held civil and criminal jurisdiction over the realigned segments? Which city collected taxes? Where did the residents vote? Could population be forcibly relocated? If so, what of the property they owned, some of it of considerable value? Involved in the answers were precedents concerning other involuntary transfers of land wrought by changes in the river's channel.

A 1911 attempt at arbitration collapsed when the United States refused to accept the decree of the international board. The case then entered the murky realms of national pride and dragged on until 1963, when President Kennedy of the United States and President López Mateos of Mexico agreed that international amity demanded a solution. Long discussions ended in the major part of the disputed area being awarded to Mexico. So that the Rio Grande would remain the boundary, the two governments shared the cost of digging a new river channel to set off the transferred area and fortified it against future floods. Highways were realigned, new bridges built. Realistic formulas were devised to settle questions of citizenship and property rights. Except for one element—a willingness to negotiate as friends—all of this had been implicit half a century earlier in the abortive arbitration decree of 1911. Once that ingredient was added, the boundary commissions of the two nations had little difficulty in handling another 220 lesser cases involving 30,000 acres along the lower river.

Mexico considered the Chamizal settlement a victory and in a burst of pride launched a border improvement program that lined the Juárez side of the "rectified" river with parks, museums, and handsomely landscaped roadways. On a fifty-five-acre tract on its side of the stream the United States erected a striking Chamizal National Memorial heralding the triumph of good sense over a stubborn insistence on "rights." The gesture was reassuring, for by then a flood of impoverished Mexican immigrants was pouring across the border and raising new problems whose solution would require new measures of patience and understanding.

## The Brown Tide

An elegant example of the pitfalls of prophecy appeared in the San Diego *Union* on March 5, 1872. During the course of a story describing four-year-old Phoenix for the newspaper, an Arizona correspondent remarked, "The Indian is now a nuisance and the Sonorian [sic] a decided annoyance, but both are sure to disappear before civilization 'as snow before the noonday sun.' " A century of experience has taught us better. Indians and persons of Mexican extraction are ineradicably established not only in Phoenix but in most of the major urban centers of the United States. If present trends continue, people whose origins reach back to the Spanish-speaking nations of the Western Hemisphere will soon replace blacks as the largest American minority.

Of this minority more than 60 percent are Mexican. They crossed the border at all points between Brownsville, Texas, near the mouth of the Rio Grande, and San Ysidro near the Pacific. More went north through southern Texas and southern California than through New Mexico or Arizona, but the latter two states have shared fully with their neighbors the continuing shocks of the still unabated flood. Before considering the problems, however, let us note briefly the circumstances that made the influx inevitable.

Anglos have always depended on a constantly replenished supply of cheap labor to perform the unskilled, unattractive tasks involved in exploiting their part of the North American continent. In the North, for example, Irish were used for building railroads; in the West, Chinese were utilized. As an equivalent to those groups, Jack Swilling's ditch company, nourisher of the seed that became Phoenix, hired Indians and Mexicans to do the hard part of the canal digging. The Hispanos involved had probably been living in the Gadsden Purchase area for generations. Five years later, however, the Lesinsky brothers had to go into Mexico itself for laborers to extract and smelt the ore of their pioneering copper mines in the Clifton-Morenci district of Arizona.

These tiny movements gained momentum when, in 1882, the United States initiated the first of a long series of laws designed to restrict immigration regarded as undesirable. That year Chinese, criminals, paupers, and mental defectives were banned. In 1907–08, the prohibition was extended, through a "gentleman's agreement" engineered by Theodore Roosevelt, to Japanese coolies.

It chanced that during that same period the Southwest was experiencing its first significant economic gains. As soon as transcontinental railroads made commercial agriculture profitable, land promoters brought into production tens of thousands of irrigated acres of vegetables, sugar beets, and cotton whose thinning and harvesting required laborious amounts of handwork. Simultaneously new technologies in the copper industry were opening new mines and smelters, expanding old ones, and stimulating the construction of branch railroads for hauling coal, timber, ore, and matte. Asiatic labor being unavailable for those projects, employers turned to Mexico.

They worked through labor contractors, even though a congressional act of 1885 had outlawed labor agreements with foreign immigrants before their arrival in the United States. The American labor contractor (often of Mexican descent himself) worked in turn through a Mexican counterpart who did the actual recruiting, mostly among impoverished drifters in the rapidly growing cities of interior Mexico.

The Díaz regime, admired greatly by Anglo businessmen of the early 1900s for its stability, was creating chaos among the country's rural poor. Those who were able fled to the cities. If they found jobs, they discovered that Díaz was trying to combat inflation by imposing a lid on wages. Workingmen's lives degenerated to barest subsistence.

There was one outlet. In his drive to open the north, Díaz was pushing railroads into Chihuahua and Sonora. Before then, leaving Mexico's central agricultural regions had been physically difficult and, because of the people's strong family attachments, emotionally shattering. But jobs on the railroad (often families were allowed to go along and set up homes in boxcars) broke traditional social patterns; introduced the workers to a wage, as contrasted to a barter, economy; and brought them close enough to the international border to learn that although Mexicans in the United States earned less than Anglos, still their pay was double that allowed in their own country.

Once these desperate people had left their railroad jobs for whatever cause, they were ready to listen to recruiters from the United States. Those who took the wrenching step of signing on were put into dusty railroad cars, their worn seats smelling of stale sweat and coal smoke, taken to the border, and turned over to the American handler. (Families followed as soon as husbands earned enough to send for them, or the men returned to visit when they could. Either way was hard on deep-seated ties.) The American contractor then moved his cargo on to the employer who had hired him or passed it on to agents from other areas—from the coal mines of Raton, New Mexico, say, or the sugar-beet and melon fields of Colorado. Costs of the migration were subtracted in installments from the workers' pay. It was often a dishonest subtraction, for there was much chiseling on railroad fares and food costs, with the Mexican recruiters as adept at taking advantage of their own countrymen as Anglos were.

The first world war added tremendous incentives. Demands for cotton and copper soared. At the same time Anglo workers left mines and fields for the armed forces or for jobs in new industrial plants. To fill the void Congress in 1918 suspended its prohibitions against contract labor and for three years allowed the recruitment of unskilled Mexicans for temporary agricultural work. And so it went. Whenever cheap labor from other sources dwindled (after the imposition, in 1924, of quotas on immigration from eastern and southern Europe, and during World War II and its uneasy aftermath), Mexicans were called on to substitute. Conversely, during the economic downturns of the 1930s and 1950s hundreds of thousands were rounded up and forcibly repatriated. During the process families were often split, and because all competitive dark-skinned labor was frowned on, many a legal Mexican-American citizen was "mistakenly" included in the roundups.

Julian Samora of the University of Notre Dame has assembled some sobering figures about the extent of this flux and flow. During the last century more than 1.5 million Mexicans have settled in this country legally. Upward of 5 million laborers called *braceros* were imported between 1942 and the end of 1964 with the understanding that they would be returned home at the expiration of their contracts. An unknown number managed to evade the order and stayed behind. Most significantly, 7.3 million illegal entrants were detected by the understaffed Immigration and Naturalization Service (INS) and deported. (Several undoubtedly were repeats.) The INS itself agrees that if 7.3 million were caught, at least twice that many escaped and melted into the legal community. And whether the migrants arrived legally or illegally, they are extraordinarily prolific; family sizes tend to be two or three times that of other American groups. One can hazard a reasonable guess that Mexican immigrants and their offspring account for a full 25 percent of America's current population growth.

The border adds special problems. At least 60,000 Mexicans who have achieved the right to live in the United States as resident aliens or citizens prefer to make their homes on the south side of the border, where prices are lower, and commute to their jobs. They are called "green-card" holders because the cards that let them past border checkpoints used to be green. (They are blue now.) Others obtain cards that allow them to visit the United States to shop or attend to business. Obviously there is considerable misuse of these identification papers— counterfeiting, theft, swapping, and whatnot.

Anglos along the border seldom protest the "invasion." Workers are needed in factories, hotel kitchens, and on construction projects. In El Paso female aliens are in widespread demand as cheap domestics and baby sitters. Their presence allows thousands of Anglo women (and middle-class Mexican-American women as well) to operate small businesses of their own—beauty salons or dress shops, for example—or to work as teachers, nurses, receptionists, secretaries, and the like. If the border were to be sealed off tomorrow, one housewife told me only half facetiously, all El Paso would jar to a stop in half an hour.

Perhaps the quickest way to sum up the problem is to note that if every United States citizen—man, woman, child—were to have received as a cash gift his or her share of the country's gross national product in 1970, the sum would have been $5,353. In Mexico that same year it would have been $717. It is the greatest economic disparity between adjoining countries in the world. Of course there is a flow from less to more, and will be as long as the disparity exists.

Although the problem is international in scope, proximity has made it seem particularly acute in the border states, where, until recently, most of the newcomers clustered before being pushed deeper into the interior by later arrivals. In those states the sheer volume of aliens aroused antipathies among Anglos who feared loss of economic and political control. Fear in turn led to a search for disagreeable traits to use as excuses for restrictive measures.

Mexicans, it was widely said, were swarthy, dirty, and clannish. (Naturally. Most had a large proportion of Indian blood in their veins; the poverty that had brought them to the United States forced them to live in substandard houses and to wear cheap clothes; and traditional kinship bonds as well as the scorn of the Anglos led them to huddle together for security. As for the cleanliness of their shirts and the interior of their houses, dispassionate observers felt that the neighboring Anglos had little to feel superior about.) Mexicans, the arguments went on, had been traditional enemies in various wars and near-wars. Mexicans took away good American jobs—and, indeed, aliens recruited with no knowledge of their destination had been used as strikebreakers, particularly in the Colorado coal mining disputes of 1903–4. (But many of the strikers they replaced had also been Mexicans. Besides, the argument was a sophistry. Mexicans, like other aliens, took work that Anglos didn't really want and left the Anglos free to try for better positions.)

The dislike and the advantage taken of it were manifested in various ways. Mexicans, both citizens and aliens, had to work for lower wages than Anglos did, for if they objected, labor recruiters would bring in hungry peons from below the border who would gladly step into their shoes. Except in New Mexico, where Hispanos were numerous enough to force bilingual teaching, schools mirrored Anglo contempt by conducting classes only in English and mentioning Mexican history only in terms of defeat and loss. And even in New Mexico some Anglos were so angered by Hispanic influence in school affairs that on different occasions two counties tried to secede from the territory: Grant County in the west wanted annexation to Arizona, and Eddy County in the southeast asked to join Texas.

Such situations created problems of identity. Although the Hispanos of New Mexico felt a strong empathy for these aliens from a land they had long regarded nostalgically as home, they also sensed the contempt that native Mexicans aroused among Anglos. Noticing, too, the artistic interest that tourists were beginning to show in the remnants left by the Spanish occupation, the Hispanos tried, guiltily, to disassociate themselves from the newcomers by calling themselves Spanish Americans. Mexicans outside New Mexico who had achieved United States citizenship went through a similar process, labeling themselves and their children either as Spanish Americans or, more frequently, as Mexican Americans.

Paradoxically the migrants also sought to maintain their own culture by means of Spanish newspapers and magazines, fraternal and mutual-benefit societies, sports clubs, church affiliations, and enormous family gatherings.

Some of the societies the people founded were aggressive as well as defensive. One such was La Sociedad Alianza Hispano-Americano, established in Tucson in 1893 to "protect and fight for the rights of Spanish-Americans." From Tucson the Alliance spread across New Mexico to El Paso and even as far as Chicago. It provided health and life insurance for members, and at times seems to have functioned as a secret labor union in Arizona, where employers long refused to recognize any union labeled as such. Bolstered by the Alliance—and by the staunch wives of the workers, insists Raquel Goldsmith, a vehement Chicana activist of Tucson—the mine and smelter workers of the Clifton-Morenci district won pay scales equal to those of their Anglo counterparts. Mexican labor organizers were active during the 1930s and 1940s in forming the Mine, Mill and Smelter Workers Union of the Southwest and Rocky Mountain regions (now a part of the Steel Workers Union), and in the early 1970s a strike composed largely of Mexican women brought the mighty Farah Company of El Paso, the world's largest manufacturer of trousers, to its knees. It should be noted, by way of contrast, that Cesar Chavez's famed United Farmworkers of America as yet has had little success in either Arizona or the lower Rio Grande Valley.

Those sparks, the liberating force of World War II and the GI Bill of Rights, and the black civil rights agitation of the 1960s gave rise to the militant Chicano movement, which combined demands for social and economic justice with an insistence on the worth of the migrants' Mexican and Indian heritage. Spinoffs include La Raza Unida, a political party dedicated to supporting Chicano candidates or Anglos openly favorable to Chicano causes. Again there is divisiveness. New Mexico's Hispanos and well-entrenched, conservative Mexican Americans tend to stand back . . . but that ferment, too, has gone beyond regional to national bounds.

Meanwhile the border continues to face problems peculiarly its own. Partly as a result of the pull of the United States, the growth of northern Mexico has been phenomenal. Thirteen sets of twin cities with an aggregate population of more than five million people dot either side of the international line. In the area with which we are concerned, Mexicali, the capital of Baja California; Nogales, Sonora; and Juárez, Chihuahua, are now considerably larger than their American counterparts: Calexico, California; Nogales, Arizona; and El Paso. Cultures and economics are inextricably intertwined. Shoppers, tourists, and workers flow back and forth. A twist of a dial brings either English or Spanish radio and television broadcasts. Shopkeepers, restaurateurs, lawyers, doctors, journalists, hair stylists, and filling station operators are almost invariably bilingual.

Traffic on the highways is heavy. Sonora, for instance, has become a major producer of food, and it is an eye-opening sight to encounter, in Nogales, Arizona, the acres and acres of truck service stations, parking lots, and motels catering to truckers needing a brief nap, day or night, before they gun their mammoth refrigerated vehicles on along the pavement to markets scattered from California to Illinois.

The International Boundary Commissions of the two nations cooperate effectively to solve interrelated problems of flood control, sewage disposal, and the purity of domestic water deliveries. Less amenable to solution are matters of pollution and ground-water mining. Intent on speeding industrialization and providing jobs for one of the world's fastest-growing populations, Mexican authorities pay little attention to environmental issues. El Paso's air is so filled with Juárez's smog that the American city has been excused from meeting national clean air standards. Almost as unrestrained as air currents are underground water flows. A reckless drilling of deep wells on one side of the border could rob those on the other and result in disastrous pumping "wars." As yet, however, no organization has been formed to regulate the exploitation of that priceless resource or even to conduct a comprehensive boundary-area hydrology survey.

Crime soars. Old-time bandits and cattle rustlers have given way to car thieves, traffickers in dope, jewel smugglers, and organized *coyote* groups who clandestinely transport frightened human freight under abominable conditions to destinations as far away as Chicago. A recurrent scandal in Arizona and southern Texas is the discovery on ranches owned by respected citizens and corporations of hidden labor camps where workers paid substandard wages live in stomach-turning squalor.

Juárez adds its share. Ignorant girls barely in their teens who have left the poverty of their isolated homes in the mountains to take jobs in factories beside the border often are laid off by circumstances of which they know nothing—the failure of a garment pattern to sell, the completion of a big one-shot order for transistor radios, or the sudden devaluation of the peso. There is no place to go then but the streets and the degradation of prostitution.

Controversies wax. Labor unions used to be ambivalent about brown aliens. They wanted to organize Mexican Americans, who often proved to be effective members, but they were reluctant to stir protests by enrolling noncitizens who had exactly the same virtues. But simple head counts have altered policies: There is power in those growing numbers. The International Ladies' Garment Workers Union, for one, no longer speaks of Mexicans or Americans but only of workers. Late in 1978 other labor groups challenged, in court, the right of the INS to seize illegal immigrants for deportation by surprise sweeps through plants suspected of employing them. Figures purporting to show what it costs the country to give health care, welfare, and schooling to illegal wetback Mexicans are also being questioned. Social security and other deductions from the workers' paychecks more than offset the sums they receive, it is argued.

But none of those figures are fundamental, retort environmentalists and proponents of Zero Population Growth. The real cost is the strain that the swiftly rising numbers of migrants is placing on American resources. It's time to call a halt, they insist, and the INS moves by fits and starts to comply. Also late in 1978 announcement was made of plans to construct all but impregnable fences near San Ysidro and El Paso—El Paso, where the Chamizal National Memorial to international amity shines across the river. Chicanos are outraged. Such a fence speaks to them of the very kind of contempt they are determined to eradicate. Do Americans really still believe, as that barrier implies, that the Mexicans, who for decades labored in furnace heat and searing winds to do jobs the Anglos would not face, have nothing more to contribute to the Southwest?

## To Be Continued

One of the richest pieces of agricultural land in the United States, and hence a prime target for real estate speculators, is the Imperial Valley, stretching through southeastern California into Mexico. Frosts are rare. Soil is a deep silt deposited through the eons by the meandering Colorado River, and because the valley floor lies below sea level, it is easily irrigated—or so its original promoters believed. All they had to do was go south of the sand hills that lie between the river and the valley, open a channel along the northern rim of Baja California in Mexico, and let the diverted water gurgle through, ready for sale to eager buyers.

Prospectuses were broadcast and, in January 1901, settlers began arriving. Within two years population had reached 8,000; 75,000 acres were under cultivation, and property values were soaring. But in 1905 a flood tore away the diversion gap, and the entire Colorado River rushed into the valley. It kept rushing for sixteen months, inundating a third of a million acres and forming in the heart of the desert the still-extant Salton Sea, whose maximum depth reached 72 feet. Finally, in February 1907, the Southern Pacific Railroad, which had heavy investments in the area, managed to dump 2,581 freight-car loads of rock, gravel, and clay into the breach and turn the river back into its original channel.

No sense of security followed. Silt kept building up in the riverbed. Levees constantly had to be raised, canals constantly dredged. To complicate the work, Mexico's revolutionary government, annoyed by Pershing's excursions into Chihuahua, deliberately interfered with men and materials moving across the border to repair the threatened works.

During these crises engineers of the United States Reclamation Service came up with figures purporting to show that the problems could be solved by a dam more than 700 feet tall in Boulder Canyon, some 250 miles upstream between Nevada and Arizona. This dam would check floods, store 30 million acre feet of water, and generate enough electricity to pay the costs of the project.*What did the states through or beside which the Colorado River and its principal tributaries flowed—Wyoming, Colorado, Utah, New Mexico, Nevada, California, and Arizona—think of that?

All but California objected violently. Their anguish came from their own legal codes, for all of them subscribed, with varying modifications,

*An acre foot of water will fill 325,850 one-gallon jugs. It will take care of the water requirements of five urban dwellers for a year. If sixty-thousand toilets were to be flushed simultaneously, they would put one acre foot of water into the local sewage plant.

to a principle of water law known as the doctrine of prior appropriation. A product of societies where supplies of water seldom meet demands, the doctrine declares that the person, company, community, or state that first removes water from a stream and puts it to beneficial use in factories or on farms can hold that water against all later appropriators. When shortages occur, supplies are not divided; the original claimant takes all he is entitled to before a second claimant can touch a drop.

By the time the high dam in Boulder Canyon was proposed, California was so far ahead of the other Colorado River Basin states in wealth, population, and political clout that the latter had nightmares of its establishing beneficial claims to the bulk of the river's water before they were in a position to begin sizable developments of their own. Colorado contemplated moving water under the Rockies to the Denver area; Utah had similar dreams concerning the Wasatch Front and Salt Lake City. Still more ambitious was Arizona's hope, unflaggingly promoted by a prosperous rancher, Fred T. Colter, of building its own high dam in the vicinity of the Grand Canyon and moving practically the entire river through a series of tunnels and aqueducts into southern and central Arizona. But none of the dreams could come to pass if California succeeded in establishing prior claims.

Clearly too many aspirations of great moment were involved to let decisions depend on as narrow a base as the doctrine of prior appropriation. Gradually businessmen and politicians of the river states, linked together as the League of the Southwest, turned toward the idea of dividing the waters by means of a formal compact. Under their prodding the legislatures of the states involved arranged to send delegates to Santa Fe during November 1922 to try to work out an agreement under the chairmanship of Herbert Hoover, then Secretary of Commerce.

Jealousies between the states were so intense that the best the conference could do was to partition the Colorado's flow between Upper and Lower River Basins. The dividing point between the two regions was set at Lee's Ferry, the historic Mormon crossing of the Colorado near the mouth of the Paria River, which drains out of Utah through a most spectacular canyon. Thus the Upper Basin embraced Wyoming, Colorado, Utah, New Mexico, and a fragment of Arizona. The Lower Basin consisted of Arizona, Nevada, and California.

How much water was there to divide? The commissioners had to depend on measurements that had been kept only since 1899 at an ill-equipped gauging station near Yuma. These indicated that the Colorado, together with its principal Arizona tributary, the Gila, could be counted on each year for about 17.5 million acre feet (maf), some of which was already being diverted here and there along the river's course. Seventeen and a half for sure? The negotiators wondered, for the years they were dealing with, 1899–1920, had been unusually wet. In other words there was no more precision to that figure, 17.5 million, than there was to Colorado River quicksand. Yet they went ahead with their long division regardless, for they feared that squabbling about arithmetical uncertainties would paralyze action.

The compact they produced allotted each basin 7.5 million acre feet a year. This meant that when Colorado, Wyoming, Utah, and New Mexico got around to calculating their individual shares of Upper Basin water, their base figure would be 7.5 maf *if that much was available.* If not, too bad. The Upper Basin still had to deliver 7.5 maf to the Lower Basin, even at the cost of shorting themselves. To keep seasonal variations from creating annual contentions, the negotiators agreed to set up bookkeeping on a ten-year basis—75 million acre feet to the Lower Basin each decade, which would allow wet years to compensate for dry ones.

At that point someone raised a thorny question. Was the flow of the Gila to be charged against Arizona's share of the 7.5 maf allotted the Lower Basin?

Certainly, said the Upper Basin people, seeing a way to reduce the drain on their water treasury. Never, retorted Arizona's delegate, W. S. Norviel. The Gila and its principal tributary, the Salt, lay almost entirely within Arizona. Both streams were highly developed. Except during the spring very little of their water reached the Colorado. To include their flow as part of the 7.5 maf to be divided eventually among California, Arizona, and Nevada would sorely reduce the amount of water Arizona was counting on from the main river. Never!

To placate Norviel, the negotiators eventually allowed the Lower Basin an extra million acre feet—considerably less than the Gila actually flows. It was understood by the delegates that when the different states got around to dividing their basin's water among themselves, the extra million feet would go to Arizona, but this important point was not written into the compact, because allocation there was made solely between basins without mention of any state by name.

The allotments to the two basins thus totalled 16 million acres—surely a safe calculation even though Mexico and the several Indian tribes that lived along the river were unprovided for. But in those days few white Americans paid much attention to Mexico or Indians. Believing that their work would bring order to basin water affairs for the foreseeable future, the delegates signed the compact on November 24, 1922, and went home. Inasmuch as the economic well-being of their respective states depended in large measure on effective utilization of Colorado River water, each negotiator could expect criticism—and got it. In every case they were flayed for yielding too much to the enemy.

None suffered more than W. S. Norviel, Arizona's unhappy delegate. As his detractors instantly pointed out, the ratification of the compact would soon be followed by the construction of a high dam in Boulder Canyon, a concrete-lined All-American Canal that would avoid Mexico on its way to the Imperial Valley, and, quite probably, an aqueduct to the Los Angeles Metropolitan Water District. All this would help California, but what was in it for Arizona? There was no codicil providing for Colter's high-line canal scheme. Nothing specific had been said about protecting the meager million acre feet of Gila water that Norviel had retained. In fact, his detractors railed, there was nothing whatsoever in the document to forestall a rapacious drive by California to absorb, on the basis of prior appropriations, the lion's share of the 8.5 maf allotted the Lower Basin.

Because of those derelictions Norviel lost his state job in Arizona, the legislature refused to ratify the compact, and Fred Colter went forth like a whirlwind to file preliminary claims, in the name of the people of Arizona, on enough Colorado River water to feed forty different diversion projects. Because no possible way of financing the dream existed, non-Arizonians looked on the rancher as a half insane, wholly dangerous obstructionist. Inside Arizona, however, he wore shining armor. His constituents sent him to the state legislature six times, and although he had no platform other than the water issue, he once came within a handful of votes of being elected governor.

After considerable squabbling, the legislatures of the other states ratified the document, and Congress accepted it as binding despite Arizona's abstention. The next step, taken in the face of stubborn opposition by private utility companies fearful of federal entry into power generation, was the authorization of Boulder Dam. A necessary preliminary was an understanding of how much water California would be entitled to take from the lower river. Congress arbitrarily settled matters by granting 300,000 acre feet to Nevada (behold Las Vegas as one result), 4.4 million acre feet to California (which had expected more) and 2.8 million to Arizona, plus a promise to Arizona that no Gila River water would have to be used in meeting future national commitments to Mexico.

Thoroughly disgruntled and insisting that she needed 3.5 million acre feet, not counting the Gila, Arizona entered suit in the United States Supreme Court to block work on Boulder Dam (begun actually in Black

Canyon in 1930 and finished in 1935). That failing, the state next attacked Parker Dam, the diversion point for an aqueduct to Los Angeles. *Opéra bouffe* followed. Declaring that Parker Dam had not been properly authorized by Congress, which was true, Governor Benjamin Moeur dispatched the Arizona National Guard to the river to halt the project. Although guardsmen on a sinking barge had to be rescued by the cheering enemy, their presence did delay work until a red-faced Congress rushed through an authorization bill that remedied the earlier oversight. So in the end Arizona lost that round, too.

Meantime the very massiveness of Boulder Dam was bolstering the spirits of a nation stunned by the catastrophic economic depression of the 1930s. Poets indited paeans; newsreel cameramen exposed countless feet of film picturing daredevil highscalers and blasters at work. If technology could achieve such a triumph as that dam in such dark times, then not all was lost.

During the excitement California quietly signed contracts with the Department of the Interior for the construction, by the Bureau of Reclamation, of delivery systems capable of transporting 5.26 million acre feet of water to her insatiable cities and valleys. This was 0.75 million more feet than the Boulder Canyon Project Act allowed, but Arizona had no prospects, yet, of being able to divert her share. Why let all that precious water go to waste? Secretary of the Interior Ray Lyman Wilbur, a Californian, agreed (he had to start water flowing to generate the electricity that would pay for the dam), but stated clearly that delivery did not constitute an establishment of rights. Few people in chronically suspicious Arizona believed him.

Other blows during the next nine years softened the state's intransigence. Obstructionist Fred Colter died. Wartime needs for metals and fiber created demands for water that Arizona could meet only by sinking wells deeper and deeper into dwindling ground-water tables. The same war also created worries about a possible Japanese landing on the coast of Mexico. Anxious for good will, the United States awarded its neighbor on the south, by a treaty signed in February 1944, more Colorado River water than most Westerners believed was necessary—1.5 maf a year. Meanwhile the river's flow was shrinking, California was hogging more than the law had said it could, and doomsayers were predicting a crisis. In order to have a voice in future proceedings, Arizona's legislature at last knuckled under and, three weeks after the signing of the Mexican treaty, ratified the Colorado River Compact of 1922.

Other major events followed inexorably—the 1948 compact by which the states of the Upper Basin divided the waters allotted them; the building during the 1950s and 1960s of an almost unbelievable series of upper river storage dams for hoarding every drop of runoff (much of which was then lost to evaporation); and finally Arizona's eleven-year, $5 million lawsuit to settle once and for all the state's continuing dispute with California.

In 1963 the Supreme Court declared that the amounts of water allocated to the Lower Basin states by the Boulder Canyon Project Act should prevail: 4.4 million feet to California, 2.8 million to Arizona, and 300,000 to Nevada. To California, then drawing more than 5 million feet from the river, the reduction would have been painful indeed if state water engineers, preparing for the worst, had not already launched plans for transporting huge amounts of water from the wet northern part of the state to the arid south. Even so, Californians extracted their pound of flesh. The state's strong bloc of Congressmen refused to support bills authorizing the staggering aqueducts and dams of the Central Arizona Project (CAP) until Arizona had *guaranteed* California 4.4 million acre feet of Colorado River water. That is, if the river ever fails to deliver enough water to meet the allotments granted the Lower Basin, California will have first call on what flow exists, no matter how parched Arizona becomes.

Desperate for water by then, Arizona had to agree. She had to give ground, too, to the demands of environmentalists that no high dams be built that would in any way impair the natural setting of the Grand Canyon—dams whose electric power was to have helped pay CAP's billion-dollar costs. Those concessions made, Congress authorized the project in 1968, and engineers began work on a giant aqueduct designed to draw water from Lake Havasu behind Parker Dam—a dam Arizona had tried to block a third of a century earlier with lawsuits and a contingent of floundering guardsmen.

Certainly Arizona needs water. According to figures released in November 1978 by the U.S. Geological Survey, much of the land in Maricopa and Pinal counties, homes of Phoenix and Tucson, has sunk an average of *7 feet* because of the withdrawal by pumps of 35.5 million gallons of ground water. But will CAP and its spaghetti bowl of reservoirs and conduits find water enough to halt further collapse? It seems unlikely. Original commitments of Colorado River water to the Upper and Lower Basins, it will be remembered, totaled 16 maf. In 1963 another 1 million feet were added for Indian reservations—and dissatisfied Navajos are threatening to sue for more.

To lighten the load created by the Indian allocation, the United States government has agreed that the nation and not just the Colorado

River states will assume responsibility for the 1.5 million acre feet granted to Mexico by treaty. Just where the water is to come from after CAP starts drawing off almost that much in the mid 1980s is still up in the air. Importations from the Columbia River? The Pacific Northwest is adamantly opposed.

But let's leave Mexico's 1.5 maf out of our calculations. Seventeen million acre feet are still committed to the two basins and the Indians. But there simply are not 17 maf, year in and year out, in the Colorado River. As the original negotiators of the 1922 compact had suspected, the flow figures on which they had based their work were indeed the result of heavy rainfall and inadequate gauges. Because of their doubts they had allotted a total of only 16 maf to the two contending basins—surely a safe figure, they thought. Subsequent calculations have shown, however, that between 1922 and 1972 the annual flow past Lee's Ferry has averaged only 13.8 maf. Farther downstream the Gila theoretically adds another million feet, but in some years every drop is consumed before the river reaches the Colorado. Moreover, extrapolations made at the Laboratory of Tree-Ring Research at the University of Arizona indicate that during the past 400 years, the average annual runoff of the Colorado River past Lee's Ferry has been a skimpy 13 million acre feet. So there is no use calling out the rain dancers. The odds are absolutely against any of the Colorado River states being able to do all the things with water they had planned when the 1922 compact was signed.

The situation on the Rio Grande, whose waters were apportioned between Colorado, New Mexico, Texas, and Old Mexico by compacts and treaties ratified in 1938–41, is no more heartening. Because of overgrazing on critical watersheds and an unforeseen orgy of ground-water pumping that dried up many springs, Colorado fell far in arrears on its scheduled deliveries to the lower states. A severe drought from 1951 to 1956 sharpened the crisis. Elephant Butte Reservoir went dry, and although a frantic pumping of deep wells farther down the river saved some valuable cotton fields, it destroyed others because of the salinity in the runoff water that percolated on downstream. New Mexico and Texas joined hands to sue Colorado (meantime Texas was also suing New Mexico over the Pecos), and Colorado has had to launch expensive rehabilitation programs along the upper Rio Grande in order to forestall punitive action.

Meanwhile farmers on the Southern High Plains (the once-dreaded Llano Estacado of eastern New Mexico and the Texas Panhandle) thought they had stumbled onto an inexhaustible bonanza—the vast, deep Ogallala aquifer. First windmills and then, after 1940, giant pumps, driven by either gasoline or electricity, began bringing up from the buried sandstone glistening surges of water. Soon 5.5 million acres were under intensive irrigation—and the wells began to show the strain, particularly in the southern reaches around Lubbock. Driven deeper, they produced less. An areawide survey (again we are speaking of averages) showed that whereas a single well in 1950 would irrigate 140 acres, the figure had dropped to 84 acres by 1970.

So what do you do? Most southwesterners are inclined to follow frontier tradition: off beyond the next hill the old dream of limitless gold will somehow be fulfilled. But now instead of going to the shining river, they want to bring the river to them. Faith in technology: in the mid-1960s Texas engineers proposed spending $3.5 billion on a mammoth double-barreled project to transport water from the Mississippi River to both the High Plains and the lower Rio Grande. In 1968 the voters defeated the necessary bond issues by less than 1 percent of the 625,000 ballots cast. But as the Rio Grande thins out and the Panhandle wells begin sucking sand, the idea stirs again.

The rest of the Southwest's water hustlers look toward the Saskatchewan in Canada and the Columbia in the Pacific Northwest. Listen to this utterance from Joseph Jensen, longtime chairman (since retired) of the Los Angeles Metropolitan Water District. Southern California, Arizona, and southern Nevada, Jensen has predicted, will eventually support 50 million people: "Some day there will be a river flowing across Nevada and all our beautiful interior valleys will be available. . . . You can just move in and put up a city without rough work or grading. . . . The Pacific Northwest will be . . . helpless in avoiding it." Perhaps. But the Pacific Northwest is resisting, nevertheless. As its price for not blocking the Central Arizona Project in 1968, it exacted a promise that the Bureau of Reclamation would not launch feasibility studies for such a transfer of Columbia River water for at least ten years, a time limit that has now expired.

During those ten years, many southwesterners began questioning priorities. The cost of the energy that would be required for transferring rivers—or desalinated sea water—has assumed staggering proportions. Under the circumstances, and even granting the region's favorable hothouse climate, should subsidized agriculture still be fostered? According to *Aridity and Man*, a study issued in 1963 by the American Association for the Advancement of Science, water used in agriculture produces a basic income of $212 per acre foot, whereas the same quantity used in light manufacturing produces up to $3,025. Dov Nir, in *The Semi-Arid*

*World* (1974), uses a somewhat different approach to reach the same conclusion. The farmers of the Tucson area, he says, constitute 9.6 percent of the active population, produce 7.2 percent of the region's income—but consume 46 percent of its water. That is to say, water put to other uses than agriculture can produce eleven times as much income for the region as a whole. Why foster agriculture?

What social wrenches will be involved in making so drastic a decision? The late John Fischer, a native of the Texas Panhandle and long-time editor of *Harper's Magazine,* saw the Llano Estacado returning to a livestock–dry farming economy, but with this difference. Research will have produced hardier crops and hardy animals. A living, yes, but not as rich a living as one based in large part on the land values rising under the magic of ample water. The slowdown will be hard on towns that once supplied a water-buoyed economy and on the schools and other public services that depended on the tax revenues generated by that economy, but might not water from the Mississippi in its way impose even greater tax hardships?

In other regions, where stream water does replenish itself, supplies can be—are being—stretched. Irrigation techniques are more efficient; seepage is being reduced; studies are underway concerning means for inhibiting evaporation and transpiration through plants. Still more promising are increased uses of recycled water—treated sewage, for example —and of desalination plants that will make "return water" (runoff, often underground, from irrigated areas) usable over and over. Conservation, however, can go only so far, and then the trade-offs have to begin.

How many cotton fields or coal gasification plants, another insatiable gulper of water, should be exchanged for plants manufacturing electronic devices? How many garment factories and white-collar companies—movie and TV companies, financial institutions, and insurance firms—can be lured in before the employees' homes, lawns, and swimming pools start demanding as much water as did the farmers they replaced? For that matter, need there be eastern-style lawns and Hollywood-style pools?

Recreation and site-seeing (I *mean* site: London Bridge rebuilt at Lake Havasu, an Arizona tourist attraction second only to the Grand Canyon; the lovely arches of San Xavier del Bac; the mute stones of Chaco Canyon; the Hopi towns on their rooster-crested mesas; the sweet-smelling bundles of grass in Papago trading posts where baskets are sold; candy-striped, hot-air balloons rising like colored soap bubbles into the blue enameled sky above Albuquerque; the thunderous surge of Lava Falls beneath a bucking raft in the Grand Canyon) are flourishing and take no more water than is presently available. Summer heat, boasts *Arizona Highways*, a glossy official state publication, is no longer a problem. Play while the mornings are crisp; relax in balmy air-conditioned breezes at noon. *Voilà!* Two major service organizations, Lions International and Kiwanis International, have done the unthinkable and have scheduled annual conventions for midsummer in the early 1980s in —that's right—Phoenix itself.

So the alternatives are not as radical or as far away as the familiar dig-it-out-quick frontier attitudes might suggest. It is just a question of whether, in the pinch, people will opt for a slowdown that will leave the rest of the land relatively unscathed or for accelerating water importations that may keep paychecks winging higher and higher but bring with them more burdens than even the Southwest's sun-dazzled spaciousness and compelling beauties will be able to absorb.

And the ancient Tewa chant returns:

*Oh, our mother, the earth; oh, our father, the sky,*
*Your children are we, and with tired backs*
*We bring you the gifts that you love.*
*Then weave for us a garment of brightness;*
*May the warp be of the white light of the morning,*
*May the weft be of the red light of evening,*
*May the fringes be the falling rain,*
*May the border be the standing rainbow.*
*Thus weave for us a garment of brightness*
*That we may walk fittingly where the birds sing,*
*That we may walk fittingly where the grass is green,*
*Oh, our mother the earth; oh, our father the sky.*

# BIBLIOGRAPHY AND ACKNOWLEDGMENTS

Most of the multitude of books on the Southwest have been printed or reprinted in or near the area. The University of Oklahoma Press in Norman, Oklahoma (the unadorned word "Norman" in the bibliography refers to that press), leads the list in quantity. Next comes the University of New Mexico Press in Albuquerque, which brings out both originals and reprints. Tucson boasts two active publishers, the University of Arizona Press and the Arizona Historical Society. Though other notable regional houses exist, the four mentioned produced the bulk of the volumes I consulted. The publication date that follows each title in the bibliography indicates the edition I used; often it was a paperback reprint rather than a difficult-to-obtain original.

## ABBREVIATIONS

To avoid constant repetition of the most commonly cited periodicals, I have resorted to the following abbreviations: *NMHR* for the *New Mexico Historical Review; AW* for *Arizona and the West; JW* for *Journal of the West; JAH* for *Journal of Arizona History.*

## INTERVIEWS

Normally the thanks due other people for help rendered during the quest for material would appear in a section of acknowledgments. In this case, however, many contributions deserve as much recognition as is accorded to printed material, and so I have listed interviews in the appropriate sections of the following bibliography. In addition, I would like to express gratitude to Norman Cleaveland of Santa Fe, Marc Simmons of Cerrillos, New Mexico, and Joe B. Frantz of the University of Texas for letting me use material of theirs that would not otherwise have been available at the time I needed it. Denise Miller of the Thacher School Library, Ojai, California, saved me much traveling by using interlibrary loans to bring the resources of distant libraries close to my home.

## Regional and Local Histories, Geographies, Surveys, and Anthologies

### INTERVIEWS

Much of my feeling for the sweep and special quality of the Southwest came from wide-ranging discussions and guided tours offered by a variety of knowledgeable people. Unhappily I do not recall every name I should, but among those walking anthologies who enriched my appreciation of the region are the following. In Lake Havasu City, Roger Johnson. In Tucson, James S. and Loma Griffith, the former a professor at the University of Arizona; C. L. Sonnichsen and A. Tracy Rowe of the *Journal of Arizona History;* Bernard L. Fontana, ethnologist at the Arizona State Museum; Barclay Goldsmith of Pima College and his wife Raquel Goldsmith; and Lawrence Clark Powell, most urbane of western essayists. In Phoenix, G. Wesley Johnson, Jr., director of the Phoenix History Project. In El Paso, Leon Metz of the University of Texas, and Julie Lama. In Taos, Phaedra and James Levy, the latter director of the Harwood Foundation. In Santa Fe, Peggy Pond Church and Shirley Mudd, artist, and Harvey Mudd, poet and environmentalist. In Albuquerque, Richard N. Ellis and Don Cutter, history department, University of New Mexico; Ted Martinez and his father, who delightfully recalled Hispanic days and ways in Albuquerque's old *colonia* of Martinez Town; John Taylor of Sandia Corporation; and, most especially, Jack Rittenhouse of the University of New Mexico Press, who loaded me with material and led my wife and me through all kinds of urban, rural, and literary byways.

### BOOKS

Landmarks along this part of the trail include *Aridity and Man*, Publication 74 of the American Association for the Advancement of Science (Washington, 1963), edited by Carle Hodge and containing a provocative collection of essays by a variety of experts about Indian and Hispanic adaptations to the Southwest, soil, irrigation, and erosion problems, water worries, and whatnot. Howard Lamar in *The Far Southwest, 1846–1912* (paperback, New York, 1970) lucidly untangles the complex rivalries that marked and marred the territorial period of the southwestern states. An outstanding geographic overview in small compass is D. W. Meinig's *Southwest: Three People in Geographic Change* (New York, 1971). The prose in Paul Horgan's *Great River: The Rio Grande in*

*North American History* (New York, 1954) occasionally grows empurpled, and the author has a predilection for aristocratic cavaliers, gently padding priests, and devout Indians. Catherine Mandel of the University of Texas at El Paso has even obtained a master's degree in part for belaboring him in her thesis, "Paul Horgan and the Indian: *Great River* as a Historical Failure" (1971), but the book is nevertheless a noteworthy addition to the history of the area. Another remarkable volume, necessary for grasping the full scope of the interpenetration between Mexican and Anglo cultures is Cecil Robinson's *Mexico and the Hispanic Southwest in American Literature* (Tucson, 1977), a broader study than the title may indicate. Curious, discursive, and often penetrating is Fray Angelico Chavez's *My Penitente Land: Reflections on Spanish New Mexico* (Albuquerque, 1974). Finally, the faculty of the University of Arizona has put together a bulky, well-illustrated, far-ranging, and useful compendium, *Arizona, Its People and Resources* (Tucson, 1972).

Other general overviews that have proved useful to my account follow:

Abbott, Carl. *Colorado, A History of the Centennial State.* Boulder, Colo., 1976.

Bancroft, Hubert Howe. *History of Arizona and New Mexico, 1530–1888.* San Francisco, 1889.

Barnes, Will C. *Arizona Place Names,* revised and enlarged by Byrd Granger. Tucson, 1960.

Beck, Warren A. *New Mexico: A History of Four Centuries.* Norman, 1962.

Bunting, Bainbridge, and others. *Taos Adobes.* Santa Fe, 1964.

Calvin, Ross. *Sky Determines.* Albuquerque, 1965.

Christiansen, Paige, and Frank Kottlowski, eds. *Mosaic of New Mexico Scenery, Rocks, and History.* Socorro, N. Mex., 1964.

Corle, Edwin. *Desert Country.* New York, 1941.

———. *The Gila: River of the Southwest.* New York, 1951.

Dunbier, Roger. *The Sonoran Desert: Its Geography, Economy, and People.* Tucson, 1968.

Ellis, Richard N. *New Mexico Past and Present: A Historical Reader.* Albuquerque, 1971.

Emmett, Chris. *Fort Union and the Winning of the Southwest.* Norman, 1965.

Faulk, Odie B. *Arizona, a Short History.* Norman, 1970.

———. *Land of Many Frontiers: A History of the American Southwest.* New York, 1968.

Fehrenbach, T. E. *Fire and Blood: A History of Mexico.* New York, 1973.

Fergusson, Erna. *New Mexico, A Pageant of Three Peoples.* Albuquerque, 1973.

Fischer, John. *From the High Plains.* New York, 1978.

Frantz, Joe B. *Texas: A Bicentennial History.* New York, 1976.

Garcia, F. Chris, and Paul L. Haine. *New Mexico Government.* Albuquerque, 1976.

Gonzales, Nancie L. *The Spanish Americans of New Mexico.* Albuquerque, 1969.

Hillerman, Tony, ed. *The Spell of New Mexico.* Albuquerque, 1976.

Hollon, Eugene W. *The Southwest, Old and New.* New York, 1961.

——. *The Great American Desert.* New York, 1966.

Jenkins, Myra Ellen, and Albert H. Schroeder. *A Brief History of New Mexico.* Albuquerque, 1974.

Krutch, Joseph Wood. *The Desert Year.* New York, 1952.

McWilliams, Carey. *North from Mexico.* New York, 1968.

Moquin, Wayne, with Charles Van Doren, eds. *A Documentary History of the Mexican-Americans.* New York, 1971.

Perrigo, Lynn. *Our Spanish Southwest.* Dallas, 1960.

Powell, Lawrence Clark. *Arizona: A Bicentennial History.* New York, 1976.

Rathjen, Frederick W. *The Texas-Panhandle Frontier.* Austin, Tex., 1973.

Rusho, W. L., and Gregory Crampton. *Desert River Crossing . . . Lee's Ferry.* Salt Lake City and Santa Barbara, 1975.

Sanchez, George I. *Forgotten People: A Study of New Mexicans.* Albuquerque, 1967.

Shelton, Napier. *Saguaro National Monument.* Washington, 1972.

Simmons, Marc. *New Mexico: A Bicentennial History.* New York, 1976.

Simpson, Leslie Byrd. *Many Mexicos.* Berkeley, Calif., 1967.

Sonnichsen, C. L. *Pass of the North.* El Paso, 1968.

——. *Tularosa.* New York, 1963.

Spicer, Edward H., and Raymond H. Thompson, eds. *Plural Society in the Southwest.* Albuquerque, 1972.

Swadesh, Frances Leon. *Los Primeros Pobladores.* Notre Dame, Ind., 1974.

Taylor, Frank C. *Colorado South of the Border.* Denver, 1963.

Trimble, Marshall. *Arizona.* New York, 1977.

Tuan, Yi-Fu, and others. *The Climate of New Mexico.* Santa Fe, 1969.

Twitchell, Frank Emerson. *The Leading Facts of New Mexican History,* 2 vols. Albuquerque, 1963.

Vogt, Evon Z., and Ethel M. Albert. *People of the Rimrock.* Cambridge, Mass., 1966.

Wachholtz, Florence, ed. *Arizona, the Grand Canyon State,* 2 vols. Westminster, Colo., 1975.

Wagoner, Jay J. *Arizona Territory, 1863–1912.* Tucson, 1970.

——. *Early Arizona: Prehistory to Civil War.* Tucson, 1974.

Watkins, T. H., and others. *The Grand Colorado: The Story of a River and Its Canyon.* Palo Alto, Calif., 1969.

Webb, Walter Prescott. *The Great Plains,* Boston, 1931.

Weber, David J., ed. *Foreigners in their Native Land: Historical Roots of the Mexican Americans.* Albuquerque, 1973.

Weigle, Marta. *Hispanic Villages of Northern New Mexico.* Santa Fe, 1975.

Wentworth, Edward N. *America's Sheep Trails.* Ames, Iowa, 1948.

White, Jon Manchip. *A World Elsewhere.* New York, 1975.

Wyllys, Rufus. *Arizona: The History of a Frontier State.* Phoenix, 1950.

ARTICLES

Carlson, Alvar Ward. "New Mexico's Sheep Industry." *NMHR*, Jan. 1969.
Noggle, Burl. "Anglo Observers of the Southwest Borderlands, 1825–1890."
  *AW*, Summer 1959.


## Prehistory

A lay reader—and I am one—will often find accounts of archaeological delvings
tedious and couched in arcane language. One way to break through the barrier
is to examine the fine displays in such museums as the Laboratory of Anthropology in Santa Fe; the Museum of Northern New Mexico, Flagstaff; the Arizona
State Museum, Tucson; and the museum in Mesa Verde National Park, Colorado.
Another resource is C. W. Ceram's popularly written but fascinating introduction to the subject, *The First American* (paperback, New York, 1972). Otherwise
I relied on the summaries presented in accounts listed elsewhere in this bibliography (for instance, Emil W. Haury's "Before History" in *Arizona: Its People
and Resources*); a lengthy interview with Dr. Robert Lister of the Chaco Canyon
Research Center, University of New Mexico, Albuquerque; and the following:


BOOKS

Gladwin, Harold S. *A History of the Ancient Southwest.* Portland, Maine, 1965.
Judd, Neil M. *The Material Culture of Pueblo Bonito.* Washington, 1954.
McNitt, Frank. *Richard Wetherill: Anasazi.* Albuquerque, 1966.


ARTICLES

Breternitz, David A., and Jack E. Smith. "Mesa Verde," in *Rocky Mountain and
  Mesa Verde National Parks.* Casper, Wyo., 1972.
Brody, J. J. "The Mimbres Paradox." *New Mexico Magazine,* Oct. 1977.
Euler, Robert C. "The Canyon Dwellers." *American West,* May 1967.
Haury, Emil W. "First Masters of the American Desert: the Hohokam." *Na-
  tional Geographic,* May 1967.
Moffett, Ben. "Chaco, City of Mysteries." *New Mexico Magazine,* Oct. 1977.


## The Spanish Period

A fine general introduction to Spain's northward thrust in the Americas is John
Francis Bannon's *The Spanish Borderlands Frontier, 1513–1821* (Al-
buquerque, 1974), which can be usefully supplemented by Philip W. Powell's
*Soldiers, Indians, and Silver* (Berkeley, Calif., 1952). The dean of borderland

scholars, Herbert E. Bolton, has produced three excellent studies of the leading figures of the era and region: *Anza's California Expeditions*, in five volumes, which contains the diaries of several participants (Berkeley, Calif., 1930); *Coronado, Knight of Pueblo and Plains* (New York and Albuquerque, 1949); and *Rim of Christendom*, a biography of Eusebio Kino (New York, 1960). Complementing those essential works is a plethora of more specialized studies, some of which are listed below.

## BOOKS

Adams, Eleanor B., trans. *Bishop Tamaron's Visitation of New Mexico, 1760.* Albuquerque, 1954.

Bannon, John Francis. *Bolton and the Spanish Borderlands.* Norman, 1964.

Beilharz, Edwin A. *Felipe de Neve.* San Francisco, 1971.

Benavides, Fray Alonso. *Memorial of 1630*, trans. Peter P. Forrestal. Washington, 1954.

———. *Memorial of 1634*, trans. George P. Hammond and Agapito Rey. Albuquerque, 1945.

Bolton, Herbert E. *Pageant in the Wilderness* (the Domínguez-Escalante Expedition). Salt Lake City, 1950.

———. *The Spanish Borderlands.* New Haven, 1921.

———. *Spanish Explorations in the Southwest, 1542–1706.* New York, 1916.

Castaneda, Carlos E. *Our Catholic Heritage in Texas.* Austin, Tex., 1936–1958. See the first four of the seven volumes.

Chapman, Charles E. *The Founding of Spanish California.* New York, 1916.

Chavez, Fray Angelico. *Origins of New Mexico Families.* Santa Fe, 1954.

———. *Our Lady of the Conquest.* Santa Fe, 1948.

Domínguez, Fray Francisco Atanasio. *The Missions of New Mexico, 1776*, trans. Eleanor B. Adams and Fray Angelico Chavez. Albuquerque, 1956.

Donohue, John Augustine. *After Kino: Jesuit Missions in Northwestern New Spain, 1711–1767.* St. Louis, 1969.

Espinosa, J. Manuel. *Crusaders of the Rio Grande: The Story of Don Diego de Vargas and the Reconquest and Refounding of New Mexico.* Chicago, 1942.

Forbes, Jack D. *Apache, Navajo, and Spaniard.* Norman, 1960.

Garces, Francisco. *A Record of Travels in Arizona and California, 1775–1776*, trans. and ed. John Galvin. San Francisco, 1965.

Hackett, Charles W. *Revolt of the Pueblo Indians . . . 1680–1682*, 2 vols. Albuquerque, 1942.

Hallenbeck, Cleve. *Alvar Nuñez Cabeza de Vaca: The Journey and the Route.* Glendale, Calif., 1940.

Hammond, George P., and Agapito Rey. *Narratives of the Coronado Expedition.* Albuquerque, 1940.

———. *Don Juan de Oñate, Colonizer of New Mexico, 1595–1628.* Albuquerque, 1953.

——. *The Rediscovery of New Mexico, 1580–1594.* Albuquerque, 1966.

Hammond, George P. *Don Juan de Oñate and the Founding of New Mexico.* Santa Fe, 1927.

Horgan, Paul. *Conquistadores in North American History.* New York, 1963.

Jones, Oakah L. *Pueblo Warriors and the Spanish Conquest.* Norman, 1966.

Kessell, John L. *Friars, Soldiers, and Reformers.* Tucson, 1976.

Lehmer, Donald J. "The Second Frontier: The Spanish," in Robert G. Ferris, ed., *The American West: An Appraisal.* Santa Fe, 1963.

Loomis, Noel, and Abraham P. Nasatir. *Pedro Vial and the Roads to Santa Fe.* Norman, 1967.

McCarty, Kieran, ed. *Desert Documentary: The Spanish Years, 1767–1821.* Tucson, 1976.

Moorhead, Max L. *The Apache Frontier: Jacobo Ugarte de Loyola* ... Norman, 1968.

——. *New Mexico's Royal Road: Trade and Travel on the Chihuahua Trail.* Norman, 1958.

——. *The Presidio, Bastion of the Spanish Borderlands.* Norman, 1975.

Nasatir, Abraham P. *The Borderlands in Retreat.* Albuquerque, 1976.

Pfefferkorn, Ignaz. *Sonora, A Description of the Province,* trans. Theodore E. Treutlein. Albuquerque, 1941.

Pourade, Richard F. *Anza Conquers the Desert.* San Diego, 1971.

Richman, Irving B. *California Under Spain and Mexico.* Boston, 1911.

Sauer, Carl O. *The Road to Cibola.* Berkeley, Calif., 1932.

Schroeder, Albert H., and Daniel S. Watson. *A Colony on the Move: Castaño de Sosa's Expedition, 1590–1591.* Santa Fe, 1965

Smith, Fay Jackson, and others. *Father Kino in Arizona.* Phoenix, 1966.

Thomas, Alfred B. *After Coronado: Spanish Explorations Northeast of New Mexico.* Norman, 1935.

——. *Forgotten Frontiers* (Anza in New Mexico). Norman, 1932.

——. *Teodoro de Croix and the Northern Frontier of New Spain, 1776–1788.* Norman, 1941.

Winship, George P. *The Journey of Coronado* ... New York, 1904.

ARTICLES

Benes, Roland. "Anza and Concha in New Mexico, 1787–1793." *JW,* 1965.

Bolton, Herbert E. "French Interventions in New Mexico," in *The Pacific Ocean in History.* New York, 1917.

Brinkerhoff, Sidney B. "The Last Years of Spanish Arizona." *AW,* Spring 1967.

Chavez, Fray Angelico. "Pohe-yemo's Representative and the Pueblo Revolt of 1680." *NMHR,* Jan. 1967.

Christiansen, Paige, W. "The Presidio and the Borderlands." *JW,* 1969.

Dunn, William E. "Spanish Reaction against the French Advance toward New Mexico." *NMHR,* 1915.

Faulk, Odie B. "The Presidio, Fortress or Farce?" *JW,* Jan. 1969.

Feather, Adlai. "Origin of the Name Arizona." *NMHR,* Apr. 1960.

Fireman, Bert. "Kino on the Arizona Border." *American West,* Summer 1966.

Folmer, Henri. "The Mallett Expedition . . . to Santa Fe." *Colorado Magazine,* Sept. 1939.

Greenleaf, Richard E. "Land and Water in Mexico and New Mexico, 1700–1821." *NMHR,* Apr. 1972.

Hackett, Charles W. "Retreat of the Spaniards from New Mexico in 1680 . . ." *Southwestern Historical Quarterly,* Oct. 1912, Jan. 1913.

Ivancovic, Byron. "Juan Bautista de Anza." *Arizoniana,* Winter 1960.

Ives, Ronald L. "The Quest of the Blue Shells." *Arizoniana,* Spring 1961.

Kessell, John L. "The Making of a Martyr: The Young Francisco Garces." *NMHR,* June 1970.

Moorhead, Max L. "The Soldado de Cuero." *JW,* Jan. 1969.

Scholes, France V. "Church and State in New Mexico." *NMHR,* Jan., Apr., July, Oct. 1936; Jan. 1937.

————. "Troublous Times in New Mexico, 1659–1670." *NMHR,* Apr., Oct. 1937; Jan. 1938; July, Oct. 1940; Jan., July, Oct. 1941.

————. "The Supply Service of the New Mexico Missions." *NMHR,* Jan., Apr. 1930.

Simmons, Marc. "Settlement Patterns and Village Plans in Colonial New Mexico." *JW,* Jan. 1969.

Thomas, Alfred B. "The Massacre of the Villasur Expedition . . ." *Nebraska History Magazine,* July–Sept. 1924.

————. "San Carlos: A Comanche Pueblo on the Arkansas River." *Colorado Magazine,* May 1929.

Vigness, David M. "Don Hugo Oconor and New Spain's Northwestern Frontier, 1764–1776." *JW,* 1967.

## The American Advance and the War with Mexico

### BOOKS

Some of the books listed above (among them the jumbled Loomis-Nasatir study of Pedro Vial and Nasatir's own *Borderlands in Retreat*) are appropriate introductions to the story of Spain's reaction to the Louisiana Purchase. See also Donald Jackson's meticulous editing of *The Journals of Zebulon Montgomery Pike . . .* (Norman, 1966) and the latter part of Warren L. Cook's monumental *Flood Tide of Empire* (New Haven, 1973).

The physical heralds of Manifest Destiny were of course the Santa Fe traders and the beaver hunters known as mountain men. The classic contemporary description of the former is *Josiah Gregg's Commerce of the Prairies,* ably edited by Max Moorhead (Norman, 1954). David J. Weber's almost painfully detailed *The Taos Trappers* (Norman, 1971) blankets the southwestern fur trade. My own *Bent's Fort* (New York, 1954) embraces the activities of both traders and trappers and extends on through the turmoils that preceded and accompanied the war with Mexico. A useful recent account of that conflict is John Edward Weems's *To Conquer a Peace* (New York, 1974).

LeRoy Hafen has dragooned a galaxy of writers to compose short biographical essays on practically every fur trader, famous or obscure, that trod the western soil. The results have been published in ten volumes, *The Mountain Men and the Fur Trade of the Far West* (Glendale, Calif., 1965–1972). Because the work follows no discernible organizational pattern, it is necessary to consult the index volume for whatever southwestern character you are interested in. Generally the effort is worthwhile.

For other relevant accounts on the period see:

Barreiro, Antonio. *Ojeada Sobre Nuevo-Mexico,* trans. Lansing Bloom. Santa Fe, 1928.

Camp, Charles L. *George C. Yount and His Chronicles of the West.* Denver, Colo., 1966.

Carter, Harvey L. *Dear Old Kit.* Norman, 1968.

Clarke, Dwight L. *Stephen Watts Kearny, Soldier of the West.* Norman, 1961.

Cleland, Robert Glass. *This Reckless Breed of Men: The Trappers and Fur Traders of the Southwest.* New York, 1952.

Connelly, William. *Doniphan's Expedition.* Topeka, Kans., 1907.

Cooke, Philip St. George. *The Conquest of New Mexico and California.* Chicago, 1964.

Coues, Elliott, ed. *The Journal of Jacob Fowler.* Minneapolis, 1965.

Davis, W.H.H. *El Gringo, or New Mexico and Her People.* New York, 1857.

Emory, William H. *Notes on a Military Reconnaissance.* Albuquerque, 1951.

Estergreen, M. Morgan. *Kit Carson: A Portrait in Courage.* Norman, 1963.

Foreman, Grant. *Marcy and the Gold Seekers.* Norman, 1939.

Garrard, Lewis H. *Wah-To-Yah and the Taos Trail.* Norman, 1957.

Hafen, LeRoy R., and Ann W. Hafen. *The Old Spanish Trail, Santa Fe to Los Angeles.* Glendale, 1954.

James, Thomas. *Three Years Among the Indians and Mexicans.* Philadelphia, 1962.

Kendall, George Wilkins. *Narrative of the Texas–Santa Fe Expedition,* 2 vols. New York, 1844.

Loomis, Noel M. *The Texas–Santa Fe Pioneers.* Norman, 1958.

Pattie, James O. *Personal Narrative,* ed. Timothy Flint and, subsequently, William Goetzmann. New York and Philadelphia, 1962.

Rittenhouse, Jack. *The Santa Fe Trail, A Historical Bibliography.* Albuquerque, 1971.

Ruxton, George F. *Adventures in Mexico and the Rocky Mountains.* Norman, 1950.

Van Every, Dale. *The Final Challenge.* New York, 1964.

ARTICLES

Bierck, Harold A., Jr. "Dr. James Hamilton Robinson." *The Louisiana Historical Quarterly,* July 1942.

Creer, Leland Hargrave. "Spanish-American Slave Trade in the Great Basin." *NMHR,* July 1949.

Ellis, Florence Hawley. "Tomé." *NMHR,* April 1955.

Floyd, Ewing, Jr. "The Mule as a Factor in the Development of the Southwest." *AW,* Winter 1962.

Francis, E. K. "Padre Martínez: A New Mexican Myth." *NMHR,* Oct. 1956.

Jackson, Donald. "Zebulon Pike 'Tours' Mexico." *American West,* Summer 1966.

Jenkins, Myra Ellen. "Taos Pueblo and Its Neghbors." *NMHR,* April 1966.

Marshall, Thomas M. "St. Vrain's Expedition to the Gila in 1826." *Southwest Historical Quarterly,* Jan. 1916.

Robinson, Cecil. "Spring Water with a Taste of the Land." *American West,* Summer 1966.

Romero, C. V. "Apologia of Antonio José Martínez, 1838." *NMHR,* 1928.

Vigil, Ralph. "Willa Cather and Historical Reality." *NMHR,* Apr. 1975.

## *From the Mexican War Through the Civil War*

BOOKS

This tumultuous period is well documented in William Keleher's *Turmoil in New Mexico, 1846–1868* (Santa Fe, 1952). The southwestern sections of William Goetzmann's *Exploration and Empire* (New York, 1966) ably cover the exploratory programs launched by the government to bring back information about the lands it had acquired from Mexico, as does Edward S. Wallace's sprightly *The Great Reconnaissance* (Boston, 1955). A private and fascinating prospecting exploration recorded by a participant is Daniel E. Connor's *Joseph Reddeford Walker and the Arizona Adventure* (Norman, 1956). Aurora Hunt's Civil War duo, *The Army of the Pacific* . . . (Glendale, Calif., 1951) and *Major General James H. Carleton, Frontier Dragoon* (Glendale, Calif., 1958) are exceptional treatments of the Civil War in the West, of its steely central figure, and of the concomitant Indian troubles. Other commendable accounts are listed below.

Bartlett, John Russell. *Personal Narrative of Explorations.* . . . New York, 1854.

Binkley, William Campbell. *The Expansionist Movement in Texas.* Berkeley, Calif., 1925.

Browne, J. Ross. *Adventures in the Apache Country . . . 1864,* ed. Donald Powell. Tucson, 1974.

Colton, Ray C. *The Civil War in the Western Territories.* Norman, 1959.

Faulk, Odie B. *Destiny Road: The Gila Trail . . .* New York, 1973.

Ganaway, Loomis. *New Mexico and the Sectional Controversy, 1846–1861.* Albuquerque, 1944.

Garber, Paul N. *The Gadsden Treaty.* Philadelphia, 1923.

Goetzmann, William H. *Army Exploration in the American West.* New Haven, 1959.

Hafen, LeRoy R. *The Overland Mail, 1849–1869.* Glendale, Calif., 1926.

Heyman, Max. *Prudent Soldier . . . General E.R.S. Canby.* Glendale, Calif., 1959.

Hollister, Ovando J. *Boldly They Rode.* Lakewood, Colo., 1949.

Horgan, Paul. *Lamy of Santa Fe.* New York, 1975.

Horn, Calvin. *New Mexico's Troubled Years.* Albuquerque, 1963.

Ives, Lt. Joseph C. *Report upon the Colorado River of the West, 1857–1858.* Washington, 1861.

Jackson, W. Turrentine. *Wagon Roads West.* New Haven, 1965.

Meriwether, David. *My Life in the Mountains and on the Plains.* Norman, 1965.

Moody, Ralph. *Stagecoach West.* New York, 1967.

Nevins, Allan. *Ordeal of the Union,* 2 vols. New York, 1947.

Sacks B. *Be It Enacted: The Creation of the Territory of Arizona.* Phoenix, 1964.

Sykes, Godfrey. *The Colorado River Delta.* Washington, 1937.

Wright, Arthur A. *The Civil War in the Southwest.* Denver, 1964.


ARTICLES

Altshuler, Constance W. "The Case of Silvester Mowry." *AW,* Spring and Summer 1973.

Clendenen, Clarence. "General James Henry Carleton." *NMHR,* 1955

Eaton, W. Clement. "Frontier Life in Southern Arizona . . ." *The Southwestern Historical Quarterly,* Jan. 1933.

Hall, Martin H. "The Skirmish at Mesilla." *AW,* Winter 1959.

Kibby, Leon. "A Civil War Episode in California-Arizona History." *Arizoniana,* Spring 1961.

Rodrigues, Arnold. "New Mexico in Transition." *NMHR,* July and Oct. 1949.

Sacks, B. "Sylvester Mowry: Artilleryman, Libertine, Entrepreneur." *American West,* Summer 1964.

Smith, Ralph. "The Scalp Hunters on the Borderlands, 1835–1850." *AW,* 1964.

Taylor, James Woodall. "Geographic Basis of the Gadsden Purchase." *Journal of Geography,* Nov. 1958.

Thompson, Gerald E. "Railroads and Mines in Arizona . . . 1858." *AW,* Winter 1968.

Utley, Robert M. "Fort Union and the Santa Fe Trail." *NMHR,* Jan. 1961

## *The Indian World and Its Wars*

### INTERVIEWS

The following Navajos gave generously of their time to discuss the problems and aspirations of their people: Tommy Anderson, executive assistant to the chairman, Navajo Tribal Council, Window Rock, Arizona; Samuel Pete and Jesse Thompson of the tribal government, also in Window Rock; Peggy Scott, assistant director of the Curriculum Development Center, Navajo Community College, Tsaile, Arizona; Art Allison of Navajo Agricultural Products Industry (NAPI), Farmington, New Mexico. Whites who work in close association with the Navajos were equally generous: Bill Donovan, acting general manager of the tribally owned *Navajo Times;* Martin Link, then director of the tribal museum at Window Rock; Frank D. Hardwick, public relations, Bureau of Indian Affairs, Window Rock. Also, Troy McNeill, then general manager of NAPI, and Bert Levine, Bureau of Reclamation, both of Farmington, New Mexico, and Dale Anderson, publicist for NAPI, of Durango, Colorado. In Flagstaff, Arizona, William Benjamin and Lynn Montgomery discussed Navajo-Hopi land problems, which are severe.

At Second Mesa, Hopi Reservation, Abbott Sekaquaptewa, chairman of the Hopi Tribe, talked movingly of his people's feelings and frustrations. Charles Loloma, famed Indian jewelry maker of Hotavila, talked of his Hopi roots. Kathy Whittaker, who had the unique experience of living for many months with a Hopi family at Hotavila and who is now associated with the Museum of Man in San Diego, was an inspiring "tour guide" during a 1976 trip through the Indian country with a small study group sponsored by Stanford University.

### BOOKS

Many of the titles cited in other sections of this bibliography also contain data on the Indians of the Southwest. Of numerous others devoted exclusively to Indian affairs I found Edward H. Spicer's *Cycles of Conflict: The Impact of Spain, Mexico, and the United States* (Tucson, 1962) to be indispensable to my reconstructions. Certain others stand out as sui generis in their field. Two are personal stories that reveal much about the tribes to which the subjects belong: Alice Marriott's *Maria: Potter of San Ildefonso* (Norman, 1948) and Leo Simmons's editing of Dan Talayesva's *Sun Chief: The Autobiography of a Hopi Indian* (New Haven, 1942). A rich collection of scholarly papers that is likely to stump all but specialists is *New Perspectives on the Pueblos,* edited by Alfonso Ortiz (Albuquerque, 1972). Two beautifully illustrated volumes that open clear windows on the Navajos are Ruth M. Underhill's *Here Come the Navajos!* (Lawrence, Kans., 1953) and Laura Gilpin's superb *The Enduring Navaho* (Austin, Tex., 1968).

As for Indian wars, the printed blood flows thick and generally tells more about the United States Army than about the Indians. Yet the period of fighting was critical to the Southwest and cannot be slighted. John G. Bourke's classic *On the Border with Crook* (Chicago, 1962) is as readable as any. A modern summary of Apache troubles, the fruit of many years' work in the field, is Dan Thrapp's *The Conquest of Apacheria* (Norman, 1967). A careful examination of the Bosque Redondo failure is Gerald Thompson's *The Army and the Navajo* (Tucson, 1976).

Reference books include Frederick Hodge's old but still useful *Handbook of American Indians North of Mexico* in two volumes (Washington, 1907–1919); William Brandon's beautifully illustrated *The American Heritage Book of Indians* (New York, 1961); and Alvin Josephy's sweeping *The Indian Heritage of North America* (New York, 1968). See also in the Garland Publishing Company's *American Ethnohistory Series: Indians of the Southwest* (late 1970s) the volumes—sometimes more than one—on Apache, Jicarilla Apache, Hopi, Navajo, Papago, Pima-Maricopa, Pueblo, Yavapai.

If that doesn't stop you, try the following:

Andrist, Ralph K. *The Long Death: The Last Days of the Plains Indians.* New York, 1964.

Bahti, Tom. *Southwestern Indian Tribes.* Las Vegas, Nev., 1968.

Debo, Angie. *Geronimo, The Man, His Time, His Place.* Norman, 1976.

Dozier, Edward. *The Pueblo Indians of North America.* New York, 1968.

Dunn, Dorothy. *American Indian Painting of the Southwest and Plains Areas.* Albuquerque, 1968.

Dunn, James P. *Massacres of the Mountains.* New York, 1886.

Faulk, Odie B. *Crimson Desert.* New York, 1974.

Fehrenbach, T. R. *The Comanches: The Destruction of a People.* New York, 1974.

Gilbreath, Kent. *Red Capitalism: An Analysis of the Navajo Economy.* Norman, 1973.

Hodge, F. W. *History of Hawikuh.* Los Angeles, 1937.

James, Harry C. *Pages from a Hopi History.* Tucson, 1974.

Kelly, Lawrence. *Navajo Roundup.* Boulder, Colo., 1970.

Kenner, C. L. *A History of New Mexico–Plains Indian Relations.* Norman, 1969.

Kluckhohn, Clyde, and Dorothea Leighton. *The Navaho,* rev. ed. New York, 1962.

McNitt, Frank. *The Indian Traders.* Norman, 1962.

———. *Navajo Wars: A Military History.* Albuquerque, 1976.

Minge, W. A. *Acoma, Pueblo in the Sky.* Albuquerque, 1976.

Navajo Museum, Ned A. Hatathl: Cultural Center. *Navajo Weaving,* a catalogue accompanying a splendid exhibit of the craft. Tsaile, Ariz., May 1977–Apr. 1978.

Ogle, Ralph H. *Federal Control of the Western Apaches, 1848–1886.* Albuquerque, 1970.

Owen, Roger C., and others. *The North American Indians, A Source Book.* New York, 1967.

Rath, Ida Ellen. *The Rath Trail.* Wichita, Kans., 1961.

Richardson, R. N. *The Comanche Barrier to the South Plains Settlement.* Glendale, Calif., 1933.

Sekaquaptewa, Helen. *Me and Mine,* as told to Louise Udall. Tucson, 1969.

Sonnichsen, C. L. *The Mescalero Apaches.* Norman, 1958.

Summerhayes, Martha. *Vanished Arizona.* Salem, Mass., 1911.

Underhill, Ruth M. *The Navajo,* rev. ed. Norman, 1967.

Waters, Frank. *Book of the Hopi.* New York, 1963.

Weaver, Thomas, ed. *Indians of Arizona: A Contemporary Perspective.* Tucson, 1974.

## ARTICLES

Basso, Keith. "In Pursuit of the Apaches." *Arizona Highways,* July 1977.

Broadhead, Michael J. "Elliott Coues and the Apaches." *JAH,* Summer 1973.

Chapel, William L. "Camp Rucker: Outpost in Apacheria." *JAH,* Summer 1973.

Collins, Dabney O. "The Battle for Blue Lakes." *American West,* Sept. 1971.

Kirchhoff, Paul. "Gatherers and Farmers in the Greater Southwest." *American Anthropologist,* 1954.

Kroeber, A. L. "Native American Populations." *American Anthropologist,* 1934.

Reeve, Frank D. "Navajo Foreign Affairs, 1795–1846." *NMHR,* Apr. 1971.

Russell, Frank. "The Pima Indians." *Annual Report of the Bureau of American Ethnology,* vol. 26, 1908.

Turcheneske, John A. "The Arizona Press and Geronimo's Surrender." *JAH,* Summer 1973.

Articles in the *Navajo Times,* 1977–1978, and *Qua'Toohi* ("The Eagle's Cry"), the Hopi newspaper, intermittently, 1977–78.

## *Exploiters and Victims*

The Southwest was notably lawless during the last part of the nineteenth century, and unless the disorders are examined, the culture of the area is incompletely understood. The books and articles that follow at least try to be more than simple-minded shoot-'em-ups. The best are those that deal with the land grant issue—for instance, Jim Barry Pearson's survey of *The Maxwell Land Grant* (Norman, 1961) and Richard Gardner's *Grito!,* a story of a century of injustice that culminated in Reies Tijerina's famed raid on the courthouse at Tierra Amarilla, New Mexico, in 1967. For significant bang-bangs dealing with other episodes, see Maurice Fulton's *The Lincoln County War* (Tucson, 1968) and the chapters about the Graham-Tewksbury feud in Clara T. Woody's and Milton L. Schwartz's *Globe, Arizona* (Tucson, 1978).

In addition:

## BOOKS

Brayer, Herbert O. *William Blackmore: The Spanish-Mexican Land Grants of New Mexico.* Denver, 1949.
Brown, Richard Maxwell. "The American Vigilante Tradition," in Hugh D. Graham and Ted Robert Gurr, *Violence in America,* vol. 1. Washington, 1969.
Cleaveland, Norman, with George Fitzpatrick. *The Morleys.* Albuquerque, 1971.
Dick, Everett. *The Lure of the Land.* Lincoln, Nebr., 1970.
Frantz, Joe B. "The Frontier Tradition: An Invitation to Violence," in Hugh D. Graham and Ted Robert Gurr, *Violence in America,* vol. 1. Washington, 1969.
Gibson, A.M. *The Life and Death of Colonel Albert Jennings Fountain.* Norman, 1965.
Keleher, William A. *The Maxwell Land Grant.* Santa Fe, 1942.
———. *Violence in Lincoln County.* Santa Fe, 1957.
Metz, Leon Claire. *Pat Garrett: The Story of a Western Lawman.* Norman, 1974.
———. *The Shooters.* El Paso, 1976.
Nabakov, Peter. *Tijerina and the Courthouse Raid.* Albuquerque, 1968.
Poldervaart, Arnie. *Black-Robed Justice.* Albuquerque, 1965.
Waters, Frank. *The Earp Brothers of Tombstone.* New York, 1960.
Webb, Walter Prescott. *The Texas Rangers.* Cambridge, Mass., 1935.
Westphall, Victor. *The Public Domain in New Mexico.* Albuquerque, 1965.
White, Kock, Kelley and McCarty, attorneys at law. *Land Title Study.* State Planning Office, Santa Fe, 1971.

## *Articles*

Cook, Charles A. "The Hunter Claim: A Colossal Land Scheme in the Papagueria." *AW,* Autumn 1973.
Dunham, Harold H. "New Mexico Land Grants ... The Maxwell Grant." *NMHR,* Jan. 1955.
———. "Coloradoans and the Maxwell Grant." *Colorado Magazine,* Apr. 1955.
Hinton, Howard P. "John Simpson Chisum." *NMHR,* July 1956.
Lamar, Howard. "Land Policy in the Spanish Southwest, 1846–1891." *Journal of Economic History,* Dec. 1963.
McCarty, Frankie. "Land Grant Problems in New Mexico." *Albuquerque Journal,* Sept. 28-Oct. 10, 1969.
McCourt, Purnee. "The Conejos Land Grant of Southern Colorado." *Colorado Magazine,* Winter 1975.

Miller, Dorliss A. "William Lgan Rynerson in New Mexico." *NMHR,* Apr. 1973.
Myers, John Myers. "The Prince of Swindlers." *American Heritage,* Aug. 1956.
Newman, Simeon H. "The Santa Fe Ring: A Letter to the New York *Sun." AW,*
    Autumn 1970.
Nolan, Frederick W. "A Sidelight on the Tunstall Murder." NMHR, July 1956.
Rasch, Philip J. "Exit Axtell: Enter Wallace." *NMHR,* July 1957.
———. "Chaos in Lincon County." Denver Westerners' *Brand Book.* Denver,
    1963.

## *Reaching Toward Maturity*

### Books

No single book that I know of comes to grips with the impact on the economy
of the Southwest that has been wrought by the almost simultaneous arrival of
the railroads, large-scale livestock operations, copper mining, the beginnings of
commercial agriculture, and the political struggle to achieve statehood. Accordingly, I hesitate to single out any of the following books for special notice, good
though some are within their limited fields.

Still, readers who like the personal touch will enjoy two accounts of south-
western ranch life written by two very different New Mexico women: Fabiola
Cabeza de Vaca's *We Fed Them Cactus* (Albuquerque, 1954) and Agnes Morley
Cleaveland's *No Life for a Lady* (Boston, 1951). See also the personal and often
funny sections of a book already cited under "Regional Histories" on page 319,
John Fischer's *From the High Plains* (New York, 1978).

Also:

Atherton, Lewis. *The Cattle Kings.* Lincoln, Neb., 1972.
Ball, Eve. *Ma'am Jones of the Pecos.* Tucson, 1969. Partly fictionalized.
Barnes, Will C., and William M. Raine. *Cattle.* New York, 1930.
Bryant, Keith L. *A History of the Atchison, Topeka, and Santa Fe Railroad.*
    New York, 1974.
Clelland, Robert G. *A History of Phelps Dodge.* New York, 1952.
Dunning, C. H., and Edward Peplow. *Rock to Riches.* Phoenix, 1952.
Erwin, Allan A. *The Southwest of John Slaughter, 1841–1922.* Glendale, Calif.,
    1965.
Greever, William S. *Arid Domain: The Santa Fe Railroad and Its Western
    Land Grant.* Stanford, Calif., 1954.
Haley, J. Evetts. *Charles Goodnight: Cowman and Plainsman.* Boston, 1936.
———. *George W. Littlefield, Texan.* Norman, 1943.
Joralemon, Ira B. *Copper.* San Francisco, 1973.
Keleher, William A. *The Fabulous Frontier.* Albuquerque, 1963.
Larson, Robert W. *New Mexico's Quest for Statehood, 1846–1912.* Al-
    buquerque, 1968.

Lavender, David. *The Great Persuader.* New York, 1970. About Collis P. Huntington and the Southern Pacific.

Otero, Miguel A. *My Life on the Frontier,* 2 vols. New York, 1935–37.

――――. *My Nine Years as Governor of the Territory of New Mexico.* Albuquerque, 1940.

Peterson, Charles S. *Take Up Your Mission: Mormon Colonizing Along the Little Colorado River.* Tucson, 1973.

Sonnichsen, C. L. *Colonel William Greene and the Copper Skyrocket.* Tucson, 1974.

Young, Otis. *How They Dug the Gold.* Tucson, 1967.


ARTICLES

Braemen, John. "Albert J. Beveridge and Statehood for the Southwest." *AW,* Winter 1968.

Frantz, Joe B. "Hoof and Horn on the Chisholm Trail." *American West,* Aug. 1967.

Greever, William S. "Railway Development in the Southwest." *NMHR,* Apr. 1957.

Krop, Simon. "Albert J. Fountain and the Fight for Public Education in New Mexico." *AW,* Winter 1969.

Lyon, William H. "The Corporate Frontier." *JAH,* Spring 1968.

Mawn, Geoffrey P. "Promoters, Speculators, and the Selection of the Phoenix Townsite." *AW,* Autumn 1977.

Spude, Robert L. "A Land of Sunshine and Silver." *JAH,* Spring 1975.

Tracy, Francis G., Sr. "Pecos Valley Pioneers." *NMHR,* July 1958.

Wallace, Andrew. "John W. Swilling." *Arizoniana,* Spring 1961.

## Twentieth-Century Problems


INTERVIEWS

My awareness of the problems along the international border, immigration included, was broadened by long talks with Joseph Frank Friedkin, commissioner of the United States Section, International Boundary and Water Commission, United States and Mexico, whose headquarters are in El Paso. Raquel Goldsmith of Tucson and Ted Martinez of Albuquerque added much about the problems of the immigrants themselves and the adaptations that long-established Hispanos and Mexican Americans must make to the constant flow of newcomers.

David Hale and Phil Muntz of the State Engineer's Office in Santa Fe briefed me on water affairs in New Mexico. Larry King, resident engineer of the Bureau of Reclamation in Parker, Arizona, and Walter S. Fruland, public affairs officer of the Bureau of Reclamation's Arizona Projects Office, discussed the mammoth Central Arizona Project and supplied me with material.

Richard Bise, of Sandia Corporation in Albuquerque, and Lawrence Clark Powell, from Tucson, gave graphic accounts of the problems of rapid growth that have been confronting the southwestern metropolitan areas during recent decades.

## BOOKS

Austin, Mary. *Land of Journey's Ending.* New York, 1924.
Boyle, Robert H., and others. *The Water Hustlers.* San Francisco, 1970.
Brenner, Anita. *The Wind That Swept Mexico.* Austin, Tex., 1971.
Castro, Tony. *Chicano Power.* New York, 1974.
Clendenen, Clarence. *Blood on the Border.* New York, 1969.
Colley, Charles. *The Century of Robert H. Forbes.* Tucson, 1978.
Cooney, John Patrick. "Definition of the Sociological Vector in Comprehensive Land and Water Planning." Master's Thesis, University of Texas at El Paso, 1973.
Garnsey, Morris F. *America's New Frontier: The Mountain West.* New York, 1950.
Goff, John S. *George W. P. Hunt and His Arizona.* Pasadena, Calif., 1973.
Hundley, Norris, Jr. *Water and the West.* Berkeley, Calif., 1975.
Johnson, Rich. *The Central Arizona Project, 1918–1968.* Tucson, 1977.
Kluger, James P. *The Clifton-Morenci Strike.* Tucson, 1970.
Lamont, Lansing. *Day of Trinity.* New York, 1965. The atom bomb.
Morgan, Neill. *Westward Tilt.* New York, 1963.
Nash, Gerald D. *The American West in the Twentieth Century.* Englewood Cliffs, N.J., 1973.
Smith, Courtland. *The Salt River Project.* Tucson, 1972.
Steiner, Stan. *La Raza: The Mexican Americans.* New York, 1970.
Tyler, Gus., ed. *Mexican Americans Tomorrow.* Albuquerque, 1975.

## ARTICLES

"How the Union Beat Willie Farah." *Fortune,* Aug. 1974.
"Illegal Aliens," *Jobs for Americans.* Washington, D.C.: Congressional Quarterly, 1977.
Knowlton, Clark. "The Changing Spanish American Villages of Northern New Mexico." *Sociology and Social Research,* July 1969.
"Laying the Wetback Problem on the Line." *Arizona Magazine* section of the *Arizona Republic,* February 26, 1978.
Nicklaus, Phil. "Border Pollution: A Slighted Problem." *Albuquerque Journal,* Mar. 20, 1977.
Park, Joseph F. "The 1903 'Mexican Affair' at Clifton." *JAH,* Summer 1977.

Roberts, Shirley. "Some Economic Characteristics of the Border Region." *The El Paso Economic Review,* Oct. 1976.

Severo, Richard. "The Flight of the Wetbacks." *New York Times Magazine,* Mar. 10, 1977.

# INDEX